Introduction & Order of the Universe

Informative Tables
Physical Constants, Astronomical Symbols, Planetary & Solar Data, Constellation & Star Charts

Monthly Star Charts

Observing the Moon
Map of the Moon & Lunar Phases from 2000 to 2050

Observing the Planets
Observing Tips ✦ Monthly Sunrise & Sunset Positions, Oppositions, Elongations & Conjunctions from 2000 to 2050

Observing Meteors, Comets, the Sun, Eclipses & Choosing a Telescope

25 Deep Sky Objects
Double Stars, Variable Stars, Nebulae, Planetary Nebulae, Open Clusters, Globular Clusters & Galaxies

Sunrise & Sunset
Time Zones, Universal Time, Sunrise & Sunset for more than 200 North American Cities

Astronomical G   & Index

THIS BOOK IS DEDICATED TO
my Mother and Father,
who supported and encouraged
my interest in astronomy during my youth.

Special Thanks to
Marie McFarland and Laura O'Bagy for typesetting.
Carol Costa and Marie McFarland for proofing.
Debra Niwa for the cover design.

I also wish to thank the following for their support...
My wife Suzanne for her inexhaustible patience as I wrote this book.
My astronomy friends, Dean Koenig, Scott Tucker, Larry Moore,
Joe Jakoby and David & Wendee Levy. And lastly, my astronomy mentor,
Mr. John Bussone, and my astronomy neighbor, Mr. Richard Raml.

Publisher's Cataloging-in-Publication Data
Graun, Ken
What's Out Tonight? 50 Year Astronomy Field Guide,
2000–2050 / by Ken Graun — rev.
p. cm.
Includes bibliographical references and index.
ISBN 1-928771-14-9
1. Astronomy — Observer's manuals. 2. Astronomy — Amateur's manuals.
QB64.G73 1999   520   99-90632

PUBLISHED BY
Ken Press
Tucson, Arizona

Visit us at:
www.whatsouttonight.com

Printed in the USA

1 2 3 Revised ★ April 2001

Introduction

Astronomy has the entire Universe as its theater. Every night, we can go out, look onto the stage and see what's playing. It's the grandest show. There is none larger, more spectacular or more dynamic.

Astronomy is not a simple science. It draws upon every discipline, from biology to nuclear physics, and engages the most complex mathematics in order to make sense of the Universe. However, none of this knowledge is required to go out, look up and enjoy the splendors the sky has to offer.

With this in mind, I set out and wrote this field guide so you will know the cast of characters for the next 50 years. No one wants to miss the show, so this book will be ready when you are, keeping you abreast of what's out tonight.

This field guide can be used anywhere in North America. Additionally, it is a comprehensive astronomy reference, so many of the answers to your questions about the heavens are within.

I hope you enjoy using this book as much as I have enjoyed writing it.

Best of luck in finding your way to the stars.

Ken Graun
Fall 1999

Pictured here with the author is his seven-year-old daughter, Adrea, and his favorite refractor telescope.

Ken Graun received his bachelor's in Applied Math and Physics and his master's in Counseling Psychology. He has taught mathematics at a community college and enjoys sharing astronomy with others. He lives in Tucson, Arizona along with his daughter and his wife, Suzanne.

The Order of the Universe & What's Where

Over the years I have heard people talk casually about astronomy and the objects in the night sky. And, it surprises me how often they have described or related erroneous information about the heavens. Additionally, I have noticed that most passing comments made in the mass media about astronomy are incorrect. Although the appreciation and wonder of astronomy abounds, the basics are widely misunderstood. Below, I provide a brief taxonomy of the heavens.

Basic Unit of the Universe: GALAXY

The galaxy is the basic unit of the Universe. A galaxy contains billions of stars and is thousands of light years in diameter. The stars in a galaxy are gravitationally bound and rotate about a center. Astronomers cannot count all the galaxies in the Universe, but they estimate that there are about 125 billion (125,000,000,000). Some galaxies are disk shaped with curved arms radiating from a bulged center. However, there are variations, as can be seen in the picture on the facing page.

> **Except for galaxies, everything that we see in the night sky is part of our own galaxy — called the Milky Way.**

What is between the galaxies? For all practical purposes, nothing. All of the matter in the Universe condensed into galaxy clumps shortly after the Big Bang, the explosion that essentially created the Universe.

The following objects make up galaxies: nebulae of various types (giant hydrogen gas clouds), black holes, neutron stars, white dwarfs, clusters of stars, globular clusters, stars, planets, moons, asteroids and comets. Nova and supernova explosions occur within galaxies.

Facing page. The basic unit of the Universe is the galaxy. This Hubble Space Telescope (HST) image pierces though our galaxy into the deep reaches of the Universe to show us a very small section of the sky near the handle of the Big Dipper. Every object in this image is a galaxy except for a few stars, which have the radiating spikes.

The Order of the Universe

The brightest and nearest galaxies can be viewed easily with a small telescope. One of our nearest galactic neighbors, the Andromeda galaxy, can be seen with the naked eye. The faintest and farthest galaxies require imaging from special telescopes like the orbiting Hubble Space Telescope.

Even though galaxies contain billions to hundreds of billions of brilliant stars, galaxies appear gossamer instead of solidly bright as one might guess. The reason is because galaxies are so large and the distances between the stars are so great that the light is diluted instead of concentrated. Photographs make galaxies appear brighter than they actually are because film and digital imaging devices can accumulate light — something that the eye cannot do. Our own galaxy is a good example of the gossamer nature of galaxies. Even though we reside in our galaxy, all that we can see of it is a faint band of light that stretches across the night sky. And in most cities, the Milky Way band cannot be seen because of light pollution.

Basic Unit of a Galaxy: STAR
The clumps of matter that formed the galaxies began as gigantic clouds of hydrogen gas. These hydrogen clouds condensed into the innumerable stars that make up galaxies. The Universe seems to create stars naturally.

The highest concentration of stars occur about the centers of galaxies. In established spiral galaxies, like our Milky Way galaxy, new stars are mostly born in the outer, curved arms, where the highest concentrations of hydrogen gas exist.

Stars vary in size and color. Our Sun is an average star; however, typical stars can be as little as 1/10 or greater than 40 times as massive. Diameters range from around 1/4 to over 1,500 times that of the Sun. Larger stars "burn" faster and may last only ten million (10,000,000) years. The smallest stars may last more than a trillion (1,000,000,000,000) years; and our Sun, already 4.5 billion years old, will have a total life span of 10 to 12 billion years.

About half of all stars belong to a binary or multiple star system in which two or more stars revolve around each other.

Many stars seem to have their own solar systems; that is, they have their own circling planets, comets and asteroids.

The Order of the Universe

BASIC UNIT OF THE UNIVERSE
GALAXY

Features of Galaxies
Nebulae, Planetary Nebulae
Clusters of Stars, Globular Clusters
Black Holes, Neutron Stars
White Dwarfs, Brown Dwarfs
Supergiant Stars, Novae, Supernovae
Basic unit is the Star

BASIC UNIT OF A GALAXY
STAR

Features of Stars
Planets (with moons), Asteroids, Comets
About half of all stars are part of Binary or Multiple Star Systems, in which two or more stars revolve around each other

Stars are born within hydrogen gas clouds like this. The gas concentrates into a gigantic disk out of which a star and planets emerge. This Hubble Space Telescope image shows a small portion of M16, commonly called the Eagle Nebula, located in the constellation Serpens (above Sagittarius).

Physical Constants & Measurements

Length

1 inch (in) = 25.4 millimeters exactly; 2.54 centimeters
1 centimeter (cm) = 0.394 inch; 10 millimeters
1 yard (yd) = 0.9144 meters; 36 inches
1 meter (m) = 1.094 yards; 39.37 inches; 100 centimeters; 1,000 millimeters
1 mile (mi) = 1.609344 kilometers; 5,280 feet; 1,760 yards
1 kilometer (km) = 0.621371 miles; 3,281 feet; 1,000 meters
1 astronomical unit (AU) = 92,955,800 miles; 149,597,870 kilometers;
    8.3 light-minutes; this is the average distance from the Earth to the Sun
1 light year (l.y.) = 63,240 astronomical units; almost 6 trillion miles
1 parsec (pc) = 3.26 light years; 206,265 astronomical units

Weight/Mass

1 ounce (oz) = 28.35 grams
1 gram (g *or* **gm)** = 0.0353 ounces
1 pound (lb) = 0.454 kilograms; 16 ounces
1 kilogram (kg) = 2.205 pounds; 1,000 grams
1 ton = 2,000 pounds; 907 kilograms
1 metric ton (t) = 1,000 kilograms; 2,205 pounds

Temperature

0° Fahrenheit (F) = −17.8° C; lowest temperature for mixture of water/ice/salt
0° Celsius (C) = 32° F; pure water freezes
212° Fahrenheit = 100° C; pure water boils
Absolute Zero = 0K (Kelvin); −459.7° F; −273.16° C

Volume

1 cubic inch = 16.39 cubic centimeters
1 cubic centimeter (cc, ml *or* **cm³)** = 0.061 cubic inches
1 cubic yard = 0.765 cubic meters
1 cubic meter (m³) = 1.308 cubic yards

Speed of Light

Speed of Light = 186,282 miles/second; 299,792 kilometers/second

Facing page. *The 48-inch Burrell Schmidt telescope at Kitt Peak, near Tucson, Arizona. Telescopes like this help gather astronomical data.*

Physical Constants & Measurements

Unit Abbreviations

Length		Weight/Mass		Temperature	
nm	Nanometer	oz	Ounce	F	Fahrenheit
mm	Millimeter	g *or* gm	Gram	C	Celsius
cm	Centimeter	lb	Pound	K	Kelvin
in *or* "	Inch	kg	Kilogram		
m	Meter	t	Metric Ton	**Time**	
km	Kilometer			s *or* sec	
mi	Mile	**Angular Measurements**			Second
AU	Astronomical Unit	°	Degree	m *or* min	
l.y.	Light-Year	'	Minute		Minute
pc	Parsec	''	Second	h	Hour
				d	Day
Volume		**Power**		yr *or* a	
ml	Milliliter	W	Watt		Year

Celestial Coordinates

RA or α Right Ascension[1] (Expressed using h, m and s. Example: 8h 27m 05s)
Dec or δ Declination[1] (Expressed using the ° ' " symbols. Example: 2° 04' 59")

---

[1]Right Ascension and Declination are used to define the position of all celestial objects. Right Ascension is analogous to longitude, except that it is based on 24 intervals, corresponding to the 24 hours of a day, the time it takes the celestial sphere to "rotate" one complete turn. Declination is analogous to latitude and uses the same nomenclature.

Wavelengths of Visible Light & Eye Sensitivity

Wavelength of Visible Light[1]		Approximate Visible Light Sensitivity of Eyes	
VIOLET	420 nm	Daytime ✦ RANGE Visible to Eyes	400 to 750 nm
BLUE	470 nm	Nighttime ✦ RANGE Visible to Eyes[2]	400 to 620 nm
GREEN	530 nm	Daytime PEAK Sensitivity of Eyes	555 nm
YELLOW	580 nm	Nighttime PEAK Sensitivity of Eyes[2]	510 nm
ORANGE	610 nm		
RED	660 nm		

[1]The wavelength of visible light is expressed in nanometers. A nanometer is 1 billionth (10^{-9}) of a meter. 500 nanometers is about 1/50,000 of an inch. [2]Nighttime dark adapted eyes. It takes up to 60 minutes for the eyes to reach full dark adaptation.

Symbols

Greek Alphabet[1]

ALPHA			IOTA			RHO		
	Case[2]			Case[2]			Case[2]	
	Lower	Upper		Lower	Upper		Lower	Upper
ALPHA	α	A	IOTA	ι	I	RHO	ρ	P
BETA	β	B	KAPPA	κ	K	SIGMA	σ	Σ
GAMMA	γ	Γ	LAMBDA	λ	Λ	TAU	τ	T
DELTA	δ	Δ	MU	μ	M	UPSILON	υ	Y
EPSILON	ε	E	NU	ν	N	PHI	ϕ	Φ
ZETA	ζ	Z	XI	ξ	Ξ	CHI	χ	X
ETA	η	H	OMICRON	o	O	PSI	ψ	Ψ
THETA	ϑ or θ	Θ	PI	π	Π	OMEGA	ω	Ω

[1]The lowercase letters of the Greek alphabet are used to designate the brightest stars within each constellation. For example, Polaris, the North Star is designated α Ursae Minoris. Ursae Minoris is the genitive form of Ursa Minor. This system of using the Greek letters is also known as Bayer Letters. [2]Only the lowercase is used to designate stars.

Solar System Members

SUN	☉	JUPITER	♃	MOON in General	☽
MERCURY	☿	SATURN	♄	NEW MOON	●
VENUS	♀	URANUS	♅	FIRST QUARTER	☽
EARTH	⊕	NEPTUNE	♆	FULL MOON	○
MARS	♂	PLUTO	♇	LAST QUARTER[1]	☾

[1]Also referred to as the Third Quarter.

Signs of the Zodiac[1]

1[2] PISCES	♓	5 CANCER	♋	9 SCORPIUS	♏
2 ARIES	♈	6 LEO	♌	10 SAGITTARIUS	♐
3 TAURUS	♉	7 VIRGO	♍	11 CAPRICORNUS	♑
4 GEMINI	♊	8 LIBRA	♎	12 AQUARIUS	♒

[1]The zodiacal constellations lie on the ecliptic, the apparent path the Sun traces through the sky during a year. [2]The numbers 1 through 12 represent the order the Sun passes through these constellations during the year. This list starts with Pisces, the constellation where the Sun resides at the start of spring (vernal equinox).

Notations & Temperature

Powers of 10

Throughout this field guide, very large numbers are expressed as powers of 10 (using what is known as Scientific Notation) because it is impractical to print or write long numbers. For those who are unfamiliar with Scientific Notation, the following examples are provided to give you a feel for this notation.

10^1 = 10   (also, 1 x 10^1 = 10 *and* 1.0 x 10^1 = 10)
10^2 = 100   (also, 1 x 10^2 = 100 *and* 1.0 x 10^2 = 100)
10^3 = 1,000
10^5 = 100,000 *(one hundred thousand)*
10^6 = 1,000,000 *(1 million)*
10^9 = 1,000,000,000 *(1 billion)*
10^{12} = 1,000,000,000,000 *(1 trillion)*
3.44 x 10^3 = 3,440 *(move decimal point 3 places to the right)*
9.296 x 10^7 = 92,960,000 *(move decimal point 7 places to the right)*

10^{-1} = 0.1 = $\frac{1}{10}$ (also, 1 x 10^{-1} *or* 1.0 x 10^{-1} = 0.1)
10^{-2} = 0.01 = $\frac{1}{100}$
10^{-5} = 0.00001 = $\frac{1}{100,000}$

Fahrenheit & Celsius Temperature Conversions

Below are the formulae and examples to change between the Fahrenheit and Celsius temperature scales.

The formula to change from Fahrenheit to Celsius is	The formula to change from Celsius to Fahrenheit is
°C = (°F − 32) x 0.556	°F = (°C x 1.8) + 32

EXAMPLES	EXAMPLES
A. Change 229° F to Celsius	C. Change 100° C to Fahrenheit
1. °C = (229 − 32) x 0.556	1. °F = (100 x 1.8) + 32
2. °C = (197) x 0.556	2. °F = (180) + 32
3. °C = 197 x 0.556	3. °F = 180 + 32
4. °C = 109.5	4. °F = 212
B. Change − 45° F to Celsius	D. Change − 13° C to Fahrenheit
1. °C = (− 45 − 32) x 0.556	1. °F = (− 13 x 1.8) + 32
2. °C = (− 77) x 0.556	2. °F = (− 23.4) + 32
3. °C = − 77 x 0.556	3. °F = − 23.4 + 32
4. °C = − 42.8	4. °F = 8.6

Physical Constants & Measurements

Star Magnitude ★ Scale of Brightness

In astronomy, Star Magnitude is a light intensity scale for comparing the relative brightness of the stars and other celestial objects. This scale ranges, at its brightest, from −27 for the Sun to over +30 for the faintest galaxies.

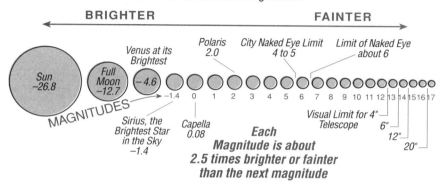

Number of Stars Visible to Magnitude...		Planets at Their Brightest		10 Brightest Stars (& Constellations)	
5	2,800	MERCURY	−1.9	SIRIUS (Canis Major)	−1.44
6	8,700	VENUS	−4.6	CANOPUS (Carina)	−0.62
7	27,000	MARS	−2.8	RIGIL KENT (Centaurus)	−0.28
8	78,000	JUPITER	−2.5	ARCTURUS (Bootes)	−0.05
9	218,000	SATURN	−0.4	VEGA (Lyra)	0.03
10	586,000	URANUS	5.7	CAPELLA (Auriga)	0.08
11	1,000,000	NEPTUNE	7.6	RIGEL (Orion)	0.18
		PLUTO	14	PROCYON (Canis Minor)	0.40
				ACHERNAR (Eridanus)	0.45
				BETELGEUSE (Orion)	0.45

NOTE: The limiting magnitude for telescopes can be greatly increased by using photographic or digital imaging to record celestial objects. The Hubble Space Telescope can record to about magnitude 30. Although the naked eye limit is normally around magnitude 6, good visibility and/or higher elevations can extend this limit to around magnitude 8.

Physical Constants & Measurements

The Universe

Age: 12 to 16 billion years (12,000,000,000 to 16,000,000,000)
Galaxy Count: upwards of 125 billion (125,000,000,000)
Chemical Composition: 75% Hydrogen, 25% Helium
Origin: created in an explosion called the "Big Bang"
Type: Astronomers do not have enough information to determine if our
   Universe will expand forever or eventually collapse back upon itself
   and possibly start over with another Big Bang.

Our Milky Way Galaxy

Type of Galaxy: moderately barred spiral
Diameter: about 100,000 light years
Central Bulge: about 10,000 light years across (within the plane of
   the Milky Way disk) and 6,500 light years thick
Mass: around 1 trillion (1,000,000,000,000) times the mass of the Sun
Number of Stars: over 100 billion and up to 300 billion
Distance from Sun to Center: about 30,000 light years
Coordinates to Center: Right Ascension: 17h 45.7m, Declination:
   −29° 00' which resides in the direction of the constellation Sagittarius
Revolution Velocity at Sun: 155 miles/sec; 250 km/sec
Revolution Period at Sun: about 220 million years
Companion Galaxies: The Large and Small Magellanic Clouds (LMC &
   SMC) are dwarf galaxies and can be seen with the naked eye from the
   southern hemisphere. The LMC, in the constellation Dorado, is 160,000
   light years away (1.6 Milky Way diameters). The SMC, in the constellation
   Tucana is 195,000 light years away.
Distance to Andromeda Galaxy (M31): about 2.3 million light years or
   23 times the diameter of our Milky Way galaxy

*The shape of our Milky Way galaxy is plainly visible in this infrared image of the
Milky Way band that circles the sky.*

Facing page. *A view of the Large Magellanic Cloud (LMC) featuring a
supernova explosion that occurred in 1987 (left of center). The LMC is
a companion galaxy to our Milky Way galaxy.*

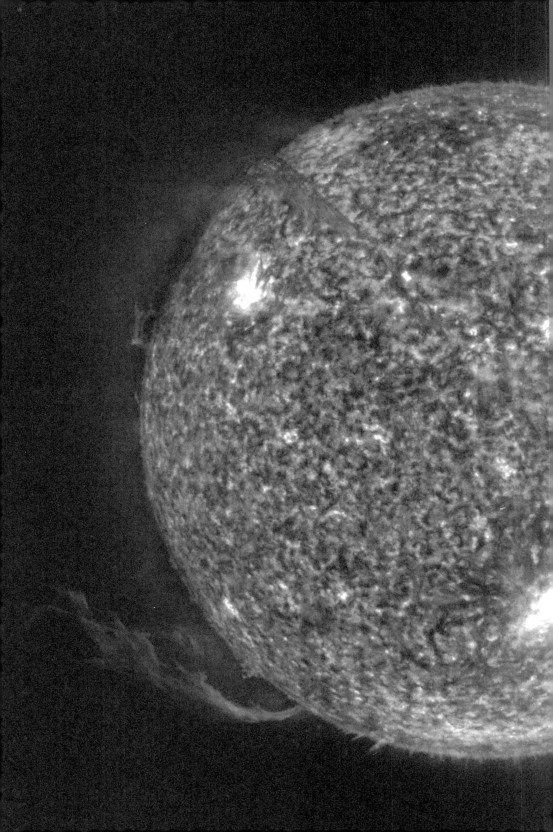

Physical Constants & Measurements

Sun

Equatorial Diameter: 864,950 miles; 1,392,000 km

Mass: 332,946.0 Earth masses or 4.3860 x 10^{30} pounds; 1.9891 x 10^{30} kg

Average Density: 1.41 gm/cm³ (water is 1.00 gm/cm³)

Rotation: 25.38 days at the equator and 35 days near the poles. Below a depth of 124,000 miles (200,000 km) the Sun appears to rotate at a stable 27 days, from equator to poles.

Inclination of Axis to Earth's Orbit: 7.25°

Visual Magnitude: −26.75

Absolute Magnitude: +4.82 (This would be the magnitude of the Sun if it were placed a distance of 10 parsecs from Earth. This distance is used to compare the actual magnitude of all stars.)

Temperatures: Surface temperature averages 10,000° F (5,500° C; 5,800K). Sunspots are cooler areas on the surface and average 6,300° F (3,500° C). The Sun's core is estimated to reach 27,000,000° F (15,000,000° C)

Star Classification: G2 V (The **G** refers to the spectral classification scale O B A F G K M R N S where O are the hottest and S the coolest stars. The **2** refers to a finer 0 – 9 subtype of the spectral scale and the Roman numeral **V** indicates that the Sun is a typical star in its class.)

Energy Output: 3.85 x 10^{26} watts. Energy just outside Earth's atmosphere is 1.37 kilowatts per square meter.

Solar Wind Speed near Earth: about 280 miles/sec; 450 km/sec. Travel time from the Sun to the Earth is about 4 days.

Composition: 92.1% Hydrogen, 7.8% Helium, with traces of Oxygen (0.061%), Carbon (0.030%), Nitrogen (0.0084%), Neon (0.0076%), Iron (0.0037%), Silicon (0.0031%), Magnesium (0.0024%), Sulfur (0.0015%), and other elements (0.0015%)

Gravity: 27.9 times the gravity of Earth

Escape Velocity: 384 miles/sec (1.4 million miles/hour); 617.5 km/sec

Sunspot Cycle: about 11.1 years, but varying from 8 to 16 years

Nearest Neighbor: Proxima Centauri, a star in the constellation Centaurus, is 4.2 light years away. Proxima is an 11th magnitude star and is not visible to the naked eye.

Age: about 4.5 billion years

Facing page. The Sun as imaged by the Solar and Heliospheric Observatory (SOHO) spacecraft. This picture shows the Sun in a very narrow band of red light, which allows easy viewing of prominences.

Physical Constants & Measurements

Earth

Equatorial Diameter: 7,926.4 miles; 12,756.3 km

Polar Diameter: 7,899.8 miles; 12,713.5 km

Mass: 1.317 x 10^{25} pounds; 5.974 x 10^{24} kg

Average Density: 5.52 gm/cm^3 (water is 1.00 gm/cm^3)

Inclination of Axis to Orbit: 23.4393° with North Pole pointing roughly
    to the star Polaris in the constellation Ursa Minor (Little Dipper)

Precession of Axis: 50.29" a year around a 47° diameter circular arc.
    Total precession period is about 25,800 years.

Day: Synodic day (time used for clocks) is 86,400 seconds or 24 hours.
    Sidereal day (one complete rotation on its axis) is
    86,164.1 seconds or 23 hours, 56 minutes, 4.1 seconds.

Year: 365.2564 days; 365 days, 6 hours, 9 minutes, 10 seconds

Average Distance from Sun: 92,955,800 miles; 149,597,870 km;
    8.3 light-minutes. This distance is also known as an astronomical unit.

Closest Distance to Sun: 91,403,000 miles; 147,099,000 km.
    The Earth is closest to the Sun on (or near) January 4th.

Farthest Distance from Sun: 94,508,000 miles; 152,096,000 km.
    The Earth is farthest from the Sun on (or near) July 4th.

Orbital Speed: 18.5 miles/sec; 29.8 km/sec

Eccentricity of Orbit: 0.017 (from the mathematical definition of eccentricity)
    or 0.015% as defined in the Orbital table on page 24

Albedo: reflects 37% of sunlight

Temperature Range: averages 59° F (15° C); highest recorded,
    136° F (58° C); lowest recorded, −129° F (−89° C)

Pressure at Sea Level: 1 atmosphere (1 bar); 14.7 pounds/$inch^2$;
    760.0 mm-Hg; 101.3 kPascals

Speed of Sound at Sea Level: 1,087 feet/sec (741.5 miles/hour);
    331.5 meters/sec

Escape Velocity at Equator: 6.96 miles/sec (25,000 miles/hour);
    11.2 km/sec

Acceleration of Gravity: 32.2 feet/sec^2; 9.81 meters/sec^2

Coordinates of Magnetic Poles: North Magnetic Pole: 76° N, 101° W.
    South Magnetic Pole: 66° S, 140° E

Age: about 4.5 billion years

Facing page. *View of Earth as seen by the Apollo 17 crew
traveling toward the Moon in 1972.*

Physical Constants & Measurements

Moon

Diameter: 2,160 miles; 3,476 km

Mass: 1.62×10^{23} pounds; 7.35×10^{22} kg

Average Density: 3.34 gm/cm^3 (water is 1.00 gm/cm^3)

Average Distance from Earth: 238,920 miles; 384,500 km

Rotation Period on Axis: The rotational period is the same as the Synodic
   Revolution, thus the same side of the Moon always faces Earth.

Inclination of Axis: 1.5° to the Moon's orbital plane

Sidereal Revolution Period (One Complete Orbit): 27.322 days

Synodic Revolution (New Moon to New Moon Period):
   29 days, 12 hours, 44 minutes, 3 seconds

Inclination of Orbit to Earth's Orbit: 5.1°

Albedo: reflects 11% of sunlight

Temperature Range: −300° F (−184° C) to 214° F (101° C);
   Poles remain at a constant −140° F (−96° C)

Magnitude at Full Moon: −12.7

Gravity: 0.17 times the gravity of Earth

Escape Velocity: 1.5 miles/sec (5,369 miles/hour); 2.4 km/sec

Age: about 4.5 billion years

Apollo 17 astronaut Harrison Schmitt walking around a boulder.

Facing page. *An image of the Moon from the Galileo spacecraft
on its journey to Jupiter in 1992.*

Solar System Data

Physical Properties of Solar System Members

	Equatorial Diameter		Mass[1] Earth = 1	Density[2] $H_2O = 1$	Gravity[3] Earth = 1	Albedo[4]
SUN	864,950 miles	1,392,000 km	332,946	1.41	27.9	n/a
MERCURY	3,032 miles	4,879 km	0.055	5.43	0.38	11%
VENUS	7,521 miles	12,104 km	0.815	5.25	0.90	65%
EARTH	7,926 miles	12,756 km	1	5.52	1.00	37%
MARS	4,222 miles	6,794 km	0.107	3.95	0.38	15%
JUPITER	88,844 miles	142,980 km	317.8	1.33	2.53	52%
SATURN	74,900 miles[5]	120,540 km[5]	95.2	0.69	1.06	47%
URANUS	31,764 miles	51,120 km	14.5	1.29	0.90	51%
NEPTUNE	30,777 miles	49,530 km	17.2	1.64	1.14	41%
PLUTO	1,429 miles	2,300 km	0.0025	2.03	0.08	30%

[1]Earth's mass is 1.32×10^{25} pounds (5.97×10^{24} kg). [2]Density per unit volume as compared to water. For comparsion, the density of alumium is 2.7 and iron is 7.7. [3]Gravity at equator. [4]Albedo is the amount of sunlight reflected by the Planet. [5]Saturn without rings. Visible rings are approximately 170,000 miles (273,600 km) in diameter.

	Rotational Period (Planet's Day)	Escape Velocity[1]		Oblateness[2]	Inclination to Orbit[3]
SUN	25 to 35 days[4]	384 miles/s	617.5 km/s	0	7.2°[5]
MERCURY	58.7 days	2.6 miles/s	4.2 km/s	0	0.0°
VENUS	243.0 days	6.5 miles/s	10.4 km/s	0	177.4°
EARTH	1 day	6.96 miles/s	11.2 km/s	0.34%	23.4°
MARS	24.62 hours	3.1 miles/s	5.0 km/s	0.65%	25.2°
JUPITER	9.84 hours	37 miles/s	59.5 km/s	6.5%	3.1°
SATURN	10.23 hours	22.1 miles/s	35.5 km/s	9.8%	25.3°
URANUS	17.9 hours	13.2 miles/s	21.3 km/s	2.3%	97.9°
NEPTUNE	19.2 hours	14.6 miles/s	23.5 km/s	1.7%	28.3°
PLUTO	6.4 days	0.8 miles/s	1.3 km/s	unknown	123°

[1]At equator. [2]Bulging at the equator caused by rotation of Planet on axis. Percentage indicates the amount of extra equatorial diameter as compared to the polar diameter. [3]Inclination of Planet's rotational axis to Planet's orbit around Sun. [4]Sun rotates about 10 days faster at its equator than at its poles. [5]Inclination of Sun's rotational axis to Earth's orbit.

Facing page. *A closeup of the Great Red Spot and surrounding clouds on Jupiter. The Great Red Spot is at the bottom of this picture and is physically larger than this Earth. This hurricane-type vortex spans 25,000 miles (40,000 kilometers).*

Solar System Data

Orbital Properties of Solar System Members

	Average Distance from Sun[1]			Eccentricity[3]
	Astronomical Units (AU)[2]	Miles	Kilometers	
MERCURY	0.387	35,980,000	57,910,000	2.2%
VENUS	0.723	67,230,000	108,200,000	0.003%
EARTH	1.000	92,955,800	149,597,870	0.015%
MARS	1.524	141,640,000	227,940,000	0.44%
JUPITER	5.203	483,630,000	778,330,000	0.16%
SATURN	9.539	886,680,000	1,426,980,000	0.16%
URANUS	19.191	1,783,950,000	2,870,990,000	0.12%
NEPTUNE	30.061	2,794,350,000	4,497,070,000	0.004%
PLUTO	39.529	3,674,490,000	5,913,520,000	3.3%

[1]The Planets' orbits around the Sun are ellipses, not circles. Thus, they have a closest and farthest distance to the Sun. [2]One astronomical unit is the average distance of the Earth to the Sun, 92,955,800 miles. [3]Eccentricity is normally expressed as a decimal and represents the elongation of a Planet's elliptical orbit. Ellipses have both a major (longer) and minor (shorter) axis. For clarity, I have expressed eccentricity as a percentage indicating how much longer the major axis is as compared to the minor axis. Although the Planets' orbits are ellipses, all nine have orbits that are very close to circles. Seven of the Planets have eccentricities less than 1%.

	Revolution Around Sun (Planet's Year)	Average Orbital Velocity		Inclination of Orbit to Earth's Orbit
MERCURY	87.97 days	29.76 miles/s	47.89 km/s	7.00°
VENUS	224.70 days	21.77 miles/s	35.03 km/s	3.39°
EARTH	365.26 days	18.51 miles/s	29.79 km/s	0.00°
MARS	686.98 days	14.99 miles/s	24.13 km/s	1.85°
JUPITER	11.86 years	8.12 miles/s	13.06 km/s	1.31°
SATURN	29.42 years	5.99 miles/s	9.64 km/s	2.49°
URANUS	83.75 years	4.23 miles/s	6.81 km/s	0.77°
NEPTUNE	163.73 years	3.37 miles/s	5.43 km/s	1.77°
PLUTO	248.03 years	2.95 miles/s	4.74 km/s	17.15°

Solar System Data

Atmospheres of Solar System Members

	Description of Atmosphere	Temperature
MERCURY	No atmosphere[1]	800° F Day (427° C)
		−300° F Night (−184° C)
VENUS	96% Carbon Dioxide, 3.5% Nitrogen	Averages 900° F (482° C)
	Atmospheric Pressure: 90 bars	
EARTH	77% Nitrogen, 21% Oxygen,	Averages 59° F (15° C)
	1% Water, 1% Argon	Highest 136° F (58° C)
	Atmospheric Pressure: 1 bar	Lowest −129° F (−89° C)
MARS[2]	95% Carbon Dioxide, 2.7% Nitrogen,	Averages −81° F (−63° C)
	1.6% Argon, 0.2% Oxygen	High 72° F (22° C)
	Atmospheric Pressure: 0.007 bar	Low −274° F (−140° C)
JUPITER[3]	90% Hydrogen Gas, 10% Helium Gas	−243° F (−153° C)
		just below cloudtops
SATURN[3]	97% Hydrogen Gas, 3% Helium Gas	−301° F (−185° C)
		just below cloudtops
URANUS[3]	83% Hydrogen Gas, 15% Helium Gas	−323° F (−197° C)
	2% Methane Gas	just below cloudtops
NEPTUNE[3]	74% Hydrogen Gas, 25% Helium Gas	−373° F (−225° C)
	1% Methane Gas	just below cloudtops
PLUTO	100% Methane Gas? Some Nitrogen?	−419° F (−233° C)
	Very low atmospheric pressure	

[1]Mercury has no atmosphere in the conventional sense; however, there are trace quantities of Helium, Sodium and Oxygen and an atmospheric pressure of 10^{-15} bars. [2]With the landing of Pathfinder and accompanying rover on Mars in 1998, temperatures of 23° F (−5° C) during the day and −112° F (−80° C) at night were measured. Since the atmospheric pressure on Mars is low, temperature decreased by as much as 18 F° (10 C°) from the surface to a height of just 3 feet (1 meter). [3]Jupiter, Saturn, Uranus and Neptune are gas giants and thus do not have, in the conventional sense, a surface below the clouds. Therefore, they do not have a reference point from which to measure a standard atmospheric pressure.

Solar System Data

Major Moons of the Planets[1]

	Moon Name	Average Distance from Planet[2]	Revolution Period[3]	Diameter	Visual Magnitude[4]
MERCURY	Mercury has no moons				
VENUS	Venus has no moons				
EARTH	Earth has 1 moon				
	Moon	238,920 miles	27.3 days	2,160 miles	−12.7
		384,500 km		3,476 km	
MARS	Mars has 2 moons				
	Phobos	5,830 miles	7.7 hours	17 x 13 miles	11.6
		9,380 km		27 x 21 km	
	Deimos	14,580 miles	1.3 days	10 x 8 miles	12.7
		23,460 km		16 x 13 km	
JUPITER	Jupiter has 28 known moons[5] (This count will most likely rise)				
	Io	262,000 miles	1.77 days	2,255 miles	5.0
		421,600 km		3,629 km	
	Europa	416,900 miles	3.55 days	1,950 miles	5.3
		670,900 km		3,138 km	
	Ganymede	664,900 miles	7.16 days	3,270 miles	4.6
		1,070,000 km		5,261 km	
	Callisto	1,171,000 miles	16.69 days	2,980 miles	5.6
		1,885,000 km		4,800 km	
SATURN	Saturn has 30 known moons[6] (This count will most likely rise)				
	Mimas	116,200 miles	0.9 days	242 miles	12.5
		187,000 km		390 km	
	Enceladus	147,900 miles	1.4 days	311 miles	11.8
		238,000 km		500 km	
	Tethys	183,300 miles	1.9 days	659 miles	10.3
		295,000 km		1,060 km	
	Dione	234,900 miles	2.7 days	699 miles	10.4
		378,000 km		1,120 km	
	Rhea	326,800 miles	4.5 days	951 miles	9.7
		526,000 km		1,530 km	
	Titan	758,100 miles	15.9 days	3,200 miles	8.4
		1,221,000 km		5,150 km	
	Iapetus	2,212,700 miles	79.3 days	907 miles	11.0
		3,561,000 km		1,460 km	

Facing page. *Triton, Neptune's largest moon.*

Solar System Data

Major Moons of the Planets[1]

	Moon Name	Average Distance from Planet[2]	Revolution Period[3]	Diameter	Visual Magnitude[4]
URANUS	*Uranus has 21 known moons*[7]	*(This count will most likely rise)*			
	Ariel	118,600 miles	2.5 days	721 miles	14.0
		190,900 km		1,160 km	
	Umbriel	165,300 miles	4.1 days	739 miles	14.9
		266,000 km		1,190 km	
	Titania	271,100 miles	8.7 days	1,000 miles	13.9
		436,300 km		1,610 km	
	Oberon	362,500 miles	13.5 days	963 miles	14.1
		583,400 km		1,550 km	
NEPTUNE	*Neptune has 8 known moons*[8]	*(This count will most likely rise)*			
	Triton	220,000 miles	5.9 days	1,678 miles	13.6
		354,000 km		2,700 km	
	Nereid[1]	3,423,800 miles	365.2 days	211 miles	19.7
		5,510,000 km		340 km	
PLUTO	*Pluto has 1 known moon*				
	Charon	11,900 miles	6.4 days	746 miles	17
		19,100 km		1,200 km	

NOTE: All moon data and counts are current as of spring, 2001.

[1]Data for only the major moons are provided because the lesser moons are small and require large telescopes and photographic means to identify. A typical example of these lesser moons is Nereid, Neptune's second largest moon, which is listed in this table. [2]Distance measured from center of Planet. [3]Orbit around Planet. [4]Visual magnitude from Earth at Planet's closest approach. [5]The names of the first 16 moons of **JUPITER** are (from innermost to outermost): Metis, Adrastea, Amalthea, Thebe, Io, Europa, Ganymede, Callisto, Leda, Himalia, Lysithea, Elara, Ananke, Carme, Pasiphae and Sinope. [6]The names of the first 18 moons of **SATURN** are (from innermost to outermost): Pan, Atlas, Prometheus, Pandora, Janus, Epimetheus, Mimas, Enceladus, Tethys, Telesto, Calypso, Dione, Helene, Rhea, Titan, Hyperion, Iapetus, Phoebe. [7]The names of 17 moons of **URANUS** are (from innermost to outermost): Cordelia, Ophelia, Bianca, Cressida, Desdemona, Juliet, Portia, Rosalind, Belinda, Puck, Miranda, Ariel, Umbriel, Titania, Oberon, Caliban and Sycorax. [8]The names of all the moons of **NEPTUNE** are (from innermost to outermost): Naiad, Thalassa, Despina, Galatea, Larissa, Proteus, Triton and Nereid.

Solar System Data

QUICK COMPARISON of Solar System Members

	Distance from Sun[1]		Diameter[3]	Mass[4]	Volume[5]
	Earth = 1	*Light Time[2]*	*Earth = 1*	*Earth = 1*	*Earth = 1*
SUN	n/a	n/a	109	333,000	1,300,000
MERCURY	0.4	3.2 minutes	0.4	0.06	0.06
VENUS	0.7	6 minutes	0.95	0.8	0.9
EARTH	1	8.3 minutes	1	1	1
MARS	1.5	12.7 minutes	0.5	0.1	0.15
JUPITER	5.2	43.3 minutes	11.2	318	1,326
SATURN	9.5	1h 19min	9.5	95	771
URANUS	19	2h 40min	4	15	63
NEPTUNE	30	4h 10min	3.8	17	58
PLUTO	39.5	5h 29min	0.2	0.003	0.006

[1]The average distance from the Earth to the Sun is 92,955,800 miles (149,597,870 km) and is also known as 1 astronomical unit (AU). [2]The time it takes for light to travel from the Sun to the respective Planet. Light travels at 186,282 miles/sec (299,792 km/sec). [3]Earth's equatorial diameter is 7,926 miles (12,756 km). [4]Earth's mass is 1.32×10^{25} pounds (5.97×10^{24} kg). [5]Earth's volume is 2.6×10^{11} cubic miles (1.1×10^{12} km³).

Eight of the nine Planets as imaged by spacecraft. The top four, known as the terrestrial Planets, are Mercury, Venus, Earth (our Moon is to the right of Earth) and Mars. The bottom four are the gas giants — Jupiter Saturn, Uranus and Neptune. Pluto is not pictured because it has not yet been visited and imaged by an exploratory spacecraft.

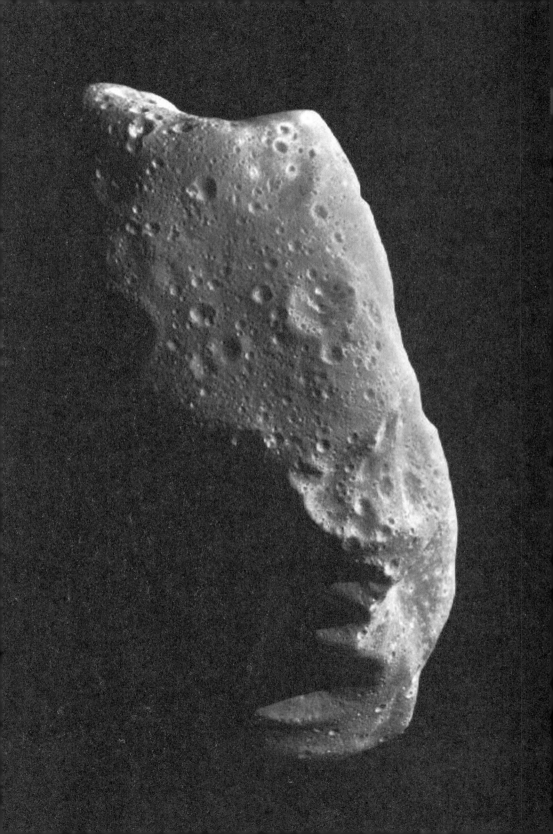

Solar System Data

Major Asteroids[1]

Name	Diameter[2]		Average Distance from Sun[3]	Orbital Period	Orbital Inclination[4]
CERES	568 miles	914 km	2.77 AU	4.61 years	10.6°
PALLAS	324 miles	522 km	2.77 AU	4.61 years	34.8°
VESTA	311 miles	500 km	2.36 AU	3.63 years	7.1°
HYGIEA	267 miles	430 km	3.14 AU	5.59 years	3.8°
DAVIDA	209 miles	336 km	3.18 AU	5.67 years	15.9°
INTERAMNIA	208 miles	334 km	3.06 AU	5.36 years	17.3°
EUROPA	194 miles	312 km	3.10 AU	5.46 years	7.4°
EUNOMIA	169 miles	272 km	2.64 AU	4.30 years	11.8°
SYLVIA	169 miles	272 km	3.49 AU	6.52 years	10.9°
PSYCHE	164 miles	264 km	2.92 AU	5.00 years	3.1°

[1]Presented here are the 10 largest asteroids in the asteroid belt between Mars and Jupiter. [2]Diameters are approximate and represent the longest axis, as most asteroids are not spherical. [3]Mars is 1.5 AU from the Sun and Jupiter is 5.2 AU from the Sun. [4]Inclination to Earth's orbit.

Near Earth Asteroids. In the last years of the 20th century, there was a heightened public awareness of the potential for asteroids to strike Earth. This concern was no doubt fueled by the impact of Comet Shoemaker-Levy 9 into Jupiter, several movies and the end-of-the-millennium mania. Three types of asteroids approach Earth and are categorized as Aten, Apollo and Amor. **Aten** asteroids, which total about 100 asteroids, orbit inside of Earth's orbit. **Apollo** asteroids have orbits that are slightly larger than Earth's, and **Amor** asteroids orbit inside of Mars' orbit. About 80 known Amor-Apollo asteroids could potentially cross Earth's orbit.

Facing page. *The asteroid Ida, the second asteroid ever to be imaged. This view of Ida was returned by the Galileo spacecraft in August 1992 on its journey to Jupiter. Ida is about 32 miles in length (52 km) and has a small moon, named Dactyl, revolving around it. Dactyl is about one mile in diameter (1.7 km).*

Page 32. *Orion is one of the most easily and widely recognized constellations. Many of the constellations that we recognize today were known in ancient times. The Egyptians not only recognized the stars that make up Orion, they used the three belt stars as a pattern for the alignment and size of the three pyramids at Giza.*

Constellations

The 88 Constellations

Constellation Name	3 & 4 Letter Abbreviation	Meaning *Latin Genitive*[1]	Page Number Reference to Constellation & Star Charts[2]
ANDROMEDA	And Andr	Daughter of Cassiopeia *Andromedae*	**42**, 47, 41
ANTLIA	Ant Antl	Air Pump *Antliae*	**45**, 46
APUS	Aps Apus	Bird of Paradise *Apodis*	**48**
AQUARIUS	Aqr Aqar	Water Bearer *Aquarii*	**42**, 43
AQUILA	Aql Aqil	Eagle *Aquilae*	**43**
ARA	Ara Arae	Altar *Arae*	**48**, 43, 44
ARIES	Ari Arie	Ram *Arietis*	**47**, 42
AURIGA	Aur Auri	Charioteer *Aurigae*	**47**, 46, 41
BOOTES	Boo Boot	Herdsman *Bootis*	**44**, 45, 41
CAELUM	Cae Cael	Engraving Tool *Caeli*	**47**, 46, 48
CAMELOPARDALIS	Cam Caml	Giraffe *Camelopardalis*	**41**
CANCER	Cnc Canc	Crab *Cancri*	**46**
CANES VENATICI	CVn CVen	Hunting Dog *Canum Venaticorum*	**45**, 44, 41
CANIS MAJOR	CMa CMaj	Big Dog *Canis Majoris*	**46**, 47
CANIS MINOR	CMi CMin	Little Dog *Canis Minoris*	**46**
CAPRICORNUS	Cap Capr	Sea Goat Capricorni	**43**, 42
CARINA	Car Cari	Ship's Keel *Carinae*	**48**
CASSIOPEIA	Cas Cass	Queen *Cassiopeiae*	**41**

[1] The Latin Genitive form is used in conjunction with the Greek letter designation of individual stars in the constellations. For example, the star Rigil Kent in Centaurus is designated α so it would be referred to as α Centauri (Alpha Centauri). [2] Bolded page numbers indicate the chart which best shows the constellation.

Constellations

The 88 Constellations

Constellation Name	3 & 4 Letter Abbreviation	Meaning *Latin Genitive*[1]	Page Number Reference to Constellation & Star Charts[2]
CENTAURUS	Cen	Centaur	**48**, 45, 44
	Cent	*Centauri*	
CEPHEUS	Cep	King	**41**
	Ceph	*Cephei*	
CETUS	Cet	Whale	**42**, 47
	Ceti	*Ceti*	
CHAMAELEON	Cha	Chameleon	**48**
	Cham	*Chamaeleontis*	
CIRCINUS	Cir	Drawing Compass	**48**
	Circ	*Circini*	
COLUMBA	Col	Dove	**46**, **47**, 48
	Colm	*Columbae*	
COMA BERENICES	Com	Berenice's Hair	**45**, 44
	Coma	*Comae Berenices*	
CORONA AUSTRALIS	CrA	Southern Crown	**43**, 44, 48
	CorA	*Coronae Australis*	
CORONA BOREALIS	CrB	Northern Crown	**44**
	CorB	*Coronae Borealis*	
CORVUS	Crv	Crow	**45**
	Corv	*Corvi*	
CRATER	Crt	Cup	**45**
	Crat	*Crateris*	
CRUX	Cru	Southern Cross	**48**
	Crux	*Crucis*	
CYGNUS	Cyg	Swan	**43**, 41
	Cygn	*Cygni*	
DELPHINUS	Del	Dolphin	**43**
	Dlph	*Delphini*	
DORADO	Dor	Goldfish	**48**
	Dora	*Doradus*	
DRACO	Dra	Dragon	**41**
	Drac	*Draconis*	
EQUULEUS	Equ	Little Horse	**43**, 42
	Equl	*Equulei*	
ERIDANUS	Eri	River Eridanus	**47**, **48**, 42
	Erid	*Eridani*	

[1]The Latin Genitive form is used in conjunction with the Greek letter designation of individual stars in the constellations. For example, the star Antares in Scorpius is designated α so it would be referred to as α Scorpii (Alpha Scorpii). [2]Bolded page numbers indicate the chart which best shows the constellation.

Constellations

The 88 Constellations

Constellation Name	3 & 4 Letter Abbreviation	Meaning *Latin Genitive*[1]	Page Number Reference to Constellation & Star Charts[2]
FORNAX	For Forn	Furnace *Fornacis*	**47**, 42
GEMINI	Gem Gemi	Twins *Geminorum*	**46**, 47
GRUS	Gru Grus	Crane *Gruis*	42, 43, 48
HERCULES	Her Herc	The Son of Zeus *Herculis*	**44**, 43
HOROLOGIUM	Hor Horo	Clock *Horologii*	**48**, 47
HYDRA	Hya Hyda	Sea Serpent *Hydrae*	**45**, **46**, 44
HYDRUS	Hyi Hydi	Water Snake *Hydri*	**48**
INDUS	Ind Indi	Indian *Indi*	**48**, 43
LACERTA	Lac Lacr	Lizard *Lacertae*	**41**, 42, 43
LEO	Leo Leon	Lion *Leonis*	**45**, 46
LEO MINOR	LMi LMin	Little Lion *Leonis Minoris*	**45**, 46
LEPUS	Lep Leps	Hare *Leporis*	**47**, 46
LIBRA	Lib Libr	Scales *Librae*	**44**, 45
LUPUS	Lup Lupi	Wolf *Lupi*	**44**, 45, 48
LYNX	Lyn Lync	Lynx *Lyncis*	**41**, 45, 46
LYRA	Lyr Lyra	Lyre *Lyrae*	**43**, 44
MENSA	Men Mens	Table Mountain *Mensae*	**48**
MICROSCOPIUM	Mic Micr	Microscope *Microscopii*	**43**, 42, 48

[1]The Latin Genitive form is used in conjunction with the Greek letter designation of individual stars in the constellations. For example, the star Enif in Pegasus is designated ε so it would be referred to as ε Pegasi (Epsilon Pegasi). [2]Bolded page numbers indicate the chart which best shows the constellation.

Constellations

The 88 Constellations

Constellation Name	3 & 4 Letter Abbreviation	Meaning Latin Genitive[1]	Page Number Reference to Constellation & Star Charts[2]
MONOCEROS	Mon Mono	Unicorn Monocerotis	**46**, 47
MUSCA	Mus Musc	Fly Muscae	**48**
NORMA	Nor Norm	Level Normae	**44**, **48**
OCTANS	Oct Octn	Octant Octantis	**48**
OPHIUCHUS	Oph Ophi	Snake Holder Ophiuchi	**44**, 43
ORION	Ori Orio	The Hunter Orionis	**47**, 46
PAVO	Pav Pavo	Peacock Pavonis	**48**
PEGASUS	Peg Pegs	The Winged Horse Pegasi	**42**, 43
PERSEUS	Per Pers	Rescuer of Andromeda Persei	**41**, 47
PHOENIX	Phe Phoe	Phoenix Phoenicis	**48**, 42, 47
PICTOR	Pic Pict	Easel Pictoris	**48**
PISCES	Psc Pisc	Fishes Piscium	**42**, 47
PISCIS AUSTRINUS	PsA PscA	Southern Fish Piscis Austrini	**42**, 43
PUPPIS	Pup Pupp	Ship's Stern Puppis	**46**, 47, 48
PYXIS	Pyx Pyxi	Ship's Compass Pyxidis	**46**
RETICULUM	Ret Reti	Eyepiece Reticle Reticuli	**48**
SAGITTA	Sge Sgte	Arrow Sagittae	**43**
SAGITTARIUS	Sgr Sgtr	Archer Sagittarii	**43**, 44

[1]The Latin Genitive form is used in conjunction with the Greek letter designation of individual stars in the constellations. For example, the star Pollux is designated β in the constellation Gemini and would be referred to as β Geminorum (Beta Geminorum). [2]Bolded page numbers indicate the chart which best shows the constellation.

The 88 Constellations

Constellation Name	3 & 4 Letter Abbreviation	Meaning *Latin Genitive*[1]	Page Number Reference to Constellation & Star Charts[2]
SCORPIUS	Sco	Scorpion	**44**, 43, 48
	Scor	*Scorpii*	
SCULPTOR	Scl	Sculptor's Apparatus	**42**
	Scul	*Sculptoris*	
SCUTUM	Sct	Shield	**43**, 44
	Scut	*Scuti*	
SERPENS[3]	Ser	Snake	**44**, 43
	Serp	*Serpentis*	
SEXTANS	Sex	Sextant	**45**, 46
	Sext	*Sextantis*	
TAURUS	Tau	Bull	**47**, 46
	Taur	*Tauri*	
TELESCOPIUM	Tel	Telescope	**48**, 43, 44
	Tele	*Telescopii*	
TRIANGULUM	Tri	Triangle	**47**, 42
	Tria	*Trianguli*	
TRIANGULUM AUSTRALE	TrA	Southern Triangle	**48**
	TrAu	*Trianguli Australis*	
TUCANA	Tuc	Toucan	**48**
	Tucn	*Tucanae*	
URSA MAJOR	UMa	Big Bear	**41**, 44, 45, 46
	UMaj	*Ursae Majoris*	
URSA MINOR	UMi	Little Bear	**41**
	UMin	*Ursae Minoris*	
VELA	Vel	Sail	**48**, 45, 46
	Velr	*Velorum*	
VIRGO	Vir	Virgin	**45**, 44
	Virg	*Virginis*	
VOLANS	Vol	Flying Fish	**48**
	Voln	*Volantis*	
VULPECULA	Vul	Little Fox	**43**
	Vulp	*Vulpeculae*	

[1]The Latin Genitive form is used in conjunction with the Greek letter designation of individual stars in the constellations. For example, the star Capella in Auriga is designated α so it would be referred to as α Aurigae (Alpha Aurigae). [2]Bolded page numbers indicate the chart which best shows the constellation. [3]The constellation Serpens is the only constellation that has two discontinous boundaries. They lie on opposite sides of Ophiuchus. The northwest portion is referred to as Serpens Caput and the southeast portion as Serpens Cauda.

Names of Stars

Commonly Used Names of Stars

Name of Star	Constellation	Greek Letter Desig[1]	Name of Star	Constellation	Greek Letter Desig[1]
ACAMAR	Eridanus	θ	ALPHEKKA	Corona Borealis	α
ACHERNAR	Eridanus	α	ALPHERATZ	Andromeda	α
ACRUX	Crux	α	ALRAKIS	Draco	μ
ACUBENS	Cancer	α	ALRESCHA	Pisces	α
ADHAFERA	Leo	ζ	ALSHAIN	Aquila	β
ADHARA	Canis Major	ε	ALTAIR	Aquila	α
ALBALI	Aquarius	ε	ALTAIS	Draco	δ
ALBIREO	Cygnus	β	ALTERF	Leo	λ
ALCHIBA	Corvus	α	ALUDRA	Canis Major	η
ALCOR	Ursa Major	80[1]	ALULA AUSTRALIS	Ursa Major	ξ
ALDEBARAN	Taurus	α			
ALDERAMIN	Cepheus	α	ALULA BOREALIS	Ursa Major	ν
ALFIRK	Cepheus	β			
ALGEDI	Capricorn	α	ALYA	Serpens	θ
ALGENIB	Pegasus	γ	ANCHA	Aquarius	θ
ALGIEBA	Leo	γ	ANKAA	Phoenix	α
ALGOL	Perseus	β	ANTARES	Scorpius	α
ALGORAB	Corvus	δ	ARCTURUS	Bootes	α
ALHENA	Gemini	γ	ARKAB	Sagittarius	β
ALIOTH	Ursa Major	ε	ARNEB	Lepus	α
ALKAID	Ursa Major	η	ASCELLA	Sagittarius	ζ
ALKALUROPS	Bootes	μ	ASELLUS AUSTRALIS	Cancer	δ
ALKES	Crater	α			
ALMAAK	Andromeda	γ	ASELLUS BOREALIS	Cancer	γ
ALNAIR	Grus	α			
ALNASL	Sagittarius	γ	ASPIDISKE	Carina	ι
ALNATH	Taurus	β	ATIK	Perseus	ζ
ALNILAM	Orion	ε	ATRIA	Triangulum Australe	α
ALNITAK	Orion	ζ	AVIOR	Carina	ε
ALPHARD	Hydra	α	AZHA	Eridanus	η

[1]The brightest stars in each constellation are designated with a lowercase Greek letter for identification. In astronomy, when a star with a Greek letter is referred to, the Latin genitive form of the constellation name is used in conjunction with the Greek letter designation. For example, the star Betelgeuse in Orion is designated α, so it would be referred to as α Orionis (Alpha Orionis). [1]Alcor does not have a Greek designation, so it is referred to here by its Flamsteed number (see Glossary), which also uses the Latin genitive form.

Names of Stars

Commonly Used Names of Stars

Name of Star	Constellation	Greek Letter Desig[1]	Name of Star	Constellation	Greek Letter Desig[1]
BATEN KAITOS	Cetus	ζ	IZAR	Bootes	ε
BEID	Eridanus	o	KAUS AUSTRALIS	Sagittarius	ε
BELLATRIX	Orion	γ	KAUS BOREALIS	Sagittarius	λ
BETELGEUSE	Orion	α	KAUS MEDIA	Sagittarius	δ
BIHAM	Pegasus	θ	KEID	Eridanus	o
CANOPUS	Carina	α	KITALPHA	Equuleus	α
CAPELLA	Auriga	α	KOCHAB	Ursa Minor	β
CAPH	Cassiopeia	β	KORNEPHOROS	Hercules	β
CASTOR	Gemini	α	KURHAH	Cepheus	ξ
CEBALRAI	Ophiuchus	β	LESATH	Scorpius	υ
CHARA	Canes Venatici	β	MARFIK	Ophiuchus	λ
CHERTAN	Leo	θ	MARKAB	Pegasus	α
COR CAROLI	Canes Venatici	α	MATAR	Pegasus	η
CURSA	Eridanus	β	MEBSUTA	Gemini	ε
DABIH	Capricornus	β	MEGREZ	Ursa Major	δ
DENEB	Cygnus	α	MEISSA	Orion	λ
DENEB ALGEDI	Capricornus	δ	MEKBUDA	Gemini	ζ
DENEB KAITOS	Cetus	β	MENKALINAN	Auriga	β
DENEBOLA	Leo	β	MENKAR	Cetus	α
DUBHE	Ursa Major	α	MENKENT	Centaurus	θ
EDASICH	Draco	ι	MENKIB	Perseus	ξ
ENIF	Pegasus	ε	MERAK	Ursa Major	β
ERRAI	Cepheus	γ	MESARTIM	Aries	γ
ETAMIN	Draco	γ	MIAPLACIDUS	Carina	β
FOMALHAUT	Piscis Austrinus	α	MINTAKA	Orion	δ
FURUD	Canis Major	ζ	MIRA	Cetus	o
GACRUX	Crux	γ	MIRACH	Andromeda	β
GIAUSAR	Draco	λ	MIRPHAK	Perseus	α
GIENAH	Corvus	ε	MIRZAM	Canis Major	β
GOMEISA	Canis Minor	β	MIZAR	Ursa Major	ζ
GRAFFIAS	Scorpius	β	MUPHRID	Bootes	η
GRUMIUM	Draco	ξ	MUSCIDA	Ursa Major	o
HAMAL	Aries	α	NASHIRA	Capricornus	γ
HOMAM	Pegasus	ζ	NEKKAR	Bootes	β

Names of Stars

Commonly Used Names of Stars

Name of Star	Constellation	Greek Letter Desig[1]	Name of Star	Constellation	Greek Letter Desig[1]
NIHAL	Lepus	β	SEGINUS	Bootes	γ
NUNKI	Sagittarius	σ	SHAULA	Scorpius	λ
NUSAKAN	Corona Borealis	β	SHEDIR	Cassiopeia	α
PEACOCK	Pavo	α	SHELIAK	Lyra	β
PHACT	Columba	α	SHERATAN	Aries	β
PHAD	Ursa Major	γ	SIRIUS	Canis Major	α
PHERKAD	Ursa Minor	γ	SKAT	Aquarius	δ
POLARIS	Ursa Minor	α	SPICA	Virgo	α
POLLUX	Gemini	β	SULAFAT	Lyra	γ
PORRIMA	Virgo	γ	SYRMA	Virgo	ι
PROCYON	Canis Minor	α	TALITHA	Ursa Major	ι
PROPUS	Gemini	η	TANIA AUSTRALIS	Ursa Major	μ
RASALAS	Leo	μ	TANIA BOREALIS	Ursa Major	λ
RASALGETHI	Hercules	α	TARAZED	Aquila	γ
RASALHAGUE	Ophiuchus	α	THUBAN	Draco	α
RASTABAN	Draco	β	UNUKALHAI	Serpens	α
REGULUS	Leo	α	VEGA	Lyra	α
RIGEL	Orion	β	VINDEMIATRIX	Virgo	ε
RIGIL KENT	Centaurus	α	WASAT	Gemini	δ
RUCHBAH	Cassiopeia	δ	WAZN	Columba	β
RUKBAT	Sagittarius	α	YED POSTERIOR	Ophiuchus	ε
SABIK	Ophiuchus	η	YED PRIOR	Ophiuchus	δ
SADACHBIA	Aquarius	γ	ZANIAH	Virgo	η
SADALBARI	Pegasus	μ	ZAURAK	Eridanus	γ
SADALMELIK	Aquarius	α	ZAVIJAVA	Virgo	β
SADALSUUD	Aquarius	β	ZOSMA	Leo	δ
SADR	Cygnus	γ	ZUBENELGENUBI	LIbra	α
SAIPH	Orion	κ	ZUBENESCHAMALI	Libra	β
SCHEAT	Pegasus	β			

[1]The brightest stars in each constellation are designated with a lowercase Greek letter for identification. In astronomy, when a star with a Greek letter is referred to, the Latin genitive form of the constellation name is used in conjunction with the Greek letter designation. For example, the star Mizar in Ursa Major is designated ζ, so it would be referred to as ζ Ursae Majoris (Zeta Ursae Majoris).

Constellation & Star Charts

The 88 Constellations and Commonly Used Names of Stars

Right Ascension
0 hours to 24 hours
Declination
+40° to +90°

NORTH CELESTIAL POLE AREA

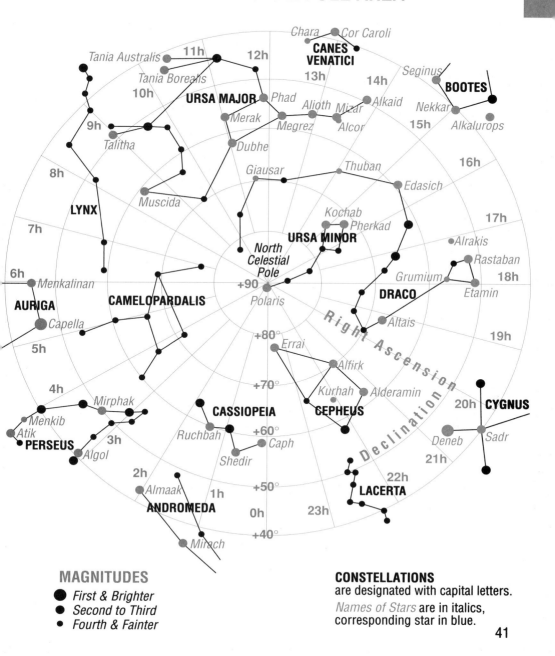

MAGNITUDES
- ● First & Brighter
- ● Second to Third
- ● Fourth & Fainter

CONSTELLATIONS
are designated with capital letters.

Names of Stars are in italics,
corresponding star in blue.

41

Constellation & Star Charts

Right Ascension
21 hours to 3 hours
Declination
−50° to +50°

The 88 Constellations and Commonly Used Names of Stars

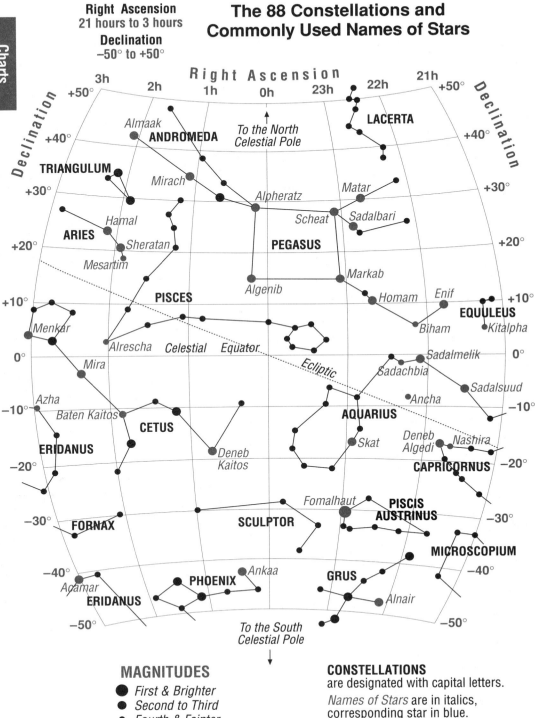

Right Ascension

To the North Celestial Pole

LACERTA

ANDROMEDA
Almaak

TRIANGULUM
Mirach
Alpheratz
Matar
Scheat
Sadalbari

ARIES
Hamal
Sheratan
Mesartim

PEGASUS
Markab

PISCES
Algenib
Homam
Enif

EQUULEUS
Biham
Kitalpha

Menkar
Alrescha Celestial Equator
Sadalmelik

Mira
Sadachbia
Sadalsuud

Azha
Baten Kaitos
Ancha

CETUS
Deneb Kaitos
AQUARIUS
Skat
Deneb Algedi
Nashira

ERIDANUS
CAPRICORNUS

Fomalhaut
PISCIS AUSTRINUS

FORNAX
SCULPTOR

MICROSCOPIUM

Ankaa
GRUS

Acamar
PHOENIX
Alnair

ERIDANUS

To the South Celestial Pole

MAGNITUDES
● First & Brighter
● Second to Third
• Fourth & Fainter

CONSTELLATIONS
are designated with capital letters.

Names of Stars are in italics, corresponding star in blue.

Constellation & Star Charts

The 88 Constellations and Commonly Used Names of Stars

Right Ascension
17 hours to 23 hours
Declination
−50° to +50°

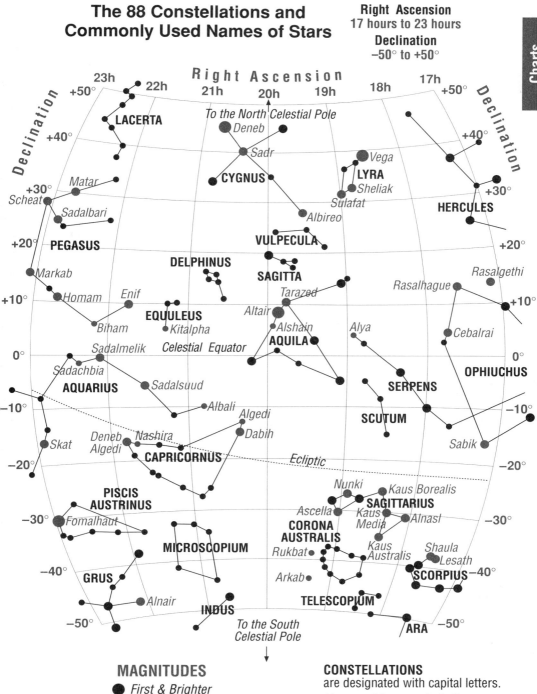

MAGNITUDES
- ● First & Brighter
- ● Second to Third
- ● Fourth & Fainter

CONSTELLATIONS
are designated with capital letters.

Names of Stars are in italics, corresponding star in blue.

43

Constellation & Star Charts

Right Ascension
13 hours to 19 hours
Declination
−50° to +50°

The 88 Constellations and Commonly Used Names of Stars

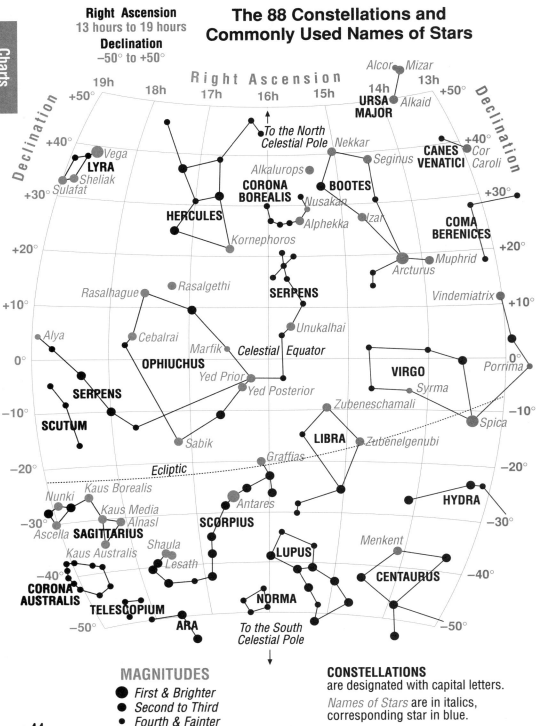

MAGNITUDES
- ● First & Brighter
- ● Second to Third
- • Fourth & Fainter

CONSTELLATIONS
are designated with capital letters.

Names of Stars are in italics,
corresponding star in blue.

Constellation & Star Charts

The 88 Constellations and Commonly Used Names of Stars

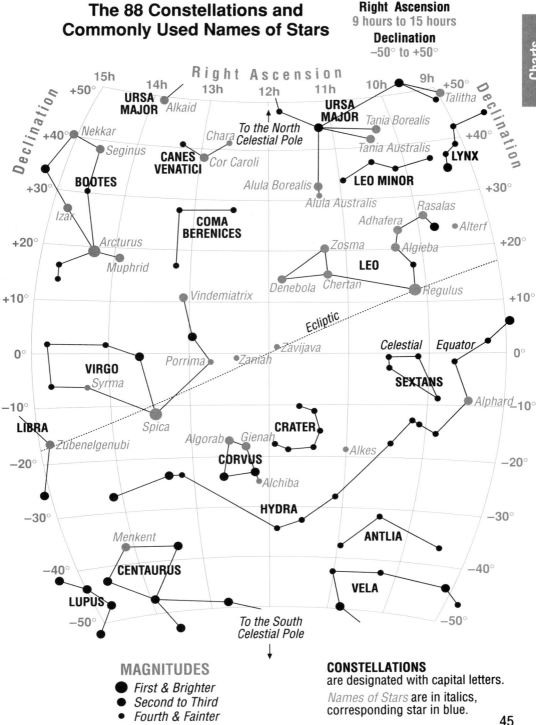

MAGNITUDES
- ● First & Brighter
- ● Second to Third
- ● Fourth & Fainter

CONSTELLATIONS
are designated with capital letters.

Names of Stars are in italics, corresponding star in blue.

45

Constellation & Star Charts

Right Ascension
5 hours to 11 hours
Declination
−50° to +50°

The 88 Constellations and Commonly Used Names of Stars

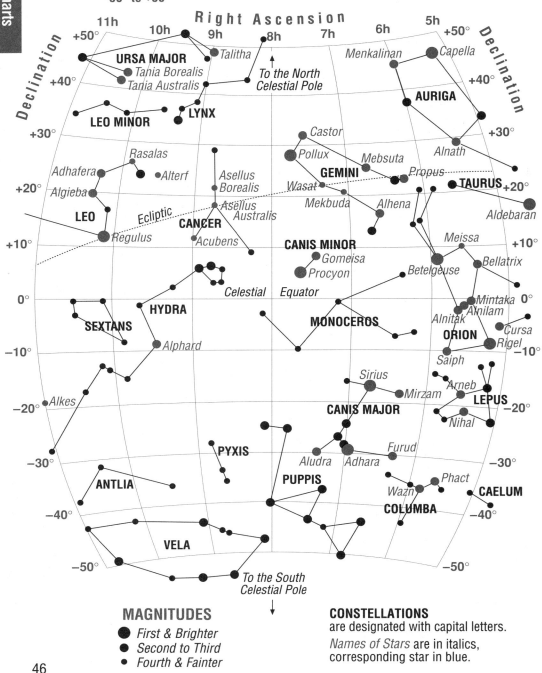

MAGNITUDES
- First & Brighter
- Second to Third
- Fourth & Fainter

CONSTELLATIONS
are designated with capital letters.

Names of Stars are in italics,
corresponding star in blue.

Constellation & Star Charts

The 88 Constellations and Commonly Used Names of Stars

Right Ascension
1 hour to 7 hours
Declination
−50° to +50°

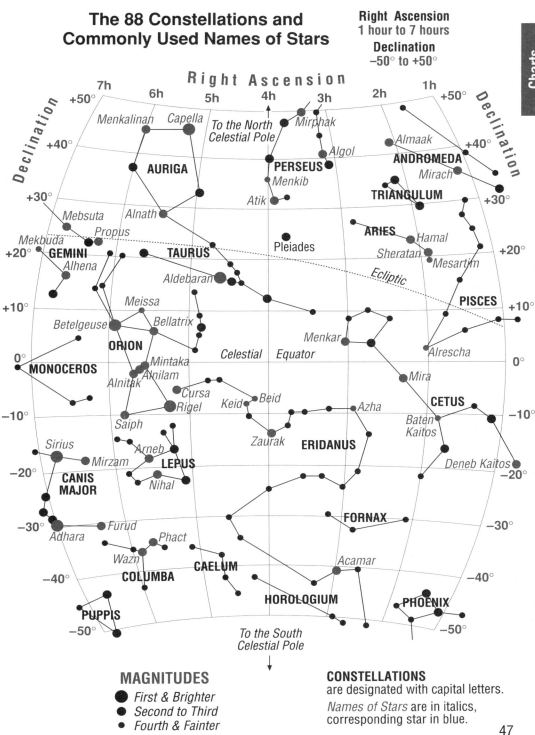

MAGNITUDES
- ● First & Brighter
- ● Second to Third
- • Fourth & Fainter

CONSTELLATIONS
are designated with capital letters.

Names of Stars are in italics,
corresponding star in blue.

47

Constellation & Star Charts

Right Ascension
0 hours to 24 hours
Declination
–40° to –90°

The 88 Constellations and Commonly Used Names of Stars

SOUTH CELESTIAL POLE AREA

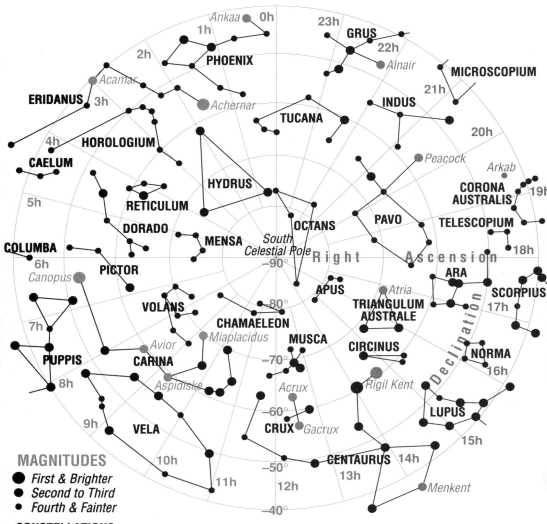

MAGNITUDES

- ⬤ First & Brighter
- ● Second to Third
- • Fourth & Fainter

CONSTELLATIONS
are designated with capital letters.

Names of Stars are in italics,
corresponding star in blue.

Facing page. *The residence and observatory of John Flamsteed (1646–1719), the first Astronomer Royal of England. It is from this site, overlooking London, that many astronomical measurements were made.*

Finding the Constellations

I f you have never found a constellation, it will take practice to orient yourself to the night skies. Even with star charts, your first times may prove frustrating. But like learning any new skill, you will become proficient if you keep practicing.

Suggestions for Those Learning to Find the Constellations

1 Jump start by enlisting the help of someone who can identify the constellations. In as little as 30 minutes, he or she can provide a framework that will last a lifetime.

2 Find a dark area and steer clear of cars and other bright or glaring lights.

3 Avoid nights when the Moon shines brightly because this will make the stars more difficult to see.

4 Stay outside at least 15 minutes for your eyes to dark adapt. You will then be able to see more stars (see the next page for information on dark adapted eyes). Also, use a red flashlight to read the star charts. This will help you keep your night vision.

5 Initially, always use star charts and face either due north or due south.

6 Try to correspond the brightest stars in the sky with the brightest stars on the star charts. Caution: Don't confuse the Planets with the brightest stars. Venus, Mars, Jupiter and Saturn normally outshine the brightest stars. Refer to the Planets at Sunrise and Sunset tables for the Planets that will be out (pages 136 to 165). If you practice facing north, you will avoid the Planets.

7 The constellations are big. With your arm extended, Orion spans one hand length and the Big Dipper over one hand length.

8 If you are having difficulty finding the constellations, *practice with many short sessions over several days, weeks or months instead of long, drawn out sessions.*

Facing page. *Star trail centered on Polaris. This 20 minute exposure shows the apparent movement of the stars around the North Celestial Pole, which is caused by the Earth's rotation on its axis.*

Night Vision

Dark Adapted Eyes — Night Vision

One night I mentioned to my wife and six-year old daughter that I was going out to observe. My daughter immediately perked up and said, "I want to go with you, Daddy." We went downstairs and I set my 4-inch scope on the porch. "I'm going to turn the lights off now," I said to her and we started to observe. After about ten minutes, she remarked, "It's getting lighter out here." I said, "No, it's not getting lighter, your eyes are opening up and you can now see better in the dark." I got no response from this statement and felt that she did not quite understand. About five minutes later, she enthusiastically said, "It's even lighter now." And so, my daughter discovered the process of her eyes "dark adapting." And I mused with joy in her observations.

It takes about 15 minutes for the eyes to become initially dark adapted. You will notice a difference in as little as five minutes. A "deeper" dark adaptation takes from 30 to 60 minutes.

If you plan to observe the night sky for an extended period of time, take care to preserve your night vision. If exposed to bright lights, your eyes will lose their dark adaptation.

Dark adapted eyes are essential for observing the fainter deep sky objects (see pages 231 to 277). You simply will not be able to see these objects if your eyes are not dark adapted.

Use a Red Flashlight to Read the Star Charts

A red light flashlight will help preserve your night vision. Use only a red light to read star charts because this color does not affect dark adapted eyes as much as other colors. If you use a regular (white light) flashlight, your eyes will lose their dark adaptation, making it difficult to see the stars. Red flashlights can be pur-chased at your local telescope shop or from advertisers in the popular monthly astronomy magazines.

The Basic Movement of the Heavens

Two major factors create most of the movement observed in heavenly bodies: the rotation of the Earth on its axis (causing our day) and the revolution of the Earth around the Sun (creat-ing our year). Remember, since the stars are very far away, they appear fixed and stationary in relationship to any move-ment of the Earth and the Solar System members.

Movement of the Stars

Movements in the Sky

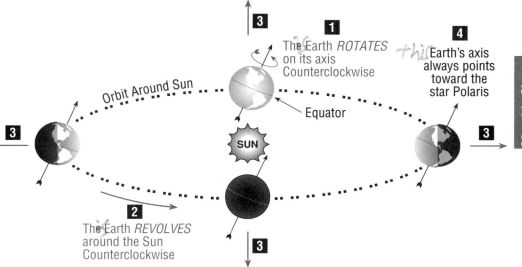

1 Our days and nights, as well as the daily rising and setting of the Sun, Moon and stars, happen because the Earth rotates on an axis.

2 The Earth's revolution around the Sun creates our year and is the reason that the stars change from month to month.

3 The night side of the Earth points in a slightly different direction every night of the year; however, it takes about a month for us to notice any change in the evening stars.

4 The Earth acts like a gyroscope as it spins daily on its axis. One property of a gyroscope is that, as it spins, its axis will always point in the same direction even if the gyroscope is moved about. So, even though the Earth revolves around the Sun, its axis always points in the same direction, and the star Polaris just happens to be near to where it points.

Our day is based on the rotation of the Earth on its axis. This rotation creates the illusion that the Sun, Moon and stars circle the sky once a day. Also, because the Earth's axis points very close to the star Polaris in the constellation Ursa Minor, all the stars in the sky appear to revolve around Polaris. The Earth's axis

Milky Way and Ecliptic

always points in the same direction (toward Polaris). This is because all spinning objects act like gyroscopes in that the spinning axis always points in the same direction even if the gyroscope is moved (like the Earth revolving around the Sun).

The Earth revolves around the Sun once a year. This movement causes the Earth's nighttime side to face a slightly different direction each night. However, it takes about a month for observers to notice any real difference in the direction that the night side is facing.

Monthly Charts

The Milky Way

The Milky Way is a band of light spanning the night sky and dividing it roughly into halves. Composed of countless stars, all too faint for our eyes to see individually, it represents the majority of stars comprising our galaxy.

The Milky Way shows considerable irregularity in its path through the sky. The thickest and brightest part, near the constellation Sagittarius, is the direction towards the center of our Galaxy. The Milky Way is not visible in large cities because light pollution easily obscures the band. Outside of metropolitan areas, the Milky Way is prominent.

The Ecliptic: Where the Planets Roam

The ecliptic is the apparent path that the Sun describes against the background stars over the course of a year. This path circles the sky and crosses the 12 constellations known as the zodiac. Its most northern point is in the constellation Taurus (Summer Solstice) and its most southern point is in Sagittarius (Winter Solstice). It crosses the celestial equator in Pisces (Vernal Equinox) and Virgo (Autumnal Equinox).

The Planets are always very close to the ecliptic because they orbit the Sun in nearly the same plane as the Earth (see bottom of page 116). This makes the ecliptic helpful in locating the Planets. If you know where the ecliptic is, you know the Planets will be somewhere near this path.

Using the Monthly Star Charts

Please follow these Instructions to get the most out of using the Monthly Star Charts

Due **East**
USE **SOUTH** CHART
AS INDICATED IN OVAL

North

Due **West**
USE **SOUTH** CHART
AS INDICATED IN OVAL

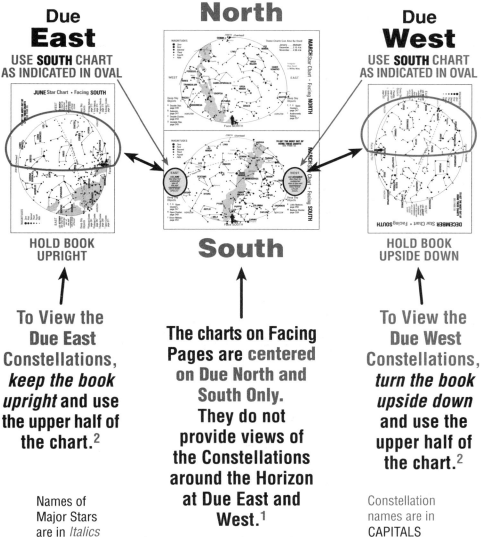

HOLD BOOK
UPRIGHT

South

HOLD BOOK
UPSIDE DOWN

To View the
Due East
Constellations,
*keep the book
upright* and use
the upper half of
the chart.[2]

**The charts on Facing
Pages are centered
on Due North and
South Only.
They do not
provide views of
the Constellations
around the Horizon
at Due East and
West.**[1]

To View the
Due West
Constellations,
*turn the book
upside down*
and use the
upper half of
the chart.[2]

Names of
Major Stars
are in *Italics*

Constellation
names are in
CAPITALS

Charts show stars 2 hours after sunset

[1] These monthly charts were designed specifically to provide undistorted shapes of the constellations. Although using the charts to identify the constellations due East and West may seem awkward at first, this method ensures that the constellations on the charts match the shape of the constellations in the sky. [2] Book may have to be rotated a little to the left or right for best orientation.

JANUARY Star Chart ★ Facing NORTH

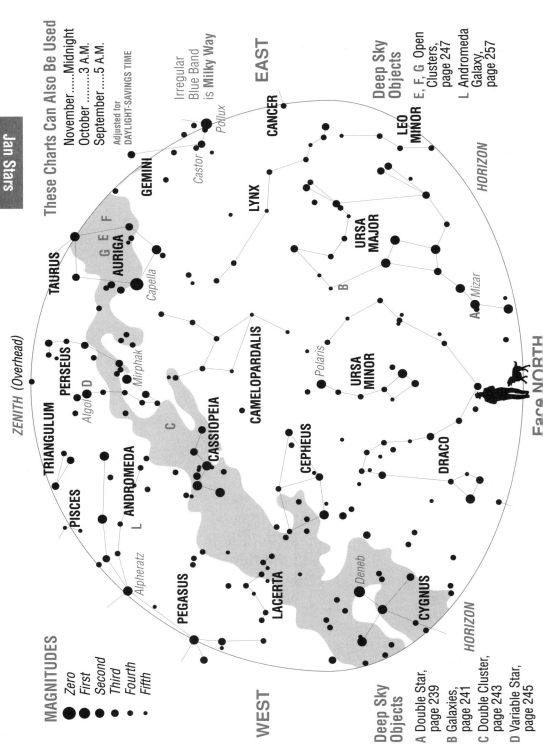

Jan Stars

ZENITH (Overhead)

These Charts Can Also Be Used

November.....Midnight
October.........3 A.M.
September.....5 A.M.

Adjusted for
DAYLIGHT-SAVINGS TIME

Irregular
Blue Band
is Milky Way

EAST

CANCER

CASTOR

GEMINI

Pollux

Castor

LEO
MINOR

Deep Sky
Objects

E, F, G Open
Clusters,
page 247

L Andromeda
Galaxy,
page 257

HORIZON

LYNX

URSA
MAJOR

B

Mizar

A

TAURUS

AURIGA

G E F

Capella

PERSEUS

Mirphak

Algol D

TRIANGULUM

ANDROMEDA

C

CAMELOPARDALIS

Polaris

URSA
MINOR

PISCES

L

CASSIOPEIA

CEPHEUS

DRACO

PEGASUS

Alpheratz

LACERTA

Deneb

CYGNUS

Face NORTH

WEST

HORIZON

MAGNITUDES

Zero
First
Second
Third
Fourth
Fifth

Deep Sky
Objects

A Double Star,
  page 239

B Galaxies,
  page 241

C Double Cluster,
  page 243

D Variable Star,
  page 245

JANUARY Star Chart ★ Facing SOUTH

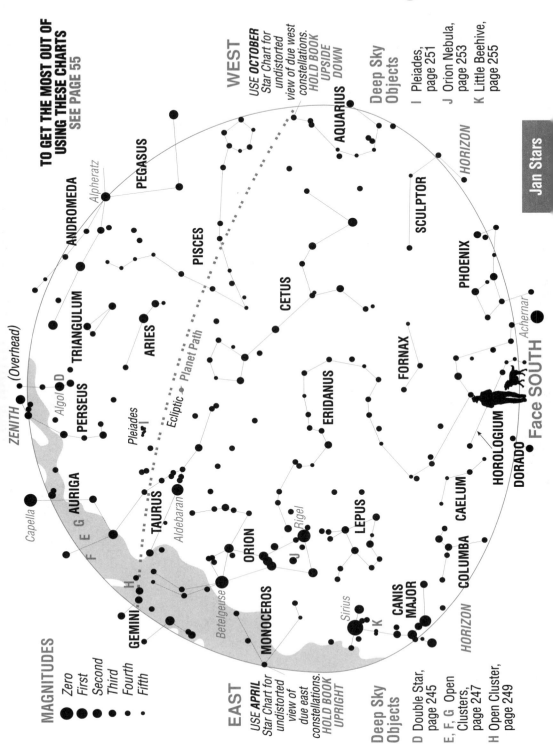

TO GET THE MOST OUT OF USING THESE CHARTS
SEE PAGE 55

WEST

USE OCTOBER Star Chart for undistorted view of due west constellations. HOLD BOOK UPSIDE DOWN

Deep Sky Objects

I Pleiades, page 251

J Orion Nebula, page 253

K Little Beehive, page 255

Jan Stars

HORIZON

PEGASUS

Alpheratz

ANDROMEDA

AQUARIUS

SCULPTOR

PHOENIX

PISCES

CETUS

Achernar

TRIANGULUM

ARIES

FORNAX

Algol D

PERSEUS

Pleiades I

ERIDANUS

HOROLOGIUM

DORADO

ZENITH (Overhead)

AURIGA

F E G

Capella

TAURUS

Aldebaran

ORION

Rigel

LEPUS

CAELUM

COLUMBA

Betelgeuse

H

GEMINI

MONCEROS

J

K

CANIS MAJOR

Sirius

Face SOUTH

Ecliptic • Planet Path

HORIZON

MAGNITUDES

Zero
First
Second
Third
Fourth
Fifth

EAST

USE APRIL Star Chart for undistorted view of due east constellations. HOLD BOOK UPRIGHT

Deep Sky Objects

D Double Star, page 245

E, F, G Open Clusters, page 247

H Open Cluster, page 249

FEBRUARY Star Chart ★ Facing NORTH

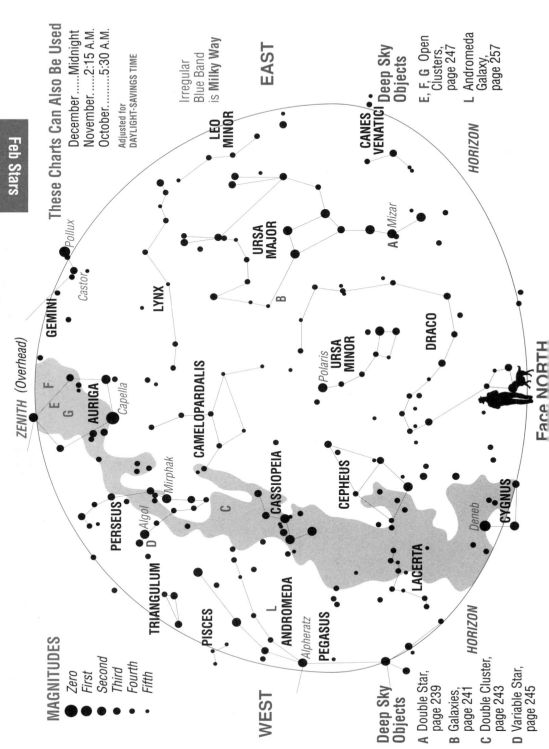

Feb Stars

These Charts Can Also Be Used

December.....Midnight
November.....2:15 A.M.
October.......5:30 A.M.

Adjusted for
DAYLIGHT-SAVINGS TIME

Irregular
Blue Band
is Milky Way

EAST

Deep Sky
Objects

E, F, G Open
Clusters,
page 247

L Andromeda
Galaxy,
page 257

HORIZON

Face NORTH

ZENITH (Overhead)

MAGNITUDES

Zero
First
Second
Third
Fourth
Fifth

Deep Sky
Objects

A Double Star,
page 239

B Galaxies,
page 241

C Double Cluster,
page 243

D Variable Star,
page 245

WEST

HORIZON

Constellations and stars labeled:
GEMINI — Pollux, Castor
LYNX
LEO MINOR
URSA MAJOR — Mizar (A), B
CANES VENATICI
DRACO
URSA MINOR — Polaris
AURIGA — Capella, E, F, G
CAMELOPARDALIS
CASSIOPEIA — C
CEPHEUS
CYGNUS — Deneb
PERSEUS — Mirphak, Algol (D)
TRIANGULUM
PISCES
ANDROMEDA — Alpheratz, L
PEGASUS
LACERTA

FEBRUARY Star Chart ★ Facing SOUTH

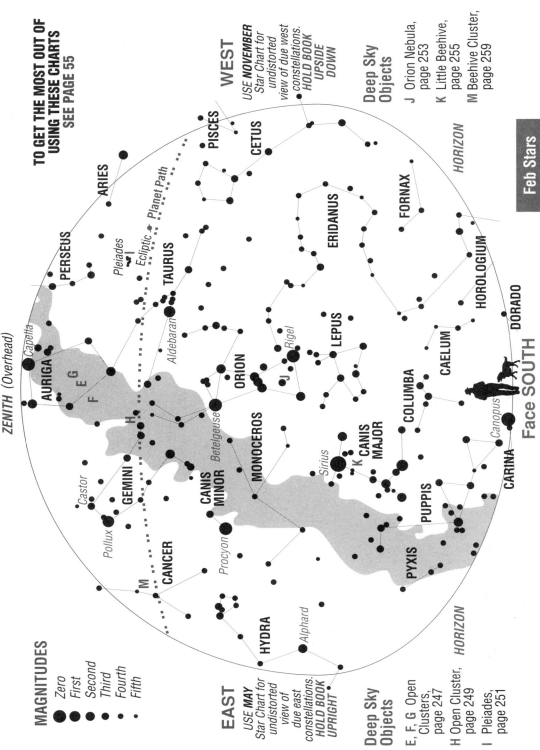

TO GET THE MOST OUT OF USING THESE CHARTS
SEE PAGE 55

ZENITH *(Overhead)*

Face SOUTH

WEST
*USE **NOVEMBER** Star Chart for undistorted view of due west constellations.*
HOLD BOOK UPSIDE DOWN

Deep Sky Objects
J Orion Nebula, page 253
K Little Beehive, page 255
M Beehive Cluster, page 259

EAST
*USE **MAY** Star Chart for undistorted view of due east constellations.*
HOLD BOOK UPRIGHT

Deep Sky Objects
E, F, G Open Clusters, page 247
H Open Cluster, page 249
I Pleiades, page 251

MAGNITUDES

- ● Zero
- ● First
- ● Second
- ● Third
- • Fourth
- · Fifth

Constellations & stars: PISCES, CETUS, ARIES, PERSEUS, Pleiades, Ecliptic, Planet Path, TAURUS, Aldebaran, AURIGA, Capella, ERIDANUS, FORNAX, HOROLOGIUM, DORADO, LEPUS, Rigel, ORION, Betelgeuse, CAELUM, COLUMBA, Canopus, CARINA, MONOCEROS, CANIS MAJOR, Sirius, CANIS MINOR, GEMINI, Castor, Pollux, CANCER, Procyon, PUPPIS, PYXIS, HYDRA, Alphard, *HORIZON*

MARCH Star Chart ★ Facing NORTH

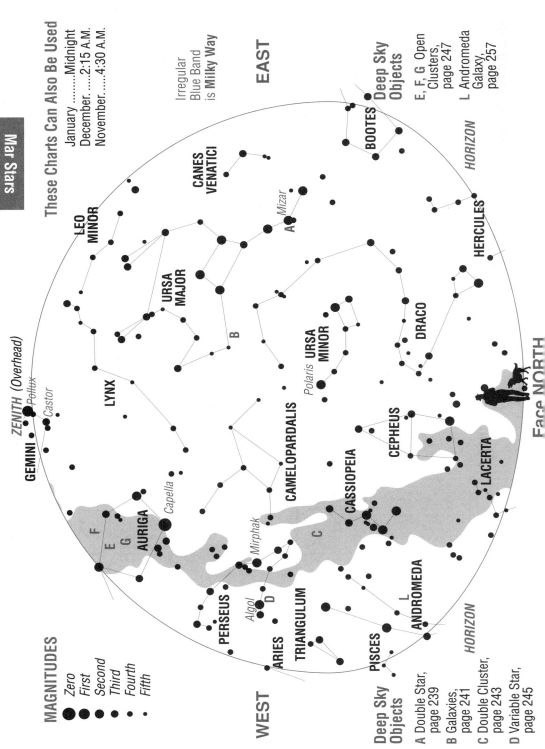

Mar Stars

These Charts Can Also Be Used

January ....Midnight
December ....2:15 A.M.
November.....4:30 A.M.

Irregular
Blue Band
is Milky Way

EAST

Deep Sky
Objects

E, F, G Open
Clusters,
page 247

L Andromeda
Galaxy,
page 257

HORIZON

BOOTES

HERCULES

CANES
VENATICI

Mizar

A

LEO
MINOR

URSA
MAJOR

DRACO

B

Polaris URSA
MINOR

LYNX

ZENITH (Overhead)

Pollux

Castor

GEMINI

CAMELOPARDALIS

CEPHEUS

LACERTA

Face NORTH

Capella

CASSIOPEIA

AURIGA

F

E

G

Mirphak

C

ANDROMEDA

L

PERSEUS

Algol

D

TRIANGULUM

PISCES

ARIES

MAGNITUDES

Zero
First
Second
Third
Fourth
Fifth

WEST

Deep Sky
Objects

A Double Star,
page 239

B Galaxies,
page 241

C Double Cluster,
page 243

D Variable Star,
page 245

HORIZON

MARCH Star Chart ★ Facing SOUTH

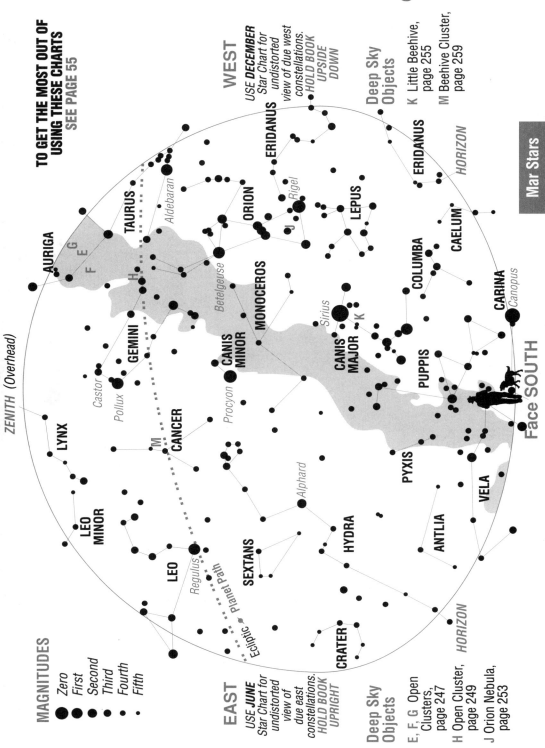

TO GET THE MOST OUT OF
USING THESE CHARTS
SEE PAGE 55

MAGNITUDES
- Zero
- First
- Second
- Third
- Fourth
- Fifth

ZENITH (Overhead)

WEST
USE **DECEMBER**
Star Chart for
undistorted
view of due west
constellations.
HOLD BOOK
UPSIDE
DOWN

Deep Sky
Objects

K Little Beehive,
page 255
M Beehive Cluster,
page 259

Mar Stars

HORIZON

EAST
USE **JUNE**
Star Chart for
undistorted
view of due east
constellations.
HOLD BOOK
UPRIGHT

Deep Sky
Objects

E, F, G Open
Clusters,
page 247
H Open Cluster,
page 249
J Orion Nebula,
page 253

HORIZON

Face SOUTH

AURIGA
TAURUS
Aldebaran
ERIDANUS
ORION
Rigel
LEPUS
ERIDANUS
CAELUM
COLUMBA
CARINA
Canopus
GEMINI
Castor
Pollux
Betelgeuse
MONOCEROS
CANIS
MINOR
Sirius
CANIS
MAJOR
PUPPIS
LYNX
CANCER
Procyon
PYXIS
VELA
LEO
MINOR
M
Alphard
LEO
Regulus
SEXTANS
HYDRA
ANTLIA
Ecliptic
Planet Path
CRATER

APRIL Star Chart ★ Facing NORTH

ZENITH (Overhead)

These Charts Can Also Be Used

February ...... 12:30 A.M.
January .... 3 A.M.
December. .... 5 A.M.

Irregular
Blue Band
is Milky Way

EAST

Deep Sky Objects

D Variable Star, page 245

E, F, G Open Clusters, page 247

N, O Globular Clusters, page 261

HERCULES

CORONA BOREALIS

BOOTES

N

O

Vega

LYRA

HORIZON

CANES VENATICI

Mizar

A

DRACO

CYGNUS

Deneb

URSA MINOR

Polaris

URSA MAJOR

B

CEPHEUS

LACERTA

LEO MINOR

CAMELOPARDALIS

CASSIOPEIA

C

Face NORTH

LYNX

ANDROMEDA

Pollux
Castor

GEMINI

Capella

Mirphak

PERSEUS

Algol

D

HORIZON

MAGNITUDES

Zero
First
Second
Third
Fourth
Fifth

F

E G

AURIGA

WEST

Deep Sky Objects

A Double Star, page 239

B Galaxies, page 241

C Double Cluster, page 243

APRIL Star Chart ★ Facing SOUTH

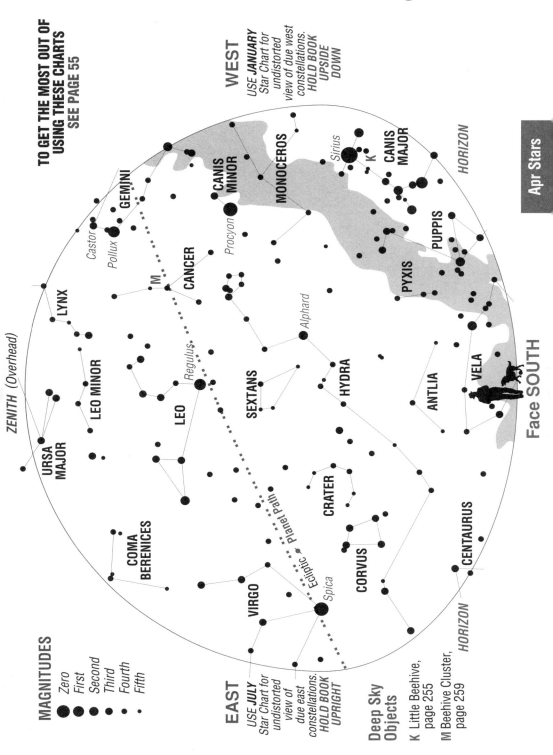

TO GET THE MOST OUT OF
USING THESE CHARTS
SEE PAGE 55

WEST
USE JANUARY
Star Chart for
undistorted
view of due west
constellations.
HOLD BOOK
UPSIDE
DOWN

HORIZON

Apr Stars

ZENITH (Overhead)

Face SOUTH

GEMINI
Castor
Pollux
CANIS MINOR
Procyon
MONOCEROS
Sirius
K
CANIS MAJOR
PUPPIS
PYXIS
LYNX
M
CANCER
Alphard
URSA MAJOR
LEO MINOR
LEO
Regulus
SEXTANS
HYDRA
ANTLIA
VELA
COMA BERENICES
CRATER
CENTAURUS
VIRGO
Spica
Ecliptic
Planet Path
CORVUS
HORIZON

MAGNITUDES
● Zero
● First
● Second
• Third
· Fourth
· Fifth

EAST
USE JULY
Star Chart for
undistorted
view of
due east
constellations.
HOLD BOOK
UPRIGHT

Deep Sky Objects
K Little Beehive,
page 255
M Beehive Cluster,
page 259

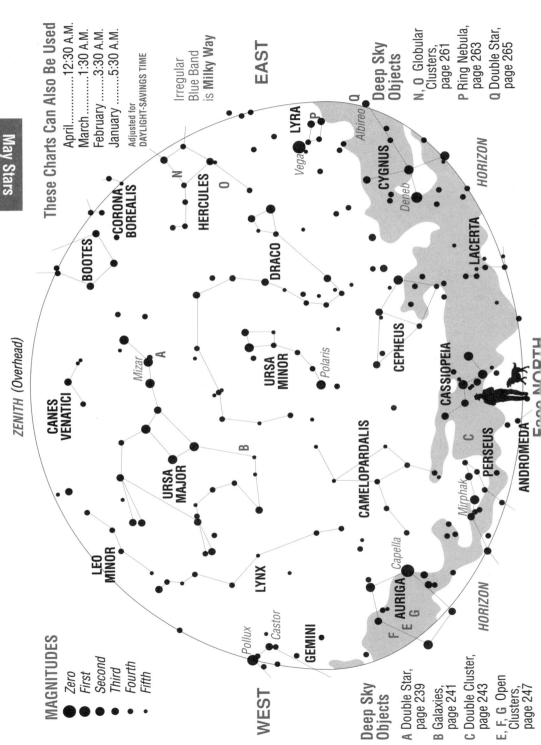

MAY Star Chart ★ Facing NORTH

May Stars

ZENITH (Overhead)

These Charts Can Also Be Used

April..........12:30 A.M.
March..........1:30 A.M.
February.......3:30 A.M.
January........5:30 A.M.

Adjusted for
DAYLIGHT-SAVINGS TIME

Irregular
Blue Band
is Milky Way

EAST

WEST

EAST NORTH

HORIZON

HORIZON

MAGNITUDES
· Zero
· First
· Second
· Third
· Fourth
· Fifth

Deep Sky Objects

A Double Star, page 239
B Galaxies, page 241
C Double Cluster, page 243
E, F, G Open Clusters, page 247

Deep Sky Objects

N, O Globular Clusters, page 261
P Ring Nebula, page 263
Q Double Star, page 265

LYRA
Vega
HERCULES
CORONA BOREALIS
BOOTES
DRACO
CANES VENATICI
Mizar
A
URSA MAJOR
B
LEO MINOR
LYNX
Castor
Pollux
GEMINI
AURIGA
Capella
F
E
G
CAMELOPARDALIS
URSA MINOR
Polaris
CEPHEUS
CASSIOPEIA
PERSEUS
Mirphak
ANDROMEDA
C
LACERTA
CYGNUS
Deneb
Albireo
Q
P
N
O
HORIZON

MAY Star Chart ★ Facing SOUTH

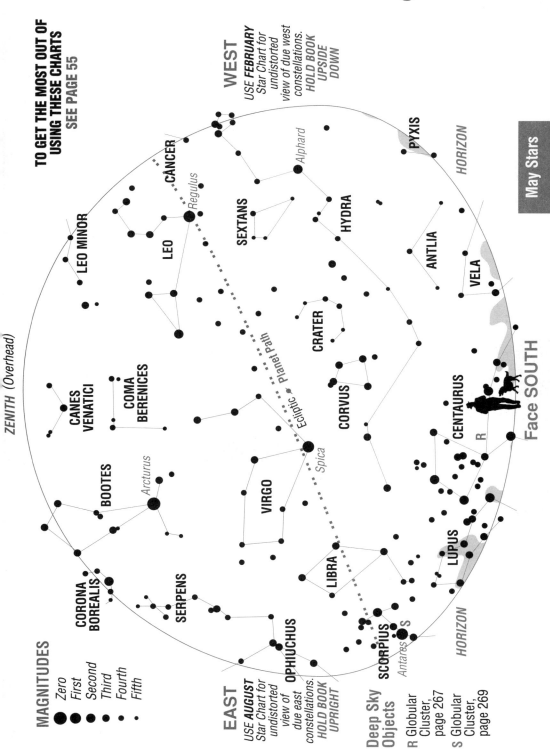

TO GET THE MOST OUT OF USING THESE CHARTS
SEE PAGE 55

WEST
USE *FEBRUARY* Star Chart for undistorted view of due west constellations.
HOLD BOOK UPSIDE DOWN

May Stars

ZENITH *(Overhead)*

EAST
USE *AUGUST* Star Chart for undistorted view of due east constellations.
HOLD BOOK UPRIGHT

MAGNITUDES
- Zero
- First
- Second
- Third
- Fourth
- Fifth

Deep Sky Objects

R Globular Cluster, page 267

S Globular Cluster, page 269

PYXIS

HORIZON

CANCER

Regulus

LEO MINOR

LEO

SEXTANS

Alphard

HYDRA

ANTLIA

VELA

CRATER

COMA BERENICES

CANES VENATICI

BOOTES

Arcturus

Ecliptic · Planet Path

Spica

VIRGO

CORVUS

CENTAURUS

R

Face SOUTH

CORONA BOREALIS

SERPENS

OPHIUCHUS

LIBRA

LUPUS

SCORPIUS

Antares

S

HORIZON

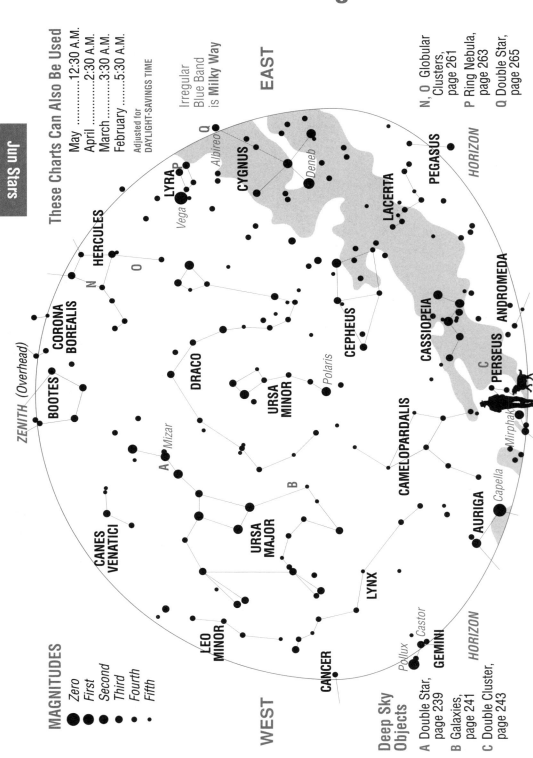

JUNE Star Chart ★ Facing SOUTH

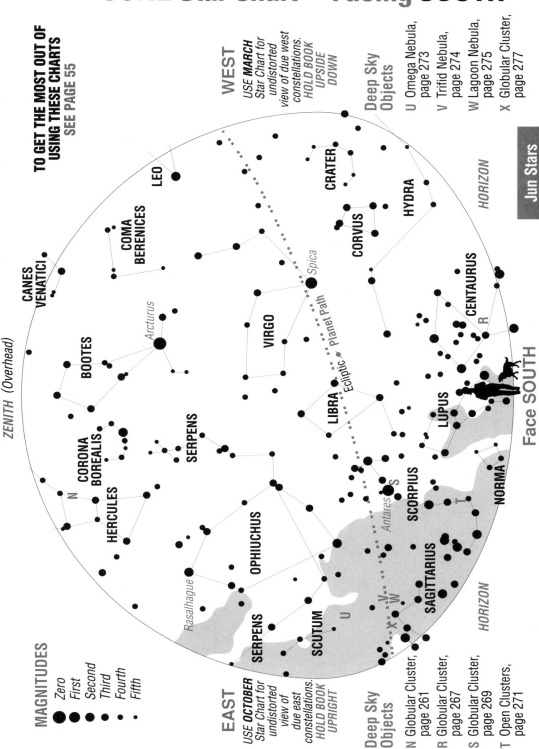

TO GET THE MOST OUT OF USING THESE CHARTS
SEE PAGE 55

ZENITH *(Overhead)*

WEST

USE **MARCH** Star Chart for undistorted view of due west constellations.
HOLD BOOK UPSIDE DOWN

Deep Sky Objects

U Omega Nebula, page 273
V Trifid Nebula, page 274
W Lagoon Nebula, page 275
X Globular Cluster, page 277

Jun Stars

HORIZON

LEO

COMA BERENICES

CANES VENATICI

CRATER

HYDRA

CORVUS

BOOTES

Arcturus

Spica

VIRGO

CENTAURUS

R

CORONA BOREALIS

N

HERCULES

SERPENS

Planet Path

Ecliptic

LIBRA

LUPUS

Face SOUTH

OPHIUCHUS

Rasalhague

SERPENS

SCUTUM

U

Antares

S

SCORPIUS

NORMA

T

V
W

X

SAGITTARIUS

HORIZON

MAGNITUDES

● Zero
● First
● Second
● Third
· Fourth
· Fifth

EAST

USE **OCTOBER** Star Chart for undistorted view of due east constellations.
HOLD BOOK UPRIGHT

Deep Sky Objects

N Globular Cluster, page 261
R Globular Cluster, page 267
S Globular Cluster, page 269
T Open Clusters, page 271

JULY Star Chart ★ Facing NORTH

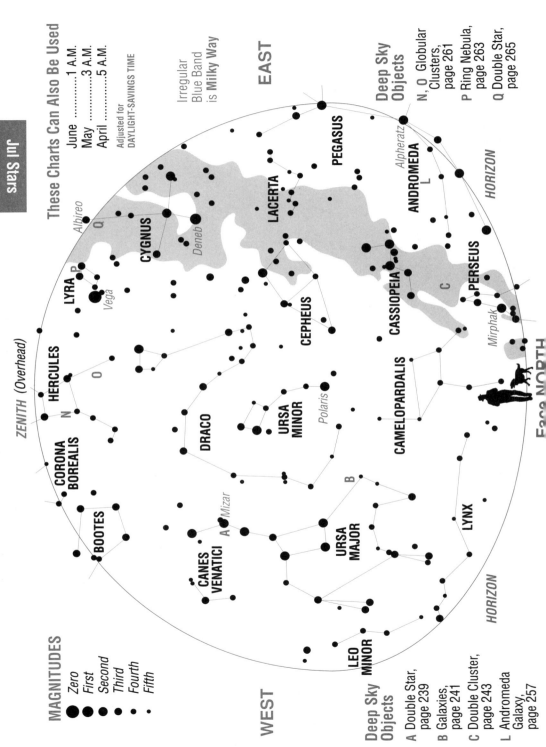

These Charts Can Also Be Used

June ....1 A.M.
May ....3 A.M.
April ....5 A.M.

Adjusted for
DAYLIGHT-SAVINGS TIME

Irregular
Blue Band
is Milky Way

EAST

ZENITH (Overhead)

WEST

HORIZON

HORIZON

Face NORTH

Deep Sky Objects

N, O Globular
Clusters,
page 261

P Ring Nebula,
page 263

Q Double Star,
page 265

Deep Sky Objects

A Double Star,
page 239

B Galaxies,
page 241

C Double Cluster,
page 243

L Andromeda
Galaxy,
page 257

MAGNITUDES

● Zero
● First
● Second
● Third
· Fourth
· Fifth

Jul Stars

Constellations and stars labeled on chart:
PEGASUS, LACERTA, ANDROMEDA, Alpheratz, CYGNUS, Deneb, Albireo, CASSIOPEIA, PERSEUS, Mirphak, LYRA, Vega, CEPHEUS, HERCULES, DRACO, URSA MINOR, Polaris, CORONA BOREALIS, CAMELOPARDALIS, BOOTES, CANES VENATICI, Mizar, URSA MAJOR, LYNX, LEO MINOR

JULY Star Chart ★ Facing SOUTH

TO GET THE MOST OUT OF USING THESE CHARTS
SEE PAGE 55

Deep Sky Objects

S Globular Cluster, page 269
T Open Clusters, page 271

WEST

USE **APRIL** *Star Chart for undistorted view of due west constellations.*
HOLD BOOK UPSIDE DOWN

Deep Sky Objects

U Omega Nebula, page 273
V Trifid Nebula, page 274
W Lagoon Nebula, page 275
X Globular Cluster, page 277

Jul Stars

MAGNITUDES

● Zero
● First
● Second
● Third
· Fourth
· Fifth

ZENITH (Overhead)

Arcturus

Spica
Ecliptic — Planet Path

VIRGO

BOOTES

CORONA BOREALIS

N

O

HERCULES

SERPENS

OPHIUCHUS

LIBRA

HYDRA

Vega

LYRA

P

Q

Albireo

CYGNUS

VULPECULA

SAGITTA

Rasalhague

SERPENS

SCUTUM

Altair

AQUILA

DELPHINUS

Antares S

SCORPIUS

LUPUS

NORMA

CENTAURUS

HORIZON

U

T

X W

SAGITTARIUS

CORONA AUSTRALIS

ARA

TELESCOPIUM

Face SOUTH

CAPRICORNUS

AQUARIUS

MICROSCOPIUM

HORIZON

EAST

USE **NOVEMBER** *Star Chart for undistorted view of due east constellations.*
HOLD BOOK UPRIGHT

Deep Sky Objects

N, O Globular Clusters, page 261
P Ring Nebula, page 263
Q Double Star, page 265

AUGUST Star Chart ★ Facing NORTH

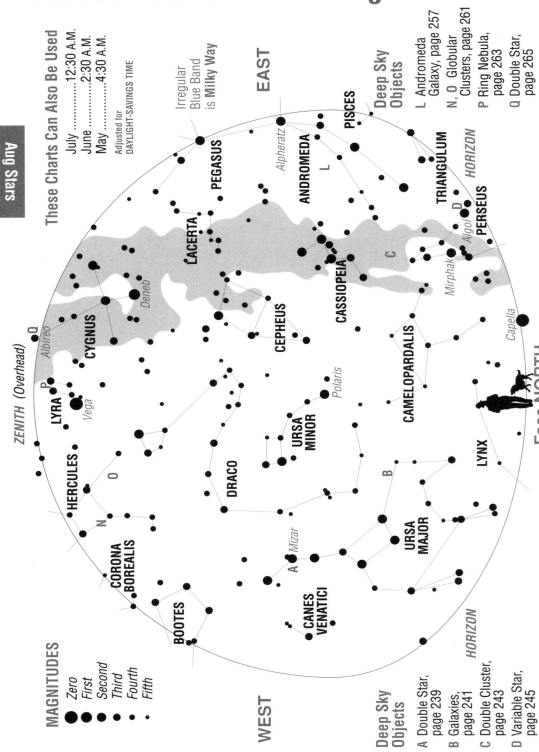

Aug Stars

These Charts Can Also Be Used

July ....12:30 A.M.
June ....2:30 A.M.
May ....4:30 A.M.

Adjusted for
DAYLIGHT-SAVINGS TIME

Deep Sky Objects

L Andromeda
  Galaxy, page 257
N, O Globular
  Clusters, page 261
P Ring Nebula,
  page 263
Q Double Star,
  page 265

MAGNITUDES

Zero
First
Second
Third
Fourth
Fifth

Deep Sky Objects

A Double Star,
  page 239
B Galaxies,
  page 241
C Double Cluster,
  page 243
D Variable Star,
  page 245

EAST

PISCES
Alpheratz
ANDROMEDA
L
TRIANGULUM
D
PERSEUS
Algol
Mirphak
HORIZON
C
CASSIOPEIA
PEGASUS
LACERTA
Irregular
Blue Band
is Milky Way
Deneb
CEPHEUS
CYGNUS
Albireo
P
LYRA
Vega
Q
ZENITH (Overhead)
HERCULES
O
N
CORONA
BOREALIS
BOOTES
Mizar
A
CANES
VENATICI
URSA
MAJOR
DRACO
URSA
MINOR
Polaris
B
CAMELOPARDALIS
Capella
LYNX
Face NORTH
HORIZON

WEST

AUGUST Star Chart ★ Facing SOUTH

TO GET THE MOST OUT OF USING THESE CHARTS
SEE PAGE 55

Deep Sky Objects

S Globular Cluster, page 269
T Open Clusters, page 271

WEST

*USE **MAY** Star Chart for undistorted view of due west constellations.*
HOLD BOOK UPSIDE DOWN

Deep Sky Objects

U Omega Nebula, page 273
V Trifid Nebula, page 274
W Lagoon Nebula, page 275
X Globular Cluster, page 277

Aug Stars

HORIZON

ZENITH (Overhead)

VIRGO
LIBRA
CORONA BOREALIS
SERPENS
N
O
HERCULES
OPHIUCHUS
LUPUS
SCORPIUS
Antares
S
NORMA
Vega
LYRA
P
Rasalhague
SAGITTARIUS
TELESCOPIUM
ARA
VULPECULA
SERPENS
SCUTUM
U
CYGNUS
Albireo Q
SAGITTA
DELPHINUS
AQUILA
X W V
CORONA AUSTRALIS
Deneb
Altair
CAPRICORNUS
INDUS
EQUULEUS
MICROSCOPIUM
GRUS
PEGASUS
AQUARIUS
Ecliptic Planet Path
PISCIS AUSTRINUS
Fomalhaut
HORIZON

Face SOUTH

MAGNITUDES

Zero
First
Second
Third
Fourth
Fifth

EAST

*USE **DECEMBER** Star Chart for undistorted view of due east constellations.*
HOLD BOOK UPRIGHT

Deep Sky Objects

N, O Globular Clusters, page 261
P Ring Nebula, page 263
Q Double Star, page 265

SEPTEMBER Star Chart ★ Facing NORTH

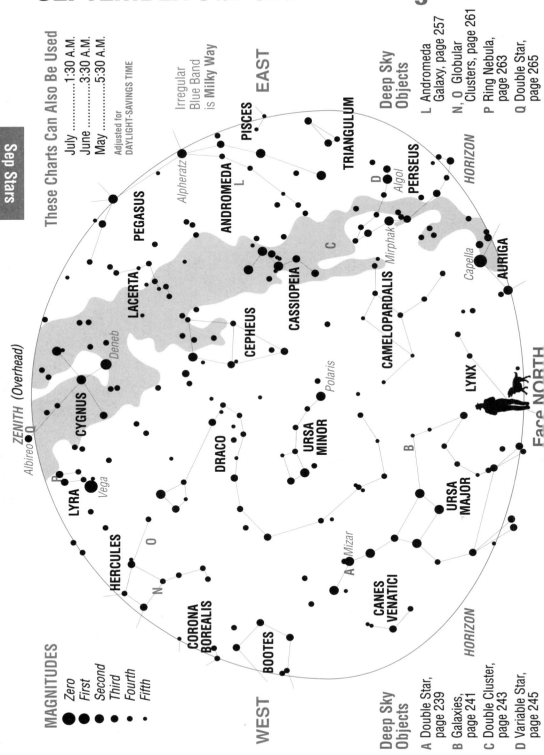

Sep Stars

These Charts Can Also Be Used

July .... 1:30 A.M.
June .... 3:30 A.M.
May .... 5:30 A.M.

Adjusted for
DAYLIGHT-SAVINGS TIME

Irregular
Blue Band
is Milky Way

EAST

Deep Sky
Objects

L Andromeda
  Galaxy, page 257
N, O Globular
  Clusters, page 261
P Ring Nebula,
  page 263
Q Double Star,
  page 265

HORIZON

PISCES
TRIANGULUM
PERSEUS
ANDROMEDA
L
Alpheratz
D
Algol
PEGASUS
C
CASSIOPEIA
Mirphak
LACERTA
CEPHEUS
CAMELOPARDALIS
Capella
AURIGA
Deneb
CYGNUS
LYNX
Polaris
DRACO
URSA
MINOR
B
LYRA
Vega
P
Q
Albireo
ZENITH (Overhead)
URSA
MAJOR
HERCULES
O
A Mizar
CANES
VENATICI
N
CORONA
BOREALIS
BOOTES
A
HORIZON
Face NORTH

WEST

MAGNITUDES

● Zero
● First
● Second
• Third
· Fourth
· Fifth

Deep Sky
Objects

A Double Star,
  page 239
B Galaxies,
  page 241
C Double Cluster,
  page 243
D Variable Star,
  page 245

SEPTEMBER Star Chart ★ Facing SOUTH

TO GET THE MOST OUT OF
USING THESE CHARTS
SEE PAGE 55

WEST

USE *MAY*
Star Chart for
undistorted
view of due west
constellations.
HOLD BOOK
UPSIDE
DOWN

Deep Sky
Objects

U Omega Nebula,
page 273

V Trifid Nebula,
page 274

W Lagoon Nebula,
page 275

X Globular Cluster,
page 277

Sep Stars

ZENITH (Overhead)

MAGNITUDES

- Zero
- First
- Second
- Third
- Fourth
- Fifth

EAST

USE *JANUARY*
Star Chart for
undistorted
view of
due east
constellations.
HOLD BOOK
UPRIGHT

Deep Sky
Objects

P Ring Nebula,
page 263

Q Double Star,
page 265

S Globular Cluster,
page 269

T Open Clusters,
page 271

HERCULES

OPHIUCHUS

Rasalhague

Vega

LYRA
P

VULPECULA

Albireo Q

SAGITTA

CYGNUS

Deneb

SERPENS

SCUTUM

Altair

AQUILA

LACERTA

DELPHINUS

EQUULEUS

PEGASUS

AQUARIUS

PISCES

Fomalhaut

PISCIS AUSTRINUS

CAPRICORNUS

Ecliptic • *Planet Path*

MICROSCOPIUM

SCULPTOR

HORIZON

Antares
S

SCORPIUS

X
W

U

SAGITTARIUS

CORONA
AUSTRALIS

TELESCOPIUM

HORIZON

T

GRUS

Alnair

INDUS

Face SOUTH

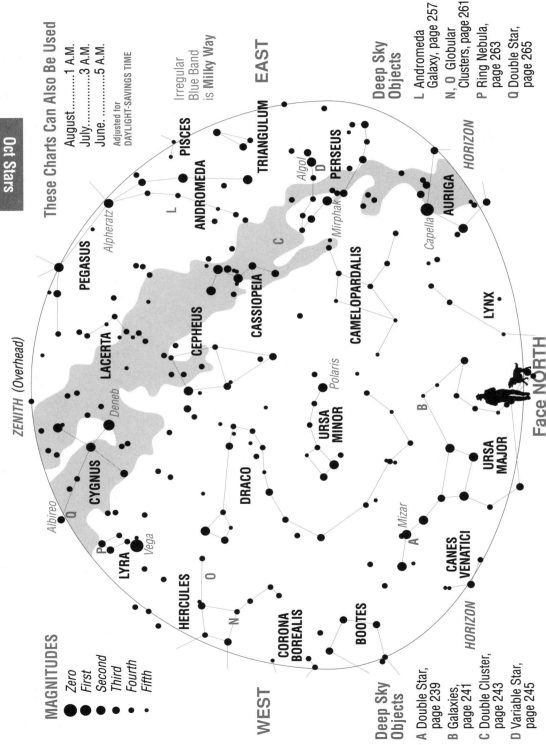

OCTOBER Star Chart ⋆ Facing NORTH

MAGNITUDES

Zero
First
Second
Third
Fourth
Fifth

These Charts Can Also Be Used

August........1 A.M.
July............3 A.M.
June. ....5 A.M.

Adjusted for
DAYLIGHT-SAVINGS TIME

Irregular
Blue Band
is Milky Way

ZENITH (Overhead)

WEST

EAST

Face NORTH

HORIZON

HORIZON

Deep Sky Objects

A Double Star, page 239
B Galaxies, page 241
C Double Cluster, page 243
D Variable Star, page 245

Deep Sky Objects

L Andromeda Galaxy, page 257
N, O Globular Clusters, page 261
P Ring Nebula, page 263
Q Double Star, page 265

PEGASUS
Alpheratz
PISCES
ANDROMEDA
TRIANGULUM
Algol
PERSEUS
Mirphak
AURIGA
Capella
HORIZON
LACERTA
CEPHEUS
CASSIOPEIA
CAMELOPARDALIS
LYNX
Deneb
Polaris
URSA MINOR
CYGNUS
Albireo
DRACO
Mizar
URSA MAJOR
Vega
LYRA
HERCULES
CORONA BOREALIS
BOOTES
CANES VENATICI

OCTOBER Star Chart ★ Facing SOUTH

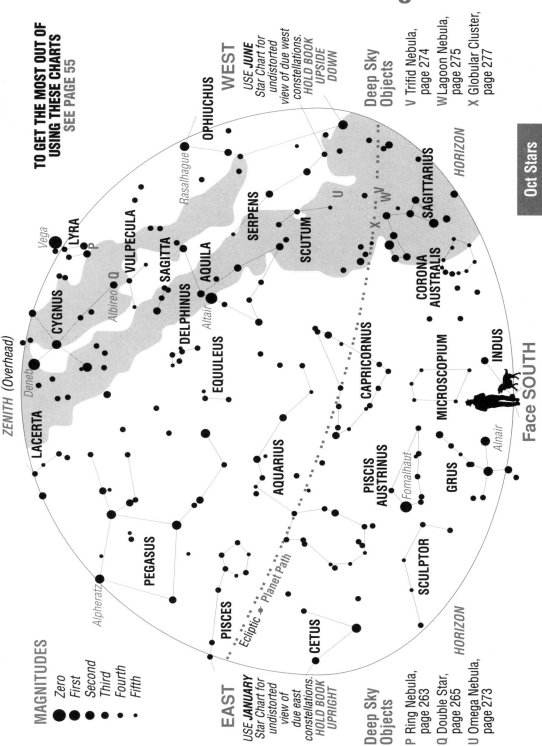

Oct Stars

TO GET THE MOST OUT OF
USING THESE CHARTS
SEE PAGE 55

MAGNITUDES

- Zero
- First
- Second
- Third
- Fourth
- Fifth

ZENITH *(Overhead)*

WEST

USE JUNE Star Chart for undistorted view of due west constellations. HOLD BOOK UPSIDE DOWN

Deep Sky Objects

V Trifid Nebula, page 274

W Lagoon Nebula, page 275

X Globular Cluster, page 277

HORIZON

Face SOUTH

HORIZON

EAST

USE JANUARY Star Chart for undistorted view of due east constellations. HOLD BOOK UPRIGHT

Deep Sky Objects

P Ring Nebula, page 263

Q Double Star, page 265

U Omega Nebula, page 273

Constellations and stars

OPHIUCHUS · Rasalhague · Vega · LYRA · P · VULPECULA · SAGITTA · SERPENS · AQUILA · SCUTUM · U · W · X · SAGITTARIUS · CORONA AUSTRALIS · Albireo · Q · CYGNUS · DELPHINUS · Altair · LACERTA · Deneb · EQUULEUS · CAPRICORNUS · MICROSCOPIUM · INDUS · Alnair · AQUARIUS · PISCIS AUSTRINUS · Fomalhaut · GRUS · PEGASUS · Alpheratz · SCULPTOR · PISCES · CETUS · Ecliptic · Planet Path

NOVEMBER Star Chart ★ Facing NORTH

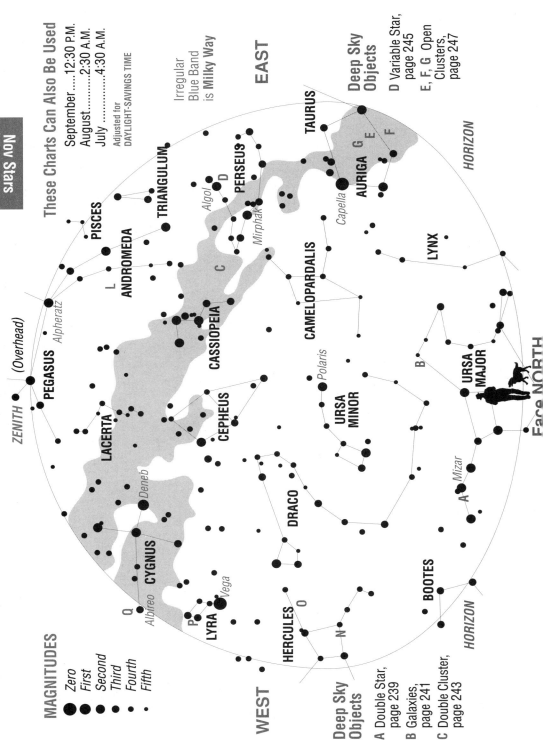

These Charts Can Also Be Used

September.....12:30 P.M.
August.........2:30 A.M.
July ....4:30 A.M.

Adjusted for
DAYLIGHT-SAVINGS TIME

Irregular
Blue Band
is Milky Way

EAST

Deep Sky
Objects

D Variable Star,
page 245
E, F, G Open
Clusters,
page 247

HORIZON

TAURUS

PERSEUS

AURIGA G E F

Capella

Algol

Mirphak

TRIANGULUM

PISCES

ANDROMEDA

L

Alpheratz

CAMELOPARDALIS

LYNX

PEGASUS

ZENITH (Overhead)

CASSIOPEIA

Polaris

URSA
MINOR

URSA
MAJOR

B

Face NORTH

CEPHEUS

LACERTA

Deneb

DRACO

Mizar

A

CYGNUS

Albireo

Vega

LYRA

P

Q

HERCULES

O

N

BOOTES

HORIZON

MAGNITUDES

Zero
First
Second
Third
Fourth
Fifth

WEST

Deep Sky
Objects

A Double Star,
page 239
B Galaxies,
page 241
C Double Cluster,
page 243

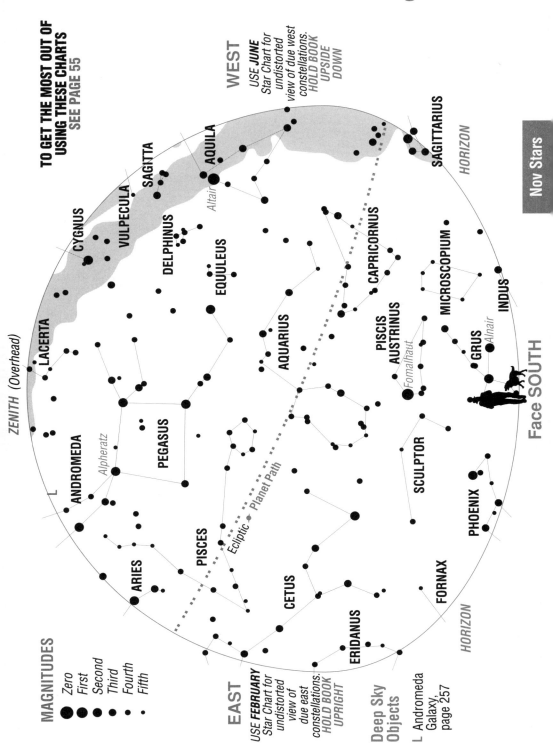

NOVEMBER Star Chart ★ Facing SOUTH

TO GET THE MOST OUT OF
USING THESE CHARTS
SEE PAGE 55

WEST

USE *JUNE*
Star Chart for
undistorted
view of due west
constellations.
*HOLD BOOK
UPSIDE
DOWN*

Nov Stars

HORIZON

ZENITH *(Overhead)*

SAGITTARIUS

CYGNUS

LACERTA

VULPECULA

SAGITTA

AQUILA

Altair

DELPHINUS

EQUULEUS

CAPRICORNUS

MICROSCOPIUM

INDUS

Alnair

ANDROMEDA

Alpheratz

PEGASUS

AQUARIUS

PISCIS
AUSTRINUS

Fomalhaut

GRUS

Face SOUTH

L

Ecliptic ● Planet Path

SCULPTOR

ARIES

PISCES

CETUS

PHOENIX

ERIDANUS

FORNAX

HORIZON

MAGNITUDES

Zero
First
Second
Third
Fourth
Fifth

EAST

USE *FEBRUARY*
Star Chart for
undistorted
view of
due east
constellations.
*HOLD BOOK
UPRIGHT*

Deep Sky
Objects

L Andromeda
Galaxy,
page 257

DECEMBER Star Chart ★ Facing NORTH

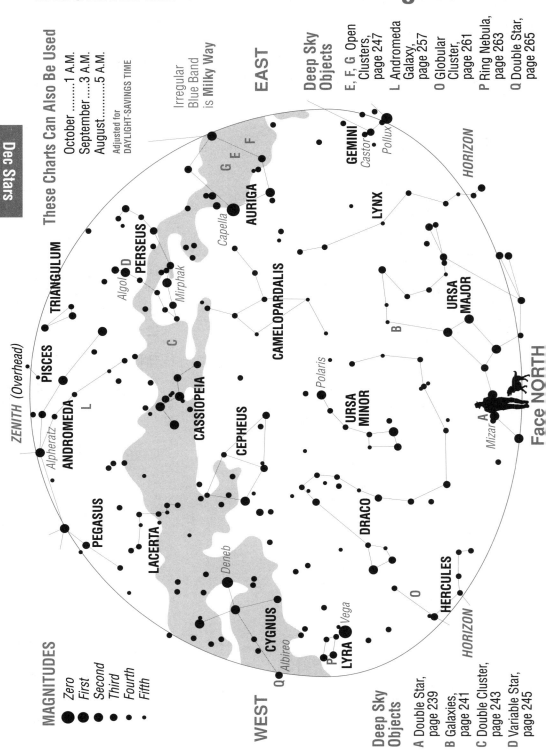

These Charts Can Also Be Used

October ......1 A.M.
September ....3 A.M.
August ....5 A.M.

Adjusted for
DAYLIGHT-SAVINGS TIME

Irregular
Blue Band
is **Milky Way**

EAST

Deep Sky Objects

E, F, G Open Clusters, page 247
L Andromeda Galaxy, page 257
O Globular Cluster, page 261
P Ring Nebula, page 263
Q Double Star, page 265

ZENITH (Overhead)

MAGNITUDES

Zero
First
Second
Third
Fourth
Fifth

WEST

Deep Sky Objects

A Double Star, page 239
B Galaxies, page 241
C Double Cluster, page 243
D Variable Star, page 245

Face NORTH

GEMINI — *Castor*, *Pollux*
LYNX
URSA MAJOR
AURIGA — *Capella*
PERSEUS — *Mirphak*, *Algol* D
TRIANGULUM
CAMELOPARDALIS
Polaris
URSA MINOR
Mizar A
PISCES
ANDROMEDA — *Alpheratz*, L
CASSIOPEIA
CEPHEUS
DRACO
PEGASUS
LACERTA
Deneb
CYGNUS — *Albireo*
HERCULES O
LYRA — *Vega*, P
HORIZON

DECEMBER Star Chart ★ Facing SOUTH

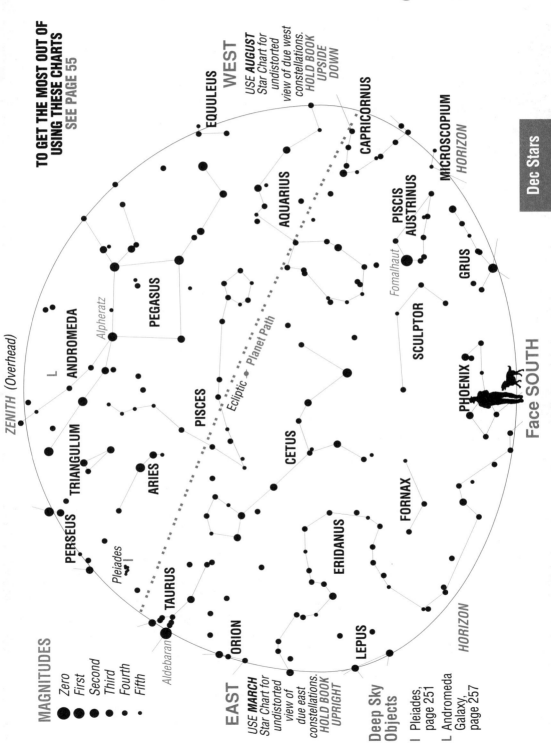

TO GET THE MOST OUT OF
USING THESE CHARTS
SEE PAGE 55

MAGNITUDES

- Zero
- First
- Second
- Third
- Fourth
- Fifth

WEST

USE *AUGUST* Star Chart for undistorted view of due west constellations. *HOLD BOOK UPSIDE DOWN*

EAST

USE *MARCH* Star Chart for undistorted view of due east constellations. *HOLD BOOK UPRIGHT*

Deep Sky Objects

I Pleiades, page 251

L Andromeda Galaxy, page 257

ZENITH (Overhead)

Dec Stars

Face SOUTH

HORIZON

EQUULEUS
CAPRICORNUS
MICROSCOPIUM
AQUARIUS
PISCIS AUSTRINUS
GRUS
PEGASUS
ANDROMEDA
Alpheratz
Fomalhaut
SCULPTOR
PISCES
CETUS
PHOENIX
FORNAX
PERSEUS
TRIANGULUM
ARIES
ERIDANUS
Pleiades
TAURUS
Aldebaran
ORION
LEPUS

Ecliptic — Planet Path

HORIZON

Earth's Moon

T here are two objects in the sky that command our unanimous attention: the Sun and the Moon. Ruling by night, the Moon is in stark contrast to the Sun. Waxing and waning through phases, from magnificent crescents to a brilliant disk, the Moon is an integral part of all our lives, gracing our skies with a splendor unmatched by any other celestial body.

I have often wondered what people in the past thought of the Moon, ever changing, disappearing and obliterating. To me, the Moon would have been absolutely haunting and mysterious. I am glad I live in a time when mostly rational thought rules and we can appreciate the Moon for what it is, a planetary satellite, inextricably bound to us by gravity, but beautiful to behold.

Where did the Moon come from?
The most accepted theory is that the Moon is the result of a Mars-sized object colliding with Earth "shortly" after the formation of our Solar System 4.5 billion years ago. This catastrophic impact caused the Mars-sized object, along with part of Earth's crust and mantle, to disintegrate and later recombine to form the Moon. Crustal and mantle materials from the Earth have been identified in the Moon rocks retrieved from the Apollo landings, lending support to this theory.

It is simply amazing that we have just one moon which not only perfectly eclipses the Sun but also keeps the same side facing us.

The Moon can be seen during the day!
An astronomy professor I had in college said he regularly received telephone calls from concerned members of the community. They would ask if something was wrong because the Moon was out during the daytime. He always assured them this was normal and that they had probably never noticed the Moon during the day.

When my daughter was two, we were driving around and I pointed the Moon out to her, plainly visible as a white crescent against the blue daytime sky. Regularly after that, and to my

Facing page. *Footprints in the Moon dust. Apollo 15 lunar mission. The surface of the Moon is covered with a fine grained soil called regolith.*

Earth's Moon

surprise, she would stretch out her arm and point her finger, and say only as a two year old can, "Moooon." Her ability to find the Moon during the day became uncanny. Once, I told her, "No, that's not the Moon;" but on closer examination, I noticed that she was right.

When you start noticing the Moon during the day, you will see it there often. In fact, about the only time that you cannot see the Moon during the day is around New Moon. From New Moon to Full Moon, the Moon trails the Sun. From Full Moon to New Moon, it precedes the Sun.

The same side always faces us. What's on the back?
Why does the same side of the Moon always face the Earth? Because the Moon's rotation on its axis is synchronized with its revolution around the Earth. This is not a coincidence. Tidal and other forces have "locked in" one side of the Moon so it always faces the Earth.

What's on the other side? The back side of the Moon is almost completely covered with craters. There are a few small maria (dark plains), but they are indistinct. The Earth-facing side is by far the more interesting side.

A glimpse of the back side of the Moon. The left side of this photograph shows the heavily cratered back side. On the right side are the maria of the Earth-facing side.

Earth's Moon

Full Moon Names. Once in a Blue Moon. Man in the Moon.
There is probably more lore associated with the Moon than any
other celestial body. Every culture has its myths and traditions;
however, the Moon's most important impact is the division of
the year into months.

In the past, the Moon was given 12 nicknames, one for each
month of the year. The nicknames that have survived are Harvest,
Hunter, Moon Before Yule and Moon After Yule (Yule refers to
Christmas). The Harvest Moon is the Full Moon closest to the
Autumnal Equinox (about September 23). The Hunter's Moon
follows Harvest; next comes Moon Before Yule, then Moon After
Yule.

The origin of the phrase "Once in a Blue Moon" is uncertain,
however it means very seldom. The modern day definition of a
Blue Moon refers to the occurrence of two full Moons in a month.
This happens about once every three years. In the not too distant
past, when the Moon had 12 nicknames, "Blue Moon" was the
name given to the third Full Moon in a season (any of the four
seasons) that had four Full Moons. A season, which spans three
months, normally has three Full Moons.

What about the Man in the Moon? The darker plains (maria)
and the lighter cratered areas (terrae) have given rise to people
seeing a host of figures in the Full Moon. These include a rabbit,
donkey, jack-o'-lantern, woman, man, and a girl reading. Let me
caution you that seeing these figures or any other requires a bit
of imagination.

 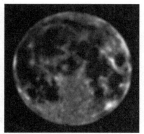 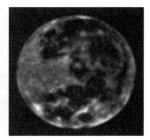

*Three orientations of the Moon as it can appear in the sky. Can you see any
figures in these Moons? I think a rabbit is the easiest to see (Does this say
something about me?). These images have been purposely blurred to help
you focus on finding a figure.*

Earth's Moon

The Moon: Bane of Deep Sky Objects

Dark skies are needed for the best viewing of the fainter deep sky objects like galaxies and nebulae. A bright Moon hinders observing these objects because it "white washes" the sky by scattering its light, preventing us from seeing the fainter celestial objects. Additionally, when the Moon is bright, our eyes cannot fully adapt to the darkness — and dark adapted eyes are essential for viewing deep sky objects. So, unless you want to observe the Planets or Moon, you must work around the Moon's schedule to view the deep sky objects.

Water on the Moon. Moon Colonies

What is humankind's future with the Moon? All but abandoned after our visits in the early 1970s, the Moon regained the interest of scientists at the end of the twentieth century. The *Lunar Prospector* satellite placed in orbit around the Moon in early 1998 provided evidence that frozen water probably exists at the poles. However, this water, which is debris from cometary impacts, is most likely mixed with the lunar soil material and may require processing to extract. Despite this obstacle, there appears to be enough water to support the air and water requirements of a colony for an extended period of time.

Eclipses

Why don't we have both a solar and lunar eclipse every month? Because the Moon's orbit is tilted 5.1° to the Earth's orbit. This usually places the Moon above or below the Earth's shadow and Sun during Full Moon and New Moon. See page 206 for more information.

If you were on the Moon, the Earth would appear to remain stationary in the sky. It would not rise or set, but hover and cycle through phases like the Moon does in the Earth's sky.

Observing the Moon

OBSERVING THE MOON: PHASES

The Moon cycles through phases as it orbits the Earth. The phases represent the *portion* of the lighted side of the Moon that we see from Earth. If you were on the Sun, and were looking at the Earth and the Moon, both would always appear full. Below is an illustration that may help explain the phases, and on the following page is a table that indicates when the phased Moon is visible.

PAGES 98 TO 111 LIST PHASES OF THE MOON FROM 2000 TO 2051

The Phases of the Moon

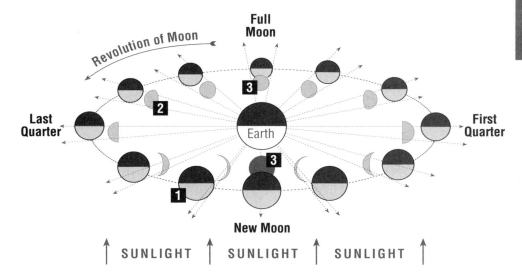

Lunar phases occur as the Moon revolves around the Earth.

1 One half of the Moon is always lighted by the Sun (just like the Earth's day).

2 The phases represent the portion of the lighted side of the Moon that we can see from Earth, which varies from a crescent to a full disk as indicated by the blue dotted lines.

3 Eclipses do not occur regularly at New Moon and Full Moon because the Moon's orbit is tilted slightly, which almost always places the Moon above or below the Earth's shadow and Sun.

Moon

85

Observing the Moon

Observing the Moon's Phases

Phase of Moon	Rises in East	Sets in West	Visible During Day
TO FIRST QUARTER	Shortly After Sunrise	Shortly After Sunset	Trails Sun[1]
FIRST QUARTER ☽	At Noon	At Midnight	Noon to Sunset[2]
FULL MOON ○	At Sunset	At Sunrise	Not Visible During the Day
LAST QUARTER ☾	At Midnight	At Noon	Sunrise to Noon[3]
TO NEW MOON	Shortly Before Sunrise	Shortly Before Sunset	Precedes Sun[4]
NEW MOON ●	*Not visible at all — in line with the Sun*		

[1]Visible for most of the day, trailing the Sun.
[2]Visible in the eastern or morning half of sky.
[3]Visible in the western or afternoon half of sky.
[4]Visible for most of the day, preceding the Sun.

THE MOON RISES
about 50 minutes
later each day

OBSERVING THE MOON: THROUGH A TELESCOPE

The prime time to observe the Moon is during its waxing and waning phases. Waxing means "adding on" and waning means "subtracting from." The terminator, the "line" separating the lighted side from the dark side, is present when the Moon is waxing and waning. Craters appear their best (sharpest) when near the terminator because the contrast from the shadows makes them more pronounced. Magnifications from 40x to 250x are recommended.

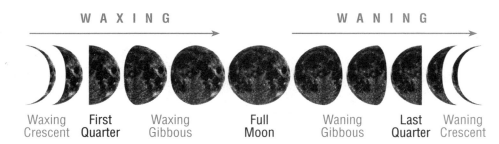

WAXING   WANING

Waxing Crescent | First Quarter | Waxing Gibbous | Full Moon | Waning Gibbous | Last Quarter | Waning Crescent

Moon

Observing the Moon

The Moon is disappointing to observe around Full Moon. During this time, the entire surface, along with most features, is "washed out." However, at this time, the rays of craters are at their most pronounced. The crater Tycho's rays stretch halfway across the hemisphere.

Want to observe the dark side of the Moon? This side of the Moon is slightly lighted by reflected light from Earth called Earthshine. Some features on the dark side are visible in a telescope when the Moon is a crescent. Try it — it is a pretty sight!

MAJOR FEATURES OF THE MOON

The Moon's surface has brighter cratered highlands called terrae and smoother darker plains known as maria. Most of the Moon's craters were formed from meteoroid or cometary impacts during its early history, from 3.8 to 4 billion years ago. The maria are a result of volcanic lava flow and appear darker than the terrae because of a higher iron content. They are a little older than three billions years. The Moon is no longer geologically active.

Craters. Huge bowl-like depressions on the Moon. All of the craters on the Moon were formed from meteoroid or cometary impact. Most of these impacts occurred during the early history of the Solar System.

Rays. Bright streaks that radiate from some craters. They are a result of the ejection of reflective material during the formation of craters (from a cometary or meteoroid impact). They are most pronounced around Full Moon. The crater Tycho has the longest rays, spanning one-quarter of the globe. It is estimated that rayed craters are less than one billion years old because the rays of older craters have been eroded by micrometeorites.

This image of the Moon shows the rays emanating from the crater Tycho, near the bottom, and the low contrast, "washed out" look of a fully illuminated Moon.

Observing the Moon

Maria. A term coined by Galileo meaning "seas." Maria are the darker, smoother areas of the Moon and represent 16% of its surface. Almost all of the maria are on the hemisphere facing Earth. They average 500 to 600 feet thick (150 to 180 meters). The maria are the result of impacts from large asteroids or comets creating fractures to the once molten interior, releasing basalt lava, which flowed upward and outward to create the great plains.

Rille. A long cliff or split in the maria, up to hundreds of miles or kilometers in length. Rilles are easy to see in a telescope. They are the result of cracks, fractures or collapses in the maria.

Terminator. The border or "line" separating the lighted side from the dark side. The terminator is absent during Full Moon. Craters appear at their sharpest near the terminator.

Regolith. A fine grained "soil" that covers the surface of the Moon. Created from the bombardment of the surface by micrometeorites, the regolith varies in depth from 6.5 to 26 feet (2 to 8 meters) in the maria, and to a possible 49 feet (15 meters) in the highlands. The micrometeorites that bombard Earth burn up in the atmosphere.

Moon

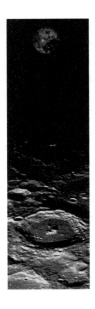

Left. Closeup of the crater Tycho as imaged by the Clementine spacecraft on March 15, 1994.

Right. Earth over the Moon. Note the high contrast of the craters because they are on the terminator.

Index of Moon's Craters

Below is an index of the major craters on the Moon. They are alphabetized and referenced by quadrant for easier identification. Several craters are referenced to two quadrants because these craters fall on the terminator.

NUMBERED CRATERS ARE ON PAGES 94 & 95

1 Abenezra (IV)
2 Abulfeda (IV)
3 Agatharchides (III)
4 Agrippa (I)
5 Albategnius (III)(IV)
6 Alexander (I)
7 Alfraganus (IV)
8 Aliacensis (III)(IV)
9 Almanon (IV)
10 Alpetragius (III)
11 Alphonsus (III)
12 Anaxagoras (II)
13 Anaximenes (II)
14 Apianus (IV)
15 Apollonius (I)
16 Arago (I)
17 Archimedes (II)
18 Archytas (I)
19 Ariadaeus (I)
20 Aristarchus (II)
21 Aristillus (I)
22 Aristoteles (I)
23 Arzachel (III)
24 Asclepi (IV)
25 Atlas (I)
26 Autolycus (I)
27 Azophi (IV)
28 Baco (IV)
29 Bailly (III)
30 Ball (III)
31 Barocius (IV)
32 Barrow (I)
33 Bayer (III)
34 Beaumont (IV)
35 Bernouilli (I)
36 Berosus (I)
37 Berzelius (I)
38 Bessarian (II)

39 Bessel (I)
40 Bettinus (III)
41 Bianchini (II)
42 Biela (IV)
43 Billy (III)
44 Birmingham (II)
45 Birt (III)
46 Blancanus (III)
47 Blanchinus (III)

Quadrant Reference

48 Bode (II)
49 Bohnenberger (IV)
50 G. Bond (I)
51 W. Bond (II)
52 Bonpland (III)
53 Borda (IV)
54 Boscovich (I)
55 Bouguer (II)
56 Boussingault (IV)
57 Brayley (II)
58 Briggs (II)
59 Buch (IV)

60 Bullialdus (III)
61 Burckhardt (I)
62 Bürg (I)
63 Büsching (IV)
64 Byrgius (III)
65 La Caille (III)
66 Calippus (I)
67 Campanus (III)
68 Capella (IV)

69 Capuanus (III)
70 Cardanus (II)
71 Carpenter (II)
72 Cassini (I)
73 Catharina (IV)
74 Cavalerius (II)
75 Cavendish (III)
76 Celsius (IV)
77 Cepheus (I)
78 Chacornac (I)
79 Cichus (III)
80 Clairaut (IV)

Moon

89

Index of Moon's Craters

Maria ★ Oceans, Seas, Lakes & Channels

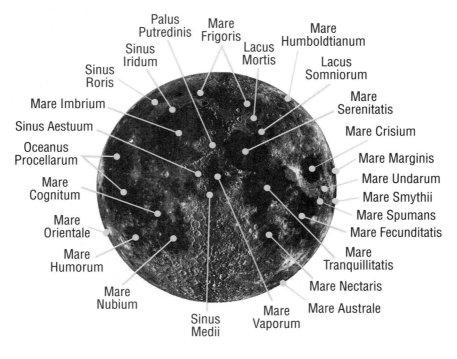

Palus Putredinis
Mare Frigoris
Sinus Iridum
Lacus Mortis
Mare Humboldtianum
Sinus Roris
Lacus Somniorum
Mare Imbrium
Mare Serenitatis
Sinus Aestuum
Mare Crisium
Oceanus Procellarum
Mare Marginis
Mare Cognitum
Mare Undarum
Mare Smythii
Mare Orientale
Mare Spumans
Mare Fecunditatis
Mare Humorum
Mare Tranquillitatis
Mare Nubium
Mare Nectaris
Mare Australe
Sinus Medii
Mare Vaporum

Moon

Index of Moon's Craters

Mountain Ranges & Associated Features

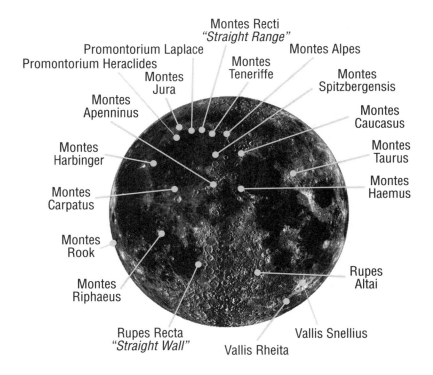

Montes Recti *"Straight Range"*
Promontorium Laplace
Montes Alpes
Promontorium Heraclides
Montes Teneriffe
Montes Spitzbergensis
Montes Jura
Montes Apenninus
Montes Caucasus
Montes Harbinger
Montes Taurus
Montes Carpatus
Montes Haemus
Montes Rook
Rupes Altai
Montes Riphaeus
Rupes Recta *"Straight Wall"*
Vallis Snellius
Vallis Rheita

Moon

Index of Moon's Craters

Moon

Index of Moon's Craters

Moon

Apollo Lunar Landings 1969 to 1972

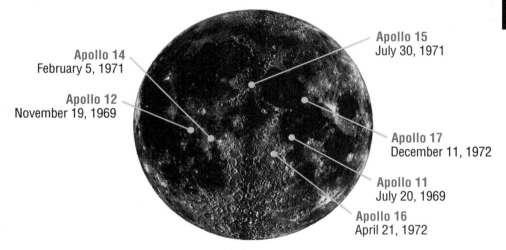

Apollo 14
February 5, 1971

Apollo 15
July 30, 1971

Apollo 12
November 19, 1969

Apollo 17
December 11, 1972

Apollo 11
July 20, 1969

Apollo 16
April 21, 1972

MISSION CREWS

Apollo 11 Neil Armstrong[1] Edwin Aldrin *Michael Collins*[2]	**Apollo 15** David Scott[1] James Irwin *Alfred Worden*[2]
Apollo 12 Charles Conrad[1] Alan Bean *Richard Gordon*[2]	**Apollo 16** John Young[1] Charles Duke *Thomas Mattingly*[2]
Apollo 14 Alan Shepard[1] Edgar Mitchell *Stuart Roosa*[2]	**Apollo 17** Eugene Cernan[1] Harrison Schmitt *Ronald Evans*[2]

Apollo 13 Mission aborted en route to Moon because of equipment failure.
Crewed by James Lovell, Fred Haise & John Swigert.

[1]Commander. [2]Remained aboard Command Module orbiting Moon.

Map of the Moon

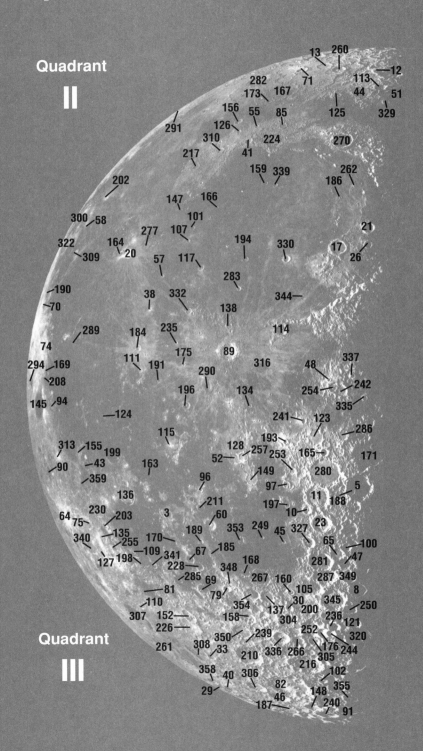

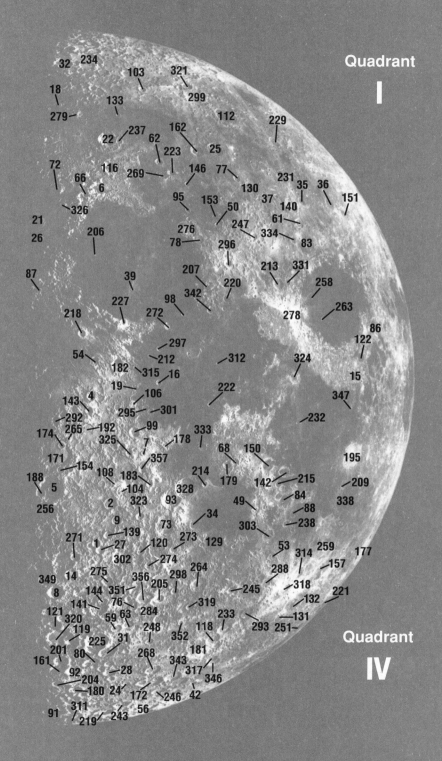

Map of the Moon

Moon

Moon

Phases of the Moon 2000 – 2003

Date of Phase Based on Mountain Standard Time

		NEW MOON ○	FIRST QTR ◗	FULL MOON ●	LAST QTR ◖
2000	JAN	6	14	◐20	28
	FEB	5	12	19	26
	MAR	5	12	19	27
	APR	4	11	18	26
	MAY	3	10	18	26
	JUN	2	8	16	24
	JUL	1&30❺	8	◐16	24
	AUG	29	6	14	22
	SEP	27	5	13[1]	20
	OCT	27	5	13	20
	NOV	25	4	11	18
	DEC	❺25	3	11	17

2001	JAN	24	2	9	16
	FEB	23	1	8	14
	MAR	24	2	9	16
	APR	23	1&30	7	15
	MAY	22	29	7	15
	JUN	21	27	5	13
	JUL	20	27	◐5	13
	AUG	18	25	3	12
	SEP	17	24	2	10
	OCT	16	23	2[1]&31[2]	9
	NOV	14	22	30	8
	DEC	❺14	22	30	7

		NEW MOON ○	FIRST QTR ◗	FULL MOON ●	LAST QTR ◖
2002	JAN	13	21	28	5
	FEB	12	20	27	4
	MAR	13	21	28	5
	APR	12	20	26	4
	MAY	12	19	26	4
	JUN	❺10	17	24	2
	JUL	10	16	24	2
	AUG	8	15	22	1&30
	SEP	6	13	21[1]	29
	OCT	6	12	21	28
	NOV	4	11	19	27
	DEC	4	11	19	26

2003	JAN	2	10	19	25
	FEB	1	9	18	23
	MAR	2	11	16	24
	APR	1	9	18	23
	MAY	1&30❺	9	◐15	22
	JUN	29	7	14	21
	JUL	29	6	13	21
	AUG	27	5	11	19
	SEP	25	3	10[1]	18
	OCT	25	2&31	10	18
	NOV	23	30	◐8	16
	DEC	23	30	8	16

[1]Harvest Moon. [2]Blue Moon month.
❺ Solar Eclipse. ◐ Lunar Eclipse. *For time and location, see pages 210 to 214.*

Phases of the Moon 2004 – 2007

Date of Phase Based on Mountain Standard Time

	NEW MOON ○	FIRST QTR ◐	FULL MOON ●	LAST QTR ◑
2004 JAN	21	28	7	14
FEB	20	27	6	13
MAR	20	28	6	13
APR	19	27	5	11
MAY	18	27	4	11
JUN	17	25	2	9
JUL	17	24	2&31[2]	9
AUG	15	23	29	7
SEP	14	21	28[1]	6
OCT	13	20	●27	6
NOV	12	18	26	4
DEC	11	18	26	4

	NEW MOON ○	FIRST QTR ◐	FULL MOON ●	LAST QTR ◑
2006 JAN	29	6	14	22
FEB	27	4	12	21
MAR	29	6	●14	22
APR	27	5	13	20
MAY	26	4	13	20
JUN	25	3	11	18
JUL	24	3	10	17
AUG	23	2&31	9	15
SEP	22	30	7	14
OCT	21	29	6[1]	13
NOV	20	27	5	12
DEC	20	27	4	12

	NEW MOON ○	FIRST QTR ◐	FULL MOON ●	LAST QTR ◑
2005 JAN	10	16	25	3
FEB	8	15	23	2
MAR	10	17	25	3
APR	☉8	16	24	1&30
MAY	8	16	23	30
JUN	6	14	21	28
JUL	6	14	21	27
AUG	4	12	19	26
SEP	3	11	17[1]	24
OCT	3	10	●17	24
NOV	1	8	15	23
DEC	1&31	8	15	23

	NEW MOON ○	FIRST QTR ◐	FULL MOON ●	LAST QTR ◑
2007 JAN	18	25	3	11
FEB	17	24	1	10
MAR	18	25	●3	11
APR	17	23	2	10
MAY	16	23	2&31[2]	9
JUN	14	22	30	8
JUL	14	21	30	7
AUG	12	20	●28	5
SEP	11	19	26[1]	3
OCT	10	19	25	3
NOV	9	17	24	1
DEC	9	17	23	1&31

Moon Phases

[1] Harvest Moon. [2] Blue Moon month.
☉ Solar Eclipse. ● Lunar Eclipse. *For time and location, see pages 210 to 214.*

Phases of the Moon 2008 – 2011

Date of Phase Based on Mountain Standard Time

		NEW MOON ○	FIRST QTR ◗	FULL MOON ●	LAST QTR ◖
2008	JAN	8	15	22	29
	FEB	6	13	☾20	28
	MAR	7	14	21	29
	APR	5	12	20	28
	MAY	5	11	19	27
	JUN	3	10	18	26
	JUL	2	9	18	25
	AUG	1&30	8	16	23
	SEP	29	7	15[1]	21
	OCT	28	7	14	21
	NOV	27	5	12	19
	DEC	27	5	12	19

		NEW MOON ○	FIRST QTR ◗	FULL MOON ●	LAST QTR ◖
2010	JAN	15	23	29	7
	FEB	13	21	28	5
	MAR	15	23	29	7
	APR	14	21	28	6
	MAY	13	20	27	5
	JUN	12	18	☾26	4
	JUL	11	18	25	4
	AUG	9	16	24	2
	SEP	8	14	23[1]	1&30
	OCT	7	14	22	30
	NOV	5	13	21	28
	DEC	5	13	☾21	28

		NEW MOON ○	FIRST QTR ◗	FULL MOON ●	LAST QTR ◖
2009	JAN	26	4	10	17
	FEB	24	2	9	16
	MAR	26	4	10	18
	APR	24	2	9	17
	MAY	24	1&30	8	17
	JUN	22	29	7	15
	JUL	☉21	28	7	15
	AUG	20	27	5	13
	SEP	18	25	4	11
	OCT	17	25	3[1]	11
	NOV	16	24	2	9
	DEC	16	24	2&31[2]	8

		NEW MOON ○	FIRST QTR ◗	FULL MOON ●	LAST QTR ◖
2011	JAN	4	12	19	26
	FEB	2	11	18	24
	MAR	4	12	19	26
	APR	3	11	17	24
	MAY	2	10	17	24
	JUN	1	8	15	23
	JUL	1&30	7	14	22
	AUG	28	6	13	21
	SEP	27	4	12[1]	20
	OCT	26	3	11	19
	NOV	24	2	10	18
	DEC	24	2&31	☾10	17

[1]Harvest Moon. [2]Blue Moon month.
☉Solar Eclipse. ☾Lunar Eclipse. *For time and location, see pages 210 to 214.*

Phases of the Moon 2012 – 2015

Date of Phase Based on Mountain Standard Time

2012	NEW MOON ○	FIRST QTR ◐	FULL MOON ●	LAST QTR ◑
JAN	23	30	9	16
FEB	21	29	7	14
MAR	22	30	8	14
APR	21	29	6	13
MAY	⑤ 20	28	5	12
JUN	19	26	ⓛ 4	11
JUL	18	26	3	10
AUG	17	24	1&31[2]	9
SEP	15	22	29[1]	8
OCT	15	21	29	8
NOV	13	20	ⓛ 28	6
DEC	13	19	28	6

2013	NEW MOON ○	FIRST QTR ◐	FULL MOON ●	LAST QTR ◑
JAN	11	18	26	4
FEB	10	17	25	3
MAR	11	2&31	27	4
APR	10	19	25	2
MAY	⑤ 9	17	24	2&31
JUN	8	18	23	29
JUL	8	15	22	29
AUG	6	14	20	28
SEP	5	12	19[1]	26
OCT	4	11	18	26
NOV	3	9	17	25
DEC	2	9	17	25

2014	NEW MOON ○	FIRST QTR ◐	FULL MOON ●	LAST QTR ◑
JAN	1&30	7	15	23
FEB	—	6	14	22
MAR	1&30	8	16	23
APR	28	7	ⓛ 15[3]	22
MAY	28	6	14	21
JUN	27	5	12	19
JUL	26	5	12	18
AUG	25	3	10	17
SEP	23	2	8[1]	15
OCT	⑤ 23	1&30	ⓛ 8	15
NOV	22	29	6	14
DEC	21	28	6	14

2015	NEW MOON ○	FIRST QTR ◐	FULL MOON ●	LAST QTR ◑
JAN	20	26	4	13
FEB	18	25	3	11
MAR	20	27	5	13
APR	18	25	ⓛ 4	11
MAY	17	25	3	11
JUN	16	24	2	9
JUL	15	23	1&31[2]	8
AUG	14	22	29	6
SEP	12	21	ⓛ 27[1]	5
OCT	12	20	27	4
NOV	11	18	25	3
DEC	11	18	25	3

Moon Phases

[1]Harvest Moon. [2]Blue Moon month. [3]Lunar Eclipse occurs at Midnight on April 14.
⑤ Solar Eclipse. ⓛ Lunar Eclipse. *For time and location, see pages 210 to 214.*

Phases of the Moon 2016 – 2019

Date of Phase Based on Mountain Standard Time

2016	NEW MOON ○	FIRST QTR ◗	FULL MOON ●	LAST QTR ◖
JAN	9	16	23	1&31
FEB	Ⓢ 8	15	22	—
MAR	8	15	23	1&31
APR	7	13	21	29
MAY	6	13	21	29
JUN	4	12	20	27
JUL	4	11	19	26
AUG	2	10	18	24
SEP	1&30	9	16[1]	23
OCT	30	8	15	22
NOV	29	7	14	21
DEC	28	7	13	20

2017	NEW MOON ○	FIRST QTR ◗	FULL MOON ●	LAST QTR ◖
JAN	27	5	12	19
FEB	26	3	❶ 10	18
MAR	27	5	12	20
APR	26	2	10	19
MAY	25	2	10	18
JUN	23	1&30	9	17
JUL	23	30	8	16
AUG	Ⓢ 21	29	7	14
SEP	19	27	6	12
OCT	19	27	5[1]	12
NOV	18	26	3	10
DEC	17	26	3	10

2018	NEW MOON ○	FIRST QTR ◗	FULL MOON ●	LAST QTR ◖
JAN	16	24	1&31[2] ❶	8
FEB	15	23	—	7
MAR	17	24	1&31[2]	9
APR	15	22	29	8
MAY	15	21	29	7
JUN	13	20	27	6
JUL	12	19	27	6
AUG	11	18	26	4
SEP	9	16	24[1]	2
OCT	8	16	24	2&31
NOV	7	15	22	29
DEC	7	15	22	29

2019	NEW MOON ○	FIRST QTR ◗	FULL MOON ●	LAST QTR ◖
JAN	5	13	❶ 20	27
FEB	4	12	19	26
MAR	6	14	20	27
APR	5	12	18	26
MAY	4	11	17	26
JUN	3	9	17	25
JUL	2&31	9	16	24
AUG	30	7	15	23
SEP	28	5	13[1]	21
OCT	27	5	13	21
NOV	26	4	12	19
DEC	25	4	11	18

[1] Harvest Moon. [2] Blue Moon month.
Ⓢ Solar Eclipse. ❶ Lunar Eclipse. *For time and location, see pages 210 to 214.*

Phases of the Moon 2020 – 2023

Date of Phase Based on Mountain Standard Time

2020	NEW MOON ○	FIRST QTR ◗	FULL MOON ●	LAST QTR ◖
JAN	23	2	10	17
FEB	24	1	9	15
MAR	24	2	9	16
APR	22	1&30	7	14
MAY	22	29	7	14
JUN	20	28	5	12
JUL	20	27	4	12
AUG	18	25	3	11
SEP	17	23	1	10
OCT	16	23	1[1]&31[2]	9
NOV	14	21	30	8
DEC	14	21	29	7

2022	NEW MOON ○	FIRST QTR ◗	FULL MOON ●	LAST QTR ◖
JAN	2&31	9	17	25
FEB	—	8	16	23
MAR	2&31	10	18	24
APR	30	8	16	23
MAY	30	8	◐15	22
JUN	28	7	14	20
JUL	28	6	13	20
AUG	27	5	11	18
SEP	25	3	10[1]	17
OCT	25	2&31	9	17
NOV	23	30	◐8	16
DEC	23	29	7	16

2021	NEW MOON ○	FIRST QTR ◗	FULL MOON ●	LAST QTR ◖
JAN	12	20	28	6
FEB	11	19	27	4
MAR	13	21	28	5
APR	11	20	26	4
MAY	11	19	◐26	3
JUN	◉10	17	24	2
JUL	9	17	23	1&31
AUG	8	15	22	30
SEP	6	13	20[1]	28
OCT	6	12	20	28
NOV	4	11	◐19	27
DEC	4	10	18	26

2023	NEW MOON ○	FIRST QTR ◗	FULL MOON ●	LAST QTR ◖
JAN	21	28	6	14
FEB	20	27	5	13
MAR	21	28	7	14
APR	19	27	5	13
MAY	19	27	5	12
JUN	17	26	3	10
JUL	17	25	3	9
AUG	16	24	1&30	8
SEP	14	22	29[1]	6
OCT	◉14	21	28	6
NOV	13	20	27	5
DEC	12	19	26	4

[1]Harvest Moon. [2]Blue Moon month.
◉ Solar Eclipse. ◐ Lunar Eclipse. *For time and location, see pages 210 to 214.*

Moon Phases

Phases of the Moon 2024 – 2027

Date of Phase Based on Mountain Standard Time

		NEW MOON ○	FIRST QTR ◗	FULL MOON ●	LAST QTR ◖
2024	JAN	11	17	25	3
	FEB	9	16	24	1
	MAR	10	16	❶25³	3
	APR	❸8	15	23	1
	MAY	7	15	22	1&30
	JUN	6	13	21	28
	JUL	5	13	21	27
	AUG	4	12	19	26
	SEP	2	10	17¹	24
	OCT	❸2	10	17	24
	NOV	1&30	8	15	22
	DEC	30	8	15	22
2025	JAN	29	6	13	21
	FEB	27	5	12	20
	MAR	29	6	❶13	22
	APR	27	4	12	20
	MAY	26	4	12	20
	JUN	25	2	11	17
	JUL	24	2	10	18
	AUG	22	1&30	9	15
	SEP	21	29	7	14
	OCT	21	29	6¹	13
	NOV	20	27	5	11
	DEC	19	27	4	11

		NEW MOON ○	FIRST QTR ◗	FULL MOON ●	LAST QTR ◖
2026	JAN	18	25	3	10
	FEB	17	24	1	9
	MAR	18	25	❶3	11
	APR	17	23	1	9
	MAY	16	23	1&31²	9
	JUN	14	21	29	8
	JUL	14	21	29	7
	AUG	❸12	19	❶27	5
	SEP	10	18	26¹	4
	OCT	10	18	25	3
	NOV	9	17	24	1&30
	DEC	8	16	23	30
2027	JAN	7	15	22	29
	FEB	6	14	20	27
	MAR	8	15	22	29
	APR	6	13	20	28
	MAY	6	12	20	28
	JUN	4	11	18	26
	JUL	3	10	18	26
	AUG	2&31	8	17	24
	SEP	29	7	15¹	23
	OCT	29	7	15	22
	NOV	27	6	13	20
	DEC	27	5	13	20

Moon Phases

¹Harvest Moon. ²Blue Moon month. ³Lunar Eclipse occurs at Midnight on March 24.
❸ Solar Eclipse. ❶ Lunar Eclipse. *For time and location, see pages 210 to 214.*

Facing page. Face to face. Apollo 12 lunar mission.

Phases of the Moon 2028 – 2031

Date of Phase Based on Mountain Standard Time

2028	NEW MOON ○	FIRST QTR ◗	FULL MOON ●	LAST QTR ◖
JAN	S 26	4	L 11	18
FEB	25	3	10	17
MAR	25	4	10	17
APR	24	2	9	16
MAY	24	1&31	8	16
JUN	22	29	6	14
JUL	21	28	6	14
AUG	20	26	5	13
SEP	18	25	3	11
OCT	17	24	3[1]	11
NOV	16	23	2	9
DEC	15	23	1&31[2] L	8

2030	NEW MOON ○	FIRST QTR ◗	FULL MOON ●	LAST QTR ◖
JAN	3	11	19	26
FEB	2	10	17	24
MAR	3	12	19	26
APR	2	10	17	24
MAY	2&31	10	17	23
JUN	30	8	15	22
JUL	30	8	14	22
AUG	28	6	13	20
SEP	27	4	11[1]	19
OCT	26	3	11	19
NOV	24	2	11	18
DEC	24	1&31	L 9	19

2029	NEW MOON ○	FIRST QTR ◗	FULL MOON ●	LAST QTR ◖
JAN	S 14	22	29	7
FEB	13	21	28	5
MAR	14	23	29	7
APR	13	21	28	5
MAY	13	20	27	5
JUN	S 11	19	L 25	3
JUL	11	18	25	3
AUG	9	16	23	2&31
SEP	8	14	22[1]	30
OCT	7	14	22	30
NOV	5	12	20	28
DEC	5	12	20	28

2031	NEW MOON ○	FIRST QTR ◗	FULL MOON ●	LAST QTR ◖
JAN	22	30	8	16
FEB	21	28	7	14
MAR	22	30	8	15
APR	21	29	7	14
MAY	21	29	6	13
JUN	19	27	5	11
JUL	19	27	4	11
AUG	17	25	2	9
SEP	16	23	1&31[1&2]	8
OCT	16	23	30	8
NOV	S 14	21	28	7
DEC	14	20	28	6

[1] Harvest Moon. [2] Blue Moon month.
S Solar Eclipse. L Lunar Eclipse. *For time and location, see pages 210 to 214.*

Phases of the Moon 2032 – 2035

Date of Phase Based on Mountain Standard Time

Moon Phases

2032	NEW MOON ○	FIRST QTR ◗	FULL MOON ●	LAST QTR ◖		2034	NEW MOON ○	FIRST QTR ◗	FULL MOON ●	LAST QTR ◖
JAN	12	19	27	5		JAN	20	27	4	12
FEB	10	17	26	4		FEB	18	25	3	11
MAR	11	18	26	4		MAR	20	26	4	12
APR	9	17	●25	3		APR	18	25	3	11
MAY	9	17	24	2&31		MAY	17	24	3	11
JUN	7	15	23	29		JUN	16	23	1	8
JUL	7	15	22	29		JUL	15	23	1&30[2]	9
AUG	5	14	20	27		AUG	13	21	29	6
SEP	4	12	19[1]	26		SEP	12	20	27[1]	5
OCT	4	11	18	25		OCT	12	20	27	4
NOV	2	10	16	24		NOV	10	18	25	2
DEC	2	9	16	24		DEC	10	18	25	2

2033	NEW MOON ○	FIRST QTR ◗	FULL MOON ●	LAST QTR ◖		2035	NEW MOON ○	FIRST QTR ◗	FULL MOON ●	LAST QTR ◖
JAN	1&30	7	15	23		JAN	9	16	23	1&30
FEB	—	6	14	22		FEB	8	15	22	—
MAR	1&30⊙	7	15	23		MAR	9	16	23	1&31
APR	28	6	14	22		APR	8	14	22	30
MAY	28	5	14	21		MAY	7	14	21	30
JUN	26	4	12	19		JUN	5	12	20	28
JUL	26	4	12	18		JUL	5	12	20	27
AUG	24	3	10	17		AUG	3	10	●18[1]	26
SEP	23	1	8[1]	15		SEP	⊙1	9	17	24
OCT	23	1&30	●8	14		OCT	1&30	9	16	23
NOV	21	29	6	13		NOV	29	7	15	21
DEC	21	29	6	13		DEC	29	7	14	21

[1]Harvest Moon. [2]Blue Moon month.
⊙ Solar Eclipse. ● Lunar Eclipse. *For time and location, see pages 210 to 214.*

Phases of the Moon 2036 – 2039

Date of Phase Based on Mountain Standard Time

2036	NEW MOON ○	FIRST QTR ◗	FULL MOON ●	LAST QTR ◖
JAN	28	6	13	21
FEB	26	5	11	18
MAR	27	5	12	19
APR	26	3	10	18
MAY	25	2	10	18
JUN	23	1&30	8	16
JUL	23	29	8	16
AUG	ⓢ21	28	ⓛ6	14
SEP	19	26	5	13
OCT	19	26	5[1]	12
NOV	17	25	3	10
DEC	17	25	3	10

2038	NEW MOON ○	FIRST QTR ◗	FULL MOON ●	LAST QTR ◖
JAN	ⓢ5	13	20	27
FEB	3	12	19	26
MAR	5	13	20	27
APR	4	12	19	25
MAY	4	11	18	25
JUN	2	10	16	24
JUL	ⓢ2&31	9	16	23
AUG	30	7	14	22
SEP	28	5	13[1]	21
OCT	27	5	12	21
NOV	26	3	11	19
DEC	25	3	11	19

2037	NEW MOON ○	FIRST QTR ◗	FULL MOON ●	LAST QTR ◖
JAN	16	24	1&31ⓛ	8
FEB	14	22	—	6
MAR	16	24	1&31	8
APR	15	22	29	7
MAY	14	22	28	6
JUN	13	20	27	5
JUL	12	19	ⓛ26	5
AUG	11	17	25	4
SEP	9	16	24[1]	2
OCT	8	15	23	2&31
NOV	7	14	22	29
DEC	6	14	22	29

2039	NEW MOON ○	FIRST QTR ◗	FULL MOON ●	LAST QTR ◖
JAN	24	2&31	10	17
FEB	22	—	8	15
MAR	24	2	10	17
APR	23	1	8	15
MAY	22	1&30	8	14
JUN	ⓢ21	29	6	13
JUL	21	28	5	12
AUG	19	26	4	11
SEP	18	24	2	10
OCT	17	24	2[1]&31[2]	10
NOV	15	22	ⓛ30	8
DEC	15	22	30	8

[1] Harvest Moon. [2] Blue Moon month.
ⓢ Solar Eclipse. ⓛ Lunar Eclipse. *For time and location, see pages 210 to 214.*

Moon Phases

Phases of the Moon 2040 – 2043

Date of Phase Based on Mountain Standard Time

		NEW MOON ○	FIRST QTR ◐	FULL MOON ●	LAST QTR ◑
2040	JAN	13	20	29	7
	FEB	12	19	27	5
	MAR	12	20	28	6
	APR	11	19	26	4
	MAY	10	19	● 26	3
	JUN	9	17	24	1
	JUL	9	17	23	1&30
	AUG	9	15	22	29
	SEP	6	13	20¹	27
	OCT	5	13	19	27
	NOV	⑤ 4	11	18	26
	DEC	4	10	18	26

		NEW MOON ○	FIRST QTR ◐	FULL MOON ●	LAST QTR ◑
2042	JAN	21	28	6	14
	FEB	20	26	4	13
	MAR	21	28	6	14
	APR	⑤ 19	26	● 5	13
	MAY	19	26	4	12
	JUN	17	25	2	10
	JUL	16	24	3	11
	AUG	15	23	1&30	8
	SEP	14	22	29¹	6
	OCT	13	21	28	7
	NOV	12	20	26	4
	DEC	12	19	26	4

		NEW MOON ○	FIRST QTR ◐	FULL MOON ●	LAST QTR ◑
2041	JAN	2&31	9	17	25
	FEB	—	7	15	23
	MAR	2&31	9	17	25
	APR	30	8	16	23
	MAY	29	7	● 15	22
	JUN	28	6	14	20
	JUL	27	6	13	20
	AUG	26	4	11	18
	SEP	25	3	10¹	16
	OCT	⑤ 24	2	9	16
	NOV	23	1&30	● 7	15
	DEC	23	29	7	15

		NEW MOON ○	FIRST QTR ◐	FULL MOON ●	LAST QTR ◑
2043	JAN	10	18	24	2
	FEB	9	16	23	1
	MAR	11	17	● 25	3
	APR	⑤ 9	16	24	2
	MAY	8	15	23	2&31
	JUN	7	14	22	29
	JUL	6	13	21	29
	AUG	4	12	20	27
	SEP	3	11	● 18¹	25
	OCT	2	11	18	24
	NOV	1	11	16	23
	DEC	1&31	9	16	22

¹Harvest Moon. ²Blue Moon month.
⑤ Solar Eclipse. ● Lunar Eclipse. *For time and location, see pages 210 to 214.*

Moon Phases

Phases of the Moon 2044 – 2047

Date of Phase Based on Mountain Standard Time

2044	NEW MOON ○	FIRST QTR ◑	FULL MOON ●	LAST QTR ◖
JAN	29	7	14	21
FEB	28	6	12	20
MAR	29	6	13	21
APR	27	4	12	20
MAY	26	4	13	19
JUN	25	2	10	18
JUL	24	1&31	9	17
AUG	◉ 22	30	8	16
SEP	21	29	◐ 7	14
OCT	20	28	7[1]	13
NOV	19	27	5	12
DEC	19	27	4	11

2046	NEW MOON ○	FIRST QTR ◑	FULL MOON ●	LAST QTR ◖
JAN	6	15	22	28
FEB	◉ 5	13	20	27
MAR	7	15	22	29
APR	6	13	20	27
MAY	5	13	19	27
JUN	4	11	18	26
JUL	3	10	◐ 17	25
AUG	2&31	8	16	24
SEP	29	7	14[1]	23
OCT	29	6	14	22
NOV	27	5	13	20
DEC	27	5	13	20

2045	NEW MOON ○	FIRST QTR ◑	FULL MOON ●	LAST QTR ◖
JAN	17	25	3	9
FEB	◉ 16	24	1	8
MAR	18	25	3	10
APR	17	24	30	9
MAY	16	23	30	8
JUN	14	21	29	7
JUL	14	20	28	7
AUG	◉ 12	19	27	5
SEP	10	17	25[1]	4
OCT	10	17	25	3
NOV	8	16	24	1
DEC	8	16	23	1&30

2047	NEW MOON ○	FIRST QTR ◑	FULL MOON ●	LAST QTR ◖
JAN	25	3	◐ 11	18
FEB	24	2	10	16
MAR	26	4	11	18
APR	24	3	10	16
MAY	24	2	9	16
JUN	23	1&30	7	15
JUL	22	29	◐ 7	14
AUG	21	27	5	13
SEP	19	26	4	12
OCT	18	25	3[1]	11
NOV	17	24	2	10
DEC	16	23	2&31[2] ◐	10

[1] Harvest Moon. [2] Blue Moon month.
◉ Solar Eclipse. ◐ Lunar Eclipse. *For time and location, see pages 210 to 214.*

Phases of the Moon 2048 – 2051

Date of Phase Based on Mountain Standard Time

2048	NEW MOON ○	FIRST QTR ◑	FULL MOON ●	LAST QTR ◐	2050	NEW MOON ○	FIRST QTR ◑	FULL MOON ●	LAST QTR ◐
JAN	15	22	30	8	JAN	22	29	7	15
FEB	13	21	29	6	FEB	21	28	6	14
MAR	14	22	29	7	MAR	22	29	8	16
APR	12	21	28	5	APR	21	28	7	14
MAY	12	20	27	4	MAY	20	28	6	13
JUN	S11	19	L25	3	JUN	19	27	5	11
JUL	10	18	25	2	JUL	18	26	4	11
AUG	9	16	23	1&31	AUG	17	25	2	9
SEP	7	14	21[1]	29	SEP	15	23	1&30[1,2]	7
OCT	7	14	21	29	OCT	15	23	L29	7
NOV	5	12	20	28	NOV	S14	21	28	6
DEC	5	12	L19	28	DEC	13	20	27	5

2049	NEW MOON ○	FIRST QTR ◑	FULL MOON ●	LAST QTR ◐	2051	NEW MOON ○	FIRST QTR ◑	FULL MOON ●	LAST QTR ◐
JAN	3	10	18	26	JAN	12	19	26	4
FEB	2	9	17	25	FEB	10	17	25	3
MAR	3	11	19	26	MAR	12	19	27	5
APR	2	10	17	24	APR	S10	17	L25	4
MAY	1&31S	9	17	23	MAY	10	17	25	3
JUN	29	8	15	22	JUN	8	15	23	1
JUL	29	8	14	21	JUL	7	15	23	1&30
AUG	28	6	13	20	AUG	6	14	21	28
SEP	26	4	11[1]	18	SEP	4	13	20[1]	26
OCT	26	4	10	18	OCT	4	12	19	26
NOV	24	2	9	17	NOV	3	11	17	24
DEC	24	1&31	9	17	DEC	3	10	17	24

[1] Harvest Moon. [2] Blue Moon month.
S Solar Eclipse. L Lunar Eclipse. *For time and location, see pages 210 to 214.*

Moon Phases

111

Observing the Planets

Like the Earth, asteroids and comets, the Planets are part of our Solar System, all gravitationally bound to the star that we call the Sun.

In ancient times, the Planets were known as five wandering stars because their true nature was not understood. These stars did not stay put like the other stars and they also changed brightness. It was not until Galileo and others began observing them with telescopes that their actual nature became clear: that they were companions of Earth and circled the Sun.

The dawning of the space age in the 1960s opened the doors to our Solar System. Our knowledge of the Planets took off, as exploratory spacecraft encountered every Planet except Pluto. We received unprecedented close-up images of the Planets and their moons, revealing detail that no telescope could approach. For the first time, humankind was seeing the Solar System as it actually existed. The centuries of speculation and conjecture were over.

During the 1990s, astronomers found planets orbiting other stars. It is believed that most stars have planets. The question begging to be answered is, "Is there life in any of these solar systems?" Answers may be found during the next 50 years.

In ancient times, the five Planets were puzzling stars because they did not stay in place like the others but wandered among them.

How are planets formed?
Planets form with stars, condensing out of protoplanetary disks. These disks, which have been imaged by the Hubble Space Telescope, are gigantic clouds of hydrogen and other elements, including ices and minerals, that slowly condense by gravity into a star and planets. Our Sun is known as a second generation star because it contains heavier elements, like gold, that can only be

Facing page. Saturn and its magnificent rings. Saturn personifies our idea of a planet; however, it is not like the Earth. Saturn is one of the Solar System's four gas giants, composed mainly of hydrogen gas and having a solid hydrogen core. It has no surface as we think of one, just an extended atmosphere. In this image, all the major divisions of the rings can be seen as detailed on page 130.

Planet Position Terms

created by a supernova explosion of a star. Our Sun's protoplanetary disk contained debris from such explosions.

OBSERVING THE PLANETS: SOME TERMINOLOGY

Elongation. The arc angle distance in the sky that separates a Planet from the Sun. This term is often applied to the inferior Planets — Mercury and Venus. These Planets are at Greatest Eastern Elongation or Greatest Western Elongation when they appear, from Earth, the farthest away from the Sun. Elongation is a perspective view from the Earth.

Mercury or Venus at Greatest Elongations and Inferior & Superior Conjunction

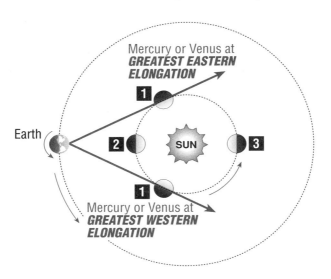

1 **Greatest Eastern or Western Elongation** is the farthest Mercury or Venus appears from the Sun in the sky.

2 **Inferior Conjunction.** Neither Mercury nor Venus are visible at this time because they are in line with the Sun. Both rise and set with the Sun.

3 **Superior Conjunction.** Neither Mercury nor Venus are visible at this time because they are in line with the Sun. Both rise and set with the Sun.

Planet Position Terms

Opposition. Refers to the superior Planets, Mars through Pluto. A superior Planet is at opposition if it is rising in the east as the Sun is setting; that is, it is on the opposite side of the Earth from the Sun. The superior Planets are closest to the Earth at opposition; hence they will appear their largest in a telescope and be at their brightest. Opposition places a superior Planet at its highest in the sky (near the zenith) around midnight.

The Superior Planets at Opposition

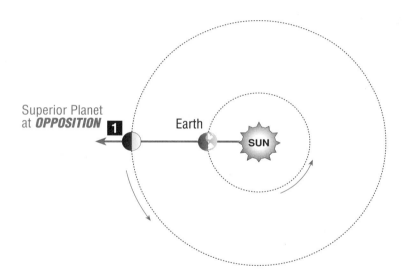

Superior Planet at *OPPOSITION* **1**

Earth

SUN

1 The Superior Planets are the Planets Mars through Pluto. These Planets are at opposition when they are directly opposite the Sun from Earth. At opposition, the Planets appear their largest and brightest. They rise in the east as the Sun sets in the west and are overhead at midnight.

Conjunction. Term often used to indicate when two or more Planets, or a Planet and the Moon appear close to one another in the sky. Conjunctions are beautiful sights, as little can compare to the brilliant glow of Venus standing next to a crescent Moon. Conjunctions are a perspective alignment as viewed from Earth and do not represent the Planet(s) and/or Moon *(Continues on page 118)*

Solar System Comparison

Comparative Orbit Sizes of Our Nine Planets

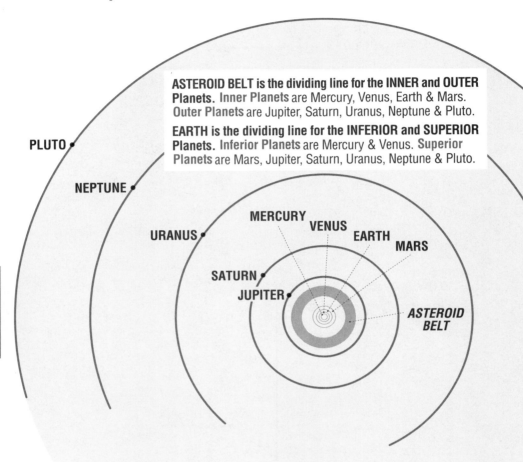

ASTEROID BELT is the dividing line for the INNER and OUTER Planets. Inner Planets are Mercury, Venus, Earth & Mars. Outer Planets are Jupiter, Saturn, Uranus, Neptune & Pluto.

EARTH is the dividing line for the INFERIOR and SUPERIOR Planets. Inferior Planets are Mercury & Venus. Superior Planets are Mars, Jupiter, Saturn, Uranus, Neptune & Pluto.

PLUTO

NEPTUNE

URANUS

MERCURY VENUS EARTH MARS

SATURN

JUPITER

ASTEROID BELT

Inclination of Orbits Compared to Earth's

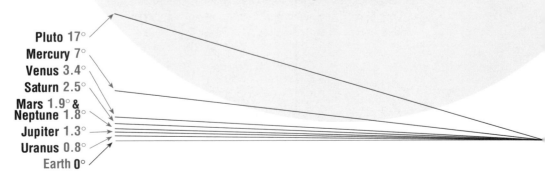

Pluto 17°
Mercury 7°
Venus 3.4°
Saturn 2.5°
Mars 1.9° & Neptune 1.8°
Jupiter 1.3°
Uranus 0.8°
Earth 0°

Solar System Comparison

QUICK COMPARISON of Solar System Members

| | Distance from Sun[1] | | Diameter[3] | Mass[4] | Volume[5] |
	Earth=1	Light Time[2]	Earth=1	Earth=1	Earth=1
SUN	n/a	n/a	109	333,000	1,300,000
MERCURY	0.4	3.2 minutes	0.4	0.06	0.06
VENUS	0.7	6 minutes	0.95	0.8	0.9
EARTH	1	8.3 minutes	1	1	1
MARS	1.5	12.7 minutes	0.5	0.1	0.15
JUPITER	5.2	43.3 minutes	11.2	318	1,326
SATURN	9.5	1h 19min	9.5	95	771
URANUS	19	2h 40min	4	15	63
NEPTUNE	30	4h 10min	3.8	17	58
PLUTO	39.5	5h 29min	0.2	0.003	0.006

[1]The average distance from the Earth to the Sun is 92,955,800 miles (149,597,870 km) and is also known as 1 astronomical unit (AU). [2]The time it takes for light to travel from the Sun to the respective Planet. Light travels at 186,282 miles/sec (299,792 km/sec). [3]Earth's equatorial diameter is 7,926 miles (12,756 km). [4]Earth's mass is 1.32×10^{25} pounds (5.97×10^{24} kg). [5]Earth's volume is 2.6×10^{11} cubic miles (1.1×10^{12} km^3).

Comparative Sizes of Our Sun & Nine Planets

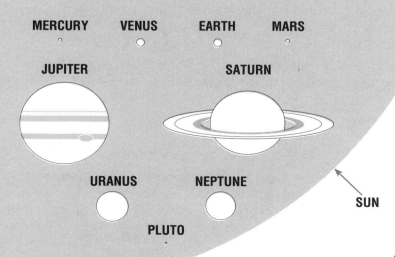

MERCURY   VENUS   EARTH   MARS

JUPITER   SATURN

URANUS   NEPTUNE

PLUTO

SUN

Viewing Considerations

physically getting close to one another. See the Glossary for an expanded definition of Conjunction.

Retrograde Motion. An apparent backward movement of the superior Planets (Mars through Pluto). Normally, these Planets move slowly eastward in the sky (against the stationary background stars) because of their revolutions around the Sun. However, as the Earth "passes" them in their orbits, they appear to travel backwards or westward for several months before resuming their eastward course. This backward, retrograde motion is a perspective view from Earth, and occurs because the Earth travels around the Sun more quickly than the superior Planets. It is similar to the view seen from one automobile that is passing another.

OBSERVING THE PLANETS: SOME CONSIDERATIONS

Binoculars. Most 7x50 binoculars (7x magnification with 50mm diameter lenses) will not be useful to view any detail of the Planets; however, you will be able to see Venus when crescent and the four Galilean moons of Jupiter. Additionally, binoculars are helpful in locating Mercury, Uranus and Neptune.

Telescope Magnification. Useful magnifications for observing the Planets are from 60x to 300x. Depending on your telescope size, quality of the optics and atmospheric conditions, magnifications from 150x to 300x may not provide good images.

Viewing/Seeing Conditions. Because of changing weather conditions, some nights are just better than others to view the Planets. Observing as often as possible will increase your chance of encountering good seeing conditions.

Seeing conditions are poor near the horizon because light passes through more atmosphere and turbulence. Through a telescope, Planets near the horizon look like they are bubbling.

And then there are moments of clarity when, just for a instant, you can clearly see details on the Planets. These moments last just a fraction of a second but occur frequently.

No Dark Adapted Eyes Needed. The Planets are bright enough that dark adapted eyes are not a requirement for viewing, so the Moon and outdoor lights will not readily interfere with observing the Planets.

Relative Sizes of Planets

Planet Size/Detail. When I show the Planets to others, a comment I often hear is, "It's pretty small." Don't expect any of the Planets to appear large in smaller telescopes. The amount of detail will also be limited. However, through repetitive viewing, the occasional crystal clear night, moments of clarity and familiarity, you will be able to see much more than you think.

Relative Sizes of the Planets at 100x Magnification

Smallest & Largest Appearances

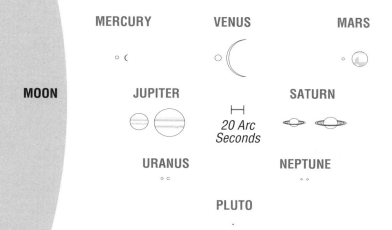

Arc Angle Sizes of Planets in Sky

Planet	Smallest / Largest Arc Angle Size[1]	Planet	Smallest / Largest Arc Angle Size[1]
MERCURY	5" / 13"	SATURN	15" / 21" (Rings 35"/50")
VENUS	10" / 64"	URANUS	3.4" / 4"
MARS	4" / 25"	NEPTUNE	2.2" / 2.4"
JUPITER	31" / 50"	PLUTO	0.16" / 0.28"

[1]Indicated in arc seconds ("). The Moon extends an arc angle of 1,800" or 30' (minutes) or about 1/2 degree. There are 60 arc seconds in an arc minute and 60 arc minutes in an arc degree. The Planets appear their smallest when they are away from Earth, on the other side of the Sun, and appear their largest near inferior conjunction (for Mercury and Venus) or at opposition (for Mars through Pluto).

Observing Mercury

OBSERVING THE PLANETS

THE PLANET MERCURY

 Mercury is the one Planet that is best viewed by eye or with binoculars. It is never far from the Sun — always low in the sky — making it difficult to view as a disk through a telescope because of atmosphere turbulence. The farthest it gets from the Sun is about 28°, less than one-third the distance from the horizon to the zenith. For me, the most exciting part about observing Mercury is finding it.

The little that was known about Mercury before *Mariner 10* visited this Planet in 1974 and 1975 was through telescopic observations made during the day. It is possible to observe, through a telescope, the brighter stars and Planets during the day if you know where to look. During the day, Mercury can more easily be studied in the higher, steadier sky.

> **CAUTION:** Permanent eye damage can result from using binoculars or a telescope near the Sun!
> Use these instruments to find or observe
> Mercury ONLY when the Sun is below the horizon!

Locating Mercury

1 Consult the Mercury at Greatest Elongation tables to find the best observing dates (**bolded entries** on pages 171 to 177). Mercury can only be seen around the time of Greatest Eastern or Western Elongation, when it is farthest from the Sun. And, it cannot be viewed at every elongation. Some elongations place Mercury farther above the horizon than others. Mercury's distance above the horizon varies depending on your latitude, the Sun's inclination to the horizon and where Mercury is in its highly inclined orbit.

2 Start your search for Mercury about one week prior to Greatest Eastern or Western Elongation. The window of opportunity to see Mercury is about one week on either side of the elongation date. Low lying clouds and an obstructed horizon can easily foil your attempt to locate Mercury.

Observing Mercury & Venus

3 **For Eastern Elongations**, search for Mercury in the evening. Start about 30 minutes after sunset. You will have about 1/2 hour to see Mercury.

4 **For Western Elongations**, search for Mercury in the morning. Start about one hour and fifteen minutes prior to sunrise.

5 Mercury will appear as bright as magnitude –2 above and near the sunrise/sunset point. Since it is visible during twilight, it will most likely be the only visible "star," making it difficult to confuse with anything else. At times Mercury is plainly visible to the naked eye, but more often, you will need *binoculars* to help locate it because it is easily missed unless you are looking *directly* at it. Mercury will be *as much as* a pencil height above the horizon when your arm is fully extended.

Observing Mercury. Since Mercury is always low in the sky where atmospheric turbulence is the greatest, it is not worthwhile to view it through a telescope where it will only appear as a bright, bubbling, color changing spot of light (pretty in its own right). Because of the turbulence, no disk or phase can be discerned.

THE PLANET VENUS

 One cold, moonless, winter night in Milwaukee, I went outside to look at the stars. Snow covered the back yard and Venus was high and bright. Something that night seemed different. I noticed the shadows of the lilac branches, plainly visible on the snow. Venus was casting shadows.

Venus has the distinction of being the brightest Planet in our sky, reaching magnitude –4.6. It is often referred to as the morning or evening star because it hugs close to the Sun's rising and setting. Since Venus orbits inside Earth's orbit, it also cycles through phases.

In the past, Venus was referred to as Earth's sister Planet because the diameters of the two Planets are almost the same. This connotation vanished when we discovered that Venus is totally inhospitable to life; so much so, that even scientific probes can only last several minutes on its surface. Its atmosphere is 96% carbon dioxide with temperatures soaring over 900° F (482° C). This temperature is more than hot enough to melt lead,

Observing Venus & Mars

zinc or tin. Its atmospheric pressure is 90 times Earth's, equivalent to water pressure at 3,000 feet (915 meters) below sea level. Venus' day is longer than its year, and in comparison to all the other Planets, it rotates on its axis almost upside down.

Locating Venus. Venus is very easy to find in the sky because of its brightness and close proximity to the rising or setting Sun. Reaching magnitude –4.6, Venus easily outshines all the other stars and Planets. See the Planets at Sunrise and Sunset tables (pages 136 to 165) to locate Venus. The Venus at Greatest Elongation tables (pages 179 to 181) provide the dates when Venus appears the farthest from the Sun in the sky.

Observing Venus. With a small telescope (4-inch) and moderate magnifications of 50x to 100x, Venus appears brilliantly white and featureless because of its thick cloud cover. Since this Planet is inside Earth's orbit, it cycles through phases just like the Moon. However, unlike the Moon, it varies in size. Venus is at its largest and brightest when a crescent. This occurs about a month after Greatest Eastern Elongation and a month before Greatest Western Elongation. The crescent phase of Venus can be seen in binoculars. At Greatest Eastern or Western Elongation, Venus' phase is about half.

THE PLANET MARS

 We identify with Mars more than any other Planet because Mars might have harbored or still may harbor life. In the first half of this century, the United States and other countries will deluge Mars with numerous exploratory vehicles and possibly a manned mission to answer this question. Additionally, Mars is the second most hospitable Planet in the Solar System — the only Planet that humankind might be able to colonize. It has an abundance of frozen water at its north pole, the one element needed to sustain a colony.

What happened to the canals? Mars never had any canals! During the late 1800s and early 1900s, several astronomers thought they saw a network of lines interlacing the surface of Mars, which became known as "canals." Maps of the canals were even drawn and published. However, no evidence was ever found for the canals. They are believed to be an honest mistake — the result of active imaginations. None of the exploratory spacecraft sent to Mars have found anything that could even be misconstrued as canals.

Mars Facts

+ Next to Earth, Mars is the **most hospitable Planet** in our Solar System

+ **Temperature** varies from −274° F to 72° F

+ **Atmosphere** is 95% Carbon Dioxide, 2.7% Nitrogen, 1.6% Argon and 0.2% Oxygen

+ Atmospheric **pressure** is 1/100 of Earth's

+ **Rotates** on axis in 24 hours, 37 minutes

+ **Revolves** around Sun in 1.9 years or 687 days

+ **Tilt on axis** is 25.2°

+ **Gravity** is 1/3 of Earth's

+ Mars' **moons**, Phobos and Deimos, are most likely **captured asteroids**

+ Mars has the **largest inactive volcano** in the Solar System, named Olympus Mons (page 145), more than 15 miles high and 55 miles across at its center

+ Mars' **atmosphere** was most likely much **denser in the past**

+ Closeup images of Mars indicate that **canyons may have been carved by water** — massive quantities of water

Mars

Locating Mars. Mars is easy to find in the sky near opposition because it is bright and red in color, shining steadily around magnitude −2. When Mars is not at opposition, its magnitude and conspicuousness fade to +2. See the Planets at Sunrise and Sunset tables (pages 136 to 165) to locate Mars.

Observing Mars

Most Favorable Times to View Mars. Mars is small, so it is best observed around opposition when it is closest to the Earth and appears its largest. Oppositions with Mars occur about every 26 months; however, some oppositions bring us much closer to Mars than others. This is because of the elliptical shape of orbits. The distance between Earth and Mars at opposition can vary from 35,000,000 to 63,000,000 miles (56,000,000 to 101,000,000 km). This difference effectively doubles the size of Mars in a telescope. The table below indicates the most favorable oppositions from 2000 to 2052 to view Mars.

Best Viewing of Mars ★ When Mars is Largest

These are the dates when Mars is closest to Earth and will appear its largest. The optimal viewing period is from three weeks before to three weeks after these opposition dates. Mars will be at it brightest during these times.

	Date	Arc Angle Size of Mars[1]		Date	Arc Angle Size of Mars[1]
2001	June 13	21"	2033	June 27	22"
2003	August 28	25"	2035	September 15	25"
2005	November 7	19"	2048	June 3	19"
2018	July 26	24"	2050	August 14	25"
2020	October 13	23"	2052	October 28	21"

[1]Indicated in arc seconds ("). See page 119 for a comparison of Planet sizes as they appear in the sky. Magnifications of 150x to 300x are recommended to see the most detail on Mars.

Features on Mars. Although surface coloration and the North Polar Cap can be seen in small to moderately sized telescopes (4-inch to 6-inch), they are subtle. For this reason, Mars is often disappointing to first time observers. Here are some suggestion to help maximize your viewing of Mars' surface features.

1   Try to observe Mars often from one month before to one month after opposition. Repetitive viewing will increase your familiarity with this Planet and increase your chance of observing on a good night. Additionally, you will be able

to see the different sides and all of the surface markings on Mars if you observe over a period of time.

2 Use a minimum magnification of 100x; however, 200x to 300x is preferable. Achieving higher magnifications is dependant on your telescope and atmospheric conditions.

3 Observe Mars when it is highest in the sky in order to minimize atmospheric disturbance. This will occur around midnight during opposition. It is more difficult to see the surface markings when Mars is low in the sky. The worst part about observing at midnight is staying up or waking up. But, it is worth it. Mars is only at opposition every couple of years.

4 When you are looking at Mars through a telescope, you will notice that there are split-second moments when the view of the surface appears clear. It is during these moments of clarity that the best glimpses will occur. It is a rare night when you can look directly at Mars and plainly see the subtleties of the surface markings.

5 & 6 on next page

Mars

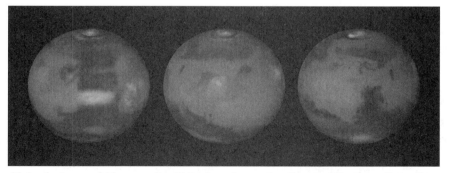

Major features of Mars are its distinct surface coloration and Northern Polar Cap. The dark surface colors represent slight variations in the color of the soil and rock and are not a distinction in features as with Earth's Moon. These three photos show the entire surface of Mars. The North Polar Cap is clearly visible at the top of Mars. In the left image, the light area just below the middle is called Chryse and the dark mass above it is called Mare Acidalium. The middle image shows the side with few surface colorations. The right image shows a whitish area near the southern polar region. This is not the Southern Polar Cap, but a scar, called Hellas, created from a meteoroid or cometary impact. The dark appendage above Hellas is named Syrtis Major.

Observing Mars & Jupiter

5 Several months preceding opposition, the popular monthly astronomy magazines carry in-depth articles which should prove invaluable. Often, they include current maps of the surface markings and charts to calculate the side of Mars that will be facing toward Earth when you observe.

6 If you follow the suggestions above and still cannot see surface markings, here are some possible reasons why. a) Wind storms on Mars could be kicking up dust and obliterating the surface markings. Review the popular monthly astronomy magazines for the latest internet sites to check on current weather conditions on Mars. b) Your telescope optics may not be adequate or your optics may not be properly aligned. Ask someone at a telescope store to check out your telescope. c) The turbulence in Earth's atmosphere may be affecting telescope image quality, so keep trying. d) Finally, remember that if you take your telescope from the warm interior of your home to the cold outside, it will take at least fifteen minutes for the telescope optics to cool and settle down. The image of Mars during this time will be blurry.

THE PLANET JUPITER

Jupiter is the largest Planet in our Solar System and the easiest to observe. Jupiter was also one of the first objects that Galileo pointed his small telescope toward in 1610. It was his observations of the revolution of Jupiter's four brightest moons that validated the heliocentric concept of the Solar System — that the Earth was not the center of the Universe, but revolved around the Sun. In his honor, these four moons are called the Galilean moons.

Jupiter is the largest of the four gas giants, namely Jupiter, Saturn, Uranus and Neptune. Much of our information about Jupiter has come from the fly-bys of *Voyager 1* and *Voyager 2* in 1979. These two exploratory spacecraft provided photos of unprecedented detail of Jupiter's cloud belts and Galilean moons.

Voyager 2 also provided conclusive proof that Jupiter has a very faint ring system. This ring system cannot be seen with Earth based telescopes.

Observing Jupiter

The gas giants do not have a familiar surface like the Earth and other terrestrial Planets. They are mainly balls of hydrogen gas. Jupiter does have a "solid" metallic hydrogen core.

In July of 1994, comet Shoemaker-Levy 9 slammed into Jupiter's atmosphere, creating dark patches in the clouds. This collision provided direct evidence that Jupiter may have served as a "cometary magnet" during the early evolution of our Solar System, giving life the chance to develop on Earth.

Locating Jupiter. This amber jewel is easy to find in the sky because it is bright and prominent. It shines boldly above magnitude −2 most of the time. See the Planets at Sunrise and Sunset tables (pages 136 to 165) to locate Jupiter. The Superior Planet Oppositions table on page 167 indicates when Jupiter appears its brightest and largest in the sky; however, Jupiter varies little in size and magnitude compared to some of the other Planets.

The Galilean Moons. The four Galilean moons are easily visible with binoculars. They are recapped in the table below.

Galilean Moons

Moon[1]	Average Distance from Planet[2]	Revolution Period[3]	Diameter	Visual Magnitude[4]
IO (I)	262,000 miles	1.77 days	2,255 miles	5.0
	421,600 km		3,629 km	
EUROPA (II)	416,900 miles	3.55 days	1,950 miles	5.3
	670,900 km		3,138 km	
GANYMEDE (III)[5]	664,900 miles	7.16 days	3,270 miles	4.6
	1,070,000 km		5,261 km	
CALLISTO (IV)	1,171,000 miles	16.69 days	2,980 miles	5.6
	1,885,000 km		4,800 km	

[1]The Roman numeral designation frequently used for these moons is also noted. [2]Distance measured from center of Planet. [3]Orbit around Planet. [4]Visual magnitude from Earth at Jupiter's closest approach (opposition). The Galilean moons are visible with binoculars and would be visible to the naked eye if they were not close to Jupiter's bright glare. [5]Ganymede is the largest moon in our Solar System and is larger than Mercury and Pluto.

Jupiter

Observing Jupiter

The brightness of the Galilean moons combined with their rapid revolution around Jupiter creates beautiful, ever changing patterns. Movement of these inner moons can be noticed in as little as 15 minutes. There are also transits, that is, the passing of these moons in front of Jupiter. During a transit, the moon's shadow is easily seen moving across the cloud belts; however, the actual moon is usually more difficult to see. When Jupiter is visible in the sky, the popular monthly astronomy magazines publish a graph indicating the daily positions of the four moons.

Jupiter's Belts & Spot

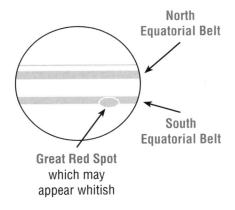

North Equatorial Belt

South Equatorial Belt

Great Red Spot which may appear whitish

Although Jupiter has dozens of moons, only the four Galilean moons are easily observed. Amalthea, Jupiter's fifth brightest moon, shines at magnitude 14.1 — as faint as Pluto. Magnitude 14 is the visual *limit* of a 12-inch telescope.

Cloud Belts. The North and South Equatorial Belts are the two most distinguished cloud belts on Jupiter. They are plainly visible in small telescopes. A narrow band just above the North Equatorial Belt can also be seen. Turbulence within the cloud belts is visible with higher magnification, larger aperture telescopes, or good seeing conditions.

Great Red Spot. The Great Red Spot is a giant circulating vortex located on the southern edge of the South Equatorial Belt. The color of the Great Red Spot changes over time. It was barely discernible in 1999 because it was light in color and blended in with the surrounding clouds. Hopefully, it will darken again to become as prominent and majestic as in the past. This oval spot is approximately 25,000 miles (40,000 km) across by 20,000 miles (32,000 km) high — larger than Earth.

Observing Saturn

THE PLANET SATURN

 The magnificent rings of Saturn make this Planet visually unique. When Galileo first looked upon Saturn, he thought he saw three orbs, two smaller orbs on opposite sides of a larger one. Galileo had no context to describe what he saw, that is, rings surrounding a Planet. So he drew what seemed to make the most sense at the time.

In 1980 and 1981, the *Voyager* missions provided close up views of Saturn's rings that answered long standing questions. The rings were thinner than expected, varying from 33 to 330 feet (10 to 100 meters). They are composed of countless ringlets, made of small chunks of ice, most less than an inch across. The entire ring system, which extends beyond the visible rings, has a diameter of about 596,000 miles (960,000 km).

Why does Saturn have a ring system? The total amount of material in the rings is small and would be equivalent to a comet about 60 miles (97 km) in diameter. The rings are positioned close to the Planet where the tidal (gravitational) forces of Saturn could tear apart a small moon. Therefore, the rings represent material that was unable to accrete into a moon because of its location. All of the gas giants in our Solar System have ring

Saturn

Saturn's Brightest Moons

Moon	Average Distance from Planet[1]	Revolution Period[2]	Diameter	Visual Magnitude[3]
ENCELADUS	147,900 miles	1.4 days	311 miles	11.8
	238,000 km		500 km	
TETHYS	183,300 miles	1.9 days	659 miles	10.3
	295,000 km		1,060 km	
DIONE	234,900 miles	2.7 days	699 miles	10.4
	378,000 km		1,120 km	
RHEA	326,800 miles	4.5 days	951 miles	9.7
	526,000 km		1,530 km	
TITAN[4]	758,100 miles	15.9 days	3,200 miles	8.4
	1,221,000 km		5,150 km	

[1]Distance measured from center of Planet. [2]Orbit around Planet. [3]Visual magnitude from Earth at Saturn's closest approach (opposition). The visual limit of a 4-inch telescope is magnitude 12. [4]Titan is the second largest moon in our Solar System and is larger than Mercury and Pluto.

Observing Saturn

systems, but none compares to Saturn's. Ring systems are most likely a natural feature of larger gaseous Planets.

Locating Saturn. This yellowish/amber colored Planet is easy to find in the sky with the naked eye because it shines steadily with an average magnitude of 0. See the Planets at Sunrise and Sunset tables (pages 136 to 165) to locate Saturn. The Superior Planet Oppositions table on page 167 indicates when Saturn will appear its brightest and largest in the sky.

Saturn's Moons. Titan, Saturn's largest moon, is also the second largest moon in our Solar System after Jupiter's Ganymede. Titan is easy to see but can appear fairly far away from Saturn. Much closer to Saturn are four moons which can be glimpsed with a small telescope. These moons are much fainter than the Galilean moons of Jupiter and are very close to the ring system, resembling little specs of light. When Saturn is visible in the sky, the popular monthly astronomy magazines publish a graph indicating the daily position of the five moons. Statistics on these moons are provided on the previous page.

The Rings. Saturn's rings are easily seen in a small telescope with magnification as little as 40x. Higher magnifications will reveal more detail.

Rings of Saturn

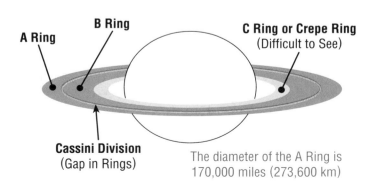

A Ring

B Ring

C Ring or Crepe Ring
(Difficult to See)

Cassini Division
(Gap in Rings)

The diameter of the A Ring is
170,000 miles (273,600 km)

Saturn

Observing Saturn

When Galileo first observed Saturn in 1610, the rings were plainly visible. But several years later in 1612, the rings were edge-on and could not be seen. This no doubt created a stir and was, to say the least, puzzling. Although Saturn is synonymous with its ring system, these rings do turn edge-on every 14 years and effectively disappear for about a year. This is not the time to show your friends Saturn because they will not believe that what they are looking at is the ringed Planet. Instead, they are more likely to think that you don't know what you are talking about.

Orientation of Saturn's Rings

Date	Orientation of Rings
2000 – 2005	Rings Open Southward
January 2009[1]	**Rings Edge-On**
2014 – 2020	Rings Open Northward
July 2024[1]	**Rings Edge-On**
2030 – 2035	Rings Open Southward
April 2039[1]	**Rings Edge-On**
2040 – 2053	Rings Open Northward
April 2054[1]	**Rings Edge-On**

[1]Rings not visible for about 6 months before and after these dates.

Saturn's rings are visible most of the time. As Saturn circles the Sun, the rings vary to the degree that they are "open," or inclined toward Earth. Also, we see the top side of the rings for one-half of Saturn's 29 year revolution about the Sun and the bottom side for the other half.

There are three major divisions in the visible rings, labeled from outermost to innermost A, B and C. Between the A and B rings, there is a 2,900 mile (4,700 km) gap, called the Cassini Division. This gap is visible in small telescopes and most apparent when the rings are opened. The middle B ring is the widest and brightest of the three rings and overwhelms the innermost C ring (known as the "crepe" ring), making it difficult to see in smaller telescopes.

Cloud Belts. Saturn's cloud belts are not as distinct as Jupiter's. Close up pictures of Saturn by *Voyager 1* and *2* also revealed that the clouds are not as complex. You should, however, be able to see several light colored belts when observing Saturn with a small telescope.

Saturn

131

Observing Uranus & Neptune

THE PLANET URANUS

 Uranus is the seventh Planet and shines at about 6th magnitude, making it just visible to the naked eye. Since it is just visible to the eye, I have, over the years, encountered references suggesting that some ancient civilizations knew of Uranus. Nevertheless, in 1781, the English astronomer William Herschel officially discovered Uranus.

Uranus is a gas giant similar in size and composition to its farther neighbor Neptune. Blue-green in color from a small amount of methane in its atmosphere, Uranus has a faint ring system. One unusual characteristic of Uranus is that it rotates on its side. Its axis is tilted 98° from a perpendicular to its orbit.

Locating Uranus. Although Uranus can just be seen with the unaided eye, it is indistinguishable from other 5th and 6th magnitude stars. The easiest way to find Uranus is to use a GO TO telescope as described on page 221. Otherwise, plan ahead, for at least yearly, the popular monthly astronomy magazines publish detailed star charts indicating the locations and movement of Uranus and Neptune. During the years 2000 to 2050, Uranus moves east from the constellation Capricornus to Leo.

Observing Uranus. Uranus' pale blue color slightly distinguishes it from surrounding stars; however, this Planet appears starlike since magnifications of about 100x are required to discern even a small disk. Uranus' rings and other surface features cannot be seen in amateur telescopes.

THE PLANET NEPTUNE

 Neptune is the farthest gas giant in our Solar System and has a faint ring system. The rings are narrow and contain areas of concentrated particles called ring arcs. Like Uranus, it has a blue-green tinted atmosphere from a small quantity of methane. Neptune was discovered or found in the fall of 1846 by German astronomer Johann Galle from a predicted position calculated by Urbain Le Verrier of France and John Adams of England. The existence of Neptune was discerned from anomalies in Uranus' orbit.

Observing Neptune & Pluto

Locating Neptune. Neptune requires some persistence to find since it is not visible to the naked eye. The easiest way to find Neptune is to use a GO TO telescope as described on page 221. Otherwise, plan ahead, for at least yearly, the popular monthly astronomy magazines publish detailed star charts indicating the locations and movement of Uranus and Neptune. During the years 2000 to 2050, Neptune moves east from the constellation Capricornus to just inside the boundary of Taurus.

Observing Neptune. Neptune is an 8th magnitude object and cannot be seen with the unaided eye; however, it is visible with binoculars or a small telescope.

To my eyes, Neptune has slightly more blue coloring than Uranus; however, this Planet often appears indistinguishable from other stars since magnifications of about 200x are required to discern a hint of a disk. Neptune's rings and other surface features cannot be seen in amateur telescopes.

THE PLANET PLUTO

Pluto is difficult to locate because it is so faint, about magnitude 14, and requires at least a 12-inch telescope. Pluto does not appear as a disk and its moon, Charon cannot be seen. A large telescope, detailed star charts and three to four days of comparative viewing are required to ferret Pluto out from among the other faint stars. Once a year, the popular monthly astronomy magazines provide a star chart to help locate Pluto. Needless to say, Pluto is an object for the better equipped and more advanced amateur.

During the years 2000 to 2050, Pluto slowly moves east from the constellation Ophiuchus to Aquarius.

As shown on page 116, Pluto's orbit is highly inclined to the other planets. Also, its orbit is *not* concentric with Neptune's as pictured on pages 116 and 192. Instead, for about 20 of the 248 years that it take to circle the Sun, Pluto's orbit is closer in than Neptune's.

Pluto was found by Clyde Tombaugh in 1930 after an exhaustive photographic search. Little is known about Pluto because of its distance and small size. It is smaller than many of the moons in our Solar System. Until an exploratory spacecraft can be sent to Pluto, its secrets will remain out of reach.

Page 134. *The best 20th century image of Pluto and its moon Charon.*

Using the SUNRISE/SET Planet Tables

Please follow these Guidelines to get the most out of using the Planets at Sunrise/Sunset tables

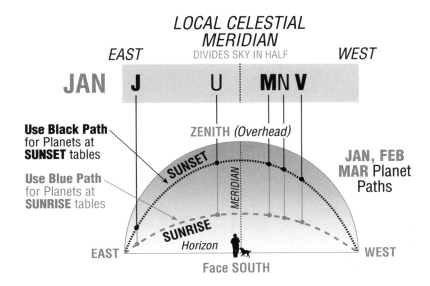

LOCAL CELESTIAL MERIDIAN
DIVIDES SKY IN HALF

EAST   *WEST*

JAN   **J**   U   **MN V**

Use Black Path for Planets at **SUNSET** tables

ZENITH *(Overhead)*

Use Blue Path for Planets at **SUNRISE** tables

MERIDIAN

SUNSET

SUNRISE

Horizon

JAN, FEB MAR Planet Paths

EAST   WEST

Face SOUTH

INSTRUCTIONS: The example above shows how the positions of the Planets on the bar correspond to the arced Planet Path for the respective month and time. The correspondence will become more obvious as you become familiar with using the tables. The Planet Path is indicated on the Monthly Star Charts.

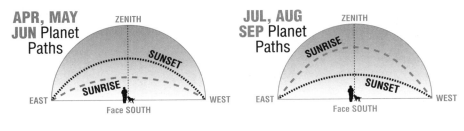

APR, MAY JUN Planet Paths

ZENITH

SUNSET

SUNRISE

EAST   WEST

Face SOUTH

JUL, AUG SEP Planet Paths

ZENITH

SUNRISE

SUNSET

EAST   WEST

Face SOUTH

HEIGHT OF PLANET PATHS. Planet Paths are drawn for the mid-latitude of 39° N (Kansas City). They will arc higher in the sky for lower latitudes and lower in the sky for higher latitudes.

MOVEMENT OF PLANETS. Depending on your location and time of year, it can take a few to 6 or more hours for a Planet to move from the horizon to the meridian.

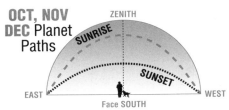

OCT, NOV DEC Planet Paths

ZENITH

SUNRISE

SUNSET

EAST   WEST

Face SOUTH

Planets at SUNRISE 2000 – 2003

Relative Positions on the 1st of Each Month
FACING SOUTH

2000 — EAST ← CELESTIAL MERIDIAN (DIVIDES SKY IN HALF) → WEST

Month	Positions (East → West)
JAN	V
FEB	V
MAR	VN
APR	U N
MAY	U N
JUN	JS · · U N
JUL	JS · · U N
AUG	JS · · U N
SEP	M · J S
OCT	M · J S
NOV	M · J S
DEC	M · · J

2002 — EAST ← CELESTIAL MERIDIAN (DIVIDES SKY IN HALF) → WEST

Month	Positions (East → West)
JAN	J
FEB	
MAR	N
APR	U N
MAY	U N
JUN	U N
JUL	S · · U N
AUG	S · · U N
SEP	J · S · U
OCT	M J S
NOV	M J · S
DEC	VM · J · S

2001 — EAST ← CELESTIAL MERIDIAN (DIVIDES SKY IN HALF) → WEST

Month	Positions (East → West)
JAN	M
FEB	M
MAR	N · M
APR	U N · M
MAY	V U N · M
JUN	V U N · M
JUL	S V · U N
AUG	JV S · U N
SEP	V J S
OCT	V · J · S
NOV	V · · J S
DEC	J S

2003 — EAST ← CELESTIAL MERIDIAN (DIVIDES SKY IN HALF) → WEST

Month	Positions (East → West)
JAN	VM · J
FEB	V M · J
MAR	N V M
APR	VU N M
MAY	V U N M
JUN	V U M N
JUL	M U N
AUG	S · M U N
SEP	S · M U
OCT	J S
NOV	J · S
DEC	J · S

See Instructions on Page 135

See Instructions on Page 135

NOTE — Planet Positions are for 1 hour before Sunrise and 1 hour after Sunset

V=Venus, **M**=Mars, **J**=Jupiter, **S**=Saturn, U=Uranus, N=Neptune
Uranus and Neptune are very faint compared to the other Planets listed in these tables. For **Mercury**, see tables starting on page 171.

Planets Rise/Set

136

Planets at SUNSET 2000 – 2003

Relative Positions on the 1st of Each Month
FACING SOUTH

In each chart the LOCAL MERIDIAN (divides sky in half) runs vertically between EAST (left) and WEST (right). The "|" marks the meridian.

2000

Month	EAST — MERIDIAN — WEST
JAN	S J | M U N
FEB	S J | M
MAR	| S J M
APR	| SJM
MAY	| M
JUN	
JUL	
AUG	U N |
SEP	U N | V
OCT	U N | V
NOV	| U N V
DEC	J S | U N V

2001

Month	EAST — MERIDIAN — WEST
JAN	J S | V U N
FEB	J S | V
MAR	| J S V
APR	| J S
MAY	| JS
JUN	
JUL	M |
AUG	U N M |
SEP	U N | M
OCT	U N | M
NOV	U | N M
DEC	S | M U N

2002

Month	EAST — MERIDIAN — WEST
JAN	J S | M U N
FEB	J S | M
MAR	| J S M
APR	| J S M V
MAY	| J SMV
JUN	| JV M
JUL	| V
AUG	U N | V
SEP	U N | V
OCT	U N | V
NOV	| U N
DEC	| U N

2003

Month	EAST — MERIDIAN — WEST
JAN	S | U N
FEB	J S | U
MAR	J | S
APR	J | S
MAY	| J S
JUN	| J S
JUL	| J
AUG	N |
SEP	MU N |
OCT	MU N |
NOV	| MU N V
DEC	| M U N V

See Instructions on Page 135

V=Venus, **M**=Mars, **J**=Jupiter, **S**=Saturn, U=Uranus, N=Neptune
Uranus and ***Neptune*** *are very faint compared to the other Planets listed in these tables.* For **Mercury**, see tables starting on page 171.

Planets Rise/Set

Planets at SUNRISE 2004 – 2007

Relative Positions on the 1st of Each Month
FACING SOUTH

Each chart shows planet positions from EAST (left) to WEST (right). The CELESTIAL MERIDIAN divides the sky in half (dashed line).

2004

Month	Planet positions (East → West)
JAN	J · S
FEB	J
MAR	N · · · · J
APR	U N
MAY	U N
JUN	U N
JUL	V · · U N
AUG	S V · · · · U N
SEP	SV · · · · · U
OCT	V S
NOV	MJV · · S
DEC	MV · J · · S

2005

Month	Planet positions (East → West)
JAN	V M · · J · · · S
FEB	M · · J
MAR	N M · · · J
APR	U NM · · · J
MAY	U MN
JUN	M U · N
JUL	M U · N
AUG	M · · U · N
SEP	S · M · · U
OCT	S · · M
NOV	S · · · M
DEC	J · · · S

2006

Month	Planet positions (East → West)
JAN	J · · S
FEB	V · J · · · · S
MAR	NV · · J
APR	U VN · · · J
MAY	VU N · · · · J
JUN	V · U · N
JUL	V · · U · N
AUG	V · · · · U · N
SEP	VS · · · · · · U
OCT	S
NOV	· · S
DEC	M · · S

2007

Month	Planet positions (East → West)
JAN	MJ · · · S
FEB	M · J · · · S
MAR	M · J
APR	U MN · · J
MAY	MU N · · · J
JUN	M · U · N · · · J
JUL	M · · U · N
AUG	M · · U · N
SEP	V · M · · U
OCT	SV · M
NOV	V S · · M
DEC	V · S · · M

V=Venus, **M**=Mars, **J**=Jupiter, **S**=Saturn, U=Uranus, N=Neptune
Uranus and **Neptune** are very faint compared to the other Planets listed in these tables. For **Mercury**, see tables starting on page 171.

See Instructions on Page 135

NOTE
Planet Positions are for 1 hour before Sunrise and 1 hour after Sunset

Planets at SUNSET 2004 – 2007

Relative Positions on the 1st of Each Month
FACING SOUTH

V=Venus, M=Mars, J=Jupiter, S=Saturn, U=Uranus, N=Neptune

2004 — LOCAL MERIDIAN DIVIDES SKY IN HALF (EAST ← → WEST)

Month	Positions (East → West)
JAN	S · · M U VN
FEB	· S · M V U
MAR	J · S · M V
APR	J · · S MV
MAY	· J · S MV
JUN	· · J MS
JUL	· · J M
AUG	N · · J
SEP	U N · ·
OCT	· U N ·
NOV	· U N ·
DEC	· · U N

2006 — LOCAL MERIDIAN DIVIDES SKY IN HALF (EAST ← → WEST)

Month	Positions (East → West)
JAN	· M · U N V
FEB	S · M · U
MAR	S · M
APR	· S · M
MAY	J · S M
JUN	· J · S M
JUL	· J · MS
AUG	N · · J M
SEP	U N · · J
OCT	U N · · J
NOV	· U N ·
DEC	· U N

2005 — LOCAL MERIDIAN DIVIDES SKY IN HALF (EAST ← → WEST)

Month	Positions (East → West)
JAN	S · · U N
FEB	· S · U
MAR	· S
APR	J · S
MAY	· J · S
JUN	· · J S V
JUL	· · J V
AUG	N · · J V
SEP	U N · · JV
OCT	· U N · V
NOV	M U N V
DEC	· M U N V

2007 — LOCAL MERIDIAN DIVIDES SKY IN HALF (EAST ← → WEST)

Month	Positions (East → West)
JAN	· · U N V
FEB	S · · U V
MAR	S · · V
APR	· S · V
MAY	· · S V
JUN	J · S V
JUL	· J · SV
AUG	N · J ·
SEP	U N · J
OCT	U N · J
NOV	· U N · J
DEC	· U N · J

See Instructions on Page 135

V=Venus, M=Mars, J=Jupiter, S=Saturn, U=Uranus, N=Neptune
Uranus and Neptune are very faint compared to the other Planets listed in these tables. For **Mercury**, see tables starting on page 171.

Planets at SUNRISE 2008 – 2011

Relative Positions on the 1st of Each Month
FACING SOUTH

2008

	EAST	CELESTIAL MERIDIAN (DIVIDES SKY IN HALF)	WEST
JAN	V	S	
FEB	VJ		S
MAR	V J		S
APR	N J		
MAY	U N J		
JUN	U N	J	
JUL		U N	J
AUG		U N	
SEP			U
OCT	S		
NOV	S		
DEC		S	

2010

	EAST	CELESTIAL MERIDIAN (DIVIDES SKY IN HALF)	WEST
JAN		S M	
FEB			S M
MAR			S
APR	J N		S
MAY	U J N		
JUN	U J N		
JUL		J U N	
AUG		J U N	
SEP			J U N
OCT			U J
NOV	S		
DEC	V S		

See Instructions on Page 135

2009

	EAST	CELESTIAL MERIDIAN (DIVIDES SKY IN HALF)	WEST
JAN		S	
FEB			S
MAR	J		S
APR	M N J		S
MAY	M V U N J		
JUN	M V U	J N	
JUL	V M	U	J N
AUG	V M	U	N J
SEP	V M		U
OCT	V M		
NOV	V S M		
DEC		S	M

2011

	EAST	CELESTIAL MERIDIAN (DIVIDES SKY IN HALF)	WEST
JAN	V S		
FEB	V	S	
MAR	V		S
APR	V N		S
MAY	V U N		
JUN	V M J U N		
JUL	M J	U N	
AUG	M J	U N	
SEP	M		J U N
OCT		M	J U
NOV	S M		J
DEC		S M	

V=Venus, M=Mars, J=Jupiter, S=Saturn, U=Uranus, N=Neptune
Uranus and *Neptune* are very faint compared to the other Planets listed in these tables. For **Mercury**, see tables starting on page 171.

Planets at SUNSET 2008 – 2011

Relative Positions on the 1st of Each Month
FACING SOUTH

CELESTIAL MERIDIAN (DIVIDES SKY IN HALF) — EAST on the left, WEST on the right.

2008

Month	EAST ———————— MERIDIAN ———————— WEST
JAN	M · · · · U N
FEB	· M · · · U
MAR	S · M
APR	· S · M
MAY	· · S · M
JUN	· · · S M
JUL	J · · · · SM
AUG	N · J · · · M S
SEP	U N · J · · MV
OCT	· U N · J · V
NOV	· · U N · J · V
DEC	· · · U · N · VJ

2009

Month	EAST ———————— MERIDIAN ———————— WEST
JAN	· · · U VN J
FEB	· · · V U
MAR	S · · · V
APR	· S
MAY	· · S
JUN	· · · S
JUL	· · · S
AUG	NJ · · · · S
SEP	U NJ
OCT	· U NJ
NOV	· · U NJ
DEC	· · · U NJ

2010

Month	EAST ———————— MERIDIAN ———————— WEST
JAN	· · · · U JN
FEB	M · · · · U J
MAR	· M · · · U
APR	S · M · · · V
MAY	· · S · M V
JUN	· · · S M V
JUL	· · · · S M V
AUG	N · · · MS V
SEP	JU N · · · VMS
OCT	UJ N · · · VM
NOV	· UJ · N · · M
DEC	· · UJ · N

2011

Month	EAST ———————— MERIDIAN ———————— WEST
JAN	· · · JU · N
FEB	· · · JU · N
MAR	· · · JU
APR	S
MAY	· S
JUN	· · S
JUL	· · · S
AUG	N · · · · S
SEP	N · · · · S
OCT	U · N
NOV	J U · N · · V
DEC	· J · U · N · V

See Instructions on Page 135

V=Venus, **M**=Mars, **J**=Jupiter, **S**=Saturn, **U**=Uranus, **N**=Neptune
Uranus and **Neptune** *are very faint compared to the other Planets listed in these tables.* For **Mercury**, see tables starting on page 171.

Planets Rise/Set

Planets at SUNRISE 2012 – 2015

Relative Positions on the 1st of Each Month
FACING SOUTH

See Instructions on Page 135

Columns read EAST → (CELESTIAL MERIDIAN DIVIDES SKY IN HALF) → WEST

2012

Month	EAST			MERIDIAN			WEST
JAN			S	M			
FEB				S	M		
MAR					S	M	
APR	N					S	
MAY	U	N					S
JUN		U	N				
JUL	VJ		U	N			
AUG	VJ			U	N		
SEP		V	J		U	N	
OCT		V		J		U	
NOV		V			J		
DEC	VS					J	

2013

Month	EAST			MERIDIAN			WEST
JAN	V	S					
FEB			S				
MAR				S			
APR	N				S		
MAY	U	N					S
JUN		U	N				
JUL	M		U	N			
AUG	MJ			U	N		
SEP	M	J			U	N	
OCT		M	J				U
NOV			M		J		
DEC	S		M			J	

2014

Month	EAST			MERIDIAN			WEST
JAN		S	M				J
FEB	V		S	M			
MAR	V			S	M		
APR	N V					S	M
MAY	U V N						S
JUN	V U	N					
JUL	V		U	N			
AUG	V				U	N	
SEP	V J					U	N
OCT		J					U
NOV			J				
DEC	S			J			

2015

Month	EAST			MERIDIAN			WEST
JAN		S				J	
FEB			S				J
MAR				S			
APR	N				S		
MAY	U	N				S	
JUN	U	N					S
JUL			U	N			
AUG					U	N	
SEP	MV					U	N
OCT	JMV						U
NOV	MVJ						
DEC		V	M	J			

V=Venus, M=Mars, J=Jupiter, S=Saturn, U=Uranus, N=Neptune
Uranus and **Neptune** are very faint compared to the other Planets listed in these tables. For **Mercury**, see tables starting on page 171.

Planets at SUNSET 2012 – 2015

Relative Positions on the 1st of Each Month
FACING SOUTH

Legend of columns: **EAST** — *CELESTIAL MERIDIAN (DIVIDES SKY IN HALF)* — **WEST**

Planets are listed below in order from East (left) to West (right) as plotted on each chart; the `|` marks the celestial meridian.

2012

Month	East ←		Meridian		→ West
JAN		J	U	N V	
FEB		J	U V N		
MAR	M		J V	U	
APR	M			V J	
MAY	S	M		V	
JUN	S		M		
JUL		S M			
AUG			S M		
SEP	N			M S	
OCT	U N				M
NOV	U N				M
DEC	J	U	N		M

2013

Month	East ←		Meridian		→ West
JAN	J		U	N	M
FEB		J	U N		
MAR		J	U		
APR			J		
MAY	S			J	
JUN		S			V
JUL		S			V
AUG			S		V
SEP	N			S V	
OCT	U N			V S	
NOV	U N		V		
DEC		U	N		V

2014

Month	East ←		Meridian		→ West
JAN	J		U	N	V
FEB		J	U N		
MAR		J	U		
APR	M		J		
MAY	S M			J	
JUN	S		M		J
JUL		S M			
AUG			S M		
SEP	N			M S	
OCT	U N			M S	
NOV	U N		M		
DEC		U	N	M	

2015

Month	East ←		Meridian		→ West
JAN			U	N	M V
FEB	J			U	M V N
MAR	J			U V M	
APR	J			V M	
MAY			J	V	
JUN	S			J V	
JUL		S			J V
AUG			S		
SEP	N			S	
OCT	U N				S
NOV	U N				S
DEC		U	N		

See Instructions on Page 135

Page 144. *One of the best images of Mars from the Hubble Space Telescope.*
Page 145. *Olympus Mons on Mars is the largest volcano in the Solar System.*

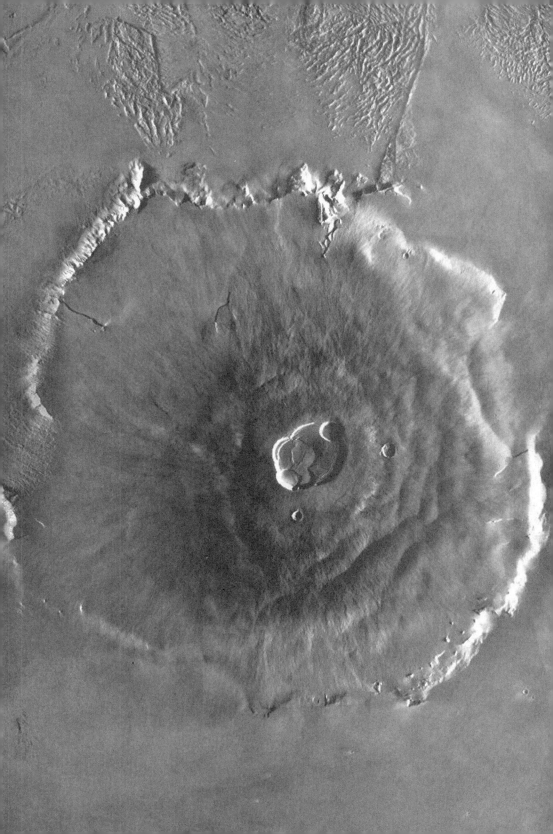

Planets at SUNRISE 2016 – 2019

Relative Positions on the 1st of Each Month
FACING SOUTH

2016 — EAST → CELESTIAL MERIDIAN (DIVIDES SKY IN HALF) → WEST

Month	Positions (EAST → WEST)
JAN	S V M J
FEB	V S M J
MAR	V S M J
APR	N S M J
MAY	N S M
JUN	U N S M
JUL	U N
AUG	U N
SEP	U N
OCT	U
NOV	J
DEC	J

2017 — EAST → CELESTIAL MERIDIAN (DIVIDES SKY IN HALF) → WEST

Month	Positions (EAST → WEST)
JAN	S J
FEB	S J
MAR	S J
APR	N S J
MAY	V N S
JUN	UV N S
JUL	V U N
AUG	V U N
SEP	V U N
OCT	MV U
NOV	V M
DEC	J M

2018 — EAST → CELESTIAL MERIDIAN (DIVIDES SKY IN HALF) → WEST

Month	Positions (EAST → WEST)
JAN	JM
FEB	S M J
MAR	S M J
APR	N SM J
MAY	N M S J
JUN	U N M S
JUL	U N M S
AUG	U N M
SEP	U N
OCT	U
NOV	U
DEC	V

2019 — EAST → CELESTIAL MERIDIAN (DIVIDES SKY IN HALF) → WEST

Month	Positions (EAST → WEST)
JAN	J V
FEB	S V J
MAR	V S J
APR	V S J
MAY	V N S J
JUN	VU N S J
JUL	U N S
AUG	U N
SEP	U N
OCT	U
NOV	M U
DEC	M

See Instructions on Page 135

NOTE Planet Positions are for 1 hour before Sunrise and 1 hour after Sunset

V=Venus, **M**=Mars, **J**=Jupiter, **S**=Saturn, U=Uranus, N=Neptune
Uranus and *Neptune* are very faint compared to the other Planets listed in these tables.* For **Mercury**, see tables starting on page 171.

Planets at SUNSET 2016 – 2019

Relative Positions on the 1st of Each Month
FACING SOUTH

Columns run from EAST (left) to WEST (right); the CELESTIAL MERIDIAN divides the sky in half.

2016 — EAST · CELESTIAL MERIDIAN · WEST

Month	East → West positions
JAN	U N
FEB	U N
MAR	J … U
APR	J
MAY	J
JUN	S M … J
JUL	S M … J
AUG	S M … J
SEP	N … M S … V
OCT	U N … M S … V
NOV	U N … M … V S
DEC	U N … M V

2017 — EAST · CELESTIAL MERIDIAN · WEST

Month	East → West positions
JAN	U … M N V
FEB	U M V N
MAR	M U V
APR	J … M
MAY	J … M
JUN	S … J … M
JUL	S … J … M
AUG	S … J
SEP	N … S J
OCT	U N … S
NOV	U N … S
DEC	U N … S

2018 — EAST · CELESTIAL MERIDIAN · WEST

Month	East → West positions
JAN	U N
FEB	U N
MAR	U
APR	V U
MAY	J … V
JUN	J … V
JUL	S … J … V
AUG	M S … J V
SEP	N … M S … J V
OCT	N … M … S … J V
NOV	U N M … S
DEC	U N M … S

2019 — EAST · CELESTIAL MERIDIAN · WEST

Month	East → West positions
JAN	U … M N
FEB	U M … N
MAR	M U
APR	M U
MAY	M
JUN	J … M
JUL	S J … M
AUG	S … J
SEP	N … S J
OCT	N … S J
NOV	U N … S J V
DEC	U N … S V J

See Instructions on Page 135

V=Venus, M=Mars, J=Jupiter, S=Saturn, U=Uranus, N=Neptune
Uranus and *Neptune* are very faint compared to the other Planets listed in these tables. For **Mercury**, see tables starting on page 171.

Planets at SUNRISE 2020 – 2023

Relative Positions on the 1st of Each Month
FACING SOUTH

CELESTIAL MERIDIAN DIVIDES SKY IN HALF
EAST — WEST

2020

Month	East → West
JAN	M
FEB	J M
MAR	S JM
APR	MJS
MAY	N M SJ
JUN	U NM SJ
JUL	V U MN SJ
AUG	V U M N S
SEP	V U M N
OCT	V U M
NOV	V U
DEC	V

2021

Month	East → West
JAN	V
FEB	
MAR	JS
APR	J S
MAY	N J S
JUN	U N J S
JUL	U N J S
AUG	U N J S
SEP	U N
OCT	U
NOV	U
DEC	M

2022

Month	East → West
JAN	M
FEB	VM
MAR	VM
APR	VSM
MAY	VJNMS
JUN	UV MJN S
JUL	V U M J N S
AUG	V UM J N S
SEP	V M U J N
OCT	M U J
NOV	M U
DEC	M

2023

Month	East → West
JAN	
FEB	
MAR	
APR	S
MAY	N S
JUN	UJ N S
JUL	UJ N S
AUG	U J N S
SEP	V U J N S
OCT	V U J N
NOV	V U J
DEC	V

See Instructions on Page 135

V=Venus, **M**=Mars, **J**=Jupiter, **S**=Saturn, U=Uranus, N=Neptune
Uranus and ***Neptune*** *are very faint compared to the other Planets listed in these tables.* For **Mercury**, see tables starting on page 171.

Planets at SUNSET 2020 – 2023

Relative Positions on the 1st of Each Month
FACING SOUTH

2020 — EAST … CELESTIAL MERIDIAN (DIVIDES SKY IN HALF) … WEST

Month	East ←→ West (meridian marked with │)
JAN	U │ N V
FEB	U │ V N
MAR	U V │
APR	V │ U
MAY	V │
JUN	
JUL	J │
AUG	S J │
SEP	N S J │
OCT	M N S J │
NOV	U M N S J │
DEC	U M N │ S J

2022 — EAST … CELESTIAL MERIDIAN (DIVIDES SKY IN HALF) … WEST

Month	East ←→ West (meridian marked with │)
JAN	U │ N J S
FEB	U │ N J
MAR	U │
APR	│ U
MAY	
JUN	
JUL	
AUG	S │
SEP	N S │
OCT	J N S │
NOV	U JN S │
DEC	M U J N │ S

2021 — EAST … CELESTIAL MERIDIAN (DIVIDES SKY IN HALF) … WEST

Month	East ←→ West (meridian marked with │)
JAN	U M │ N J S
FEB	M U │ N
MAR	M U │
APR	M │ U
MAY	M │
JUN	M │ V
JUL	M V │
AUG	J S │ V M
SEP	N J S │ V
OCT	N J S │ V
NOV	U N J │ S V
DEC	U N │ J S V

2023 — EAST … CELESTIAL MERIDIAN (DIVIDES SKY IN HALF) … WEST

Month	East ←→ West (meridian marked with │)
JAN	M U │ J N S V
FEB	M │ U J N V
MAR	M │ U VJN
APR	M │ VU
MAY	M V │
JUN	│ MV
JUL	│ MV
AUG	│ M
SEP	N S │ M
OCT	N S │
NOV	UJ N S │
DEC	UJ N │ S

See Instructions on Page 135

V=Venus, **M**=Mars, **J**=Jupiter, **S**=Saturn, U=Uranus, N=Neptune
Uranus and ***Neptune*** *are very faint compared to the other Planets listed in these tables.* For **Mercury**, see tables starting on page 171.

Planets at SUNRISE 2024 – 2027

Relative Positions on the 1st of Each Month
FACING SOUTH

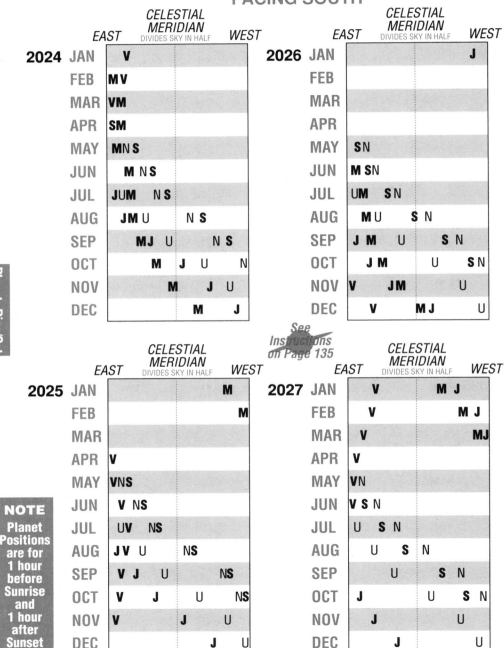

2024	EAST	CELESTIAL MERIDIAN (DIVIDES SKY IN HALF)	WEST
JAN	V		
FEB	M V		
MAR	V M		
APR	S M		
MAY	MN S		
JUN	M N S		
JUL	JUM	N S	
AUG	JM U	N S	
SEP	MJ U	N S	
OCT	M	J U	N
NOV	M	J	U
DEC		M	J

2026	EAST	CELESTIAL MERIDIAN (DIVIDES SKY IN HALF)	WEST
JAN			J
FEB			
MAR			
APR			
MAY	S N		
JUN	M SN		
JUL	UM	S N	
AUG	M U	S N	
SEP	J M	U	S N
OCT	J M		U	S N
NOV	V	JM	U
DEC	V	M J	U

See Instructions on Page 135

2025	EAST	CELESTIAL MERIDIAN (DIVIDES SKY IN HALF)	WEST
JAN			M
FEB			M
MAR			
APR	V		
MAY	VNS		
JUN	V NS		
JUL	UV NS		
AUG	JV U	NS	
SEP	V J	U	NS
OCT	V	J	U	NS
NOV	V	J	U
DEC		J	U

2027	EAST	CELESTIAL MERIDIAN (DIVIDES SKY IN HALF)	WEST
JAN	V	M J	
FEB	V	M J	
MAR	V	MJ	
APR	V		
MAY	VN		
JUN	V S N		
JUL	U S N		
AUG	U S N		
SEP	U	S N	
OCT	J	U	S N
NOV	J	U	
DEC	J	U	

V=Venus, **M**=Mars, **J**=Jupiter, **S**=Saturn, **U**=Uranus, **N**=Neptune
Uranus and ***Neptune*** *are very faint compared to the other Planets listed in these tables.* For **Mercury**, see tables starting on page 171.

Planets Rise/Set

150

Planets at SUNSET 2024 – 2027

Relative Positions on the 1st of Each Month
FACING SOUTH

2024 — EAST · CELESTIAL MERIDIAN (DIVIDES SKY IN HALF) · WEST

Month	Positions (East → West)
JAN	U J N S
FEB	U J N S
MAR	U J N
APR	UJ
MAY	
JUN	
JUL	
AUG	
SEP	NS V
OCT	NS V
NOV	U N S V
DEC	J U N S V

2026 — EAST · CELESTIAL MERIDIAN (DIVIDES SKY IN HALF) · WEST

Month	Positions (East → West)
JAN	J U NS
FEB	J U NS
MAR	J U SN
APR	J U V
MAY	J VU
JUN	JV
JUL	V J
AUG	V
SEP	V
OCT	SN
NOV	SN
DEC	U SN

2025 — EAST · CELESTIAL MERIDIAN (DIVIDES SKY IN HALF) · WEST

Month	Positions (East → West)
JAN	J U N S V
FEB	M J U VNS
MAR	M J U VN
APR	M J U
MAY	M J
JUN	M J
JUL	M
AUG	M
SEP	S M
OCT	NS M
NOV	NS
DEC	U NS

2027 — EAST · CELESTIAL MERIDIAN (DIVIDES SKY IN HALF) · WEST

Month	Positions (East → West)
JAN	U S N
FEB	J U S N
MAR	MJ U S N
APR	MJ U
MAY	M J U
JUN	M J
JUL	M J
AUG	M J
SEP	M
OCT	S N M
NOV	S N MV
DEC	U S N VM

See Instructions on Page 135

V=Venus, **M**=Mars, **J**=Jupiter, **S**=Saturn, U=Uranus, N=Neptune
Uranus and **Neptune** are very faint compared to the other Planets listed in these tables. For **Mercury**, see tables starting on page 171.

Planets at SUNRISE 2028 – 2031

Relative Positions on the 1st of Each Month
FACING SOUTH

2028 — EAST ← CELESTIAL MERIDIAN (DIVIDES SKY IN HALF) → WEST

Month	Sky (East → West)
JAN	J
FEB	J
MAR	J
APR	J
MAY	N
JUN	S N
JUL	M U V S N
AUG	M V U S N
SEP	M V U S N
OCT	V M U S N
NOV	J V M U S
DEC	V J M U

2030 — EAST ← CELESTIAL MERIDIAN (DIVIDES SKY IN HALF) → WEST

Month	Sky (East → West)
JAN	J
FEB	V J
MAR	V J
APR	V J
MAY	N V J
JUN	V N
JUL	U V S N
AUG	M V U S N
SEP	V M U S N
OCT	M U S N
NOV	M U S
DEC	M U S

2029 — EAST ← CELESTIAL MERIDIAN (DIVIDES SKY IN HALF) → WEST

Month	Sky (East → West)
JAN	V J M
FEB	J M
MAR	J M
APR	J M
MAY	N J
JUN	S N
JUL	U S N
AUG	U S N
SEP	U S N
OCT	U S N
NOV	U S
DEC	J U

2031 — EAST ← CELESTIAL MERIDIAN (DIVIDES SKY IN HALF) → WEST

Month	Sky (East → West)
JAN	J M
FEB	J M
MAR	J M
APR	J M
MAY	N J M
JUN	N J
JUL	U S N
AUG	U S N
SEP	V U S N
OCT	V U S N
NOV	V U S
DEC	V U S

See Instructions on Page 135

NOTE
Planet Positions are for 1 hour before Sunrise and 1 hour after Sunset

V=Venus, **M**=Mars, **J**=Jupiter, **S**=Saturn, U=Uranus, N=Neptune
Uranus and **Neptune** *are very faint compared to the other Planets listed in these tables.* For **Mercury**, see tables starting on page 171.

Planets at SUNSET 2028 – 2031

Relative Positions on the 1st of Each Month
FACING SOUTH

The charts run from **EAST** (left) to **WEST** (right); the dashed **CELESTIAL MERIDIAN** (marked ¦) divides the sky in half.

2028

Month	East ← Positions → West
JAN	U S N ¦ V M
FEB	U ¦ S N V
MAR	J .... U ¦ VS N
APR	J ...... U V ¦ S
MAY	J ...... ¦ VU
JUN	...... J ¦
JUL	...... ¦ J
AUG	...... ¦ J
SEP	
OCT	N
NOV	S N
DEC	U S N

2029

Month	East ← Positions → West
JAN	U S ¦ N
FEB	U ¦ S N
MAR	U S ¦ N
APR	J M ...... U ¦ S
MAY	J M ...... ¦ U
JUN	..... J ¦ M V
JUL	..... ¦ J M V
AUG	¦ MJ V
SEP	¦ M JV
OCT	N ¦ M V
NOV	S N ¦ MV
DEC	U S N ¦ MV

2030

Month	East ← Positions → West
JAN	U S ¦ N M
FEB	U ¦ S N M
MAR	U S ¦ N M
APR	U ¦ S
MAY	J ¦ .... U S
JUN	J ¦
JUL	...... ¦ J
AUG	...... ¦ J
SEP	¦ J
OCT	N ¦ J
NOV	N ¦ J
DEC	U S N ¦

2031

Month	East ← Positions → West
JAN	U S ¦ N V
FEB	U S ¦ N V
MAR	U S ¦ VN
APR	¦ U S V
MAY	M ¦ .... VU S
JUN	J ...... M ¦ V
JUL	J ...... ¦ M V
AUG	...... J ¦ M
SEP	¦ J M
OCT	N ¦ MJ
NOV	N ¦ M J
DEC	US N ¦ M J

See Instructions on Page 135

V=Venus, **M**=Mars, **J**=Jupiter, **S**=Saturn, U=Uranus, N=Neptune
Uranus and ***Neptune*** are very faint compared to the other Planets listed in these tables. For **Mercury**, see tables starting on page 171.

Planets at SUNRISE 2032 – 2035

Relative Positions on the 1st of Each Month
FACING SOUTH

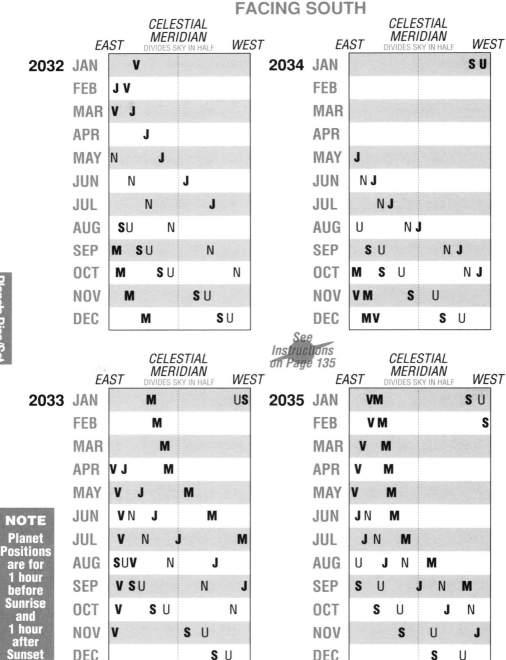

2032

	EAST	CELESTIAL MERIDIAN (DIVIDES SKY IN HALF)	WEST
JAN	V		
FEB	J V		
MAR	V J		
APR	J		
MAY	N	J	
JUN	N		J
JUL	N		J
AUG	S U N		
SEP	M S U	N	
OCT	M S U		N
NOV	M	S U	
DEC	M		S U

2034

	EAST	CELESTIAL MERIDIAN (DIVIDES SKY IN HALF)	WEST
JAN			S U
FEB			
MAR			
APR			
MAY	J		
JUN	N J		
JUL	N J		
AUG	U	N J	
SEP	S U		N J
OCT	M S U		N J
NOV	V M	S U	
DEC	M V		S U

2033

	EAST	CELESTIAL MERIDIAN (DIVIDES SKY IN HALF)	WEST
JAN	M		U S
FEB	M		
MAR	M		
APR	V J	M	
MAY	V J	M	
JUN	V N J		M
JUL	V N	J	M
AUG	S U V	N	J
SEP	V S U	N	J
OCT	V	S U	N
NOV	V	S U	
DEC			S U

2035

	EAST	CELESTIAL MERIDIAN (DIVIDES SKY IN HALF)	WEST
JAN	V M		S U
FEB	V M		S
MAR	V M		
APR	V	M	
MAY	V	M	
JUN	J N	M	
JUL	J N	M	
AUG	U	J N M	
SEP	S U	J N	M
OCT	S U		J N
NOV		S U	J
DEC			S U

See Instructions on Page 135

See Instructions on Page 135

NOTE
Planet Positions are for 1 hour before Sunrise and 1 hour after Sunset

V=Venus, **M**=Mars, **J**=Jupiter, **S**=Saturn, U=Uranus, N=Neptune
Uranus and **Neptune** are very faint compared to the other Planets listed in these tables. For **Mercury**, see tables starting on page 171.

Planets at SUNSET 2032 – 2035

Relative Positions on the 1st of Each Month
FACING SOUTH

2032

Month	EAST ←→ CELESTIAL MERIDIAN (DIVIDES SKY IN HALF) ←→ WEST
JAN	US ... N ... M
FEB	US ... N M
MAR	US ... MN
APR	US ... M
MAY	US M
JUN	
JUL	J
AUG	J
SEP	J ... V
OCT	N ... J ... V
NOV	N ... J ... V
DEC	N ... JV

2033

Month	EAST ←→ CELESTIAL MERIDIAN (DIVIDES SKY IN HALF) ←→ WEST
JAN	SU ... N ... V J
FEB	SU ... N V
MAR	SU ... N V
APR	SU
MAY	SU
JUN	SU
JUL	M
AUG	M
SEP	J ... M
OCT	N ... J ... M
NOV	N ... J M
DEC	N ... JM

2034

Month	EAST ←→ CELESTIAL MERIDIAN (DIVIDES SKY IN HALF) ←→ WEST
JAN	SU ... N ... M J
FEB	SU ... NM J
MAR	SU ... M N V
APR	SU ... M V
MAY	SU MV
JUN	SVMU
JUL	V M
AUG	V
SEP	V
OCT	NJ
NOV	N J
DEC	N J

2035

Month	EAST ←→ CELESTIAL MERIDIAN (DIVIDES SKY IN HALF) ←→ WEST
JAN	U ... N J
FEB	S U ... N J
MAR	S U ... NJ
APR	S U
MAY	S U
JUN	S U
JUL	S
AUG	
SEP	
OCT	N M
NOV	JN M ... V
DEC	J N M ... V

See Instructions on Page 135

Page 156 & 157. Images from Voyager of Uranus (left) and Neptune (right).

Planets at SUNRISE 2036 – 2039

Relative Positions on the 1st of Each Month
FACING SOUTH

See Instructions on Page 135

2036 — EAST → *CELESTIAL MERIDIAN (DIVIDES SKY IN HALF)* → WEST

	1 (EAST)	2	3	4 ‖	5	6	7	8 (WEST)
JAN							S	U
FEB							S	
MAR								
APR								
MAY								
JUN	N							
JUL	JV	N						
AUG	U	VJ	N					
SEP	S V U	J			N			
OCT	VS	U	J			N		
NOV	MV	S			U	J		
DEC	MV		S		U	J		

2038 — EAST → *CELESTIAL MERIDIAN (DIVIDES SKY IN HALF)* → WEST

	1 (EAST)	2	3	4 ‖	5	6	7	8 (WEST)
JAN						S	JU	
FEB	V					S		
MAR	V						S	
APR	V							
MAY	V							
JUN	VN							
JUL	V	N						
AUG	UV		N					
SEP	VJ	U			N			
OCT	S	J	U			N		
NOV		S	J	U				N
DEC			S	J	U			

2037 — EAST → *CELESTIAL MERIDIAN (DIVIDES SKY IN HALF)* → WEST

	1 (EAST)	2	3	4 ‖	5	6	7	8 (WEST)
JAN	V M					S	U	
FEB	M						S	
MAR	M						S	
APR	M							
MAY	M							
JUN	N	M						
JUL		N M						
AUG	UJ		M	N				
SEP		UJ		M	N			
OCT	S	JU		M		N		
NOV		S		JU		M	N	
DEC			S		JU			

2039 — EAST → *CELESTIAL MERIDIAN (DIVIDES SKY IN HALF)* → WEST

	1 (EAST)	2	3	4 ‖	5	6	7	8 (WEST)
JAN	M					S	J	U
FEB	M						S J	U
MAR	M						S	J
APR	M							S
MAY	M							
JUN	N M							
JUL		M N						
AUG			M	N				
SEP	V U		M		N			
OCT	J V	U	M			N		
NOV	S JV				U	M		N
DEC	V S	J				U M		

NOTE
Planet Positions are for 1 hour before Sunrise and 1 hour after Sunset

V=Venus, **M**=Mars, **J**=Jupiter, **S**=Saturn, U=Uranus, N=Neptune
Uranus and ***Neptune*** are very faint compared to the other Planets listed in these tables. For **Mercury**, see tables starting on page 171.

Planets at SUNSET 2036 – 2039

Relative Positions on the 1st of Each Month
FACING SOUTH

2036 — EAST ←→ CELESTIAL MERIDIAN (DIVIDES SKY IN HALF) ←→ WEST

Month	East	Meridian	West
JAN	U	J NM	V
FEB	S U	JMN	V
MAR	S U	MJ VN	
APR	S U	M VJ	
MAY	S	U MVJ	
JUN		S MU	
JUL		SM	
AUG			
SEP			
OCT	N		
NOV	N		
DEC	J	N	

2038 — EAST ←→ CELESTIAL MERIDIAN (DIVIDES SKY IN HALF) ←→ WEST

Month	East	Meridian	West
JAN	JU M N		
FEB	JU M	N	
MAR	S UJ	M N	
APR	S	JU M N	
MAY	S	JU M	
JUN		S MJU	
JUL		SMJ	
AUG		SM	
SEP			
OCT	N		
NOV	N		
DEC		N	

2037 — EAST ←→ CELESTIAL MERIDIAN (DIVIDES SKY IN HALF) ←→ WEST

Month	East	Meridian	West
JAN	U J	N	
FEB	U J	N	
MAR	S U J	N	
APR	S U J		
MAY	S U J		
JUN		S UJV	
JUL		S V	
AUG		VS	
SEP		V	
OCT	N	V	
NOV	N	V	
DEC	M N	V	

2039 — EAST ←→ CELESTIAL MERIDIAN (DIVIDES SKY IN HALF) ←→ WEST

Month	East	Meridian	West
JAN		N	V
FEB	U	N	V
MAR	J U	N V	
APR	S J U	V N	
MAY	S J U V		
JUN		S J VU	
JUL		S JV	
AUG		SJ	
SEP		S	
OCT			
NOV	N		
DEC	N		

See Instructions on Page 135

V=Venus, **M**=Mars, **J**=Jupiter, **S**=Saturn, U=Uranus, N=Neptune
Uranus and *Neptune* are very faint compared to the other Planets listed in these tables.* For **Mercury**, see tables starting on page 171.

159

Planets at SUNRISE 2040 – 2043

Relative Positions on the 1st of Each Month
FACING SOUTH

(EAST ← CELESTIAL MERIDIAN divides sky in half → WEST)

2040

Month	EAST ———————— MERIDIAN ———————— WEST
JAN	V · · S J · · U M
FEB	V · · · S J · U
MAR	V · · · · S J
APR	· · · · · S J
MAY	·
JUN	N
JUL	· N
AUG	· · N
SEP	U · · N
OCT	· U · · N
NOV	SJ · U · · · N
DEC	· JS · · U

2041

Month	EAST ———————— MERIDIAN ———————— WEST
JAN	· J S · · U
FEB	· · J S · U
MAR	· · J S
APR	V · · · J S
MAY	MV · · · · JS
JUN	NMV
JUL	VM N
AUG	V M · N
SEP	UV M · · N
OCT	V U M · · · N
NOV	V · UM · · N
DEC	J S · · M U

2042

Month	EAST ———————— MERIDIAN ———————— WEST
JAN	· J S · · M U
FEB	· · J S · M U
MAR	· · J S
APR	· · · J S
MAY	· · · · J S
JUN	N · · · · · J
JUL	· N
AUG	· · N
SEP	U · · N
OCT	· U · · N
NOV	V · U · · · N
DEC	S V · · U

2043

Month	EAST ———————— MERIDIAN ———————— WEST
JAN	J · V S · · U
FEB	VJ · S · · U
MAR	V · J · · S
APR	V · · J · · S
MAY	V · · J · S
JUN	MN · · · J
JUL	M N · · · · J
AUG	M · N
SEP	U M · · N
OCT	· U M · · N
NOV	· M U · · N
DEC	S · · M · U

See Instructions on Page 135

NOTE
Planet Positions are for 1 hour before Sunrise and 1 hour after Sunset

V=Venus, M=Mars, J=Jupiter, S=Saturn, U=Uranus, N=Neptune
Uranus and *Neptune* are very faint compared to the other Planets listed in these tables.* For **Mercury**, see tables starting on page 171.

Planets Rise/Set

Planets at SUNSET 2040 – 2043

Relative Positions on the 1st of Each Month
FACING SOUTH

See Instructions on Page 135

2040 — EAST · CELESTIAL MERIDIAN (DIVIDES SKY IN HALF) · WEST

Month	EAST		MERIDIAN		WEST
JAN	M	N			
FEB	U	M		N	
MAR		U M		N	
APR	S J		U M		N
MAY		S J	M U		
JUN			S J	M U	
JUL				S J M	U
AUG					S J M
SEP					S M VJ
OCT					V
NOV	N				V
DEC		N			V

2042

Month	EAST		MERIDIAN		WEST
JAN		N			
FEB	M U			N	
MAR	M U			N	V
APR			M U		N V
MAY	S			M U	V
JUN		J S			M U V
JUL			J	S	M V U
AUG				J S	M V
SEP					J S M V
OCT					J M S
NOV	N				M J
DEC		N			M

2041 — EAST · CELESTIAL MERIDIAN (DIVIDES SKY IN HALF) · WEST

Month	EAST		MERIDIAN		WEST
JAN		N		V	
FEB	U		N		V
MAR		U		N	V
APR	S		U		N
MAY	J S			U	
JUN		J S			U
JUL			J S		U
AUG				J S	
SEP					J S
OCT					J
NOV	N				
DEC		N			

2043

Month	EAST		MERIDIAN		WEST
JAN		N			
FEB	U			N	
MAR		U		N	
APR			U		N
MAY	S			U	
JUN		S			U
JUL	J			S	U
AUG		J		S	
SEP			J		S
OCT				J	S
NOV	N				J V
DEC		N			V J

V=Venus, **M**=Mars, **J**=Jupiter, **S**=Saturn, U=Uranus, N=Neptune
Uranus and *Neptune* are very faint compared to the other Planets listed in these tables.   For **Mercury**, see tables starting on page 171.

Planets at SUNRISE 2044 – 2047

Relative Positions on the 1st of Each Month
FACING SOUTH

See Instructions on Page 135

2044 — EAST ... CELESTIAL MERIDIAN (DIVIDES SKY IN HALF) ... WEST

Month	1	2	3	4	‖	5	6	7	8
JAN		S		M	‖	U			
FEB	J		S		‖		M	U	
MAR	J			S	‖	M	U		
APR		J			‖	S		M	
MAY			J		‖		S		
JUN	N			J	‖			S	
JUL	V	N		J	‖				
AUG	V		N		‖				J
SEP	U V			N	‖				
OCT	V U			N	‖				
NOV	V		U		‖		N		
DEC	V			U	‖				

2045 — EAST ... CELESTIAL MERIDIAN (DIVIDES SKY IN HALF) ... WEST

Month	1	2	3	4	‖	5	6	7	8
JAN	V S				‖		U		
FEB			S		‖		U		
MAR				S	‖			U	
APR	J			S	‖				
MAY	J				‖	S			
JUN	N		J		‖			S	
JUL	M	N		J	‖				
AUG	M		N		‖	J			
SEP	M			N	‖		J		
OCT	U M			N	‖				
NOV		M U			‖			N	
DEC			M	U	‖				

2046 — EAST ... CELESTIAL MERIDIAN (DIVIDES SKY IN HALF) ... WEST

Month	1	2	3	4	‖	5	6	7	8
JAN	S			M	‖		U		
FEB	V S				‖	M		U	
MAR	V	S			‖	M		U	
APR	V			S	‖		M		
MAY	JV				‖	S			M
JUN	NVJ				‖			S	
JUL	V	N	J		‖				
AUG	V		N	J	‖				
SEP					‖	N	J		
OCT	U				‖		N		J
NOV	U				‖			N	
DEC				U	‖				

2047 — EAST ... CELESTIAL MERIDIAN (DIVIDES SKY IN HALF) ... WEST

Month	1	2	3	4	‖	5	6	7	8
JAN					‖		U		
FEB		S			‖		U		
MAR			S		‖			U	
APR				S	‖				
MAY					‖	S			
JUN	N	J			‖			S	
JUL	NJ				‖				S
AUG		J N			‖				
SEP	M V		J N		‖				
OCT	U M V				‖		J N		
NOV	M V	U			‖			J N	
DEC	V M		U		‖				

NOTE
Planet Positions are for 1 hour before Sunrise and 1 hour after Sunset

V=Venus, **M**=Mars, **J**=Jupiter, **S**=Saturn, U=Uranus, N=Neptune
Uranus and *Neptune* are very faint compared to the other Planets listed in these tables. For **Mercury**, see tables starting on page 171.

Planets at SUNSET 2044 – 2047

Relative Positions on the 1st of Each Month
FACING SOUTH

2044 — EAST · CELESTIAL MERIDIAN (DIVIDES SKY IN HALF) · WEST

Month	East of Meridian	West of Meridian
JAN	N	V
FEB	U, N	V
MAR	M U	N V
APR	M U	V N
MAY	M U	V
JUN	S, M	U
JUL	S	M U
AUG	J	S M
SEP	J	S M
OCT	J	M S
NOV	N, J	M S
DEC	N	J M

2045 — EAST · CELESTIAL MERIDIAN (DIVIDES SKY IN HALF) · WEST

Month	East of Meridian	West of Meridian
JAN	N	J M
FEB	U, N	M
MAR	U	N M
APR	U	N
MAY	U	
JUN	S	U V
JUL	S	U V
AUG	S	V
SEP	J	S V
OCT	J	S V
NOV	N J	V S
DEC	N	J V

2046 — EAST · CELESTIAL MERIDIAN (DIVIDES SKY IN HALF) · WEST

Month	East of Meridian	West of Meridian
JAN	N	J
FEB	N	J
MAR	U	N
APR	U	N
MAY	M	U
JUN	S, M	U
JUL	S	M U
AUG	S	M
SEP		S M
OCT	J	S M
NOV	N J	M S
DEC	N J	M

2047 — EAST · CELESTIAL MERIDIAN (DIVIDES SKY IN HALF) · WEST

Month	East of Meridian	West of Meridian
JAN	N	J M V
FEB	N	J M V
MAR	U	N J V M
APR	U	V N M
MAY	U	V M
JUN		U V
JUL	S	U V
AUG	S	U
SEP	S	
OCT		S
NOV	J N	S
DEC	N J	S

See Instructions on Page 135

V=Venus, M=Mars, J=Jupiter, S=Saturn, U=Uranus, N=Neptune
Uranus and **Neptune** are very faint compared to the other Planets listed in these tables. For **Mercury**, see tables starting on page 171.

Planets Rise/Set

Planets at SUNRISE 2048 – 2051

Relative Positions on the 1st of Each Month
FACING SOUTH

V=Venus, M=Mars, J=Jupiter, S=Saturn, U=Uranus, N=Neptune

2048 — EAST ← CELESTIAL MERIDIAN (DIVIDES SKY IN HALF) → WEST

Month	Positions (East → West)
JAN	V M | U
FEB	VS M | U
MAR	V S M | U
APR	S M |
MAY	S | M
JUN	| S M
JUL	J N | S
AUG	J N |
SEP	J N |
OCT	U J | N
NOV	U | J N
DEC	| U J

2050 — EAST ← CELESTIAL MERIDIAN → WEST

Month	Positions (East → West)
JAN	M | U J
FEB	M | U J
MAR	S M | U
APR	S M |
MAY	S M |
JUN	| M S
JUL	N | M S
AUG	N | M S
SEP	J | N
OCT	U J | N
NOV	V U J | N
DEC	V U J |

2049 — EAST ← CELESTIAL MERIDIAN → WEST

Month	Positions (East → West)
JAN	| U
FEB	S | U
MAR	S | U
APR	V S |
MAY	V S |
JUN	V | S
JUL	VN | S
AUG	J V N |
SEP	V J N |
OCT	MUV J | N
NOV	VM U J | N
DEC	M U | J

2051 — EAST ← CELESTIAL MERIDIAN → WEST

Month	Positions (East → West)
JAN	V | U J
FEB	V | U J
MAR	S V | U J
APR	V S |
MAY	V S |
JUN	| S
JUL	N | S
AUG	N | S
SEP	| N
OCT	J | N
NOV	M U J | N
DEC	M J U | N

See Instructions on Page 135

NOTE Planet Positions are for 1 hour before Sunrise and 1 hour after Sunset

V=Venus, M=Mars, J=Jupiter, S=Saturn, U=Uranus, N=Neptune
Uranus and *Neptune* are very faint compared to the other Planets listed in these tables. For **Mercury**, see tables starting on page 171.

Planets Rise/Set

Planets at SUNSET 2048 – 2051

Relative Positions on the 1st of Each Month
FACING SOUTH

EAST ← CELESTIAL MERIDIAN (DIVIDES SKY IN HALF) → WEST

2048

Month	East	← Meridian →	West
JAN	NJ		
FEB		NJ	
MAR	U	JN	
APR	U		JN
MAY	U		J
JUN	M	U	
JUL	S M		U
AUG	S	M	U
SEP		S M	V
OCT		SM	V
NOV	N		M S V
DEC	N		M V S

2049

Month	East	← Meridian →	West
JAN	J N		M V
FEB	J	N	M V
MAR	U	J	N M V
APR	U	J	NM
MAY	U		J M
JUN		U	JM
JUL	S		U
AUG	S		U
SEP		S	
OCT		S	
NOV	N		S
DEC	N		S

2050

Month	East	← Meridian →	West
JAN	N		S
FEB	J	N	
MAR	U J		N V
APR	U	J	N V
MAY	U		J V
JUN		U	J V
JUL			U V J
AUG	S		VU
SEP	M S		V
OCT	M S		
NOV	N	M S	
DEC	N	M	S

2051

Month	East	← Meridian →	West
JAN	N		M S
FEB		N M	
MAR	U J		N M
APR	U J		MN
MAY	U	J	MN
JUN		U	J M
JUL			UJ M
AUG	S		U J
SEP	S		
OCT		S	
NOV		S	V
DEC	N		S V

See Instructions on Page 135

V=Venus, **M**=Mars, **J**=Jupiter, **S**=Saturn, U=Uranus, N=Neptune
Uranus and Neptune are very faint compared to the other Planets listed in these tables. For **Mercury**, see tables starting on page 171.

Superior Planet Oppositions 2000 – 2018

Best Viewing of the Superior Planets

The superior planets, Mars through Pluto, are at opposition when they are directly opposite the Sun from the Earth. At opposition, a superior planet is rising as the Sun is setting, placing it high or overhead at midnight. The superior planets are closest to the Earth at opposition. They are also at their brightest magnitude and will appear their largest in a telescope. The best time to observe a superior planet is from about one month before to one month after the opposition date; however, do not let this discourage you from observing these planets at other times!

For More Information on Oppositions, See Page 115

For MARS, the Best Opposition Years are Bolded

	MARS	JUPITER	SATURN	URANUS	NEPTUNE
2000	—	Nov 27	Nov 19	Aug 10	Jul 27
2001	**Jun 13**	Dec 31	Dec 3	Aug 15	Jul 30
2002	—	—	Dec 17	Aug 19	Aug 1
2003	**Aug 28**	Feb 2	Dec 31	Aug 24	Aug 4
2004	—	Mar 3	—	Aug 27	Aug 5
2005	**Nov 7**	Apr 3	Jan 13	Aug 31	Aug 8
2006	—	Mar 4	Jan 27	Sep 5	Aug 10
2007	Dec 24	Jun 5	Feb 10	Sep 9	Aug 13
2008	—	Jul 9	Feb 24	Sep 12	Aug 14
2009	—	Aug 14	Mar 8	Sep 17	Aug 17
2010	Jan 29	Sep 21	Mar 21	Sep 21	Aug 20
2011	—	Oct 28	Apr 3	Sep 25	Aug 22
2012	Mar3	Dec 2	Apr 15	Sep 29	Aug 24
2013	—	—	Apr 28	Oct 3	Aug 26
2014	Apr 8	Jan 5	May 10	Oct 7	Aug 29
2015	—	Feb 6	May 22	Oct 11	Aug 31
2016	May 22	Mar 8	Jun 2	Oct 15	Sep 2
2017	—	Apr 7	Jun 15	Oct 19	Sep 4
2018	**Jul 26**	May 8	Jun 27	Oct 23	Sep 7

Dates are based on Mountain Standard Time

Oppositions

Facing page. *A dark spot near the North Equatorial Belt of Jupiter.*

Superior Planet Oppositions 2019 – 2045

Best Viewing Dates

	MARS	JUPITER	SATURN	URANUS	NEPTUNE
2019	—	Jun 10	Jul 9	Oct 28	Sep 9
2020	**Oct 13**	Jul 14	Jul 20	Oct 31	Sep 11
2021	—	Aug 19	Aug 1	Nov 4	Sep 14
2022	Dec 7	Sep 26	Aug 14	Nov 9	Sep 16
2023	—	Nov 2	Aug 27	Nov 13	Sep 19
2024	—	Dec 7	Sep 7	Nov 16	Sep 20
2025	Jan 15	—	Sep 20	Nov 21	Sep 23
2026	—	Jan 10	Oct 4	Nov 25	Sep 25
2027	Feb 19	Feb 10	Oct 17	Nov 30	Sep 28
2028	—	Mar 12	Oct 30	Dec 3	Sep 29
2029	Mar 25	Apr 11	Nov 13	Dec 8	Oct 2
2030	—	May 13	Nov 27	Dec 12	Oct 4
2031	May 4	Jun 15	Dec 11	Dec 17	Oct 7
2032	—	Jun 18	Dec 24	Dec 20	Oct 8
2033	**Jun 27**	Aug 24	—	Dec 25	Oct 11
2034	—	Oct 1	Jan 7	Dec 29	Oct 13
2035	**Sep 15**	Nov 7	Jan 21	—	Oct 16
2036	—	Dec 12	Feb 4	Jan 3	Oct 17
2037	Nov 19	—	Feb 17	Jan 7	Oct 20
2038	—	Jan 14	Mar 3	Jan 12	Oct 22
2039	—	Feb 15	Mar 16	Jan 16	Oct 25
2040	Jan 2	Mar 16	Mar 28	Jan 21	Oct 26
2041	—	Apr 16	Apr 10	Jan 25	Oct 29
2042	Feb 6	May 17	Apr 23	Jan 30	Oct 31
2043	—	Jun 19	May 5	Feb 4	Nov 3
2044	Mar 11	Jul 23	May 16	Feb 9	Nov 4
2045	—	Aug 30	May 29	Feb 12	Nov 7

Dates are based on Mountain Standard Time

Oppositions

Superior Planet Oppositions 2046 – 2051

Best Viewing Dates

	MARS	JUPITER	SATURN	URANUS	NEPTUNE
2046	Apr 17	Oct 6	Jun 10	Feb 17	Nov 9
2047	—	Nov 12	Jun 22	Feb 22	Nov 12
2048	Jun 3	Dec 17	Jul 3	Feb 27	Nov 13
2049	—	—	Jul 15	Mar 3	Nov 16
2050	Aug 14	Jan 19	Jul 28	Mar 8	Nov 18
2051	—	Feb 19	Aug 9	Mar 13	Nov 21

PLUTO. Although Pluto has a yearly opposition date, I have only provided dates every tens years because it is very difficult to observe this Planet with a telescope.

2000 ✦ June 1	2030 ✦ Aug 2
2010 ✦ June 25	2040 ✦ Aug 17
2020 ✦ July 15	2050 ✦ Sep 1

Oppositions

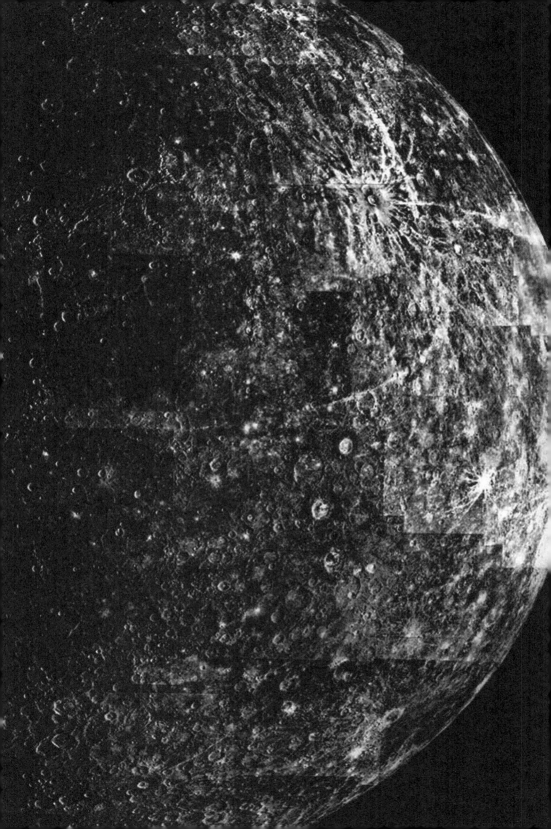

Mercury at Greatest Elong. 2000 – 2003

Mercury when Farthest from the Sun

Mercury can only be observed at or near Greatest Eastern or Western Elongation when it is farthest from the Sun, thus easiest to see. Not all Greatest Eastern or Western Elongations are favorable for observing Mercury because some factors (see page 120) contribute to placing Mercury closer to the horizon and into the glare of twilight.

TABLE NOTES: Date & Time to Observe. These tables indicate the dates of Greatest Eastern or Western Elongation. Favorable viewing is one week on either side of these dates. Elongation & *(Degrees Above Horizon)*. The East and West numbers indicate Mercury's apparent distance from the Sun. The numbers in parentheses indicate Mercury's distance above the horizon at sunrise or sunset for the *mid-latitude of 39° (Kansas City)* — the larger this number, the easier it will be and the longer you will have to see Mercury after sunset and before sunrise. LATITUDE CONSIDERATIONS: Mercury's height above the horizon varies depending on your latitude. Mercury is lower in the sky for northern latitudes and higher for southern latitudes. The bolded entries indicate the dates when Mercury is visible for most of the continental US. Those in the south should easily find Mercury but it may be more challenging for those in the north. Mercury does not get very high in the sky for upper Canada and Alaska and will be lost in the glare of twilight most of the time. Dates and times based on Mountain Standard Time.

BOLDED ENTRIES are the Best Dates to View Mercury

	Date & Time to Observe	Elongation & (Degrees Above Horizon)
2000	**Feb 14 Evening**	**18° E** *(16°)*
	Mar 28 Morning	28° W *(10°)*
	Jun 9 Evening	**24° E** *(18°)*
	Jul 27 Morning	20° W *(15°)*
	Oct 6 Evening	26° E *(8°)*
	Nov 14 Morning	**19° W** *(17°)*
2001	**Jan 28 Evening**	**18° E** *(16°)*
	Mar 10 Morning	27° W *(11°)*
	May 21 Evening	**22° E** *(19°)*
	Jul 9 Morning	21° W *(14°)*
	Sep 18 Evening	27° E *(9°)*
	Oct 29 Morning	**19° W** *(17°)*

	Date & Time to Observe	Elongation & (Degrees Above Horizon)
2002	Jan 11 Evening	19° E *(15°)*
	Feb 21 Morning	27° W *(12°)*
	May 3 Evening	**21° E** *(19°)*
	Jun 21 Morning	23° W *(13°)*
	Sep 1 Evening	27° E *(9°)*
	Oct 13 Morning	**18° W** *(17°)*
	Dec 25 Evening	20° E *(13°)*
2003	Feb 3 Morning	25° W *(13°)*
	Apr 16 Evening	**20° E** *(18°)*
	Jun 2 Morning	24° W *(11°)*
	Aug 14 Evening	27° E *(11°)*
	Sep 26 Morning	**18° W** *(17°)*
	Dec 8 Evening	21° E *(11°)*

For More Information on Observing Mercury, See Page 120

Facing page. Mercury from Mariner 10 in 1974.

Mercury at Greatest Elong. 2004 – 2011

Mercury when Farthest from the Sun

BOLDED ENTRIES are Best Dates to View Mercury

	Date & Time to Observe	Elongation & (Degrees Above Horizon)		Date & Time to Observe	Elongation & (Degrees Above Horizon)
2004	Jan 17 Morning	24° W (14°)	**2008**	Jan 21 Evening	19° E (15°)
	Mar 29 Evening	**19° E (18°)**		Mar 3 Morning	27° W (11°)
	May 14 Morning	26° W (10°)		**May 13 Evening**	**22° E (19°)**
	Jul 26 Evening	27° E (13°)		Jul 1 Morning	22° W (13°)
	Sep 9 Morning	**18° W (16°)**		Sep 10 Evening	27° E (9°)
	Nov 20 Evening	22° E (9°)		**Oct 22 Morning**	**18° W (17°)**
	Dec 29 Morning	**22° W (16°)**	**2009**	Jan 4 Evening	19° E (14°)
2005	**Mar 12 Evening**	**18° E (17°)**		Feb 13 Morning	26° W (12°)
	Apr 26 Morning	27° W (10°)		**Apr 26 Evening**	**20° E (19°)**
	Jul 8 Evening	26° E (15°)		Jun 13 Morning	23° W (12°)
	Aug 23 Morning	**18° W (16°)**		Aug 24 Evening	27° E (10°)
	Nov 3 Evening	24° E (8°)		**Oct 5 Morning**	**18° W (17°)**
	Dec 12 Morning	**21° W (17°)**		Dec 18 Evening	20° E (12°)
2006	**Feb 23 Evening**	**18° E (17°)**	**2010**	Jan 26 Morning	25° W (14°)
	Apr 8 Morning	28° W (10°)		**Apr 8 Evening**	**19° E (18°)**
	Jun 20 Evening	**25° E (17°)**		May 25 Morning	25° W (11°)
	Aug 6 Morning	**19° W (16°)**		Aug 6 Evening	27° E (12°)
	Oct 16 Evening	25° E (8°)		**Sep 19 Morning**	**18° W (17°)**
	Nov 25 Morning	**20° W (17°)**		Dec 1 Evening	21° E (11°)
2007	**Feb 7 Evening**	**18° E (16°)**	**2011**	Jan 9 Morning	23° W (15°)
	Mar 21 Morning	28° W (11°)		**Mar 22 Evening**	**19° E (18°)**
	Jun 2 Evening	**23° E (19°)**		May 7 Morning	27° W (10°)
	Jul 20 Morning	20° W (15°)		Jul 19 Evening	27° E (14°)
	Sep 29 Evening	26° E (8°)		**Sep 2 Morning**	**18° W (16°)**
	Nov 8 Morning	**19° W (17°)**		Nov 14 Evening	23° E (9°)
				Dec 22 Morning	**22° W (16°)**

For More Information on Observing Mercury, See Page 120

Mercury at Greatest Elong. 2012 – 2019

Mercury when Farthest from the Sun

BOLDED ENTRIES are Best Dates to View Mercury

	Date & Time to Observe		Elongation & (Degrees Above Horizon)
2012	**Mar 5**	**Evening**	**18° E** **(17°)**
	Apr 18	Morning	28° W (10°)
	Jun 30	**Evening**	**26° E** **(16°)**
	Aug 16	**Morning**	**19° W** **(16°)**
	Oct 26	Evening	24° E (8°)
	Dec 4	**Morning**	**21° W** **(17°)**
2013	**Feb 16**	**Evening**	**18° E** **(17°)**
	Mar 31	Morning	28° W (10°)
	Jun 12	**Evening**	**24° E** **(18°)**
	Jul 30	**Morning**	**20° W** **(16°)**
	Oct 9	Evening	25° E (8°)
	Nov 17	**Morning**	**19° W** **(17°)**
2014	**Jan 31**	**Evening**	**18° E** **(16°)**
	Mar 13	Morning	28° W (11°)
	May 25	**Evening**	**23° E** **(19°)**
	Jul 12	Morning	21° W (14°)
	Sep 21	Evening	26° E (9°)
	Nov 1	**Morning**	**19° W** **(17°)**
2015	Jan 14	Evening	19° E (15°)
	Feb 24	Morning	27° W (12°)
	May 6	**Evening**	**21° E** **(19°)**
	Jun 24	Morning	23° W (13°)
	Sep 4	Evening	27° E (9°)
	Oct 15	**Morning**	**18° W** **(17°)**
	Dec 28	Evening	20° E (13°)

	Date & Time to Observe		Elongation & (Degrees Above Horizon)
2016	Feb 6	Morning	26° W (13°)
	Apr 18	**Evening**	**20° E** **(19°)**
	Jun 5	Morning	24° W (12°)
	Aug 16	Evening	27° E (11°)
	Sep 28	**Morning**	**18° W** **(17°)**
	Dec 10	Evening	21° E (12°)
2017	Jan 19	Morning	24° W (14°)
	Apr 1	**Evening**	**19° E** **(18°)**
	May 17	Morning	26° W (10°)
	Jul 29	Evening	27° E (13°)
	Sep 12	**Morning**	**18° W** **(16°)**
	Nov 23	Evening	22° E (10°)
2018	**Jan 1**	**Morning**	**23° W** **(16°)**
	Mar 15	**Evening**	**18° E** **(17°)**
	Apr 29	Morning	27° W (10°)
	Jul 11	Evening	26° E (15°)
	Aug 26	**Morning**	**18° W** **(16°)**
	Nov 6	Evening	23° E (9°)
	Dec 15	**Morning**	**21° W** **(17°)**
2019	**Feb 26**	**Evening**	**18° E** **(17°)**
	Apr 11	Morning	28° W (10°)
	Jun 23	**Evening**	**25° E** **(17°)**
	Aug 9	**Morning**	**19° W** **(16°)**
	Oct 19	Evening	25° E (8°)
	Nov 28	**Morning**	**20° W** **(17°)**

For More Information on Observing Mercury, See Page 120

Mercury Elong

173

Mercury at Greatest Elong. 2020 – 2027

Mercury when Farthest from the Sun

BOLDED ENTRIES are Best Dates to View Mercury

	Date & Time to Observe		Elongation & (Degrees Above Horizon)	
2020	**Feb 10**	**Evening**	**18° E**	**(16°)**
	Mar 23	Morning	28° W	(11°)
	Jun 4	**Evening**	**24° E**	**(19°)**
	Jul 22	Morning	20° W	(15°)
	Oct 1	Evening	26° E	(8°)
	Nov 10	**Morning**	**19° W**	**(17°)**
2021	Jan 23	Evening	19° E	(15°)
	Mar 6	Morning	27° W	(11°)
	May 16	**Evening**	**22° E**	**(19°)**
	Jul 4	Morning	22° W	(14°)
	Sep 13	Evening	27° E	(9°)
	Oct 24	**Morning**	**18° W**	**(17°)**
2022	Jan 7	Evening	19° E	(14°)
	Feb 16	Morning	26° W	(12°)
	Apr 29	**Evening**	**21° E**	**(19°)**
	Jun 16	Morning	23° W	(12°)
	Aug 27	Evening	27° E	(10°)
	Oct 8	**Morning**	**18° W**	**(17°)**
	Dec 21	Evening	20° E	(13°)
2023	Jan 29	Morning	25° W	(13°)
	Apr 11	**Evening**	**19° E**	**(18°)**
	May 28	Morning	25° W	(11°)
	Aug 9	Evening	27° E	(12°)
	Sep 22	**Morning**	**18° W**	**(17°)**
	Dec 4	Evening	21° E	(11°)

	Date & Time to Observe		Elongation & (Degrees Above Horizon)	
2024	Jan 12	Morning	24° W	(15°)
	Mar 24	**Evening**	**19° E**	**(18°)**
	May 9	Morning	26° W	(10°)
	Jul 22	Evening	27° E	(13°)
	Sep 4	**Morning**	**18° W**	**(16°)**
	Nov 16	Evening	23° E	(10°)
	Dec 24	**Morning**	**22° W**	**(16°)**
2025	**Mar 7**	**Evening**	**18° E**	**(17°)**
	Apr 21	Morning	27° W	(10°)
	Jul 3	**Evening**	**26° E**	**(16°)**
	Aug 19	**Morning**	**19° W**	**(16°)**
	Oct 29	Evening	24° E	(9°)
	Dec 7	**Morning**	**21° W**	**(17°)**
2026	**Feb 19**	**Evening**	**18° E**	**(17°)**
	Apr 3	Morning	28° W	(10°)
	Jun 15	**Evening**	**25° E**	**(18°)**
	Aug 2	**Morning**	**19° W**	**(16°)**
	Oct 12	Evening	25° E	(8°)
	Nov 20	**Morning**	**20° W**	**(17°)**
2027	**Feb 2**	**Evening**	**18° E**	**(16°)**
	Mar 16	Morning	28° W	(11°)
	May 28	**Evening**	**23° E**	**(19°)**
	Jul 15	Morning	21° W	(15°)
	Sep 24	Evening	26° E	(8°)
	Nov 4	**Morning**	**19° W**	**(17°)**

For More Information on Observing Mercury, See Page 120

Mercury at Greatest Elong. 2028 – 2035

Mercury when Farthest from the Sun

BOLDED ENTRIES are Best Dates to View Mercury

	Date & Time to Observe		Elongation & (Degrees Above Horizon)	
2028	Jan 17	Evening	19° E	(15°)
	Feb 27	Morning	27° W	(12°)
	May 9	**Evening**	**21° E**	**(19°)**
	Jun 26	Morning	22° W	(13°)
	Sep 6	Evening	27° E	(9°)
	Oct 17	**Morning**	**18° W**	**(17°)**
	Dec 30	Evening	20° E	(14°)
2029	Feb 8	Morning	26° W	(13°)
	Apr 21	**Evening**	**20° E**	**(19°)**
	Jun 8	Morning	24° W	(12°)
	Aug 19	Evening	27° E	(10°)
	Oct 1	**Morning**	**18° W**	**(17°)**
	Dec 13	Evening	21° E	(12°)
2030	Jan 22	Morning	24° W	(14°)
	Apr 4	**Evening**	**19° E**	**(18°)**
	May 20	Morning	26° W	(11°)
	Aug 1	Evening	27° E	(12°)
	Sep 15	**Morning**	**18° W**	**(17°)**
	Nov 26	Evening	22° E	(10°)
2031	Jan 4	Morning	23° W	(15°)
	Mar 18	**Evening**	**18° E**	**(17°)**
	May 2	Morning	27° W	(10°)
	Jul 15	Evening	27° E	(14°)
	Aug 29	**Morning**	**18° W**	**(16°)**
	Nov 9	Evening	23° E	(9°)
	Dec 18	**Morning**	**21° W**	**(17°)**

For More Information on Observing Mercury, See Page 120

	Date & Time to Observe		Elongation & (Degrees Above Horizon)	
2032	**Feb 29**	**Evening**	**18° E**	**(17°)**
	Apr 13	Morning	28° W	(10°)
	Jun 25	**Evening**	**25° E**	**(17°)**
	Aug 11	**Morning**	**19° W**	**(16°)**
	Oct 21	Evening	24° E	(8°)
	Nov 30	**Morning**	**20° W**	**(17°)**
2033	**Feb 12**	**Evening**	**18° E**	**(16°)**
	Mar 26	Morning	28° W	(11°)
	Jun 7	**Evening**	**24° E**	**(19°)**
	Jul 25	Morning	20° W	(15°)
	Oct 4	Evening	26° E	(8°)
	Nov 13	**Morning**	**19° W**	**(17°)**
2034	**Jan 26**	**Evening**	**18° E**	**(16°)**
	Mar 9	Morning	27° W	(11°)
	May 20	**Evening**	**22° E**	**(19°)**
	Jul 7	Morning	21° W	(14°)
	Sep 16	Evening	27° E	(9°)
	Oct 27	**Morning**	**18° W**	**(17°)**
2035	Jan 10	Evening	19° E	(15°)
	Feb 19	Morning	26° W	(12°)
	May 2	**Evening**	**21° E**	**(19°)**
	Jun 19	Morning	23° W	(13°)
	Aug 30	Evening	27° E	(10°)
	Oct 11	**Morning**	**18° W**	**(17°)**
	Dec 24	Evening	20° E	(13°)

Mercury Elong

Mercury at Greatest Elong. 2036 – 2043

Mercury when Farthest from the Sun

BOLDED ENTRIES are Best Dates to View Mercury

	Date & Time to Observe		Elongation & (Degrees Above Horizon)	
2036	Feb 1	Morning	25° W	(13°)
	Apr 13	**Evening**	**20° E**	**(18°)**
	May 31	Morning	25° W	(11°)
	Aug 11	Evening	27° E	(11°)
	Sep 24	**Morning**	**18° W**	**(17°)**
	Dec 6	Evening	21° E	(11°)
2037	Jan 14	Morning	24° W	(15°)
	Mar 27	**Evening**	**19° E**	**(18°)**
	May 12	Morning	26° W	(10°)
	Jul 25	Evening	27° E	(13°)
	Sep 7	**Morning**	**18° W**	**(16°)**
	Nov 19	Evening	22° E	(10°)
	Dec 28	**Morning**	**22° W**	**(16°)**
2038	**Mar 10**	**Evening**	**18° E**	**(17°)**
	Apr 24	Morning	27° W	(10°)
	Jul 6	**Evening**	**26° E**	**(16°)**
	Aug 22	**Morning**	**19° W**	**(16°)**
	Nov 1	Evening	24° E	(9°)
	Dec 10	**Morning**	**21° W**	**(17°)**
2039	**Feb 22**	**Evening**	**18° E**	**(17°)**
	Apr 6	Morning	28° W	(10°)
	Jun 18	**Evening**	**25° E**	**(18°)**
	Aug 5	**Morning**	**19° W**	**(16°)**
	Oct 15	Evening	25° E	(8°)
	Nov 23	**Morning**	**20° W**	**(17°)**

For More Information on Observing Mercury, See Page 120

	Date & Time to Observe		Elongation & (Degrees Above Horizon)	
2040	**Feb 5**	**Evening**	**18° E**	**(16°)**
	Mar 19	Morning	28° W	(11°)
	May 30	**Evening**	**23° E**	**(19°)**
	Jul 17	Morning	20° W	(15°)
	Sep 26	Evening	26° E	(8°)
	Nov 5	**Morning**	**19° W**	**(17°)**
2041	Jan 19	Evening	19° E	(15°)
	Mar 1	Morning	27° W	(11°)
	May 12	**Evening**	**22° E**	**(19°)**
	Jun 29	Morning	22° W	(13°)
	Sep 9	Evening	27° E	(9°)
	Oct 20	**Morning**	**18° W**	**(17°)**
2042	Jan 2	Evening	19° E	(14°)
	Feb 11	Morning	26° W	(13°)
	Apr 24	**Evening**	**20° E**	**(19°)**
	Jun 11	Morning	24° W	(12°)
	Aug 22	Evening	27° E	(10°)
	Oct 4	**Morning**	**18° W**	**(17°)**
	Dec 16	Evening	20° E	(12°)
2043	Jan 25	Morning	25° W	(14°)
	Apr 6	**Evening**	**19° E**	**(18°)**
	May 23	Morning	25° W	(11°)
	Aug 5	Evening	27° E	(12°)
	Sep 17	**Morning**	**18° W**	**(16°)**
	Nov 29	Evening	22° E	(10°)

Mercury at Greatest Elong. 2044 – 2051

Mercury when Farthest from the Sun

BOLDED ENTRIES are Best Dates to View Mercury

Year	Date & Time to Observe	Elongation	& (Degrees Above Horizon)
2044	Jan 7 Morning	23° W	(15°)
	Mar 20 Evening	**19° E**	**(18°)**
	May 4 Morning	27° W	(10°)
	Jul 17 Evening	27° E	(14°)
	Aug 31 Morning	**18° W**	**(16°)**
	Nov 11 Evening	23° E	(9°)
	Dec 20 Morning	**22° W**	**(16°)**
2045	**Mar 3 Evening**	**18° E**	**(17°)**
	Apr 16 Morning	28° W	(10°)
	Jun 28 Evening	**26° E**	**(17°)**
	Aug 14 Morning	**19° W**	**(16°)**
	Oct 24 Evening	24° E	(8°)
	Dec 2 Morning	**20° W**	**(17°)**
2046	**Feb 14 Evening**	**18° E**	**(16°)**
	Mar 29 Morning	28° W	(10°)
	Jun 10 Evening	**24° E**	**(18°)**
	Jul 28 Morning	20° W	(15°)
	Oct 7 Evening	25° E	(8°)
	Nov 16 Morning	**19° W**	**(17°)**
2047	**Jan 29 Evening**	**18° E**	**(16°)**
	Mar 12 Morning	28° W	(11°)
	May 23 Evening	**22° E**	**(19°)**
	Jul 10 Morning	21° W	(14°)
	Sep 19 Evening	27° E	(9°)
	Oct 30 Morning	**19° W**	**(17°)**

Year	Date & Time to Observe	Elongation	& (Degrees Above Horizon)
2048	Jan 12 Evening	19° E	(15°)
	Feb 22 Morning	27° W	(12°)
	May 4 Evening	**21° E**	**(19°)**
	Jun 21 Morning	23° W	(13°)
	Sep 1 Evening	27° E	(9°)
	Oct 13 Morning	**18° W**	**(17°)**
	Dec 26 Evening	20° E	(13°)
2049	Feb 4 Morning	25° W	(13°)
	Apr 16 Evening	**20° E**	**(19°)**
	Jun 3 Morning	24° W	(11°)
	Aug 14 Evening	27° E	(11°)
	Sep 26 Morning	**18° W**	**(17°)**
	Dec 9 Evening	21° E	(12°)
2050	Jan 17 Morning	24° W	(14°)
	Mar 30 Evening	**19° E**	**(18°)**
	May 15 Morning	26° W	(10°)
	Jul 28 Evening	27° E	(13°)
	Sep 10 Morning	**18° W**	**(16°)**
	Nov 22 Evening	22° E	(10°)
	Dec 30 Morning	**23° W**	**(16°)**
2051	**Mar 13 Evening**	**18° E**	**(17°)**
	Apr 27 Morning	27° W	(10°)
	Jul 10 Evening	26° E	(15°)
	Aug 25 Morning	**18° W**	**(16°)**
	Nov 4 Evening	23° E	(9°)
	Dec 13 Morning	**21° W**	**(17°)**

For More Information on Observing Mercury, See Page 120

Mercury Elong

Venus at Greatest Elongation 2000 – 2033

Venus when Farthest from the Sun

These tables provide the dates when Venus is at Greatest Eastern or Western Elongation — when it is farthest from the Sun. At these times, Venus appears at about half phase. About a month after Greatest Eastern Elongation and a month before Greatest Western Elongation, Venus is at its brightest, around magnitude –4.5 and appears as a large crescent, visible with binoculars. Dates and times based on Mountain Standard Time.

Year				Year			
2000	No Greatest Elongations			2017	Jan 12	Evening	47° E
2001	Jan 17	Evening	47° E		Jun 3	Morning	46° W
	Jun 7	Morning	46° W	2018	Aug 17	Evening	46° E
2002	Aug 22	Evening	46° E	2019	Jan 5	Morning	47° W
2003	Jan 10	Morning	47° W	2020	Mar 24	Evening	46° E
2004	Mar 29	Evening	46° E		Aug 12	Morning	46° W
	Aug 17	Morning	46° W	2021	Oct 29	Evening	47° E
2005	Nov 3	Evening	47° E	2022	Mar 20	Morning	47° W
2006	Mar 25	Morning	47° W	2023	Jun 4	Evening	45° E
2007	Jun 8	Evening	45° E		Oct 23	Morning	46° W
	Oct 28	Morning	47° W	2024	No Greatest Elongations		
2008	No Greatest Elongations			2025	Jan 9	Evening	47° E
2009	Jan 14	Evening	47° E		May 31	Morning	46° W
	Jun 5	Morning	46° W	2026	Aug 14	Evening	46° E
2010	Aug 19	Evening	46° E	2027	Jan 3	Morning	47° W
2011	Jan 8	Morning	47° W	2028	Mar 22	Evening	46° E
2012	Mar 27	Evening	46° E		Aug 10	Morning	46° W
	Aug 15	Morning	46° W	2029	Oct 27	Evening	47° E
2013	Nov 1	Evening	47° E	2030	Mar 17	Morning	47° W
2014	Mar 22	Morning	47° W	2031	Jun 1	Evening	45° E
2015	Jun 6	Evening	45° E		Oct 21	Morning	46° W
	Oct 26	Morning	46° W	2032	No Greatest Elongations		
2016	No Greatest Elongations			2033	Jan 7	Evening	47° E
					May 29	Morning	46° W

Facing page. Venus in ultraviolet light, which enhances the clouds.

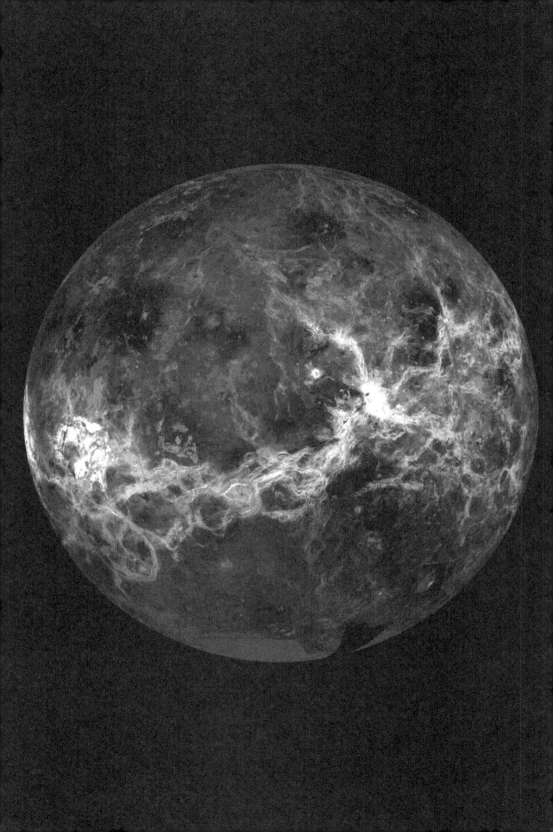

Venus at Greatest Elongation 2034 – 2051

Venus when Farthest from the Sun

Year	Date	Time	Elongation
2034	Aug 12	Evening	46° E
2035	Jan 1	Morning	47° W
2036	Mar 19	Evening	46° E
	Aug 8	Morning	46° W
2037	Oct 24	Evening	47° E
2038	Mar 15	Morning	47° W
2039	May 30	Evening	45° E
	Oct 18	Morning	46° W
2040	No Greatest Elongations		
2041	Jan 5	Evening	47° E
	May 27	Morning	46° W
2042	Aug 10	Evening	46° E
	Dec 29	Morning	47° W

Year	Date	Time	Elongation
2043	No Greatest Elongations		
2044	Mar 17	Evening	46° E
	Aug 5	Morning	46° W
2045	Oct 22	Evening	47° E
2046	Mar 12	Morning	47° W
2047	May 28	Evening	45° E
	Oct 16	Morning	46° W
2048	No Greatest Elongations		
2049	Jan 2	Evening	47° E
	May 24	Morning	46° W
2050	Aug 7	Evening	46° E
	Dec 27	Morning	47° W
2051	No Greatest Elongations		

Venus Elong

Facing page. Radar mapping of Venus produced this picture, revealing the geographical features of the Planet under its thick clouds.

Page 182. The four Galilean moons. From top to bottom, Ganymede, Callisto, Io and Europa.

Conjunctions 2000 – 2025

Planets and Moon Close Together in the Sky

When the Planets or Moon appear close to one another in the sky, they are said to be in conjunction. How close is close? For these tables, I have chosen the closest approaches, of a Moon diameter or less. Conjunctions do not hold any special astronomical significance because they represent the random alignment of the Planets and Moon as they circle the Sun or Earth. However, conjunctions are pretty. It is very striking to see two bright celestial bodies close to one another in the sky. And, all you need to enjoy the sight is your naked eyes.

SPECIAL NOTE: For many of the conjunctions listed that involve the Moon, the Planet will be occulted; that is, the Moon will pass in front of the Planet for a short period of time. Please consult the popular monthly astronomy magazines for more information about these events for your specific location.

	Date & Time to Observe		Celestial Bodies and Degrees of Separation (Moon's diameter is 0.5°)	
2000	Aug 10	Early Morning	**Mercury & Mars**	0.07°
2001	Sep 10	Early Morning	**Moon & Saturn**	0.02°
	Nov 30	Early Evening	**Moon & Saturn**	0.21°
	Dec 28	Early A.M.	**Moon & Saturn**	0.04°
2002	Jul 2	Early Morning	**Mercury & Saturn**	0.21°
2003	Jul 17	Early A.M.	**Moon & Mars**	0.48°
	Jul 26	After Sunset	**Mercury & Jupiter**	0.35°
2007	Dec 23	Early Evening	**Moon & Mars**	0.48°
2015	Feb 21	Early Evening	**Venus & Mars**	0.40°
	Jun 30	Early Evening	**Venus & Jupiter**	0.33°
2020	Feb 18	Early Morning	**Moon & Mars**	0.15°
2021	May 28	After Sunset	**Mercury & Venus**	0.39°
	Aug 18	After Sunset	**Mercury & Mars**	0.07°
2022	Dec 7	Early Evening	**Moon & Mars**	0.12°
2023	Jan 30	Late Night	**Moon & Mars**	0.17°
	May 17	Early Morning	**Moon & Jupiter**	0.08°
2024	Sep 17	Early Morning	**Moon & Saturn**	0.15°
2025	Jan 13	Evening	**Moon & Mars**	0.00°

Dates & Time are based on Mountain Standard Time

Conjunctions 2029 – 2045

Planets and Moon Close Together in the Sky

Dates & Time are based on Mountain Standard Time

	Date & Time to Observe		Celestial Bodies and Degrees of Separation (Moon's diameter is 0.5°)	
2029	Oct 10	Early Evening	**Moon & Venus**	0.18°
2033	Aug 13	Early Morning	**Venus & Saturn**	0.34°
2034	May 11	Early Evening	**Venus & Mars**	0.44°
	Sep 28	Early Morning	**Moon & Jupiter**	0.04°
2035	Nov 10	Late Night	**Moon & Mars**	0.47°
2036	Jul 19	After Sunset	**Mars & Saturn**	0.11°
	Oct 15	Early Morning	**Moon & Saturn**	0.09°
2037	Jan 5	Early Morning	**Moon & Saturn**	0.17°
	Feb 28	Early Evening	**Moon & Saturn**	0.01°
	Nov 27	Early Morning	**Moon & Jupiter**	0.38°
	Dec 24	Early Morning	**Moon & Jupiter**	0.09°
2038	Mar 15	Late Night	**Moon & Jupiter**	0.43°
	May 9	Early Evening	**Moon & Jupiter**	0.29°
	Jun 6	Late Night	**Moon & Mars**	0.15°
2039	Nov 2	Early Morning	**Venus & Jupiter**	0.21°
	Dec 3	Late Night	**Moon & Mars**	0.39°
2040	Sep 12	After Sunset	**Venus & Mars**	0.21°
	Oct 8	Early Evening	**Moon & Venus**	0.35°
	Nov 30	Early Morning	**Moon & Saturn**	0.40°
2041	Feb 20	Late Night	**Moon & Jupiter**	0.21°
	Jul 6	Late Night	**Moon & Jupiter**	0.23°
2042	Feb 4	Evening	**Moon & Mars**	0.11°
2045	Jun 21	Early Evening	**Mercury & Venus**	0.42°
	Sep 8	Early Morning	**Moon & Mars**	0.18°

Conjunctions

Conjunctions 2047 – 2051

Planets and Moon Close Together in the Sky

Date & Time to Observe		Celestial Bodies and Degrees of Separation (Moon's diameter is 0.5°)	
2047 Feb 24	Early Evening	**Venus & Mars**	0.29°
Nov 7	Early Morning	**Venus & Mars**	0.11°
2048 Jan 30	Early Morning	**Venus & Saturn**	0.07°
May 28	Early A.M.	**Moon & Mars**	0.03°
May 29	Late Night	**Moon & Saturn**	0.17°
Aug 19	Evening	**Moon & Saturn**	0.02°
Sep 29	Early Morning	**Moon & Jupiter**	0.41°
2049 Feb 11	Evening	**Moon & Jupiter**	0.31°

Dates & Time are based on Mountain Standard Time

There are no conjunctions in
2050 or 2051.

Conjunctions

Meteors & Showers

On a typical clear night, while looking at the sky, you will probably see a meteor, commonly called a shooting star. In fact, about seven meteors per hour can be seen normally. But at specific times of the year, there are meteor showers which may allow you to see 15 to 100 meteors per hour. On very rare occasions, if you are fortunate, you may encounter a storm with thousands of meteors per hour.

Meteoroid, Meteor and Meteorite

These terms are often confused. A meteoroid is a small rock in space. When a meteoroid enters the Earth's atmosphere, we view it as a white luminous streak called a meteor. If the meteoroid survives its journey through the atmosphere and happens to reach the Earth's surface as a "rock," it is then called a meteorite.

Meteoroid	Small rock in space (or grain of sand)
Meteor	White luminous streak seen in sky
Meteorite	"Space rock" on ground

Size, Speed & Height

Most meteors are caused by meteoroids the size of a grain of sand. Atmospheric speeds reach up to 45 miles per second or 162,000 miles per hour (72 km/sec or 257,500 km/hr), and trail heights range from 30 to 60 miles (48 to 96 km) above the Earth's surface.

Iron meteorite found in Antarctica. Only a few inches high, it probably is a piece from a large asteroid that broke apart.

The Bright Ones

A very bright meteor, about the brightness of Venus, is called a fireball. An exceedingly bright meteor, much brighter than a fireball, is called a bolide. If you see a bright meteor, you will not easily forget it. I remember the first time I saw a fireball, when I was growing up, riding my bicycle home one night in Milwaukee.

Facing page. *The November 1966 Leonids shower. If you were to extend these streaks back, they would intersect at a point in the constellation Leo.*

Meteor Showers

Meteor Showers

Meteor showers are caused by the sand-size silicate particles left behind by comets. A dozen meteor showers occur every year as the Earth passes through semi-permanent fields of cometary debris that also orbit the Sun.

Meteors associated with showers radiate from a spot in the sky, so showers are named after the constellation from which the meteors appear to originate. The constellation Aquarius has two associated showers which are distinguished by the Greek letter designation of the star closest to the point of origination.

New showers will be established when future cometary debris crosses Earth's orbit. Existing showers will eventually fade away as debris dissipates. The Perseids have been around for a thousand years, while there is no indication of the Quadrantids further back than 200 years.

Shower intensity varies and cannot be predicted accurately from year to year. Some forecasts are available in the popular monthly astronomy magazines.

Meteor Storms

I have never experienced a meteor storm. One of the last storms was associated with the Leonids in 1966. For a period of about an hour, more than a hundred thousand meteors pierced the sky. To say the least, watching meteors rain down, filling the entire sky would be awesome!

The Draconids and Leonids are currently the only known showers capable of storms. Storms result when the Earth hits pockets of concentrated silicate particles. The debris from future comets may also produce such displays.

Woodcut depicting the November 12, 1799 Leonids storm.

OBSERVING METEORS & SHOWERS

Meteors are observed best with the naked eye. It is not practical to view them with binoculars or a telescope because they last just a fraction of a second and extend arcs greater than what can be viewed through these instruments. Additionally, their appearance

Yearly Showers

Yearly Meteor Showers

Shower[1] (Constellation)	Date[2] Peak	(Active Period)	Hourly Rate[3]
QUADRANTIDS (Bootes)[4]	January 3	(Jan 1 – Jan 5)	60 – 200
LYRIDS (Lyra)	April 22	(Apr 16 – Apr 25)	15 – 20+
Eta (η) AQUARIDS (Aquarius)	May 5	(Apr 19 – May 28)	60
Southern Delta (δ) AQUARIDS	July 29	(Jul 12 – Aug 19)	20
PERSEIDS (Perseus)	August 12	(Jul 17 – Aug 24)	120 – 160
DRACONIDS (Draco)	October 8	(Oct 6 – Oct 10)	5[5]
ORIONIDS (Orion)	October 21	(Oct 2 – Nov 7)	20
Southern TAURIDS (Taurus)	November 5	(Oct 1 – Nov 25)	5
Northern TAURIDS	November 13	(Oct 1 – Nov 25)	5
LEONIDS (Leo)	November 17	(Nov 14 – Nov 21)	10[5]
GEMINIDS (Gemini)	December 14	(Dec 7 – Dec 17)	120
URSIDS (Ursa Minor)	December 22	(Dec 17 – Dec 26)	10+

[1]Showers have traditionally been named after the constellation they appear to radiate from. [2]Peak date is approximate and may vary by a day from year to year. [3]Hourly rate is frequency or number of meteors per hour around the Peak date. [4]The Quadrantids was named after an obsolete constellation recognized in the 1800s. Today, this shower is sometimes referred to as the Bootids, after the constellation Bootes. [5]These showers have the potential to become meteor storms, with spectacular displays of thousands of meteors per hour.

and paths in the sky cannot be predicted.

The first time you see a meteor, you will probably say, "What was that?" Unless you are looking in the direction of the meteor, you will only catch it out of the corner of your eye, but it will be exciting even then!

Meteors not associated with showers are called sporadic meteors. Both sporadic meteors and shower meteors can appear anywhere in the sky. Although the shower meteors originate from a point in the sky, this will not be immediately apparent when you watch showers. To reiterate, meteors come from small particles in the path of the Earth's orbit and not from the stars in the constellations.

The most favorable time to observe meteors or showers is from around midnight to early morning when the night side of the Earth is moving toward the meteoroids. And, the viewing is best when the Moon is not out.

Comets

C omets are spectacular to behold. They can span the sky in a splendor unequaled by any other astronomical object. What I really like about comets is not only their beauty but their accessibility. They bring astronomy to continents of people, and their grand display unites us in the awe of the Universe.

In early civilizations, comets were harbingers of the future. Something as impressive as the unexpected appearance of a comet in the sky had to be significant. Depending on the culture, a comet represented either a good or bad omen.

Today, we can enjoy comets as neither good nor bad but as the spectacular objects they are. It is good fortune when we get the opportunity to view one of these marvelous treasures.

Bright comets are like unexpected gifts — we remember them with a special fondness.

Comets of the 1980s and 1990s

Here is a recap of the major comets that graced our skies during the final years of the twentieth century.

Comet Halley. Named after the English astronomer Edmond Halley (1656–1742) who concluded that the great comet of 1682 was the same comet that appeared in 1531 and 1607. Comet Halley returns about every 76 years. Its regularity along with its brightness have made it the most familiar comet in the Solar System. During its 1986 appearance, six research spacecraft were sent out to gather data on this comet.

Comet Shoemaker-Levy 9. Discovered the night of March 23, 1993, by Gene and Carolyn Shoemaker and David Levy from photographs taken at the Palomar Observatory complex in California. On July 16, 1994, this comet, which had broken into 21 fragments, rained down on Jupiter for a week. The impacts disrupted Jupiter's clouds for almost a year, and the initial scars were visible in small telescopes. This collision was the most spectacular astronomical event of the twentieth century.

Comets

Facing page. Comet Hale-Bopp with its two tails. The top tail is the ion tail and the bottom the dust tail.

Origin of Comets

Comet Hale-Bopp. Discovered on July 22, 1995, by Alan Hale and Thomas Bopp, this comet became one of the most celebrated end-of-century splendors. Hale-Bopp's nucleus is exceptionally large for a comet and contains five times more water than all the Great Lakes combined. Thomas Bopp actually saw the comet first, but he was unable to report his finding immediately because he was out of range with his cellular phone. Hale-Bopp will return in 4390.

Comet Hyakutake. Discovered in Japan by Yuji Hyakutake on January 30, 1996, only two months before it was visible to the naked eye. This comet took astronomers by surprise because they were in the midst of planning for the arrival of Hale-Bopp.

Origin and Orbits of Comets
Comets are leftover aggregate from the formation of our Solar System. They represent matter that did not condense into the Sun, Planets or moons. They circle the Sun in very elongated, elliptical orbits with revolution periods ranging from just a few years to tens of thousands of years. Some of their orbits reach halfway to our nearest star, Proxima Centauri, four light years away.

Orbit of Halley's Comet

PLUTO's Orbit

JUPITER's Orbit

Halley's Orbit. Revolution about 76 years. Closest approach to Sun is a little farther than Mercury.

There are three major groupings of comets. Based on their orbits, they are named the Jupiter family, the Kuiper belt and the Oort cloud.

The Jupiter family contains a small number of comets with orbits that reach a little farther than Jupiter's and revolve around the Sun in as little as 3.5 years (Comet Encke for example). Jupiter's strong gravity has created this family by "roping in" longer period comets.

The Kuiper belt comets reside in a region that extends from beyond Neptune to about 1,000 astronomical units. These shorter period comets have revolution periods of 200 years or more.

Composition of Comets

Most comets have long orbital periods in the thousands of years. Their orbits take them to the outer reaches of our Solar System, into the Oort cloud. They can reach distances of 20,000 to 100,000 astronomical units (1.6 light years) from the Sun. The Oort cloud is a roughly spherical area that surrounds the Sun and contains the bulk of the comets, estimated at about a trillion.

The Size and and Composition of Comets
The nuclei of comets, that is, their solid bodies, vary in size. Diameters range from just a few to perhaps 150 miles (3 to 240 km). Comet Halley's nucleus is the only one ever imaged. It resembles a potato in shape and measures approximately 6 by 9.5 miles (9.6 by 15.3 km). Comet Hale-Bopp's nucleus is estimated to be 37 miles (60 km) in diameter, which is considered a large comet.

Comet

Jet
Visible but Intermittent

Nucleus
Obscured by Coma

← Direction to Sun

Hydrogen Cloud
Not Visible

Coma (Head)
Visible

Dust Tail
Visible

Ion Tail
Visible

Comets

The often used phrase "dirty snowball" aptly describes a comet's composition. Comets are a mixture of various ices, called ice volatiles (frozen water, ammonia, methane and other chemicals) and dust (sand-size silicate particles — the basic mineral of rocks).

Composition of Comets

As a comet approaches the Sun and heats up, the ice volatiles in the nucleus sublime (change directly from solids to gases) to become the coma and tail.

The coma can have a diameter of 125,000 to 1.2 million miles (200,000 to 2 million km) and always obscures the small nucleus. Comas start to develop at a distance around three astronomical units (between Mars and Jupiter), the tails a little farther out. In 1970, it was discovered that an invisible, tenuous hydrogen cloud extends from the coma, with a diameter in the range of millions of miles.

Comet tails can stretch for millions of miles; the longest was 1.5 astronomical units (comet Hale-Bopp). The solar wind and pressure from sunlight push the tail away from the Sun. Often, comets develop two tails: a yellowish-white dust tail and a blue ion tail (blue from fluorescing ions). Either one or both tails may be present.

A comet may exhibit a jet or jets, which are spurious eruptions that shoot out from the nucleus. They develop when pockets of ice volatiles are exposed. A jet can turn on and off, depending on the rotation of the nucleus and exposure to the Sun.

As the Comet Turns

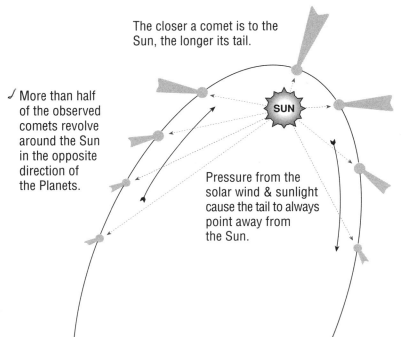

The closer a comet is to the Sun, the longer its tail.

More than half of the observed comets revolve around the Sun in the opposite direction of the Planets.

Pressure from the solar wind & sunlight cause the tail to always point away from the Sun.

SUN

Observing Comets

A comet is considered an asteroid until it develops a coma or tail. Many comets are not visible to the naked eye and require the use of a telescope.

A Comet's Legacy: Meteor Showers

Our yearly meteor showers are compliments of comets. Showers occur when the Earth passes through a comet's wake, mostly sand-size silicate particles (see page 188).

When will the next comet appear?

Astronomers cannot predict when bright, visible comets will appear. Most comets come from the outer regions of our Solar System and do not become noticeable until they get close to the Sun. They wait for individuals like David Levy to gaze up and discover them so they can be announced to the world.

Unexpected gifts are often remembered the most, and so it is with comets. These unexpected and marvelous guests leave us with the fondest memories.

OBSERVING COMETS

The naked eye, binoculars and telescopes at low magnifications can be used to observe the large visible comets. In my opinion, binoculars mounted on a tripod are the ideal observing instrument. Binoculars will enable you to see most or all of a comet in the same field of view while the tripod will help steady the binoculars and allow easy extended viewing.

When comets are in the sky, everyone starts looking up. Whether you are out in a parking lot or in your back yard, you will see eyes gazing upward to glimpse the splendor in the heavens.

Comets

The Sun

How often do we stop and think of the Sun when we think of the day? I think we take our days and nights for granted because they are natural, automatic cycles, like breathing. And, more importantly, how often do we think of the Sun when we think of life on Earth? The energy from the Sun is the reason that life developed and is sustained on Earth.

Although the Sun is special to us, it is like all the other stars in the Universe. I have always likened stars to atoms. They are the fundamental unit of the Universe, and something that the Universe naturally creates. Galaxies are the harbors of stars, the place that these fiery balls can call home.

Nuclear Fusion and the Sun's Life

Our Sun is a typical or average star. Like all stars, its energy comes from nuclear fusion. Four hydrogen atoms are fused (forced) together to create one helium atom in the core of the Sun. The mass of the resulting helium atom is 1% less than the total mass of the four hydrogen atoms. The 1% difference in mass produces the energy that we see as the blazing Sun. About five million tons (4.5 million metric tons) of matter are converted into energy every second in the core of the Sun. Fusion in the Sun is triggered by the tremendous pressure at the core, brought about by the sheer mass of the Sun. The Sun does not collapse upon itself because of the outward expansive pressure of nuclear fusion.

The Sun is about 4.5 billon years old and will last for another 5.5 billion years. Toward the end of its life, it will become a red giant with an outer atmosphere extending to about the orbit of Mercury. During its final days, the Sun will shed its outer layers in one final heave. Outwardly, this heave will produce a planetary nebula (see page 233) while the core shrinks inward to become a white dwarf, an

> **The Sun's energy is created from a 1% difference in mass that results when four hydrogen atoms fuse to make one helium atom.**

Sun

Facing page. The Sun as it appears through a regular solar filter. Sunspots are easily visible with this type of filter; however, prominences and flares can only be viewed with a special hydrogen-alpha filter. Solar filters are absolutely required to safely view the Sun through a telescope.

Structure of the Sun

object no bigger than the Earth but with significantly more mass and very low luminosity.

Structure of the Sun

Interior. Nuclear fusion occurs in the interior core where the temperature reaches 27,000,000° F (15,000,000° C). Outside the core is a radiative zone where a process of energy absorption and re-emission takes place. This zone transfers energy from the core to the convection zone that lies below the visible surface. The convection zone has huge circulating currents that transfer the energy from the radiative zone to the surface. It takes about 200,000 years for light to make its way from the core to the surface.

Surface. The visible surface, called the photosphere, is composed of a lattice of cells, each about the size of Texas, called granules. Granules are the tops of the convection currents that bring the energy from the convection zone to the surface.

Sunspots are visible on the photosphere and are associated with strong magnetic fields that restrict the convection currents, creating cooler areas that appear darker against the brighter photosphere. Sunspots are about 6,300° F (3,500° C) compared to an average surface temperature of 10,000° F (5,500° C).

Immediately above the photosphere is a thin layer of gases about 2,000 miles (3,220 km) thick called the chromosphere. The temperature there ranges from just 7,600° F (4,200° C) near the photosphere to 14,800° F (8,200° C) at its outer edge.

Beyond the chromosphere is the corona, the most tenuous part of the Sun's atmosphere. This rarified hydrogen gas reaches temperatures of up to 1,800,000° F (1,000,000° C) and extends for millions of miles from the surface. The corona is visible during total solar eclipses as the irregular halo surrounding the Moon.

Prominences (as pictured on page 16) are massive protrusions of ionized gas carried from the surface of the Sun into the corona. They can be arched, sometimes looping back to the surface. Large prominences easily extend 10 to 30 Earth diameters from the photosphere.

Solar Surface & Atmosphere

Sun Parts

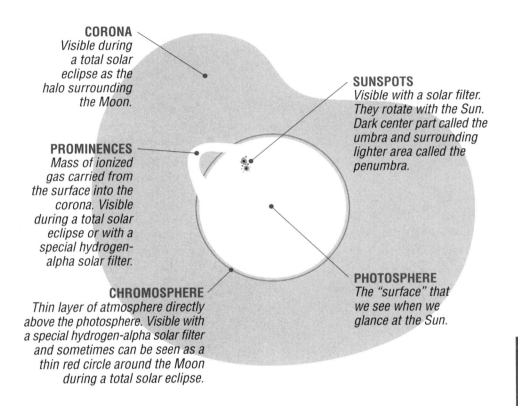

CORONA
Visible during a total solar eclipse as the halo surrounding the Moon.

SUNSPOTS
Visible with a solar filter. They rotate with the Sun. Dark center part called the umbra and surrounding lighter area called the penumbra.

PROMINENCES
Mass of ionized gas carried from the surface into the corona. Visible during a total solar eclipse or with a special hydrogen-alpha solar filter.

CHROMOSPHERE
Thin layer of atmosphere directly above the photosphere. Visible with a special hydrogen-alpha solar filter and sometimes can be seen as a thin red circle around the Moon during a total solar eclipse.

PHOTOSPHERE
The "surface" that we see when we glance at the Sun.

A flare is like a prominence but releases enormous amounts of energy and energetic particles into the Solar System, causing the aurorae on Earth as well as radio and communication disruptions.

The Sun produces a solar wind made of highly ionized gas that permeates the Solar System. This gas can reach speeds up to 435 miles per second (700 km/sec) with a density varying from 160 to 1,600 particles per cubic inch (10 to 100 particles per cubic centimeter). Additionally, sunlight itself exerts a small amount of pressure. Both the solar wind and radiating sunlight are responsible for pushing a comet's tail away from the Sun.

Safely Observing the Sun/Solar Filters

SAFELY OBSERVING THE SUN WITH SOLAR FILTERS

There is only one safe way to view the Sun with a telescope, and that is to use a solar filter that completely covers the front of the telescope (full-aperture). All other types of filters or methods are dangerous.

Solar filters can be purchased at your local telescope store or through retailers that advertise in the popular monthly astronomy magazines. DO NOT attempt to make your own filter. Solar filters transmit about 1/100,000 of the Sun's light and filter out harmful rays. The photo to the right shows a telescope fitted with a solar filter for safely viewing the Sun.

Use only full-aperture solar filters that completely cover the front of the telescope. All other filters or methods to view the Sun are dangerous. Note that the reflex sight finder is also covered.

Once the filter is fastened securely to the front of the telescope, use the telescope in a normal fashion. *IMPORTANT: Remember to cover up your finderscope or other pointing device — better yet, remove it! These also present viewing hazards and/or can be damaged by the Sun if they are not covered.* To point the telescope at the Sun, use the telescope's shadow as your guide. Move the telescope until the shadow of its tube is smallest. The Sun should then be in or near your eyepiece view.

Observing the Sun

OBSERVING THE SUN

The Sun emits so much energy that many of its features are overpowered by its brilliance. With a solar filter, only the photosphere and sunspots are visible. A special hydrogen-alpha filter is required to view prominences.

Sunspots. Sunspots are plainly visible with a regular solar filter. They form, grow and dissipate, rotating with the Sun, changing their appearance daily. The inner and darkest part of a sunspot is called the umbra, while the surrounding lighter area is called the penumbra. Sunspots often appear in groups composed of many larger and smaller spots.

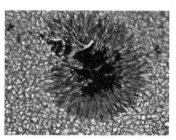

Sunspot closeup. The darkest part is called the umbra and the surrounding lighter part, which looks similar to embroidery, is the penumbra.

There is an 11 year cycle of heightened sunspot activity; however, the length of this cycle can vary by a few years. The first peak of the 21st century occurred in the year 2000.

Prominences. In order to view prominences, telescopes must be fitted with a special hydrogen-alpha filter. Unfortunately, these filters are expensive (they start at $2,000 as of this book's printing) and thus are not very common.

Hydrogen-alpha filters transmit only a very narrow range of light on the red end of the spectrum where prominences are visible. Prominences cannot be seen with regular solar filters because they get "washed out" among all the other colors that these filters transmit. Without a hydrogen-alpha filter, prominences can sometimes be seen around the edge of the Moon during a total solar eclipse.

The hydrogen-alpha filter provides incredible views of the Sun. Not only will you see prominences, but you will see the Sun's mottled surface. Changes in prominences occur hourly. I highly recommend making inquires at your local planetarium or telescope store about the possibility of observing the Sun through a hydrogen-alpha filter.

Solar & Lunar Eclipses

A total solar eclipse is one of the most spectacular natural events to behold. Those who witness total solar eclipses consider themselves fortunate. They carry an indelible impression that is as much visual as it is emotional. It is disheartening that most people never experience one of the greatest astronomical and sensory events on our planet.

It is an incredible coincidence that the Sun and Moon appear the same size in the sky. It is even more amazing that our Moon gets the chance to perfectly eclipse the Sun. The odds of this coincidence are astounding when we consider that our Moon is the only moon in the Solar System that perfectly eclipses the Sun. All the other moons of the planets are either too large or too small for their orbits to eclipse the Sun in precisely the same manner as ours.

Our Moon is the only moon in the Solar System that perfectly eclipses the Sun.

Although I emphasize the glorious nature of the total solar eclipse, I don't want to underrate the beauty of a total lunar eclipse. But they are two different kinds of events. Total lunar eclipses are more casual, because the coloration of the Moon gradually changes as it waxes and wanes through the Earth's shadow.

Overview of Solar and Lunar Eclipses

Both solar and lunar eclipses involve an alignment of the Earth, Moon and Sun. A solar eclipse is the blocking of the Sun by the Moon, either partially or totally. A lunar eclipse is the blocking of the Moon's light (from the Sun) by Earth's shadow.

Solar eclipses can occur only at the time of New Moon; lunar eclipses only at the time of Full Moon.

In order to see a total or annular solar eclipse, one must be on a narrow path that can stretch for a thousand miles or so on the Earth. Only those on the path will see the total or annular eclipse — those near it will see only a partial eclipse. On the other hand, lunar eclipses can be seen by almost everyone on the night side of the world.

Facing page. Total solar eclipse of August 11, 1999. Picture taken near Senlis, a small town northeast of Paris, France.

Solar & Lunar Eclipses

Umbra and Penumbra Shadows

These are the names of the shadows responsible for all eclipses. The umbra is the innermost and darkest shadow. The penumbra is a secondary shadow around the umbra. You will see a solar eclipse if you are in the Moon's umbra or penumbra shadow. Lunar eclipses occur when the Moon passes into Earth's umbra or penumbra shadow.

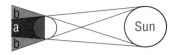

This exaggerated illustration depicts the formation of the umbra at (a) and the surrounding penumbra at (b). The geometry of these shadows is a result of the Sun's diameter.

Umbra and penumbra shadows are visible whenever it is sunny. If you look at the edge of an object's shadow, you will notice that it is fuzzy. This fuzzy edge is the penumbra and the main body of the shadow is the umbra.

Solar Eclipses

There are three types of solar eclipses: total, annular and partial. They are illustrated and explained below.

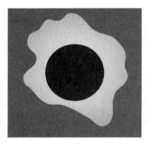

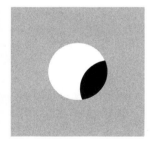

Total Solar Eclipse
Moon completely blocks Sun. The irregularly shaped halo around the Moon is the Sun's corona.

Annular Solar Eclipse
Moon moves completely in front of the Sun but does not cover the Sun.

Partial Solar Eclipse
Moon only partially blocks Sun. Those outside the path of a total or annular eclipse only see a partial eclipse.

Why do annular eclipses occur? The Moon's orbit, like those of all orbiting bodies, is an ellipse; so the distance from the Moon to the Earth varies. Annular eclipses occur when the Moon is farther away in its orbit than usual, making the apparent size of the Moon slightly smaller than the apparent size of the Sun. In these instances, the Moon is simply too small to totally block the Sun.

Eclipses

Solar & Lunar Eclipses

Total Solar Eclipses

Moon at
New Moon

← Sun

1 **UMBRA.** The darkest part of the shadow where a total eclipse can *only* be seen. On Earth, the umbra can reach 170 miles (270 km) wide and travel one-third of the way around the world in a few hours.

2 **PENUMBRA.** The secondary shadow where only a partial eclipse of the Sun will be seen. The penumbra is thousands of miles wide and straddles the path of the umbra on the Earth's surface.

3 Observers outside of the penumbra will not see the Sun eclipsed.

*The **umbra path** for the total solar eclipse of August, 2017. The penumbra stretches for thousands of miles on both sides of the umbra.*

Lunar Eclipses

Moon at
Full Moon

Penumbra

Umbra Shadow

Penumbra

← Sun

1 **TOTAL LUNAR ECLIPSES** occur when the Moon enters the Earth's umbra shadow. The Moon does not turn completely dark during a total lunar eclipse; instead, it turns a pretty red-orange color. A lunar eclipse is visible to almost half of the world.

2 **PARTIAL LUNAR ECLIPSES** occur when only part of the Moon enters the Earth's umbra shadow. Partial lunar eclipses will show one edge of the Moon turning a slight orange color.

3 **PENUMBRAL LUNAR ECLIPSES** occur when the Moon only enters the Earth's penumbra shadow. Penumbral lunar eclipses may not be noticeable.

Eclipses

Solar & Lunar Eclipses

Lunar Eclipses

Lunar eclipses can be total, partial or penumbral; however, they do not share the characteristics of solar eclipses. Total lunar eclipses turn the Moon into a dark red-orange color instead of turning it completely black. The red-orange color is caused by light refracted through the Earth's atmosphere. You see the same coloring at sunrise and sunset. Partial lunar eclipses may not be noticeable with the exception that an edge of the Moon may turn a little orange. Penumbral eclipses are usually not noticeable to the average observer.

Why Eclipses Do Not Happen Every Month

Solar and lunar eclipses do not happen every month because the Moon's orbit is tilted 5.1° to Earth's orbit, placing the Moon above or below the Sun or Earth's shadow at New Moon and Full Moon most of the time. The Moon must be positioned exactly at the point where its orbit crosses the Earth's orbit for an eclipse to occur. The Earth, Moon and Sun get perfectly aligned every 173 days, producing an eclipse somewhere on Earth.

Missed Eclipses

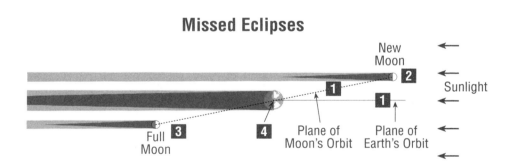

1 The Moon's orbit is tilted 5.1° to the Earth's orbit. This slight tilt is enough to place the shadows necessary for eclipses out of reach of the Earth or Moon.

2 The shadow of most **New Moons** falls either above or below the Earth.

3 At **Full Moon**, the Moon is usually above or below the Earth's shadow.

4 **Eclipses occur** when the Moon is either New or Full *and* the Moon crosses the plane of the Earth's orbit. This intersection happens every 173 days and this time interval is known as an eclipse season.

Eclipses

Observing Solar Eclipses

Frequency of Eclipses: The Saros

Up to two eclipses can occur during a 173-day eclipse season: one lunar and one solar. Anywhere from two to seven lunar and solar eclipses can therefore occur in a year. Eclipses also repeat themselves in 18 year cycles called Saros (actually 18 years, 11 days, 8 hours). So, all of the eclipses that happen in the year 2000 will repeat 18 years later in 2018. However, the 2018 eclipses will advance by 11 days and 8 hours, placing them one-third farther around the world than their previous locations. There are 42 Saros series running concurrently, providing us with an ongoing cycle of eclipses. The intensity of eclipses in a Saros (the ones that repeat every 18 years) waxes and wanes over time.

> # W A R N I N G
> **Instant blindness or serious eye injury will result from looking at or near the Sun through telescopes, binoculars or cameras that are not properly equipped with solar filters.**

OBSERVING SOLAR ECLIPSES

Safely Viewing an Eclipse. Safety of the eyes is of the utmost importance when viewing solar eclipses. Do not stare or even look directly at the Sun. Not only is this harmful to the eyes, but you cannot see the partially eclipsed Sun this way! I highly recommend using a solar or eclipse viewer/filter (like that pictured below). These inexpensive viewers are available at telescope shops, planetarium gift shops and from telescope dealers listed in the popular monthly astronomy magazines.

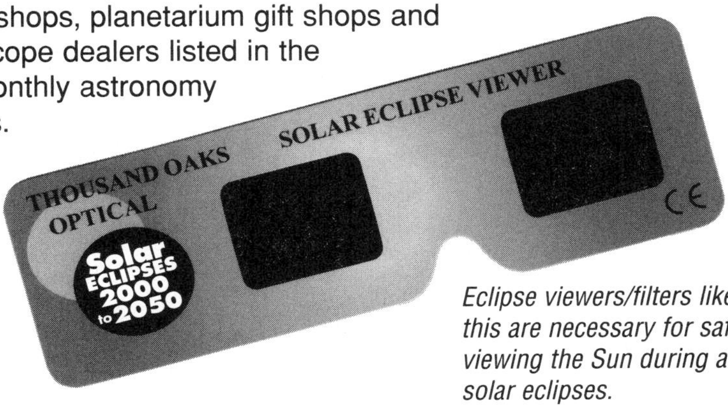

THOUSAND OAKS OPTICAL · SOLAR ECLIPSE VIEWER · Solar ECLIPSES 2000 to 2050 · CE

Eclipse viewers/filters like this are necessary for safely viewing the Sun during all solar eclipses.

Eclipses

207

Observing Solar Eclipses

During a solar eclipse, the Moon's progress can be viewed with a telescope that is properly fitted with a solar filter. Please see page 200 in this field guide on Observing the Sun for more information.

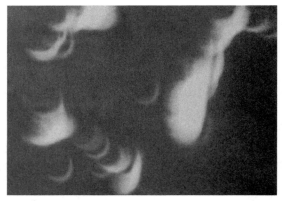

The multitude of crescents in this picture are the eclipsed Sun, projected through pinholes formed from the interweaving of leaves on a tree.

There are novel ways to view the progress of solar eclipses. My favorite is using trees. If you look at a tree's shadow (the tree must have leaves) during a solar eclipse, you will notice that mixed in with the shadow are hundreds of crescent Suns. A tree with leaves creates a multitude of pinholes that project the outline of the Sun. Some trees work better than others.

Partial and Annular Eclipses. Partial eclipses can last for several hours. They are not noticeable unless a substantial portion of the Sun is covered by the Moon. Even with half of the Sun eclipsed, you may not notice any appreciable difference in sunlight.

To observe an annular solar eclipse, consult the local media or popular monthly astronomy magazines for the location of the eclipse path. You cannot see the annular eclipse if you are not in its path. It will not get dark during an annular eclipse and the Moon will only be completely in front of the Sun for several minutes.

A solar or eclipse viewer/filter is needed to view the Sun during the entire partial and annular eclipse.

Total Solar Eclipse & Totality. Remember, to see a total solar eclipse, you must be on the eclipse path. Consult the local media or popular monthly astronomy magazines for details and locations of the path.

A total solar eclipse will last for several hours and is treated as a partial eclipse until the time of totality; that is, when the Moon completely blocks the Sun's light. During the one to five

Observing Lunar Eclipses

minutes of totality, no solar filter is required. Everyone stands and stares in wonder. Many things happen during totality. The sky darkens a little (it does not get completely dark), and almost immediately, the white shimmering corona is seen surrounding the Moon. Around the Moon's edge, the thin red ring of the chromosphere may be visible along with prominences and flares protruding outward. If you look at the sky around the Moon, you will probably see a few stars and planets (usually Venus and Mercury) and if you scan the whole sky, you will see the umbra shadow circling the sky and extending almost to the horizon. The sky near the horizon is still light but may have a red coloring like that at sunset. The entire scene is incredible. There is nothing like it! No camera can capture the experience of totality, and everyone is touched differently. People clap, cheer, cry and pray. I recommend that everyone experience a total solar eclipse.

OBSERVING LUNAR ECLIPSES

No special equipment or caution is necessary to view lunar eclipses. Binoculars and telescopes can be used to view the Moon. Lunar eclipses are especially enjoyable when you can sit outside, talk with others and casually watch the event unfold.

For the most part, the Moon will turn a dark red-orange when it is completely in Earth's umbra shadow. Various hues of red and orange will slowly dance across the Moon's surface as it enters, passes through and exits the umbra. Since the umbra is considerably larger than the Moon, total lunar eclipses can last up to 3 1/2 hours. If the Moon crosses the umbra dead center, it takes about an hour to completely enter the umbra. It will stay in the umbra for 1 1/2 hours and finish as it started, taking an hour to leave.

2000–2050 Solar and Lunar Eclipse Tables for North America
The solar and lunar eclipse tables on the following pages summarize the location and time of these events. Since the intensity of the event and the exact time vary considerably depending on your viewing location, please consult your local media for details. The popular monthly astronomy magazines also provide details on eclipses; however, their articles appear several months before the event, so please prepare in advance.

Eclipses

SOLAR Eclipses 2000 – 2031

Solar Eclipses in North America

Date of Solar Eclipse	Type of Solar Eclipse	Time of Day to View[1]	Locations[2]
July 30, 2000	Partial	Around Sunset	*Alaska*, Western Canada, Northwest
December 25, 2000	Partial	Around Noon	*Midwest*, Continental US, Southern Canada
December 14, 2001	Partial	Early to Late Afternoon	*Hawaii*, Continental US
June 10, 2002	Partial	Late Afternoon	*West*, Midwest, Hawaii, Alaska, West Canada
May 30, 2003	Partial	Around Sunset	*Alaska*
April 8, 2005	Partial	Late Afternoon	*Florida*, South, Southwest
July 21, 2009	Partial	Around Sunset	*Hawaii*
May 20, 2012	**Annular**	**Around Sunset**	**West**, Hawaii, Alaska, Western Canada
May 9, 2013	Partial	Late Afternoon	*Hawaii*
October 23, 2014	Partial	Mid Afternoon	*West*, Midwest, Alaska, Western Canada
March 8, 2016	Partial	Around Sunset	*Hawaii*, Alaska
August 21, 2017	**Total**	**Around Noon**	***Across the US!*** Hawaii, Canada & Alaska
June 10, 2021	Partial	Early Morning	*Northeast*, East
October 14, 2023	**Annular**	**Late Morning**	**West**, Continental US, Canada
April 8, 2024	**Total**	**Around Noon**	**Midwest**, Continental US, Canada, Hawaii
October 2, 2024	Partial	Early Morning	*Hawaii*
August 12, 2026	Partial	Early to Late Morning	*Alaska* to Northeast
January 26, 2028	Partial	Late Morning	*Florida*, South, East, Midwest
January 14, 2029	Partial	Around Noon	*Canada*, Continental US
June 11, 2029	Partial	Around Sunset	*Alaska*, Canada, Northwest
November 14, 2031	Partial	Mid Afternoon	*Hawaii*, Southwest, South, Florida

[1]Check media sources for specific times for your location.
[2]First listed area is most favorable viewing location.

SOLAR Eclipses 2033 – 2051

Solar Eclipses in North America

Date of Solar Eclipse	Type of Solar Eclipse	Time of Day to View[1]	Locations[2]
March 30, 2033	**Total**	**Morning**	***Alaska***, Canada, Hawaii, West, Midwest
September 1, 2035	Partial	Around Sunset	*Hawaii*
August 21, 2036	Partial	Morning	*Alaska*
January 5, 2038	Partial	Early Morning	*East*, Florida
July 2, 2038	Partial	Early Morning	*Florida*, Southeast, East
June 21, 2039	**Annular**	**Early Morning**	***Alaska***, Canada, Hawaii, West, Midwest
November 4, 2040	Partial	Around Noon	*East*, Continental US, Canada
October 24, 2041	Partial	Late Afternoon	*Hawaii*
April 19, 2042	Partial	Around Sunset	*Alaska*, Northwest Canada, Hawaii
April 9, 2043	Partial	Around Noon	*Alaska*, Western Canada, Hawaii, Northwest
August 22, 2044	**Total**	**Around Sunset**	***Northwest***, Alaska, Canada, Hawaii, West
February 16, 2045	Partial	Late Afternoon	*Hawaii*
August 12, 2045	**Total**	**Around Noon**	***South to West***, Hawaii, Canada, Alaska
February 5, 2046	**Annular**	**Mid Afternoon**	**Hawaii**, Alaska, West
June 11, 2048	**Annular**	**Early Morning**	***Northern Midwest/ Canada***, East, South, Florida
May 31, 2049	Partial	Morning	*Florida*
November 14, 2050	Partial	Early Morning	*East Canada*, Northeast
April 10, 2051	Partial	Around Sunset	*Alaska*, Northwest Canada

[1]Check media sources for specific times for your location.
[2]First listed area is most favorable viewing location.

Solar Eclipses

LUNAR Eclipses 2000 – 2021

Lunar Eclipses in North America

Date of Lunar Eclipse	Type of Lunar Eclipse	Time of Day to View[1]	Locations
January 20, 2000	Total	Around Midnight	Hawaii, Alaska, Continental US, Canada
July 16, 2000	Total	Before Sunrise	Hawaii, West Coast
July 5, 2001	Partial	Before Sunrise	Hawaii
May 15, 2003	Total	Before Midnight	Continental US, Canada
November 8, 2003	Total	Early Evening	Continental US, Canada
October 27, 2004	Total	Evening	Continental US, Canada
October 17, 2005	Penumbra	Before Sunrise	Hawaii, Alaska, West
March 14, 2006	Penumbra	Early Evening	East Coast
March 3, 2007	Total	Early Evening	East Coast
August 28, 2007	Total	Before Sunrise	Continental US, Canada
February 20, 2008	Total	Around Midnight	Continental US, Canada
June 26, 2010	Partial	Before Sunrise	Hawaii, West
December 21, 2010	Total	After Midnight	Hawaii, Alaska, Continental US, Canada
December 10, 2011	Total	Before Sunrise	Hawaii, Alaska, West
June 4, 2012	Partial	Before Sunrise	Hawaii, West
November 28, 2012	Penumbra	Before Sunrise	Hawaii, Alaska
April 14, 2014	Total	Around Midnight	Hawaii, Alaska, Continental US, Canada
October 8, 2014	Total	Before Sunrise	Hawaii, Alaska, Continental US, Canada
April 4, 2015	Total	Before Sunrise	Hawaii, Alaska, West
September 27, 2015	Total	Evening	Continental US, Canada
February 10, 2017	Penumbra	Evening	Continental US, Canada
January 31, 2018	Total	Early Morning	Hawaii, Alaska, West
January 20, 2019	Total	Around Midnight	Hawaii, Alaska, Continental US, Canada
May 26, 2021	Partial	Before Sunrise	Hawaii, Alaska, West
November 19, 2021	Almost Total	Before Sunrise	Hawaii, Alaska, Continental US, Canada

[1]Check media sources for specific times for your location.

LUNAR Eclipses 2022 – 2043

Lunar Eclipses in North America

Date of Lunar Eclipse	Type of Lunar Eclipse	Time of Day to View[1]	Locations
May 15, 2022	Total	Around Midnight	Continental US, Canada
November 8, 2022	Total	Before Sunrise	Hawaii, Alaska, Continental US, Canada
March 24, 2024	Penumbra	Around Midnight	Hawaii, Alaska, Continental US, Canada
March 13, 2025	Total	Around Midnight	Hawaii, Alaska, Continental US, Canada
March 3, 2026	Total	Before Sunrise	Hawaii, Alaska, West, Midwest, Canada
August 27, 2026	Partial	Around Midnight	Continental US, Canada
January 11, 2028	Penumbra	Around Midnight	Hawaii, Alaska, Continental US, Canada
December 31, 2028	Total	Early Evening	Hawaii, Alaska
June 25, 2029	Total	Before Midnight	Continental US, Canada
December 9, 2030	Penumbra	Early Evening	East
April 25, 2032	Total	Before Sunrise	Hawaii
October 8, 2033	Total	Before Sunrise	Hawaii, Alaska, Continental US, Canada
August 18, 2035	Penumbra	Early Evening	Midwest, East
August 6, 2036	Total	Evening	Continental US except West Coast
Janaury 31, 2037	Total	Before Sunrise	Hawaii, Alaska, West
July 26, 2037	Partial	Evening	Continental US, Canada
November 30, 2039	Partial	Early Evening	Alaska
May 26, 2040	Total	Before Sunrise	Hawaii, Alaska, West Coast
May 15, 2041	Penumbra	Early Evening	East Coast
November 7, 2041	Penumbra	Around Midnight	Hawaii, Alaska, Continental US, Canada
April 5, 2042	Penumbra	Before Sunrise	Hawaii, Alaska
March 25, 2043	Total	Before Sunrise	Hawaii, Alaska
September 18, 2043	Total	Early Evening	Midwest, East

[1]Check media sources for specific times for your location.

Lunar Eclipses

LUNAR Eclipses 2044 – 2051

Lunar Eclipses in North America

Date of Lunar Eclipse	Type of Lunar Eclipse	Time of Day to View[1]	Locations
September 7, 2044	Total	Before Sunrise	Hawaii, Alaska, West
July 17, 2046	Partial	Early Evening	East Coast
January 11, 2047	Total	Early Evening	Continental US, Canada, Alaska
July 7, 2047	Total	Before Sunrise	Hawaii, Alaska, West
December 31, 2047	Total	Around Midnight	Hawaii, Alaska, Continental US, Canada
June 25, 2048	Partial	Around Midnight	Midwest, East
December 19, 2048	Penumbra	Around Midnight	Hawaii, Alaska, Continental US, Canada
October 29, 2050	Total	Evening	Continental US, Canada, Alaska
April 25, 2051	Total	Early Evening	Continental US, Canada

[1]Check media sources for specific times for your location.

Facing page. *A sequence of photographs taken after totality of the August 11, 1999 eclipse.*

Instruments for Viewing

Anyone can participate in and enjoy astronomy without the aid of binoculars or a telescope. However, their use can heighten the experience of exploring the heavens. These instruments will open vistas unobtainable in any other manner, revealing a hidden Universe out of reach of the eye alone. It is this Universe that humankind started to explore several centuries ago, but only recently started to understand.

Telescope Overview

Refractors and reflectors are the two basic types of telescopes; although today, a hybrid of the two has become popular. Refracting telescopes utilize clear optical lenses for focusing light while reflecting telescopes use mirrors. The hybrid telescopes use mirrors for focusing light, but also employ a front "correcting lens."

Refractors. Refractors represent the most common notion of a telescope. The front lens used for focusing light is called an objective lens. Common objective diameters range from 2.4 inches (60mm) to 6 inches. Most are 3 inches (80mm) or less. Refractors are more expensive per inch of aperture than other telescopes. Small, inexpensive refractors are often purchased for children. Unfortunately, these telescopes do not perform well and very often taint first impressions of observational astronomy.

The telescope helped usher in the scientific era and has opened the doors to the Universe.

Telescopes

Reflectors. The Newtonian reflector, patterned after Newton's original design, is the most common reflector telescope. These telescopes use a concave primary mirror to focus light. Today, the most popular form of the Newtonian telescope is called a Dobsonian. The Dobsonian telescope features a Newtonian telescope with a simple altazimuth mount that allows easy vertical and horizontal movement. The simplicity of the

Facing page. Fully equipped 3.1" refractor telescope on a traditional equatorial mount. Note the eyepiece is turned 90° from the tube, with a diagonal, to make viewing easier. There is also a finderscope near the eyepiece to help aim the telescope. Traditional equatorial mounts have counterweights to balance the telescope around the polar axis.

Telescopes

Dobsonian telescope has enabled amateurs to purchase larger telescopes for the lowest cost ever. The 6-inch Dobsonian is an affordable telescope to own and is convenient to use. Dobsonians of 36 inches in diameter and larger are available.

Hybrids. Although there are several types of hybrid telescopes, the Schmidt-Cassegrain Telescope (SCT) is the most popular. The 8-inch diameter is the best selling size and provides an extremely portable observing system because of its "folded" optical system. SCTs have primary mirrors for focusing light rays, but incorporate a front correcting plate or lens, which also helps seal the optics from the environment. Per apeture inch, SCT telescopes cost less than refractors but more than Dobsonian reflectors.

Popular Types of Telescopes

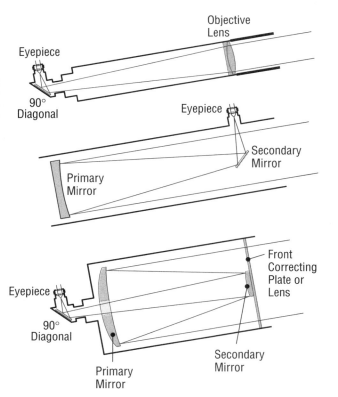

REFRACTOR

Most refractors are 3 inches or less in diameter, the largest are over 6 inches.

REFLECTOR

The Newtonian reflector is popular with amateurs. Common diameters range from 4.5 inches to over 36 inches.

SCHMIDT-CASSEGRAIN TELESCOPE (SCT)

A SCT uses two mirrors and a front correcting plate to focus light. The correcting plate helps seal the optics from the environment. The 8-inch is becoming the telescope of choice for amateurs.

Telescope Mounts

A family of Dobsonians. A Newtonian reflector in a simple mount is the hallmark of the Dobsonian telescope. Shown here are 4.5" to 17.5" diameter mirror sizes. Dobsonians use altazimuth mounts and are the lowest cost per inch of aperture of all telescopes.

Telescope Mounts

There are two basic types of telescope mounts, but many variations and options.

The simplest is the altazimuth mount. This mount is the type used with the giant binoculars attached to permanent pedestals at tourist attractions. Altazimuth mounts allow quick and easy side-to-side and up-and-down movement. I use an altazimuth mount for most of my casual observing.

The German equatorial mount is the traditional astronomical mount. Before the age of computers, this was the only mount that could be motorized to automatically follow a celestial object. Equatorial mounts have two axes. One points directly at the north

Telescopes Mounts

celestial pole (close to the star Polaris) and is called the **polar axis**. The other axis, the **declination axis**, is perpendicular to the polar axis. These mounts usually are heavy because they require extra weights to counterbalance the telescope.

The New Telescopes — Compliments of the Computer
Computer controlled telescope mounts have revolutionized astronomy for both the amateur and professional. Amateurs can enjoy the simplicity of an altazimuth mount that will automatically find and follow any celestial object. These mounts, complete with telescope, are now commonplace and inexpensive.

Professional astronomers started building and using computer controlled altazimuth mounts in the early 1970s. They quickly

Telescope Mounts

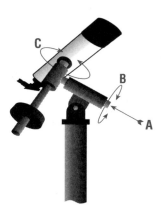

ALTAZIMUTH MOUNT
Simple, easy vertical and horizontal movement.

For amateurs, the Equatorial mount is required to take photographs of celestial objects. Altazimuth mounts can be tilted to perform just like Equatorial mounts. The largest professional telescopes are on computer controlled Altazimuth mounts.

EQUATORIAL MOUNT
Traditional telescope mount. Motors can often be added to follow stars and take photos. One axis, the Polar Axis, **A**, is pointed at the North Celestial Pole. The telescope rotates around the Polar Axis, **B** and the Declination Axis, **C**.

Telescopes

Advanced Telescope Mounts

caught on because they were considerably less expensive (and less massive) than the equatorial equivalent. These professional altazimuth mounts helped usher in the largest telescope in the world and paved the way for this technology to become available to amateurs.

Motorized Mounts & GO TO Computerized Telescopes

Slow moving motors can be attached to the axes of many altazimuth and equatorial mounts, allowing telescopes to follow celestial objects. So, instead of nudging the telescope every minute or so to keep a celestial object in view, the motorized mounts do it for you. Almost all SCTs come with motorized mounts; it is an option for most Dobsonians and some refractors. A motorized mount is one requirement needed to take photographs of celestial objects.

One of the greatest innovations for amateurs was the introduction of the GO TO computerized/motorized telescopes in the 1990s. For the first time, amateurs had telescopes that could automatically find and follow celestial objects. GO TO telescopes are controlled through a hand-controller that works similar to a cellular phone. They have a small display screen, where celestial objects, including the Planets, can be chosen from scrollable lists.

This 4-inch GO TO telescope is controlled by the detachable hand-controller located in the arm of the mount. Once this telescope is set up, a five to ten minute process, it uses its motors to automatically "go to" and follow any object selected through the hand-controller.

I have a 5-inch Celestron NexStar GO TO telescope — it works very well. After you turn the telescope on, it takes about five minutes to initially align the telescope to two bright stars. This is not a difficult task because the hand-controller walks you through the steps and

Advanced Mounts & Eyepieces

it even selects and moves the telescope close to the two stars needed for this initial alignment. All you have to do is center the bright stars in the eyepiece. After you have accomplished this five-minute alignment process, you can then spend the rest of your time observing celestial objects instead of trying to find them.

The Next Generation, GO TO, GPS Telescopes

The ultimate telescopes use computerized GO TO, GPS technology. At the flick of the "on" switch, the telescope automatically determines the time, the date and its exact position using the Global Positioning System network of satellites that orbit the Earth. It is then ready to find and follow celestial objects.

If you get frustrated or are hassled by programming your cellular phone or VCR, then the GO TO, GPS telescopes are right for you. Finally, most GO TO telescopes can take you on a guided tour (selected through the hand-controller) of the best objects in your night sky.

2001 ushered in the ultimate telescopes. Pictured is Celestron's NexStar GPS 11 with GO TO, GPS technology. This telescope has the easiest startup procedure of any telescope.

MORE ABOUT TELESCOPES

Eyepieces & The Barlow Lens

Quality eyepieces are just as important as a quality objective lens or primary mirror. Low quality eyepieces will render poor quality images. The standard eyepiece is the Plössl eyepiece (Plössl is the name of a specific lens design). Plössls are excellent eye-pieces because they provide good images across a wide field of view and are reasonably priced.

Eyepieces are identified by their focal length, which is always expressed in millimeters (mm). Focal lengths range from about 2.5mm to 55mm (0.16 inches to 2.16 inches). Shorter focal length eyepieces provide higher magnifications.

Telescopes

Magnification

The standard eyepiece barrel diameter is 1.25 inches. There is also a 2-inch size. Some inexpensive telescopes use eyepieces that have barrel diameters of 0.965 inches, but very few eyepieces are available for this smaller barrel diameter.

A family of Plössl eyepieces and a barlow lens. The barlow lens is the tall "eyepiece" in the middle.

A barlow lens can be used in conjunction with an eyepiece to double or triple its magnification. A quality barlow will not degrade the performance of an eyepiece. The barlow looks like a long eyepiece and fits into the eyepiece holder (focuser) of a telescope. Regular eyepieces are then inserted into the barlow.

Most telescopes come with at least one eyepiece. As a minimum, I recommend two Plössl eyepieces, a 10mm and 30mm, with a 2x barlow.

What are all those f/numbers about?

The f/numbers (e.g. f/4, f/5.4, f/8) associated with telescopes indicate the ratio of the telescope focal length to the aperture. In other words, the focal length of a telescope, divided by the diameter of the objective lens or primary mirror, gives you the f/number. For example, if your telescope has a focal length of 21.5 inches (540mm) and an objective lens diameter of 4 inches (100mm), then your f/number is f/5.4 (21.5 inches ÷ 4 inches = 5.4 *or* 540mm ÷ 100mm = 5.4). Telescopes with f/numbers of 5 or lower are considered rich-field telescopes (RFT) because they provide lower magnifications and wider fields of view (that is, you can see more of the sky in an eyepiece). Usually, telescope f/numbers range from f/4 to f/11. The f/number is also referred to as the focal ratio.

The Myth of Telescope Magnification

Magnification is the least important factor in choosing a telescope! But, unfortunately, the selling and marketing of many telescopes (especially those sold in department, chain or toy stores) has often been based on magnification.

Telescopes

223

Magnification & Finderscopes

Computing Telescope Magnification

Focal Length of TELESCOPE ÷ *Focal Length* of EYEPIECE = **Magnification**

NOTE: All focal lengths must be expressed in the same units — usually millimeters.

EXAMPLE 1

2032mm focal length telescope with 8mm, 15mm & 20mm eyepieces

2032mm ÷ 8mm = 254x
2032mm ÷ 15mm = 135.5x
2032mm ÷ 20mm = 101.6x

EXAMPLE 2

4-inch f/6 telescope using a 20mm eyepiece

1. Compute focal length of the telescope.
   4-inch x 6 (f/6) = 24 inch focal length
2. Change 24 inch focal length into millimeters. 24 x 25.4 (conversion factor) = 610mm focal length
3. Compute Magnification.
   610mm ÷ 20mm = 30.5x

Technically, it is possible to get any magnification out of any optical system, but there are practical limits. *Useful magnification for most observing, independent of objective lens or primary mirror size, is from 30x to 250x. I seldom use magnifications above 150x.*

The practice of selling high magnification does not seem to go away despite the repeated efforts of professional and amateur astronomers to stamp out this idea. In early 1999, I was window shopping in a national "gadget" chain store. This store had a refracting telescope on the floor with a description tag attached. The tag mentioned the "powerful" (their word on the tag) magnification of 575x that the telescope could achieve. This scope had an objective diameter of 2.4 inches (60mm). If this telescope had good optics (both objective and eyepieces), which it did not, its highest useful magnification would be about 150x, period. I doubt that this particular telescope could perform well at 60x.

Finderscopes & Reflex Sights

Have you ever tried to point a telescope at a star or Planet? It is not easy without a finderscope. A finderscope is a small, low powered telescope attached to the main telescope. It usually has cross reticles and is used to steer or target the telescope. Even economically priced finderscopes will help you enormously to guide your telescope.

Eyeglasses & Focusing

A number of finders, known as "reflex sights," project a red dot or concentric circles onto the night sky for guiding the telescope. Reflex sights are wonderful because you can quickly point a telescope to a specific spot in the night sky without having to look through the limited confines of a finderscope. Most amateurs use reflex sights instead of the traditional finderscope.

The Telrad is a very popular reflex sight finder that can be mounted on any telescope. You position your eyes a foot or so behind the slanted glass plate to view concentric circles that are used to guide your scope. They are natural and fun to use — kids really like them.

Modern Optical Quality

At the beginning of this twenty-first century, middle-of-the-line telescopes and other optical instruments perform better than the very high end telescopes of the 1970s. Modern computer technology, sophisticated production techniques and new materials give us the highest mechanical and optical quality ever.

Unfortunately, not all optics are excellent. Most telescopes sold in department and discount stores, as well as the lower end line of telescopes sold by the major telescope manufacturers, almost always exhibit lower optical quality. Don't disappoint yourself — if you are in the market to purchase binoculars or a telescope, buy at least middle-of-the-line.

Observing with Eyeglasses. Focusing.

If possible, observe without eyeglasses. If you are unsure as to whether or not you can, give it a try. Observing is more pleasant and comfortable without them. If you must use your glasses, remember that some eyepieces have a rubber guard that can be folded back to provide easier and better viewing.

Almost everyone must focus a telescope to his or her individual eyes. I am always amazed at the difference in focus from one individual to another. What may be very blurry to one is perfectly clear to another. If you are out observing with others, do not be afraid to focus the telescope (but please politely ask) because there is nothing worse than viewing a blurry image.

Telescopes

Binoculars

Upside Down and Inside Out Images

Most astronomical telescopes and finderscopes do not provide upright, correctly oriented views. For instance, refractors without the 90° diagonal provide upside down views. With the 90° diagonal, you get a mirror image — the image is upright, but left and right are reversed. SCT's provide the same orientation as a refractor with a 90° diagonal. The biggest problem with mirror image views is matching stars in the eyepiece to those printed correctly in star atlases. Newtonian reflectors provide a correctly oriented view but you would have to stand in front of the tube to see it, so these telescopes are not practical for terrestrial viewing.

The reason for reversed images is that image quality has always been more important to the astronomical community than a correctly oriented view. The extra optics required to correctly orient a view degrade optical performance. Remember, we're just looking at stars, so who cares if they are upside down?

Binoculars

Binoculars are an excellent instrument for observing the heavens. They offer the comfort of two-eye viewing and capture greater vistas than can be obtained with telescopes.

Almost all middle-of-the-line binoculars offer good optical performance. The standard configuration, 7x50, is ideal for gazing at the heavens and for daytime use. I do not recommend binoculars smaller than 40mm for astronomical use. My 10x40s provide excellent views of the brighter nebulae and star clusters; however, my 8x20 pair

Using a tripod with your binoculars will make viewing the heavens more enjoyable because your arms will not get tired from holding them. Unfortunately, some binoculars do not have a tripod socket for attachment to the tripod's head. With my 10x40s (pictured), I got creative with Velcro. With a hole punch, I punched holes in short strips of both the hook and loop pieces, which were then slipped over the 1/4-20 screw in the tripod head. A wingnut holds the Velcro pieces in place. The binoculars are secured by tightly wrapping the loose ends of the Velcro pieces around the center post of the binoculars .

Recommendations

is not adequate for these fainter objects.

Binocular Nomenclature

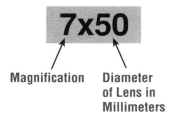

Since most binoculars are limited to magnification from 7x to 10x, they cannot provide the detail possible with telescopes. On the other hand, the wide vistas obtainable with binoculars are impossible to capture with telescopes. In my opinion, the most beautiful views of the Pleiades (M45, page 251) and the Praesepe (M44, page 259) are through binoculars. These clusters fill the binoculars' field of view and give the impression that the stars are floating in front of you. Many deep sky objects are visible with binoculars; they just appear smaller. Binoculars serve as observing adjuncts for most amateur astronomers.

A tripod is very useful when using binoculars to view the heavens. It steadies your view and gives you the opportunity to study the sky without making your arms tired. I also lean on the tripod, which makes it more comfortable for me to stand in place for a period of time. Some binoculars do not have a tripod socket to attach them easily to the tripod head. You may have to get creative to latch these binoculars to a tripod.

Telescopes

RECOMMENDATIONS & CONSIDERATIONS
The best telescope is the one that gets used the most. I have several telescopes: a 4-inch refractor, 6 and 10-inch reflectors. I use the 4-inch refractor the most because it is easy to take in and out of the house and has excellent image quality. Even though I can see a lot more with my heavy, equatorially mounted 10-inch reflector, I dislike the hassle of set up and take down associated with this large instrument.

On the next page, I have provided summaries of the three major telescopes, binoculars and eyepieces as well as some suggestions about purchasing a telescope.

Summary & Recommendations

REFRACTORS
- Highest cost per inch of aperture
- Practically maintenance free
- Diameters are small, most are 2.4 to 4 inches (60 to 100mm). Largest diameters are around 6 inches.
- Easy set up and take down for 4-inch and smaller sizes
- Various mounts available
- Smaller "entry level" refractors are inexpensive but are not a good choice for astronomical use
- Most expensive refractors (called apochromatic) provide the highest image quality of all telescopes

DOBSONIAN REFLECTORS
- Lowest cost per inch of aperture
- Optics need to be realigned frequently and cleaned occasionally
- Common diameters range from 4.5 to 36 inches
- Easy set up and take down for 10-inch and smaller sizes
- Mount limited to simple altazimuth
- Low quality components in some commercially produced units
- Larger diameter Dobsonians provide the brightest images of deep sky objects

HYBRIDS ★ SCHMIDT-CASSEGRAIN TELESCOPES (SCT)
- Per inch of aperture, SCT are more expensive than Dobsonians but less expensive than refractors
- Maintenance required occasionally
- Common diameters range from 5 to 16 inches
- Easy set up and take down for 8-inch and smaller sizes
- Front correcting plate susceptible to dew
- Come with motorized mount to follow the stars (most GO TO)
- 8-inch is telescope of choice for many amateurs

BINOCULARS
- Purchase at least middle-of-the-line binoculars. These should provide good image quality.
- 7x40, 10x40, 7x50 or 10x50 are good choices for astronomical use
- A tripod is helpful for astronomical viewing
- Some binoculars do not have a tripod socket, so you may have to get creative in latching them to a tripod's head

Telescopes

Summary & Recommendations

EYEPIECES

✦ Telescopes are only half of the equation for viewing the heavens. Good quality eyepieces are the other half.

✦ Be prepared to purchase a few with your telescope since most telescopes come with only one eyepiece

✦ Plössl is the standard eyepiece of choice

✦ A barlow lens can economically double or triple the magnification range of your set of eyepieces

Here are some of my ideas for exploring the heavens with and without your own optical instrument.

Interloper. Do not buy a telescope or binoculars, but instead attend public astronomy events that feature telescope viewing. If you "hang around" at these events, you will see more celestial objects than you ever would by yourself, and see them through larger telescopes than you would have purchased. And you won't have to do any of the work. At such gatherings, I have looked through 2 to 20-inch telescopes and have seen objects that I can't see with my own scopes.

Gathering Dust. Borrow a friend's telescope that is sitting in the garage or basement. They may not want to sell it, but they will probably let you use it.

Really Want a Telescope. Please take some time to become informed so you can choose the best telescope for your budget and interests. Read about astronomy, subscribe to one of the popular monthly astronomy magazines, visit telescope shops, attend astronomy events, join a club and ask lots of questions before you decide to buy.

Used Telescopes. Many telescope stores sell used telescopes. They usually are sold quickly because they are less expensive than new. Some stores will put your name on a waiting list.

Bottom Line Recommendation. My first recommendation would be a 6 or 8-inch Dobsonian with several quality eyepieces. This will cost around $500 to $600. For about $1,700, you can get an 8-inch GO TO SCT. The 8-inch SCT is the most versatile product for the price. Both of these telescopes can easily be sold or traded if you outgrow them.

Deep Sky Objects

D eep sky objects include nebulae, star clusters and galaxies, that is, distant objects beyond the Solar System. Binary and variable stars are not considered deep sky objects, but I have included them in this section to "round out" the kinds of objects that are observed by amateur and professional astronomers.

Galaxies

All galaxies lie outside ours, the Milky Way galaxy, at distances in the millions of light years. Galaxies harbor stars and represent the largest structures in the Universe. Many are circular in shape. The most distinct galaxies are categorized as "**spiral**," which have several curved arms radiating from a bulged center or nucleus. The picture of M101 to the right typifies a spiral galaxy.

Two other types of galaxies are elliptical and irregular. **Elliptical** galaxies look like giant elongated balls with bright neclei They have no arms and little internal structure. **Irregular** galaxies are irregular in shape, lack arms and have mottled interiors with no obvious neclei. Pictures of these types of galaxies are on the next page.

Remember, everything that we see in the night sky, except for galaxies, is part of our own Milky Way galaxy. And for all practical purposes, there is nothing between galaxies.

A spiral galaxy in Ursa Major (M101). Spiral galaxies have several arms radiating from a bright, bulging, central core. Spiral galaxies represent the most common notion of a galaxy. M101 is 17.5 million light years away and has a diameter of 142,000 light years.

Sky Objects

Facing page. *The Crab nebula in the constellation Taurus, known as M1, is a supernova remnant that exploded in 1054 A.D. In a small telescope, this nebula is faint and somewhat shaped like a flame. Although this object is easy to find because it is close to the star opposite Alnath, it is visible only in dark skies as it is easily washed out by light pollution. I have indicated its location on the Deep Sky Object chart on page 251.*

Deep Sky Objects

The elliptical galaxy M110 near the Andromeda galaxy. This type of galaxy has very little internal structure compared to spiral galaxies.

The irregular galaxy M82 in Ursa Major. Irregular galaxies have mottled interiors with no apparent core or nuclei. M82 may represent the turmoil from two galaxies that have collided and combined.

Nebulae

The word nebulae is a general term that refers to gaseous clouds composed mostly of hydrogen gas. They reside in galaxies. There are several types of nebulae: galactic clouds, planetary nebulae and supernova remnants.

Emission, reflective and dark nebulae represent three types of galactic clouds. These nebulae reside mainly in the arms of spiral galaxies. They span 100 light years or so in size and serve as cauldrons for the birth of stars. Galactic cloud nebulae represent the original matter of galaxies.

An Emission Nebula, like the Great Orion Nebula, emits its own light, stimulated by the ultraviolet radiation from nearby stars.

Reflection Nebulae are the same type of gas clouds as emission nebulae but are

The Horsehead nebula in Orion is a combination of emission and dark nebulae. The head is a dark nebula in front of a nebula stimulated by the radiation of nearby stars. This nebula is located about one arc degree south of the star Alnitak in the belt of Orion and cannot be seen with small telescopes.

visible because they only reflect light from nearby stars.
Dark Nebulae have no nearby stars to light them up. They are indirectly visible as silhouettes or dark patches against a background of stars or bright nebulae.

Planetary Nebulae are different. They represent the remains from the collapse of giant stars in their final stages of evolution. These nebulae are spherical, ringed or have diametrically opposed lobes. Like emission nebulae, ultraviolet radiation from the dying stars stimulate planetary nebulae to emit their own light.

Planetary nebulae have nothing to do with the Planets. The term was coined because the first planetary nebulae observed appeared spherical or round in shape. Many planetary nebulae are characterized by having two diametrically opposed, symmetrical lobes created by the spin and magnetic field characteristics of the dying star. Planetary nebulae are "small," only several light years in diameter or length.

The Dumbbell nebula (M27) in Vulpecula, near Cygnus. The Dumbbell is 815 light year away and has a diameter of two light years. This nebula displays more of the symmetrical lobe nature that is characteristic of many planetary nebulae; however, it is not as pronounced and elongated as some.

Supernova Remnants are nebulae created from the explosions of stars. The Crab Nebula in Taurus, pictured on page 230, is a good example of this type. Supernova remnants are rare compared to other nebulae.

Star Clusters

The term star cluster is a general term referring to an open cluster, galactic cluster or globular cluster.

Deep Sky Objects

Open Cluster. Stars are born in a group or cluster from the same nebula. Open clusters are easy to recognize since the groupings are distinct. As the stars in a cluster revolve around the galaxy, the cluster breaks up. The number of stars in a cluster varies, and can range from several dozen to a thousand or so.

Galactic Cluster. Specific term for an open cluster within an arm of a sprial galaxy. Galactic clusters are composed of young stars born from the nebulae in the arms of spiral galaxies.

Globular Cluster. Distinctly different from open or galactic clusters, a globular cluster represents a collection of upwards of a million stars compacted into the shape of a ball. In a small telescope, globular clusters look like cotton balls. In larger telescopes, they are fantastic sights because thousands of the fainter stars are resolved into pinpoints of light. Our galaxy has about 200 globular clusters that surround it in a spherical halo. Many of these clusters are outside the plane of the Milky Way.

Variable Stars
Any star that changes its actual brightness over a period of days to years is considered a variable star. Stars change in brightness for various reasons. Twinkling stars are not variable stars. Twinkling is causes by atmospheric disturbances.

Algol in Perseus (page 245) is an example of an extrinsic variable star known as an eclipsing binary. Orbiting Algol is a significantly fainter star that passes between Algol and Earth, blocking and lowering Algol's magnitude for a period of several hours.

There are also intrinsic variable stars that vary in magnitude because of physical changes that occur within the star's structure. The Cepheid variables are the best known type. These stars expand and contract, changing their overall size (by as much as 30%) and thus their brightness. They vary in brightness by about one magnitude.

As a side note, Cepheid variables have been extremely important in helping astronomers determine the distances to many star clusters, nebulae and some galaxies. There is a direct relationship between the Cepheid variable period and its actual brightness. When astronomers find a Cepheid variable, they measure how it varies in brightness, which determines its actual brightness and then use this to calculate its distance.

Deep Sky Objects

Double, Binary and Multiple Stars

Double stars can be either optical or binary. Optical double stars appear visually to be close to one another because they are in the same line of sight.

About half of all stars are binary or multiple stars. A binary is a pair of stars revolving around each other, while multiple stars represent a system of three or more stars revolving around each other. A good example is Mizar (page 239). Casually, we refer to Mizar as a binary star; however it is a multiple star system. In a small telescope at 50x, Mizar can be separated into two stars, known as Mizar A (the actual Mizar) and Mizar B. However, each of these stars has another star revolving around it. This multiple star system has a total of four stars. The two stars that make up Mizar (Mizar A) revolve around each other in 20.5 days while Mizar A and B take about 10,000 years to revolve around each other.

OBSERVING DEEP SKY OBJECTS

Deep sky objects are markedly different from the Planets, Moon and Sun, so they are observed differently. Below are some suggestions for observing these objects. On pages 238−277, I have showcased 25 deep sky objects.

1 Observe deep sky objects when the Moon is not out because the Moon whitewashes the night sky. Many deep sky objects cannot be seen when the Moon is out.

2 Stay away from bright or glaring lights.

3 In the evening, begin your observing when it is dark, after the end of astronomical twilight.

4 Once outside at your observing site, let your eyes dark adapt for a good 15 minutes before observing deep sky objects (see page 52). This will greatly increase your ability to see these fainter objects.

5 To preserve your dark adapted eyes, use only a red flashlight to refer to your reference material or for writing notes. Using a white light flashlight will destroy your night vision.

6 If you have never found a deep sky object, begin with easier objects from my selection — those that are bright and conspicuous, like the Pleiades, Mizar, Albireo, the Great

Sky Objects

Deep Sky Objects

Orion Nebula, the Andromeda Galaxy and M13. Most of the objects on pages 238–277 are fairly easy to find, but some require more diligence than others, like M81/82 and M17.

7 If you continue having difficulty finding deep sky objects, enlist the help of others. If this is not practical, search for these objects with many short sessions over several days, weeks or months instead of long, drawn out sessions.

8 If light pollution is a problem, try observing these objects when they are higher in the sky, near the zenith. Naturally, this will not be possible for the more southern objects like M8, M17 and M20. Or, go observe outside the city.

Using Averted Vision to View Deep Sky Objects
Averted vision is viewing a faint object by looking at it using peripheral vision (look to the side of the object instead of right at it). This technique will greatly enhance your ability to see faint objects. Our eyes have a reduced number of light receptacles in the center of the retina, causing a blind spot for very faint light in this area. This problem does not interfere with our daytime vision.

NOTES FOR DEEP SKY OBJECTS ON PAGES 238–277
I have chosen to highlight 25 of the biggest, brightest and "best" deep sky objects. With a little diligence, everyone should be able to find and observe these objects with binoculars or a small telescope.

Name/Designation
Some celestial objects have become popular enough to have a name (or names) associated with them. In such cases, these names have been provided.

M numbers, NGC numbers, etc. M42 and NGC 1976 are two different designations that refer to the Great Orion Nebula. In astronomy, there are many overlapping nomenclature systems that are used to designate stars and deep sky objects. For deep sky objects, the two most popular designation systems are the Messier (M) numbers and NGC numbers. The M numbers refer to 110 of the brightest deep sky objects as catalogued by Charles Messier in the 1700s. These 110 objects are very popular with

Deep Sky Objects

amateurs because all of them can be seen with a small telescope. The NGC designations are from a listing of 8,000 deep sky objects catalogued by J. L. E. Dreyer in 1888. Most of these objects are galaxies and star clusters. Larger telescopes (12-inch and larger) are needed to view all of the NGC objects.

Arc Degree Size in Sky

This measurement is provided to give you a feel for the size of the object in the sky. I have provided the Moon as a comparison. Many of the 25 objects are as large as or larger than the Moon.

Deep Sky Object Drawings

For several deep sky objects, I have included drawings (in the black circles) to provide a realistic visual appearance of these objects. These drawings were made using a 4-inch refractor and represent the minimum detail that you should see. All of the nebulae and galaxies will appear whitish — no color will be perceived and they will appear faint.

Although I have included numerous photographs of these objects, the photographs, for the most part, provide a much more intense and detailed image than can be viewed through any telescope. However, many of the open clusters look better visually through a telescope or binoculars than in photographs.

Locating Star Charts and Finding Technique

On each deep sky object page, there is a star chart detailing the exact position of the object. These charts have stars mapped to magnitude 6. The Milky Way is indicated as the irregular blue path. Use these charts in conjunction with the Monthly Star Charts to find the objects.

A simple technique for finding deep sky objects is to use basic geometry with the stars. For example, M81/82 is located about twice the bowl diagonal away from the Big Dipper (as indicated on page 239). Use your finderscope to roughly position your telescope in this area and then start moving the telescope back and forth in small steps to locate the galaxies. You will not always succeed, and if you do not, then reposition the telescope and start scanning. Depending on an object's location, I use halves and thirds of distances between bright stars, triangles or squares to help steer me in the right direction to find a deep sky object.

Mizar, Double Star in the Big Dipper

NAME/DESIGNATION: Mizar, Zeta (ζ) Ursae Majoris

DESCRIPTION: Mizar is a well known binary star with an optical counterpart, Alcor. When I was growing up, my next door neighbor said that a measure of good eyesight was being able to see Mizar and Alcor as two stars. Back then, it was easy for me to separate them; today, I need my glasses.

Distances: to Mizar, 78 light years; to Alcor, 81 light years

Magnitudes: +2.3 for Mizar, +3.95 for Mizar's companion, Mizar B and +4.0 for Alcor

Separation between Mizar & Mizar B: 14" (arc seconds) which equates to an actual separation of 334 astronomical units. Revolution period is around 10,000 years.

Summary

Easy to find binary star. Alcor is an optical counterpart.

When to Observe

March through September

Observing

Easy with a telescope around 60x

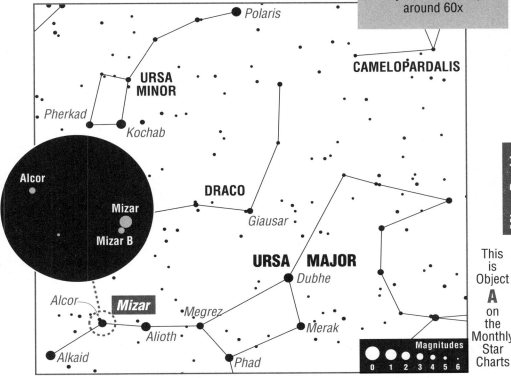

Mizar Double

This is Object **A** on the Monthly Star Charts

Facing page. The Big Dipper in the early morning.

Galaxies in Ursa Major

DESIGNATIONS: M81, NGC 3031; M82, NGC 3034

DESCRIPTION: Pair of very bright galaxies not far from the bowl of the Big Dipper. Both galaxies can be seen in the same eyepiece view at low powers and are visible in light infested areas. M81 is a spiral galaxy that appears ovalish. M82 is irregular, edge-on and cigar shaped. These galaxies are more difficult to locate than most objects in this section because they do not have a conspicuous celestial marker.

Distance to galaxies: 4.5 million light years to M81 and 17 million light years to M82

Diameter of galaxies: 35,000 light years for M81 and 54,000 light years for M82

Arc degree sizes in sky: 0.45° for M81, 0.18° for M82 (Moon is 0.5°)

Summary

Bright galaxies that can be seen in the same eyepiece view. Easy to see even in light polluted skies.

When to Observe

All year

Observing

Telescope at 50x to 100x required. Both can be seen in same eyepiece view at lower magnification.

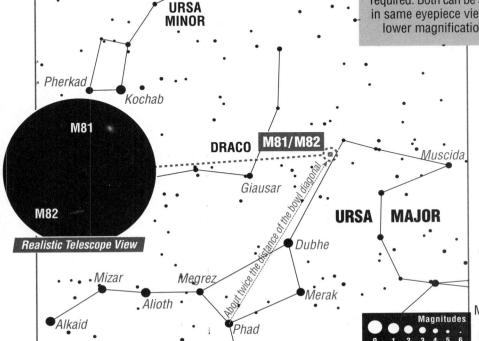

Realistic Telescope View

M81/M82

Magnitudes
0 1 2 3 4 5 6

M81/82 Gal

This is Object **B** on the Monthly Star Charts

Facing page. M81. See top of page 232 for M82.

241

Deep Sky Objects

Double Cluster in Perseus

NAME/DESIGNATIONS: Known as the "Double Cluster." Formal designations are NGC 869 & NGC 884.

DESCRIPTION: Absolutely beautiful sight! A must-see object. Although you can spot these clusters with your eyes and see them through binoculars, you need a telescope at low power to view their glory. NGC 869 is the cluster that has a higher concentration of brighter stars near its center. Can you see the faint red star halfway between the clusters?

Distance to clusters: 7,200 light years to NGC 869 and 7,500 light years to NGC 884

Size of clusters: each has several hundred stars and is about 70 light years across

Arc degree size in sky: together, these two clusters extend about 1° in the sky (2 Moons)

Summary

Must-see object! Two nice clusters side by side in same eyepiece view.

When to Observe

September through March

Observing

Best with a telescope at around 60x

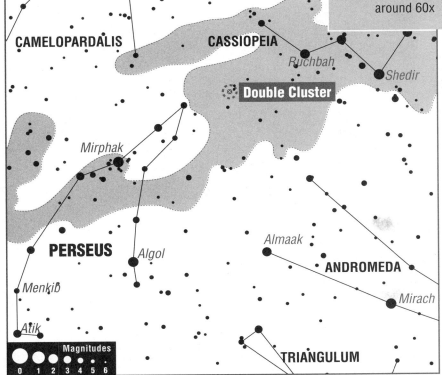

Facing page. The Double Cluster, NGC 884 above and NGC 869 below.

This is Object **C** on the Monthly Star Charts

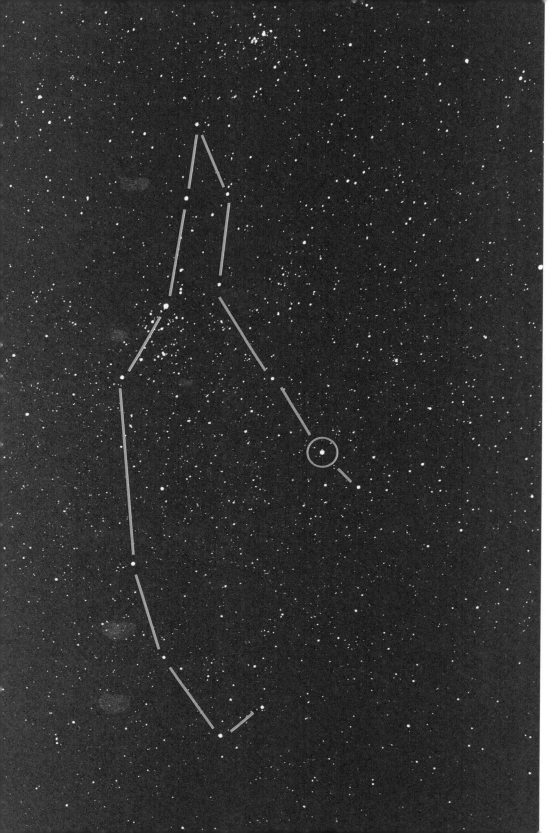

Algol, Variable Star in Perseus

NAME/DESIGNATION: Algol, Beta (β) Persei

DESCRIPTION: Most visible and dramatic variable star in the sky, as its magnitude drops by 1.3 for about two hours every three days. It takes several hours for Algol to fade and brighten. You will need to consult one of the popular monthly astronomy magazines to find exact times when its magnitude dips. These dips are referred to as the Minima of Algol.

Distance to Algol: 93 light years

Type of variable: eclipsing binary with a period of 68 hours, 48.5 minutes

Magnitudes: normally +2.1, minimum +3.4

Summary
Most visible and dramatic variable star

When to Observe
September through March

Observing
Naked eye is adequate

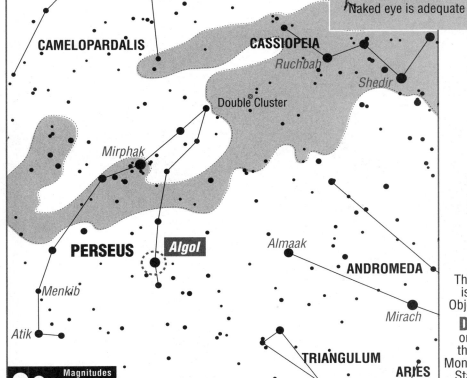

Facing page. The constellation Perseus, Algol circled, Double Cluster at top.

Algol Variable

This is Object **D** on the Monthly Star Charts

Open Clusters in Auriga

DESIGNATIONS: M36, NGC 1960; M37, NGC 2099; M38, NGC 1912

DESCRIPTION: Three clusters in Auriga. All three are visible through binoculars on a moonless night. I like M37 the most because it has a pretty red star amidst many fainter stars. M36 has many bright members, and M38 is the least attractive of the bunch.

Distance to clusters: 4,100 light years to M36, 2,200 light years to M37, 4,200 light years to M38

Sizes of clusters: M36 is 12 light years across with 60 stars, M37 is 19 light years across with nearly 2,000 stars and M38 is 18 light years across with 120 stars

Arc degree sizes in sky: 0.17° for M36, 0.25° for M37, 0.25° for M38 (Moon is 0.5°)

Summary
Three nice clusters that intertwine with Auriga

When to Observe
November through April

Observing
Visible with binoculars on moonless nights.
All 3 good with telescope around 60x.

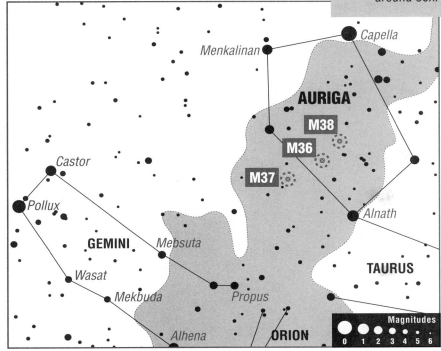

Aur Clusters

These are Objects **E,F,G** on the Monthly Star Charts

Facing page. Extreme closeup of M37.

247

Open Cluster in Gemini

DESIGNATIONS: M35, NGC 2168

DESCRIPTION: This cluster is easy to find and remember because it is at the foot of Gemini. M35 is a favorite because it is large, open, and has many bright members. If you look carefully, you may see a smaller, fainter cluster (NGC 2158) about a Moon's diameter from the center of M35. Auriga is right next to Gemini, so take some time to compare the size and brightness of M36, M37 and M38 with M35.

Distance to cluster: 2,800 light years

Size of cluster: spans 21 light years with 200 to 300 stars

Arc degree size in sky: 0.42° (Moon is 0.5°)

Summary
Large, pretty, easy to find open cluster with many bright stars

When to Observe
December through April

Observing
Visible with binoculars. Nice with a telescope from 50x to 100x.

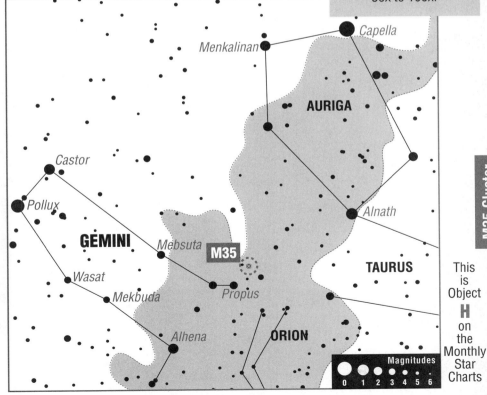

M35 Cluster

This is Object **H** on the Monthly Star Charts

Facing page. M35 with a hint of NGC 2158 to the lower left of the cluster.

249

Pleiades in Taurus

NAMES/DESIGNATION: Pleiades, Seven Sisters, M45

DESCRIPTION: Most prominent naked eye star cluster in the sky. Almost everyone has heard of the Pleiades. I frequently hear people refer to this cluster as a little dipper. While its shape is similar, it is *not* The Little Dipper. The seven sisters are the daughters of Atlas and Pleione. They were changed into doves and sent into the heavens as stars to avoid the amorous clutches of Orion. Thus, the Pleiades always rise before Orion, forever escaping him.

Distance to cluster: 407 light years

Size of cluster: spans 14 light years with 100 stars

Arc degree size in sky: 2° (4 Moon diameters)

Summary
Bright, pretty, easy to see with naked eye

When to Observe
October through March

Observing
Best with binoculars

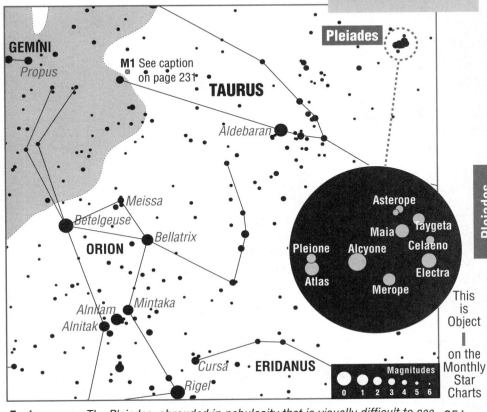

Pleiades

GEMINI
Propus

M1 See caption on page 231

TAURUS

Aldebaran

Asterope

Maia   Taygeta

Meissa

Betelgeuse

Bellatrix

ORION

Pleione   Alcyone   Celaeno

Electra

Atlas   Merope

Alnitam   Mintaka

Alnitak

Cursa   ERIDANUS

Rigel

Magnitudes
0 1 2 3 4 5 6

Pleiades

This is Object

I

on the Monthly Star Charts

Facing page. The Pleiades, shrouded in nebulosity that is visually difficult to see. 251

Great Orion Nebula

NAMES/DESIGNATIONS: Great Orion Nebula, Great Nebula, Orion Nebula, M42, NGC 1234

DESCRIPTION: Most prominent and spectacular emission nebula in the sky. Visible to the naked eye and easily seen in light infested areas. Even small telescopes will reveal subtle details and wisps. Most of its luminosity is fueled by the stimulation of the gas from four central stars known as the Trapezium, which are only a million years old. New stars are being formed and born in the Orion nebula.

Distance to nebula: 1,500 light years

Size of nebula: spans 39 light years

Arc degree size in sky: 1.5° at its widest
(3 Moon diameters)

Summary
Bright, very large, easy to find.
Best nebula in sky.

When to Observe
November through March

Observing
Visible with naked eye and binoculars.
Nice with a telescope at 40x to 100x. Need at least 50x to see the Trapezium.

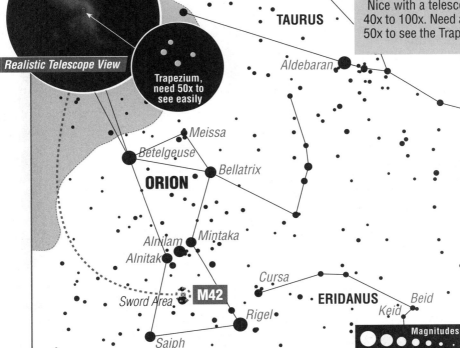

Realistic Telescope View

Trapezium, need 50x to see easily

TAURUS

Aldebaran

Meissa

Betelgeuse

Bellatrix

ORION

Alnilam *Mintaka*

Alnitak

Cursa

Sword Area **M42**

ERIDANUS *Beid*

Rigel *Keid*

Saiph

Magnitudes
0 1 2 3 4 5 6

Orion Nebula

This is Object **J** on the Monthly Star Charts

Facing page. *The Great Orion Nebula.*

253

Deep Sky Objects

Little Beehive in Canis Major

NAME/DESIGNATIONS: Little Beehive, M41, NGC 2287

DESCRIPTION: A good example of an open cluster. Easy to see because stars are sparse in this area, so this cluster pops out when you come across it. All clusters have their own characteristics. This one is more open and evenly spread out than most. M41 is an easy hop from the Great Orion Nebula.

Distance to cluster: 2,100 light years

Size of cluster: spans 24 light years with 80 stars

Arc degree size in sky: 0.67° (Moon is 0.5°)

Summary
Cluster pops out at you because it is in a sparse star area of the sky

When to Observe
December through April

Observing
Visible with binoculars as a hazy patch.
Nice with a telescope from 50x to 100x.

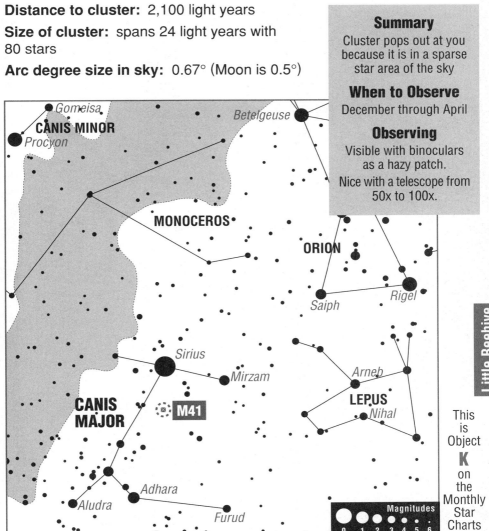

This is Object **K** on the Monthly Star Charts

Little Beehive

Facing page. *The Little Beehive, surrounded by more stars than you will see.*

255

Andromeda Galaxy

NAME/DESIGNATIONS: Andromeda Galaxy, M31, NGC 224

DESCRIPTION: This galaxy spans over six Moon diameters in the sky. However, the easily visible central portion spans only about two Moon diameters. The central area appears as a faint, softly glowing oval and can be seen with the naked eye even in light polluted areas. The Andromeda galaxy and our Milky Way galaxy are part of a group of 30 galaxies called the Local Group. Not far from M31 is M32, a very visible, small, elliptical companion galaxy to M31.

Distance to galaxy: 2.3 million light years

Diameter of galaxy: 120,000 light years

Arc degree size in sky: 3° x 1°
(6 by 2 Moon diameters)

Summary
Largest appearing galaxy in the sky!

When to Observe
September through February

Observing
Visible to the naked eye. Best with binoculars. Use low powers with telescope, 20x to 50x.

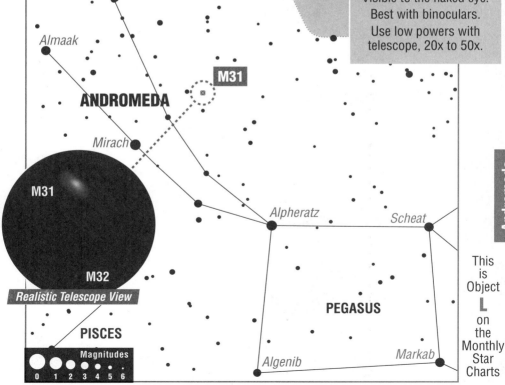

Almaak

ANDROMEDA

M31

Mirach

M31

M32

Realistic Telescope View

PISCES

Magnitudes
0 1 2 3 4 5 6

Alpheratz

Scheat

PEGASUS

Algenib

Markab

Andromeda

This is Object **L** on the Monthly Star Charts

Facing page. M31 with M32 on the galaxy's edge and M110 at the top right.

Beehive Cluster in Cancer

NAMES/DESIGNATIONS: Beehive Cluster, Praesepe, M44, NGC 2632

DESCRIPTION: Nice open cluster visible to the naked eye. This cluster is similar in size to the Pleiades but its stars are much fainter, so it appears as a fuzzy patch in the sky. Easy to locate with binoculars, it is about halfway between Regulus in Leo and Pollux in Gemini. Like the Pleiades, I like to stare at this cluster through my binoculars because these stars appear as though they are suspended in front of me. With binoculars attached to a tripod, you can leisurely look at this cluster. This is one of several clusters that looks better visually than in photographs.

Distance to cluster: 515 light years

Size of cluster: spans 11 light years with 200 stars

Arc degree size in sky: 1.2° (Moon is 0.5°)

Summary
Easy to find fuzzy patch in the sky that opens up with binoculars

When to Observe
January through May

Observing
Visible to the naked eye. Best with binoculars. Use low powers with telescope, 20x to 50x.

Beehive

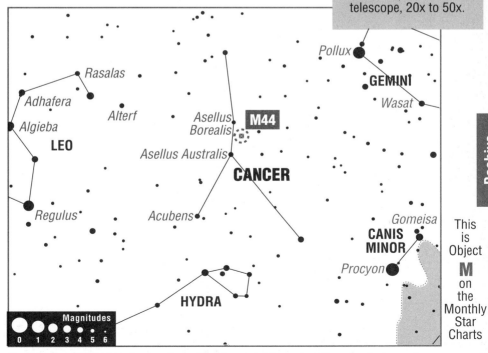

This is Object **M** on the Monthly Star Charts

Facing page. *M44 looks much prettier through binoculars than in photographs.*

Deep Sky Objects

Globular Clusters in Hercules

NAME/DESIGNATIONS: Great Hercules Cluster, M13, NGC 6205; M92, NGC 6341

DESCRIPTION: The globular cluster M13 is the largest and brightest northern globular cluster. It is easy to find because it straddles one side of Hercules' Keystone. M13 has always been a favorite to amateur astronomers. M92 always takes a back seat to M13; however, it is a spectacular globular cluster with a bright center.

Distance to clusters: 23,400 light years to M13, 25,400 light years to M92

Diameter of clusters: 143 light years for M13 and 103 light years for M92

Arc degree sizes in sky: 0.35° for M13, 0.23° for M92 (Moon is 0.5°)

Summary
Two bright and easy to find globular clusters in the same constellation

When to Observe
May through September

Observing
Both visible with binoculars.
Best with a telescope at around 100x.

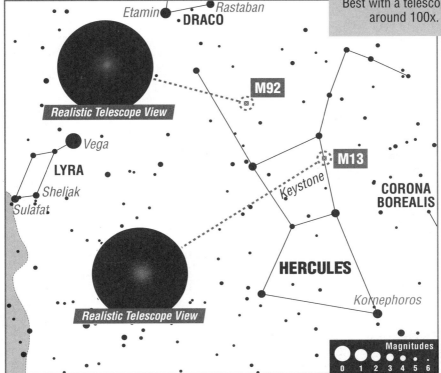

Realistic Telescope View

Etamin • DRACO • Rastaban

M92

Vega

LYRA

Sheliak

Sulafat

Realistic Telescope View

Keystone

M13

CORONA BOREALIS

HERCULES

Kornephoros

Magnitudes
0 1 2 3 4 5 6

Her Globulars

These
are
Objects
N & O
on
the
Monthly
Star
Charts

Facing page. M92, the globular cluster that takes a back seat to M13.

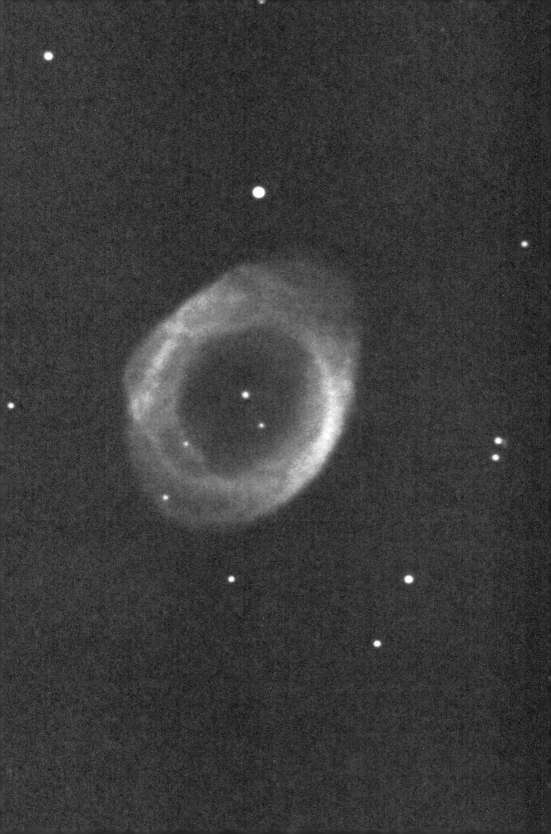

Deep Sky Objects

Ring Nebula in Lyra

NAME/DESIGNATIONS: Ring Nebula, M57, NGC 6720

DESCRIPTION: Almost everyone has seen a picture of the Ring Nebula. This planetary nebula represents the remnants of a dying star. *It is* an actual ring that just happens to be face-on toward Earth. M57 appears very small and faint compared to the other objects featured in this section; but it can be seen even in light polluted skies. Fortunately, this little wonder is easy to find because it lies between the two end stars in Lyra.

Distance to nebula: 1,140 light years

Size of nebula: 0.42 light years across, which is 335 times larger than the diameter of our Solar System

Arc degree size in sky: 76" (1.3' or 0.02°), which is about twice the size that Jupiter normally appears in a telescope, although M57 seems smaller than Jupiter because of its low luminosity

Summary
Small, faint ring that is easy to find and can be seen in light polluted skies

When to Observe
May through November

Observing
Telescope needed at 50x to 100x

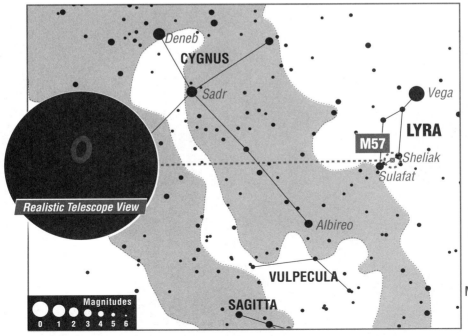

Ring Nebula

This is Object **P** on the Monthly Star Charts

Facing page. Closeup of the Ring Nebula.

263

Deep Sky Objects

Albireo, Double Star in Cygnus

NAME/DESIGNATION: Albireo, Beta (β) Cygni

DESCRIPTION: Most beautiful double star pair because of their colors, gold and blue. This double star is easy to find because it is the bottom of the Northern Cross, part of Cygnus the Swan. With the naked eye and through binoculars, this pair looks like a single star, so a telescope at low power is needed to separate them and to allow an observer to appreciate their colors. Gold colored Albireo has a diameter 50 times greater, and its blue companion about 1.5 times greater than the Sun. Astronomers are not sure whether these two stars revolve around each other.

Summary
Prettiest pair of stars because of their colors, gold and blue

When to Observe
May through November

Observing Tips
Telescope needed. Stars can be separated at 20x, but best around 80x.

Distance to stars: 385 light years

Separation of stars: 400 astronomical units

Magnitudes: gold Albireo +2, blue companion +7

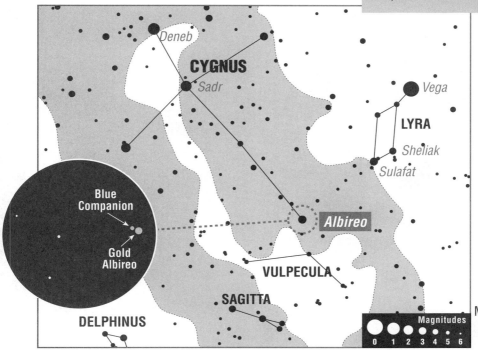

Facing page. The Northern Cross and Albireo, swathed in the Milky Way.

This is Object **Q** on the Monthly Star Charts

265

Deep Sky Objects

Omega Centauri Globular Cluster

NAME/DESIGNATION: Omega (ω) Centauri, NGC 5139

DESCRIPTION: Largest globular cluster in our skies. Omega Centauri often goes unnoticed because it can only be easily seen south of latitude 35° N (about the bottom of Tennessee) and then for only a few months around spring. Use binoculars to scan for Omega Centauri, due south and just above the horizon during May and June after it gets dark at the end of astronomical twilight. It will look like a faint cottonball. In Miami, it reaches 15° above the southern horizon.

Distance to cluster: 18,250 light years

Diameter of cluster: 350 light years

Arc degree size in sky: 1.1° (Moon is 0.5°)

Summary
Awesome. Largest globular cluster in the sky. Most visible in US from southern states.

When to Observe
April through June

Observing
Visible with naked eye. To find, scan southern horizon with binoculars. Nice in telescope at 50x to 100x.

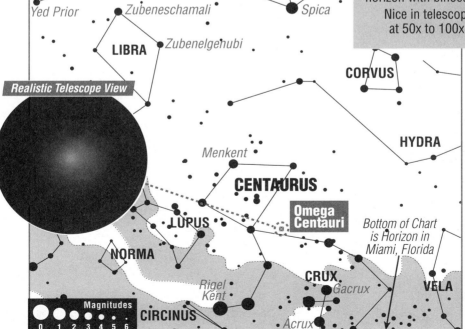

Realistic Telescope View

SERPENS · Unukalhai · VIRGO · Syrma · Spica · Yed Prior · Zubeneschamali · Zubenelgenubi · LIBRA · CORVUS · HYDRA · Menkent · CENTAURUS · Omega Centauri · Bottom of Chart is Horizon in Miami, Florida · LUPUS · NORMA · CRUX · Gacrux · VELA · Rigel Kent · CIRCINUS · Acrux

Magnitudes 0 1 2 3 4 5 6

Omega Cent

This is Object **R** on the Monthly Star Charts

Facing page. *Omega Centauri.*

Deep Sky Objects

Globular Cluster in Scorpius

DESIGNATIONS: M4, NGC 6121

DESCRIPTION: This globular cluster is easy to find because it is near the bright, 1st magnitude Antares. Fainter and more irregular than M13, this cluster is divided in half by a dark lane next to a faint line of stars. It is brighter on one side of the line than on the other. Use averted vision to see the line. With my 4-inch telescope, I find it difficult to see individual stars in M4. Many stars surround this cluster.

Distance to cluster: 6,888 light years

Diameter of cluster: 69 light years

Arc degree size in sky: 0.58° (Moon is 0.5°)

Summary
Bright, large, easy to find because it is next to Antares

When to Observe
June through September

Observing
Easy with binoculars. Best with a telescope at around 100x.

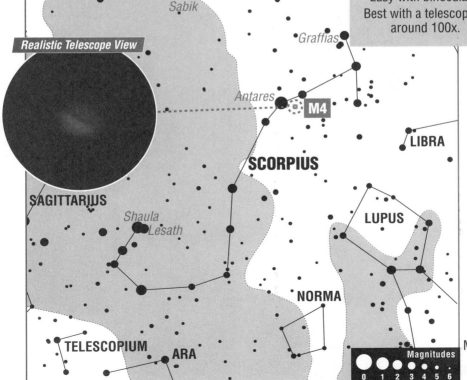

Realistic Telescope View

OPHIUCHUS
Sabik
Graffias
Antares — M4
LIBRA
SCORPIUS
SAGITTARIUS
Shaula
Lesath
LUPUS
NORMA
TELESCOPIUM
ARA
Magnitudes
0 1 2 3 4 5 6

M4 Globular

This is Object **S** on the Monthly Star Charts

Facing page. *M4, and Antares to the upper right. Note the line of stars in M4.*

Deep Sky Objects

Star Clusters in Scorpius

DESIGNATIONS: NGC 6231 and Trumpler 24

DESCRIPTION: Here are two neighboring, contrasting clusters. They are easy to find because they are very close to Zeta (ζ) Scorpii (which actually consists of three stars). Turn your binoculars toward Zeta Scorpii and the very spectacular, bright stars of NGC 6231 will pop out at you. On a line from Zeta Scorpii through NGC 6231 lies Trumpler 24, a large, spread out cluster with many faint members. Trumpler 24 is named after astronomer Robert Trumpler, who studied and catalogued star clusters in the early 1900s.

Distance to clusters: 5,800 light years

Size of clusters: NGC 6231 spans 24 light years, Trumpler 24 spans over 152 light years

Arc degree sizes in sky: 0.67° for NGC 6231, 1.5° for Trumpler 24 (Moon is 0.5°)

Summary
Beautiful and easy to find because clusters are next to Zeta Scorpii

When to Observe
June through September

Observing
NGC 6231 nice with binoculars.
For Trumpler 24, use telescope at low powers, 20x to 50x.

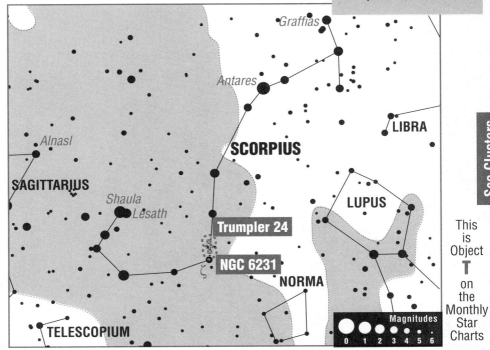

Sco Clusters

This is Object **T** on the Monthly Star Charts

Facing page. NGC 6231 is to the right and below center. Above it is Trumpler 24.

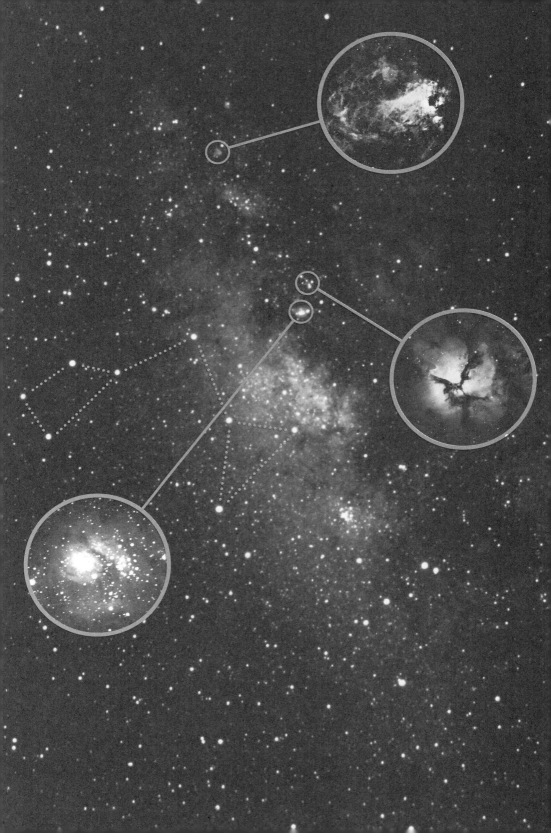

Omega Nebula in Sagittarius

NAMES/DESIGNATIONS: Omega Nebula, Horseshoe Nebula, Swan Nebula, M17, NGC 6618

DESCRIPTION: A bright, long patch of nebulosity with a hook on one end. This emission nebula is more striking and noticeable than its southern neighbors, M8 and M20. Unfortunately, M17 is more difficult to find because there are no conspicuous celestial markers. This area is saturated with Messier objects and you will probably encounter several in your search for the Omega Nebula.

Distance to nebula: 4,890 light years

Size of nebula: 57 light years across

Arc degree size in sky: 0.67° (Moon is 0.5°)

Summary
Bright, large, easy to spot with binoculars

When to Observe
June through October

Observing
Visible with binoculars but nice with a telescope at around 60x

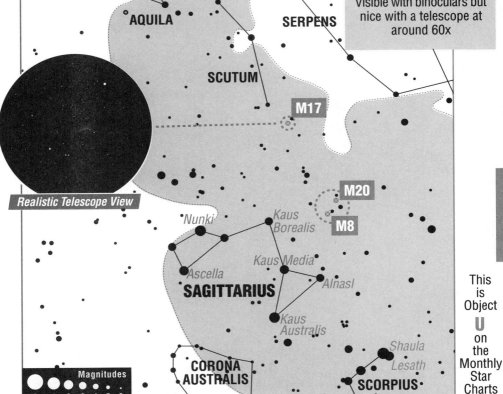

Realistic Telescope View

AQUILA SERPENS SCUTUM M17 M20 M8 Nunki Kaus Borealis Kaus Media Alnasl Ascella SAGITTARIUS Kaus Australis Shaula Lesath CORONA AUSTRALIS SCORPIUS

Magnitudes
0 1 2 3 4 5 6

Omega Neb

This is Object **U** on the Monthly Star Charts

Facing page. *From top to bottom, M17, M20 & M8.*

Deep Sky Objects

Trifid Nebula in Sagittarius

NAMES/DESIGNATIONS: Trifid Nebula, Clover, M20, NGC 6514

DESCRIPTION: In photographs, this red and blue nebula appears to be divided by dark lanes into three sections, giving it the name Trifid. Neither the divisions nor the colors can be seen in a small telescope. M20 is faint and more difficult to see than its neighbor, M8, two eyepiece views to the south. About one eyepiece view "up" from M20 is M21, a small, compact open cluster that comes alive with averted vision. Both M8 and M20 appear as a single large, bright patch in binoculars.

Distance to nebula: 5,000 light years

Size of nebula: 29 light years across

Arc degree size in sky: 0.33° (Moon is 0.5°)

Summary
Easy to find, but faint

When to Observe
June through September

Observing
Visible in binoculars but nice with a telescope around 60x

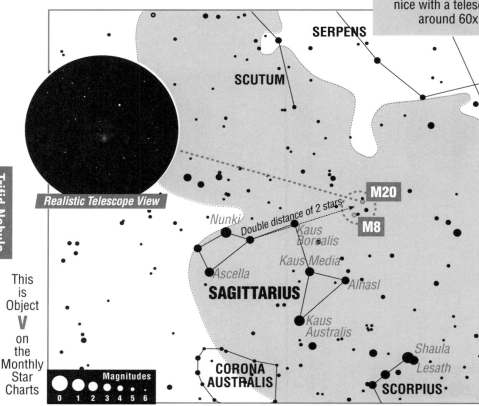

Realistic Telescope View

SERPENS

SCUTUM

M20

Double distance of 2 stars

M8

Nunki

Kaus Borealis

Kaus Media

Alnasl

Ascella

SAGITTARIUS

Kaus Australis

Shaula

Lesath

CORONA AUSTRALIS

SCORPIUS

Magnitudes
0 1 2 3 4 5 6

This is Object **V** on the Monthly Star Charts

Trifid Nebula

See page 272 for a photograph of M20.

Lagoon Nebula in Sagittarius

NAME/DESIGNATIONS: Lagoon Nebula, M8, NGC 6523

DESCRIPTION: Very large and fairly bright emission nebula in the thicket of the Milky Way. With binoculars, the Lagoon nebula, together with the Trifid, look like a large, bright patch. In fact, they appear brighter in binoculars than through a telescope. M8 is visually unique because it is nested in a cluster of stars. Take some time to study this nebula. You should see an abundance of faint nebulosity along with some dark lanes.

Distance to nebula: 5,200 light years

Size of nebula: 136 light years across

Arc degree size in sky: 1.5° (3 Moon diameters)

Summary

Very large, conspicuous nebula that looks like a large patch of the Milky Way in binoculars

When to Observe

June through September

Observing

Visible in binoculars and nice with a telescope at around 60x

Realistic Telescope View

AQUILA

SERPENS

SCUTUM

M20

M8

Nunki

Double distance of 2 stars

Kaus Borealis

Kaus Media

Ascella

Alnasl

SAGITTARIUS

Kaus Australis

Shaula

Lesath

CORONA AUSTRALIS

SCORPIUS

Magnitudes
0 1 2 3 4 5 6

Lagoon Neb

This is Object **W** on the Monthly Star Charts

See page 272 for a photograph of M8.

Globular Cluster in Sagittarius

DESIGNATIONS: M22, NGC 6656

DESCRIPTION: This is my favorite globular cluster. It hangs beautifully in the sky and has a glow unlike any of the others. I often stare at M22 through my 4-inch telescope. I can see a multitude of stars speckled against a background haze of unresolvable fainter stars. It is a beautiful sight. M22 is in the thickest part of the Milky Way which is saturated with stars, clusters and nebulae. If you scan this area with binoculars or a telescope, you will no doubt encounter many of these objects.

Distance to cluster: 10,100 light years

Diameter of cluster: 96 light years

Arc degree size in sky: 0.55° (Moon is 0.5°)

Summary
Large, bright, pretty globular that is easy to find

When to Observe
June through October

Observing
Visible with binoculars. Best with a telescope at 70x to 100x.

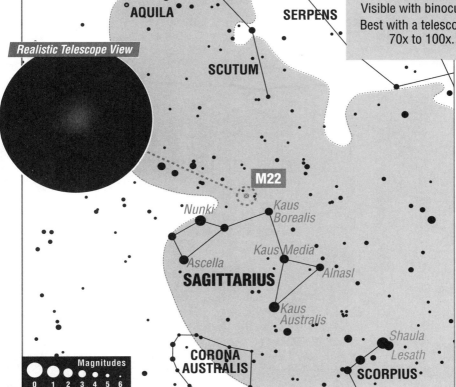

Realistic Telescope View

AQUILA
SERPENS
SCUTUM
M22
Nunki
Kaus Borealis
Kaus Media
Ascella
Alnasl
SAGITTARIUS
Kaus Australis
Shaula
Lesath
CORONA AUSTRALIS
SCORPIUS

Magnitudes
0 1 2 3 4 5 6

M22 Globular

This is Object **X** on the Monthly Star Charts

Facing page. M22 and the surrounding area.

Time and Practices

Our concept of time is rooted in the day, created from the rotation of the Earth on its axis. However, it is the "movement" of the Sun through the sky and the cycles of day and night that provide us with the sense of passing time.

I think one of humankind's most ingenious ideas was the division of the day into 24 hours, the hours into 60 minutes and the minutes into 60 seconds (seconds are further divided into tenths). With these divisions, the day can be divided into half, thirds and quarters, and the hours and minutes further divided into fifths and tenths. All of this adds up to incredible flexibility in dividing our time into convenient intervals. Although I applaud the metric system for its simplicity, it would be awkward to base our system of time on divisions of ten because decimal numbers would have to be used for many of our current divisions.

Dividing the day into 24 hours and the hours and minutes into 60 parts was pure inspiration.

The measurement of time has become very sophisticated. Today, the highest accuracy obtained is a one second error in two million years. And, as with most technological advances, this will be further refined in the years to come.

Time, Divisions & Practices

Apparent Solar Time. This is the time that is indicated on a sundial. It would be impractical to use Apparent Solar Time because cities or towns just a short distance apart would have slightly different times.

Standard Time Zones. The Earth is divided into 24 time zones, each 15° wide in longitude. Everyone in a time zone sets their clocks to the same time. The time difference between adjacent time zones is one hour. In the middle of the oceans, the time zone boundaries are straight vertical lines; however, over populated land, they are often redefined to take into account political, economical and social considerations. The continental United States is spanned by four standard time zones.

Facing page. Where time begins. The prime meridian or 0° longitude at the Old Royal Observatory in Greenwich, England, just outside of London.

Time

Universal Time

Standard Time or Local Standard Time. The time on our clocks which is based on the 24 standard time zones as defined above.

Daylight-Savings Time (DST). The practice of advancing the clocks from Standard Time by one hour from the first Sunday in April to the last Saturday in October (in the US). DST is sometimes referred to as Summer Time. Most, but not all of the world changes its clocks to Daylight-Savings Time. This practice of changing the clocks has been a societal decision. The following locations in North America do not observe DST: Hawaii; most of Arizona; most of Indiana; most of Saskatchewan, Canada; Puerto Rico; Virgin Islands and most of Mexico.

Universal Time (UT). Astronomical events are expressed in Universal Time, which is the Standard Time at the Old Royal Observatory in Greenwich, England. The location of the Old Royal Observatory was chosen to be longitude 0° in 1884. The beginning of every new day starts here.

Universal Time is not adjusted for Daylight-Savings Time. Expressed using the 24-hour clock, Universal Time must be converted to obtain Local Standard Time.

Coordinated Universal Time (UTC). In North America, the WWV radio station in Fort Collins, Colorado and the CHU radio station in Ottawa, Ontario, Canada broadcast Universal Time 24 hours a day on shortwave radio frequencies. The broadcasting of this time is known as Coordinated Universal Time. The abbreviation UTC was adopted from the French word order.

These radio broadcasts use tones to mark the seconds and have an automated voice announcement at the beginning of each minute.

Coordinated Universal Time Broadcast Frequencies

Signal Origination	Station and Location	Shortwave Broadcast Frequencies
US	WWV at Fort Collins, Colorado	2.5, 5, 10 & 20 MHz
Canada	CHU at Ottawa, Ontario	3.330, 7.335 & 14.670 MHz

Twilight

Amateur and professional astronomers use UTC to accurately record astronomical events. Additionally, many home clocks incorporate radio receivers that quietly and automatically adjust the clock's time using the UTC signals.

Greenwich Mean Time (GMT). Universal Time was originally referred to as Greenwich Mean Time. The term Universal Time was adopted in 1928 by the International Astronomical Union. UT is still occasionally referred to as GMT.

Twilight, Dawn & Dusk

Twilight is the time before sunrise and after sunset. It represents the transition period between day and night. Before sunrise, the twilight period is commonly referred to as dawn and after sunset it is called dusk. Twilight is caused by the scattering of sunlight from the atmosphere. There are three recognized twilight periods which are described below.

Civil Twilight. The period beginning at sunset and ending when the Sun is 6 arc angle degrees (12 Sun diameters) below the horizon. In the morning, before the Sun rises, Civil twilight begins when the Sun is 6 degrees below the horizon and ends at sunrise. Civil twilight is the last or first time of the day when normal daylight activities can be conducted.

Twilight Rules of Thumb

CIVIL Twilight	**Ends 30 minutes after Sunset** *Starts 30 minutes before Sunrise*
NAUTICAL Twilight	**Ends 60 minutes after Sunset** *Starts 60 minutes before Sunrise*
ASTRONOMICAL Twilight	**Ends 90 minutes after Sunset** *Starts 90 minutes before Sunrise*

Nautical Twilight. Begins in the morning or ends in the evening when the the Sun is 12 degrees below the horizon. The horizon at sea is not visible when the Sun is 12 degrees below the horizon. The brighter stars and planets are noticeable at this time.

Astronomical Twilight. The Sun must be 18 degrees below the horizon for Astronomical twilight to end in the evening and

Changing UT to Local Standard Time

begin in the morning. When the Sun is 18 or more degrees below the horizon, everyone would agree it is night and all astronomical objects are visible.

Working with Universal Time (UT)
If you read any astronomical literature, including the popular monthly astronomy magazines, you will quickly discover that Universal Time is used to express the occurrence of astronomical events. This is done to avoid confusion with time zones. But, what is the equivalent local standard time for your location? Depending on the actual Universal Time, and your location, you could witness an astronomical event as much as a day before the Universal Time noted for the event.

There are several factors that must be taken into consideration when changing Universal Time to local standard time. First is the Time Zone difference between your location and Greenwich. Second is the consideration for Daylight-Savings Time. Third is that the local standard time date may be one day prior to the UT date; and lastly, 24-hour UT time must be converted to 12-hour time.

Changing UT to Local Standard Time

a **From the last Sunday in October to the first Saturday in April**, find your location on the map on page 283 and note the BLUE Time Zone number.

b **From the first Sunday in April to the last Saturday in October**, note the **BLACK DST number** in parentheses if your location observes Daylight-Savings Time (DST).

c Subtract the Time Zone number (or DST number) from the Universal Time. Subtract whole hours only.

d If the Time Zone number is larger that the UT hour, then first add 24 to the UT hour and then subtract the Time Zone number from this larger number. When 24 is added to the UT time, the *date* of the local standard time will be *one day prior* to the UT date.

e Use the conversion table on page 284 to change 24-hour to 12-hour time.

Standard Time Zones

Universal Time Zone Differences

The numbers below the Time Zones indicate the difference in hours of Local Standard Time from Universal Time. *The number in parentheses is the difference during Daylight-Savings Time.*

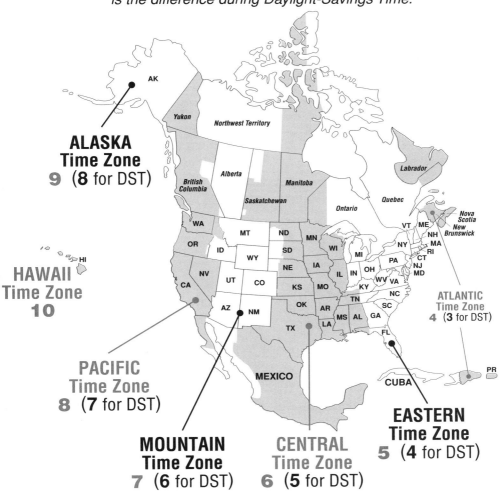

ALASKA Time Zone
9 (**8** for DST)

HAWAII Time Zone
10

PACIFIC Time Zone
8 (**7** for DST)

MOUNTAIN Time Zone
7 (**6** for DST)

CENTRAL Time Zone
6 (**5** for DST)

EASTERN Time Zone
5 (**4** for DST)

ATLANTIC Time Zone
4 (**3** for DST)

TO CHANGE...Universal Time (UT) to your Local Standard Time, *subtract* the *BLUE number* for your Time Zone from the UT. *Use the DST number* (Daylight-Savings Time number) from the first Sunday in April to the last Saturday in October.

The following locations do not observe Daylight-Savings Time: Hawaii, Most of Arizona, Most of Indiana, Most of Saskatchewan, Puerto Rico, Virgin Islands, Most of Mexico

Changing UT

Changing UT to Local Standard Time

24-Hour to 12-Hour Conversion Chart

24 Hour	12 Hour
0^1	12 MIDNIGHT[2]
1	1 A.M.
2	2 A.M.
3	3 A.M.
4	4 A.M.
5	5 A.M.
6	6 A.M.
7	7 A.M.
8	8 A.M.
9	9 A.M.
10	10 A.M.
11	11 A.M.
12	12 NOON[2]
13	1 P.M.
14	2 P.M.
15	3 P.M.
16	4 P.M.
17	5 P.M.
18	6 P.M.
19	7 P.M.
20	8 P.M.
21	9 P.M.
22	10 P.M.
23	11 P.M.

[1]Although 0 hour & 12 midnight represent the same time, the date of 12 midnight is one day prior to 0 hour. [2]You may encounter differing uses of A.M. and P.M. associated with Noon and Midnight in different sources.

Basic Example

Change the UT of August 4, 19:56 to local standard time if you are in New York.
Answer: August 4, 3:56 P.M.

1 Look up the Time Zone number on page 283 for New York (in this case, use the DST number) → **4**

2 Subtract 4 from 19:56
→ $19:56 - 4 = \textbf{15:56}$

3 Change 15:56 to 12-hour time by referring to the chart on this page
→ 15:56 = **3:56 P.M.**

4 Date does not have to be changed because the Time Zone number is less than the UT hour of 19.

Date Change Example

Change the UT of April 1, 2:38 to local standard time if you are in San Diego.
Answer: March 31, 6:38 P.M.

1 Look up the Time Zone number on page 283 for San Diego → **8**

2 You cannot subtract 8 from 2:38 because 8 is larger than 2, so add 24 to 2:38 → **26:38**

3 Now subtract 8 from 26:38
→ $26:38 - 8 = \textbf{18:38}$

4 Change 18:38 to 12-hour time by referring to the chart on this page
→ 18:38 = **6:38 P.M.**

5 **Date changes to March 31** because subtracting 8 from 2:38 UT backs into the previous day. Whenever you add 24 to the UT, the local date will always be one day prior to the UT date.

Changing UT to Local Standard Time

Practical Example

You will be visiting a friend just outside Chicago during the first half of October. Hoping for clear skies, you want to observe the variable star Algol dim to magnitude 3.4 (see page 245 in the Deep Sky Object section of this field guide). You consult the popular monthly astronomy magazine *Sky & Telescope* and find that for the first part of October, Algol will reach minima on the following dates and times:

Minima of Algol from *Sky & Telescope*	Chicago Time Zone	UT Converted to Local Standard Time
October 3, 4:05 UT	−5	October 2, 11:05 P.M.
October 6, 0:54 UT	−5	October 5, 7:54 P.M.
October 8, 21:43 UT	−5	October 8, 4:43 P.M.
October 11, 18:31 UT	−5	October 11, 1:31 P.M.

Will you be able to observe Algol dim? By converting the four UT dates, you discover that October 2nd and 5th are the only dates that will allow viewing of the minima. The other minima occur during daylight. On October 5th, the Sun sets at 5:30 P.M. and astronomical twilight ends around 7 P.M., which will, weather permitting, provide a good hour to view Algol's magnitude dip from its binary partner. If the weather is nice, you can sit outside in a chair and leisurely watch Algol since it will be low in the sky. Or, you could stay up later on the 2nd and observe the complete cycle with Algol higher up in the sky.

Using the Sunrise & Sunset Tables

Table Explanations

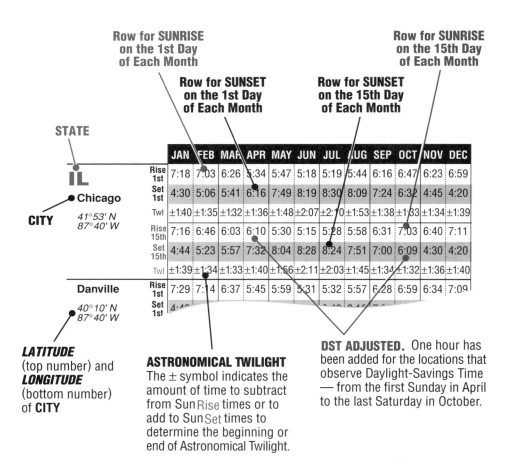

Row for SUNRISE on the 1st Day of Each Month

Row for SUNRISE on the 15th Day of Each Month

Row for SUNSET on the 1st Day of Each Month

Row for SUNSET on the 15th Day of Each Month

STATE

IL

● **Chicago**

CITY *41°53' N 87°40' W*

		JAN	FEB	MAR	APR	MAY	JUN	JUL	AUG	SEP	OCT	NOV	DEC
	Rise 1st	7:18	7:03	6:26	5:34	5:47	5:18	5:19	5:44	6:16	6:47	6:23	6:59
	Set 1st	4:30	5:06	5:41	6:16	7:49	8:19	8:30	8:09	7:24	6:32	4:45	4:20
	Twl	±1:40	±1:35	±1:32	±1:36	±1:48	±2:07	±2:10	±1:53	±1:38	±1:33	±1:34	±1:39
	Rise 15th	7:16	6:46	6:03	6:10	5:30	5:15	5:28	5:58	6:31	7:03	6:40	7:11
	Set 15th	4:44	5:23	5:57	7:32	8:04	8:28	8:24	7:51	7:00	6:09	4:30	4:20
	Twl	±1:39	±1:34	±1:33	±1:40	±1:56	±2:11	±2:03	±1:45	±1:34	±1:32	±1:36	±1:40
Danville	Rise 1st	7:29	7:14	6:37	5:45	5:59	5:31	5:32	5:57	6:28	6:59	6:34	7:09
40°10' N 87°40' W	Set 1st	4:4											

LATITUDE (top number) and **LONGITUDE** (bottom number) of **CITY**

ASTRONOMICAL TWILIGHT The ± symbol indicates the amount of time to subtract from Sun Rise times or to add to Sun Set times to determine the beginning or end of Astronomical Twilight.

DST ADJUSTED. One hour has been added for the locations that observe Daylight-Savings Time — from the first Sunday in April to the last Saturday in October.

NOTES: The sunrise and sunset times in these tables are accurate to within a few minutes. The exact time of sunrise and sunset is dependent on your location and varies because of leap year and atmospheric refraction. These tables were designed to provide reasonable accuracy for determining the beginning and end of the day. Cities were selected based on population as well as geographic considerations.

Sunrises & Sunsets

Alabama/Alaska

		JAN	FEB	MAR	APR	MAY	JUN	JUL	AUG	SEP	OCT	NOV	DEC
AL **Birmingham**	Rise 1st	6:52	6:44	6:16	5:35	5:59	5:38	5:41	6:00	6:21	6:42	6:06	6:33
	Set 1st	4:50	5:19	5:44	6:08	7:30	7:52	8:01	7:47	7:13	6:32	4:55	4:39
33°31' N 86°50' W	Twl	±1:33	±1:27	±127	±129	±1:37	±1:47	±1:49	±1:40	±1:30	±1:27	±1:29	±1:32
	Rise 15th	6:52	6:31	5:58	6:17	5:47	5:37	5:48	6:10	6:31	6:52	6:19	6:44
	Set 15th	5:02	5:32	5:55	7:18	7:41	7:59	7:58	7:33	6:54	6:14	4:45	4:41
	Twl	±1:32	±1:27	±1:27	±1:32	±1:42	±1:49	±1:45	±1:36	±1:28	±1:27	±1:30	±1:33
Mobile	Rise 1st	6:50	6:44	6:19	5:41	6:08	5:50	5:53	6:10	6:29	6:48	6:07	6:32
30°41' N 88°03' W	Set 1st	5:02	5:28	5:51	6:11	7:31	7:50	7:59	7:47	7:15	6:38	5:04	4:51
	Twl	±1:30	±1:26	±1:24	±1:25	±1:32	±1:42	±1:42	±1:35	±1:28	±1:23	±1:26	±1:29
	Rise 15th	6:50	6:33	6:02	6:25	5:58	5:49	6:00	6:19	6:36	6:55	6:18	6:42
	Set 15th	5:13	5:40	6:00	7:20	7:40	7:56	7:56	7:34	6:58	6:21	4:55	4:53
	Twl	±1:28	±1:25	±1:25	±1:28	±1:36	±1:44	±1:41	±1:32	±1:26	±1:25	±1:27	±1:30
Montgomery	Rise 1st	6:47	6:40	6:13	5:34	5:59	5:39	5:42	6:00	6:20	6:39	6:02	6:29
32°20' N 86°20' W	Set 1st	4:51	5:19	5:43	6:05	7:26	7:47	7:56	7:43	7:10	6:30	4:55	4:40
	Twl	±1:32	±1:27	±1:25	±1:28	±1:35	±1:44	±1:46	±1:38	±1:29	±1:26	±1:27	±1:31
	Rise 15th	6:47	6:28	5:56	6:16	5:47	5:38	5:49	6:09	6:29	6:49	6:15	6:39
	Set 15th	5:03	5:31	5:53	7:15	7:36	7:54	7:53	7:30	6:52	6:13	4:45	4:42
	Twl	±1:30	±1:27	±1:26	±1:30	±1:39	±1:47	±1:43	±1:34	±1:27	±1:26	±1:29	±1:32
AK **Anchorage**	Rise 1st	10:13	9:20	7:59	6:22	5:50	4:36	4:28	5:33	6:52	8:07	8:28	9:46
	Set 1st	3:54	5:08	6:26	7:46	10:05	11:20	11:38	10:37	9:05	7:30	4:57	3:51
61°10' N 149°50' W	Twl	±2:59	±2:39	±2:30	±2:59	NONE	NONE	NONE	NONE	±3:29	±2:35	±2:35	±2:56
	Rise 15th	9:56	8:41	7:16	6:38	5:12	4:21	4:52	6:09	7:27	8:43	9:06	10:09
Note: Most of Alaska does not experience an end of twilight during the summer	Set 15th	4:23	5:48	7:03	9:23	10:42	11:39	11:17	9:57	8:21	6:47	4:22	3:41
	Twl	±2:48	±2:31	±2:35	±4:39	NONE	NONE	NONE	NONE	±2:51	±2:32	±2:44	±3:02
Bethel	Rise 1st	10:57	10:05	8:46	7:10	6:40	5:27	5:20	6:23	7:41	8:54	9:14	10:30
60°50' N 161°50' W	Set 1st	4:45	5:58	7:14	8:34	10:51	12:04	12:22	11:22	9:52	8:18	5:47	4:42
	Twl	±2:57	±2:37	±2:29	±2:55	NONE	NONE	NONE	NONE	±3:23	±2:30	±2:32	±2:53

→ **Sunrises & Sunsets have been adjusted for Daylight-Savings Time**

SunRISE/SET

Sunrises & Sunsets

Alaska/Arizona

		JAN	FEB	MAR	APR	MAY	JUN	JUL	AUG	SEP	OCT	NOV	DEC
Bethel	Rise 15th	10:41	9:27	8:03	7:27	6:02	5:13	5:44	6:59	8:15	9:30	9:52	10:53
	Set 15th	5:14	6:37	7:51	10:09	11:27	12:23	12:02	10:43	9:08	7:35	5:12	4:32
	Twl	±2:48	±2:30	±2:34	±4:06	NONE	NONE	NONE	NONE	±2:44	±2:28	±2:40	±2:59
Fairbanks 64°50' N 147°50' W	Rise 1st	10:54	9:36	8:00	6:07	5:17	3:33	3:13	4:52	6:32	8:02	8:40	10:20
	Set 1st	2:57	4:35	6:09	7:45	10:22	12:09	12:36	11:01	9:08	7:18	4:29	3:01
	Twl	±3:46	±3:03	±2:53	±3:50	NONE	NONE	NONE	NONE	NONE	NONE	±2:59	±3:31
Note: Most of Alaska does not experience an end of twilight during the summer	Rise 15th	10:26	8:49	7:09	6:16	4:28	3:02	3:54	5:37	7:14	8:45	9:28	10:53
	Set 15th	3:37	5:24	6:53	9:29	11:11	12:44	11:58	10:10	8:17	6:28	3:44	2:41
	Twl	±3:23	±2:50	±3:02	NONE	NONE	NONE	NONE	NONE	±3:27	±2:54	±3:11	±3:45
Kodiak 57°30' N 152°45' W	Rise 1st	9:53	9:12	8:04	6:39	6:20	5:22	5:18	6:08	7:13	8:16	8:24	9:28
	Set 1st	4:37	5:39	6:44	7:52	9:58	10:57	11:12	10:25	9:08	7:44	5:24	4:32
	Twl	±2:35	±2:20	±2:14	±2:32	NONE	NONE	NONE	NONE	±3:36	±2:12	±2:12	±2:25
	Rise 15th	9:41	8:40	7:26	7:01	5:49	5:12	5:36	6:37	7:42	8:46	8:56	9:47
	Set 15th	5:01	6:12	7:15	9:23	10:27	11:12	10:57	9:52	8:29	7:06	4:55	4:25
	Twl	±2:29	±2:15	±2:18	±2:58	NONE	NONE	NONE	NONE	±2:28	±2:16	±2:25	±2:36
Kotzebue 66°50' N 162°40' W	Rise 1st	12:41	10:53	9:04	7:01	5:58	3:28	NONE	5:27	7:24	9:04	9:54	11:57
	Set 1st	3:09	5:17	7:03	8:50	11:40	2:09	NONE	12:24	10:15	8:15	5:14	3:23
	Twl	±4:23	±3:21	±3:06	NONE	NONE	NONE	NONE	NONE	NONE	±3:17	±3:16	±4:05
Note: Most of Alaska does not experience an end of twilight during the summer	Rise 15th	11:56	9:59	8:09	7:05	4:58	NONE	4:03	6:23	8:11	9:51	10:50	12:46
	Set 15th	4:05	6:12	7:52	10:39	12:40	NONE	1:51	11:25	9:19	7:20	4:20	2:46
	Twl	±3:51	±3:08	±3:20	NONE	NONE	NONE	NONE	NONE	±4:03	±3:09	±3:33	±4:34
AZ **Flagstaff** 35°10' N 111°40' W	Rise 1st	7:35	7:26	6:56	6:13	5:35	5:13	5:16	5:36	5:59	6:22	6:48	7:17
	Set 1st	5:26	5:55	6:22	6:48	7:13	7:36	7:45	7:30	6:53	6:10	5:32	5:15
	Twl	±1:34	±1:31	±1:29	±1:31	±1:39	±1:50	±1:53	±1:43	±1:33	±1:30	±1:30	±1:33
	Rise 15th	7:35	7:13	6:37	5:54	5:23	5:12	5:24	5:47	6:10	6:33	7:02	7:28
	Set 15th	5:38	6:09	6:35	7:00	7:24	7:43	7:41	7:15	6:33	5:51	5:21	5:16
	Twl	±1:33	±1:30	±1:28	±1:33	±1:44	±1:53	±1:50	±1:38	±1:31	±1:30	±1:32	±1:36

→ **Sunrises & Sunsets have been adjusted for Daylight-Savings Time**

Sunrises & Sunsets

Arizona/Arkansas

		JAN	FEB	MAR	APR	MAY	JUN	JUL	AUG	SEP	OCT	NOV	DEC
Phoenix	Rise 1st	7:33	7:24	6:56	6:16	5:40	5:19	5:22	5:41	6:02	6:23	6:47	7:14
33°30' N *112°10' W*	Set 1st	5:32	6:00	6:25	6:49	7:11	7:33	7:42	7:28	6:53	6:12	5:36	5:20
	Twl	±1:33	±1:29	±1:27	±1:29	±1:37	±1:47	±1:50	±1:41	±1:31	±1:28	±1:26	±1:33
	Rise 15th	7:32	7:12	6:38	5:58	5:28	5:18	5:30	5:51	6:12	6:33	7:00	7:25
	Set 15th	5:44	6:13	6:36	6:59	7:22	7:40	7:39	7:14	6:34	5:54	5:26	5:22
	Twl	±1:31	±1:28	±1:27	±1:32	±1:41	±1:49	±1:45	±1:36	±1:29	±1:28	±1:30	±1:33
Tucson	Rise 1st	7:25	7:18	6:51	6:12	5:38	5:18	5:21	5:39	5:59	6:18	6:41	7:08
32°14' N *110°59' W*	Set 1st	5:31	5:58	6:22	6:44	7:05	7:26	7:35	7:21	6:48	6:09	5:34	5:19
	Twl	±1:31	±1:27	±1:25	±1:27	±1:34	±1:43	±1:45	±1:38	±1:29	±1:26	±1:27	±1:31
	Rise 15th	7:26	7:06	6:34	5:55	5:26	5:17	5:28	5:48	6:08	6:28	6:54	7:18
	Set 15th	5:42	6:11	6:32	6:54	7:15	7:32	7:32	7:08	6:30	5:51	5:24	5:21
	Twl	±1:29	±1:26	±1:26	±1:29	±1:38	±1:46	±1:42	±1:34	±1:27	±1:26	±1:29	±1:32
Yuma	Rise 1st	7:41	7:33	7:06	6:26	5:51	5:31	5:34	5:52	6:13	6:33	6:56	7:23
32°45' N *114°37' W*	Set 1st	5:44	6:11	6:36	6:59	7:20	7:42	7:50	7:37	7:03	6:23	5:47	5:32
	Twl	±1:32	±1:28	±1:26	±1:28	±1:35	±1:45	±1:48	±1:24	±1:30	±1:27	±1:28	±1:31
	Rise 15th	7:41	7:21	6:49	6:09	5:39	5:30	5:41	6:02	6:22	6:43	7:09	7:34
	Set 15th	5:55	6:24	6:47	7:09	7:31	7:48	7:47	7:23	6:44	6:05	5:37	5:34
	Twl	±1:31	±1:27	±1:25	±1:31	±1:39	±1:47	±1:45	±1:35	±1:28	±1:27	±1:30	±1:32
AR **El Dorado**	Rise 1st	7:14	7:06	6:39	5:59	6:23	6:03	6:05	6:24	6:45	7:05	6:29	6:56
33°10' N *92°40' W*	Set 1st	5:15	5:43	6:08	6:31	7:53	8:15	8:24	8:10	7:36	6:55	5:19	5:03
	Twl	±1:32	±1:28	±1:26	±1:24	±1:35	±1:45	±1:36	±1:40	±1:30	±1:27	±1:28	±1:32
	Rise 15th	7:14	6:54	6:21	6:41	6:11	6:01	6:12	6:33	6:54	7:15	6:42	7:07
	Set 15th	5:26	5:56	6:19	7:41	8:03	8:21	8:21	7:56	7:17	6:37	5:09	5:05
	Twl	±1:32	±1:27	±1:26	±1:32	±1:41	±1:49	±1:44	±1:35	±1:28	±1:27	±1:30	±1:33
Fort Smith	Rise 1st	7:27	7:17	6:48	6:04	6:26	6:04	6:06	6:26	6:50	7:13	6:39	7:08
35°25' N *94°25' W*	Set 1st	5:16	5:46	6:13	6:39	8:04	8:27	8:37	8:21	7:45	7:02	5:23	5:05
	Twl	±1:35	±1:30	±1:29	±1:31	±1:40	±1:51	±1:54	±1:43	±1:33	±1:29	±1:30	±1:34

→ **Sunrises & Sunsets have been adjusted for Daylight-Savings Time**

SunRISE/SET

Sunrises & Sunsets

Arkansas/California

		JAN	FEB	MAR	APR	MAY	JUN	JUL	AUG	SEP	OCT	NOV	DEC
Fort Smith	Rise 15th	7:26	7:04	6:29	6:45	6:13	6:02	6:14	6:37	7:00	7:24	6:53	7:19
	Set 15th	5:28	6:00	6:25	7:51	8:15	8:34	8:33	8:07	7:25	6:43	5:11	5:06
	Twl	±1:34	±1:30	±1:29	±1:33	±1:45	±1:54	±1:50	±1:38	±1:30	±1:29	±1:32	±1:36
Little Rock	Rise 1st	7:17	7:08	6:39	5:56	6:19	5:57	5:59	6:19	6:42	7:04	6:30	6:58
34°41' N	Set 1st	5:09	5:38	6:05	6:30	7:54	8:17	8:26	8:11	7:36	6:53	5:15	4:58
92°10' W	Twl	±1:34	±1:30	±1:27	±1:30	±1:37	±1:49	±1:51	±1:42	±1:32	±1:28	±1:29	±1:33
	Rise 15th	7:16	6:55	6:20	6:38	6:06	5:55	6:07	6:29	6:52	7:15	6:43	7:09
	Set 15th	5:21	5:52	6:17	7:41	8:05	8:24	8:23	7:57	7:16	6:35	5:04	5:00
	Twl	±1:33	±1:29	±1:27	±1:33	±1:44	±1:51	±1:47	±1:37	±1:29	±1:28	±1:31	±1:33
CA **Fresno**	Rise 1st	7:12	7:01	6:30	5:45	6:05	5:42	5:44	6:05	6:31	6:55	6:23	6:54
	Set 1st	4:54	5:25	5:54	6:22	7:48	8:13	8:22	8:06	7:27	6:42	5:02	4:43
36°47' N	Twl	±1:37	±1:33	±1:30	±1:33	±1:42	±1:55	±1:58	±1:46	±1:36	±1:32	±1:32	±1:37
119°50' W	Rise 15th	7:11	6:47	6:10	6:25	5:52	5:40	5:52	6:17	6:42	7:07	6:38	7:05
	Set 15th	5:07	5:40	6:07	7:34	8:00	8:20	8:18	7:50	7:07	6:23	4:50	4:44
	Twl	±1:35	±1:31	±1:30	±1:36	±1:48	±1:58	±1:54	±1:41	±1:32	±1:31	±1:34	±1:38
Los Angeles	Rise 1st	6:59	6:50	6:21	5:40	6:04	5:43	5:45	6:04	6:27	6:48	6:13	6:41
34°00' N	Set 1st	4:55	5:24	5:50	6:14	7:37	7:59	8:08	7:54	7:18	6:37	5:00	4:44
118°10' W	Twl	±1:33	±1:28	±1:26	±1:29	±1:37	±1:47	±1:49	±1:40	±1:31	±1:28	±1:29	±1:32
	Rise 15th	6:58	6:37	6:03	6:22	5:51	5:41	5:53	6:15	6:36	6:58	6:26	6:51
	Set 15th	5:07	5:37	6:01	7:25	7:48	8:06	8:05	7:40	6:59	6:19	4:49	4:45
	Twl	±1:32	±1:28	±1:27	±1:31	±1:41	±1:50	±1:46	±1:35	±1:29	±1:27	±1:31	±1:33
Redding	Rise 1st	7:33	7:19	6:43	5:53	6:08	5:41	5:43	6:07	6:37	7:06	6:40	7:14
40°30' N	Set 1st	4:54	5:28	6:01	6:35	8:06	8:34	8:44	8:24	7:41	6:51	5:06	4:44
122°25' W	Twl	±1:42	±1:38	±1:35	±1:37	±1:50	±2:08	±2:12	±1:57	±1:42	±1:36	±1:38	±1:41
	Rise 15th	7:31	7:03	6:21	6:31	5:53	5:39	5:52	6:21	6:51	7:21	6:56	7:26
	Set 15th	5:08	5:45	6:17	7:49	8:20	8:42	8:39	8:07	7:18	6:29	4:52	4:44
	Twl	±1:41	±1:36	±1:35	±1:43	±1:58	±2:13	±2:06	±1:49	±1:38	±1:36	±1:40	±1:43

➝ **Sunrises & Sunsets have been adjusted for Daylight-Savings Time**

Sunrises & Sunsets

California/Colorado

		JAN	FEB	MAR	APR	MAY	JUN	JUL	AUG	SEP	OCT	NOV	DEC
Sacramento	Rise 1st	7:24	7:11	6:38	5:51	6:09	5:43	5:45	6:08	6:35	7:02	6:33	7:05
38°33' N 121°30' W	Set 1st	4:56	5:28	5:59	6:30	7:58	8:25	8:34	8:16	7:36	6:48	5:06	4:45
	Twl	±1:39	±1:35	±1:32	±1:35	±1:45	±2:00	±2:04	±1:51	±1:38	±1:34	±1:34	±1:39
	Rise 15th	7:22	6:57	6:17	6:30	5:54	5:41	5:54	6:20	6:48	7:15	6:48	7:17
	Set 15th	5:09	5:44	6:13	7:43	8:11	8:32	8:30	8:00	7:14	6:28	4:53	4:46
	Twl	±1:37	±1:33	±1:32	±1:39	±1:52	±2:04	±1:58	±1:44	±1:35	±1:33	±1:37	±1:39
San Diego	Rise 1st	6:51	6:43	6:16	5:36	6:01	5:41	5:44	6:02	6:23	6:43	6:06	6:33
32°43' N 117°10' W	Set 1st	4:53	5:21	5:46	6:09	7:30	7:52	8:00	7:46	7:13	6:33	4:57	4:42
	Twl	±1:33	±1:28	±1:26	±1:28	±1:35	±1:45	±1:48	±1:39	±1:30	±1:27	±1:28	±1:32
	Rise 15th	6:51	6:31	5:58	6:18	5:49	5:40	5:51	6:12	6:32	6:53	6:19	6:43
	Set 15th	5:05	5:34	5:56	7:19	7:40	7:58	7:57	7:33	6:54	6:15	4:47	4:44
	Twl	±1:31	±1:27	±1:27	±1:31	±1:41	±1:47	±1:45	±1:35	±1:28	±1:27	±1:30	±1:32
San Francisco	Rise 1st	7:25	7:14	6:41	5:55	6:14	5:49	5:52	6:13	6:40	7:06	6:35	7:07
37°47' N 122°30' W	Set 1st	5:02	5:34	6:04	6:33	8:00	8:26	8:36	8:18	7:39	6:52	5:11	4:51
	Twl	±1:38	±1:34	±1:31	±1:34	±1:45	±1:59	±2:01	±1:49	±1:37	±1:33	±1:33	±1:38
	Rise 15th	7:24	6:59	6:21	6:34	6:00	5:47	6:00	6:25	6:52	7:18	6:50	7:18
	Set 15th	5:15	5:49	6:17	7:45	8:13	8:33	8:31	8:02	7:17	6:32	4:58	4:52
	Twl	±1:36	±1:33	±1:32	±1:39	±1:50	±2:02	±1:57	±1:44	±1:35	±1:33	±1:35	±1:39
CO **Denver**	Rise 1st	7:21	7:08	6:33	5:44	6:00	5:34	5:36	5:59	6:28	6:56	6:29	7:02
39°45' N 105° 00' W	Set 1st	4:46	5:20	5:52	6:24	7:54	8:22	8:32	8:13	7:31	6:42	4:58	4:36
	Twl	±1:41	±1:37	±1:34	±1:37	±1:49	±2:05	±2:08	±1:55	±1:41	±1:35	±1:36	±1:40
	Rise 15th	7:19	6:52	6:11	6:22	5:45	5:31	5:45	6:12	6:41	7:10	6:45	7:14
	Set 15th	5:00	5:37	6:07	7:38	8:08	8:30	8:27	7:56	7:08	6:20	4:44	4:36
	Twl	±1:40	±1:34	±1:34	±1:41	±1:56	±2:10	±2:03	±1:47	±1:37	±1:35	±1:39	±1:42
Grand Junction	Rise 1st	7:33	7:20	6:46	5:58	6:16	5:50	5:52	6:15	6:43	7:10	6:42	7:14
39°00' N 108°30' W	Set 1st	5:03	5:36	6:07	6:38	8:07	8:34	8:44	8:25	7:44	6:56	5:13	4:52
	Twl	±1:39	±1:34	±1:33	±1:36	±1:47	±2:02	±2:05	±1:53	±1:39	±1:34	±1:35	±1:39

➡ **Sunrises & Sunsets have been adjusted for Daylight-Savings Time**

SunRISE/SET

291

Sunrises & Sunsets

Colorado/Connecticut

		JAN	FEB	MAR	APR	MAY	JUN	JUL	AUG	SEP	OCT	NOV	DEC
Grand Junction	Rise 15th	7:31	7:05	6:25	6:37	6:01	5:48	6:01	6:28	6:56	7:24	6:57	7:26
	Set 15th	5:16	5:52	6:21	7:51	8:20	8:41	8:39	8:09	7:22	6:35	5:00	4:53
	Twl	±1:38	±1:33	±1:33	±1:40	±1:54	±2:06	±2:00	±1:45	±1:36	±1:34	±1:37	±1:40
Julesberg 41°00' N 102°20' W	Rise 1st	7:14	7:00	6:23	5:32	5:47	5:19	5:21	5:45	6:16	6:46	6:20	6:55
	Set 1st	4:32	5:07	5:41	6:15	7:46	8:15	8:25	8:05	7:22	6:31	4:45	4:22
	Twl	±1:43	±1:38	±1:35	±1:39	±1:52	±2:11	±2:14	±1:59	±1:42	±1:37	±1:38	±1:42
	Rise 15th	7:12	6:43	6:01	6:10	5:31	5:17	5:30	5:59	6:30	7:01	6:37	7:07
	Set 15th	4:46	5:24	5:56	7:29	8:01	8:23	8:20	7:48	6:59	6:09	4:31	4:22
	Twl	±1:41	±1:36	±1:37	±1:44	±2:00	±2:16	±2:08	±1:50	±1:38	±1:36	±1:40	±1:44
CT **Hartford** 41°47' N 72°41' W	Rise 1st	7:18	7:03	6:25	5:33	5:47	5:18	5:20	5:45	6:17	6:48	6:23	6:59
	Set 1st	4:31	5:06	5:41	6:16	7:49	8:19	8:29	8:09	7:24	6:32	4:45	4:21
	Twl	±1:44	±1:40	±1:37	±1:41	±1:54	±2:14	±2:19	±2:00	±1:45	±1:38	±1:40	±1:44
	Rise 15th	7:16	6:46	6:02	6:10	5:31	5:15	5:29	5:59	6:31	7:03	6:40	7:11
	Set 15th	4:45	5:24	5:58	7:32	8:04	8:27	8:24	7:51	7:00	6:09	4:30	4:21
	Twl	±1:43	±1:38	±1:37	±1:45	±2:03	±2:20	±2:11	±1:52	±1:41	±1:38	±1:42	±1:45
New Haven 41°20' N 72°54' W	Rise 1st	7:18	7:03	6:26	5:35	5:49	5:21	5:22	5:47	6:18	6:48	6:23	6:58
	Set 1st	4:33	5:08	5:43	6:17	7:49	8:19	8:29	8:08	7:24	6:33	4:47	4:23
	Twl	±1:44	±1:39	±1:35	±1:40	±1:53	±2:12	±2:16	±1:59	±1:44	±1:37	±1:38	±1:44
	Rise 15th	7:15	6:46	6:03	6:12	5:33	5:18	5:31	6:01	6:32	7:04	6:40	7:11
	Set 15th	4:47	5:26	5:58	7:32	8:04	8:27	8:23	7:51	7:01	6:11	4:32	4:23
	Twl	±1:42	±1:36	±1:37	±1:45	±2:01	±2:17	±2:10	±1:51	±1:39	±1:37	±1:41	±1:44
Norwich 41°33' N 72°05' W	Rise 1st	7:15	7:00	6:23	5:31	5:45	5:17	5:18	5:43	6:14	6:45	6:20	6:56
	Set 1st	4:29	5:04	5:39	6:14	7:46	8:16	8:26	8:06	7:21	6:30	4:43	4:19
	Twl	±1:44	±1:39	±1:36	±1:40	±1:53	±2:12	±2:18	±2:00	±1:45	±1:37	±1:39	±1:44
	Rise 15th	7:13	6:43	6:00	6:08	5:29	5:14	5:27	5:57	6:29	7:00	6:37	7:08
	Set 15th	4:44	5:22	5:55	7:29	8:01	8:24	8:21	7:48	6:58	6:07	4:28	4:19
	Twl	±1:42	±1:37	±1:37	±1:45	±2:02	±2:19	±2:11	±1:51	±1:41	±1:37	±1:41	±1:44

➙ **Sunrises & Sunsets have been adjusted for Daylight-Savings Time**

District of Columbia/Delaware/Florida

		JAN	FEB	MAR	APR	MAY	JUN	JUL	AUG	SEP	OCT	NOV	DEC
DC **Washington** *38°52' N* *77°00' W*	Rise 1st	7:27	7:14	6:40	5:53	6:10	5:45	5:46	6:09	6:37	7:04	6:35	7:08
	Set 1st	4:57	5:30	6:01	6:32	8:01	8:27	8:37	8:19	7:38	6:51	5:07	4:46
	Twl	±1:40	±1:35	±1:32	±1:35	±1:46	±2:02	±2:05	±1:51	±1:39	±1:33	±1:35	±1:39
	Rise 15th	7:25	6:59	6:19	6:31	5:55	5:42	5:55	6:22	6:50	7:18	6:51	7:19
	Set 15th	5:10	5:46	6:15	7:45	8:14	8:35	8:32	8:03	7:16	6:29	4:54	4:47
	Twl	±1:38	±1:33	±1:33	±1:40	±1:53	±2:06	±2:01	±1:43	±1:36	±1:34	±1:38	±1:40
DE **Dover** *39°10' N* *75°31' W*	Rise 1st	7:22	7:09	6:35	5:46	6:04	5:38	5:40	6:02	6:31	6:58	6:30	7:03
	Set 1st	4:50	5:23	5:55	6:26	7:55	8:22	8:32	8:14	7:33	6:45	5:01	4:40
	Twl	±1:40	±1:36	±1:33	±1:36	±1:47	±2:03	±2:06	±1:53	±1:39	±1:34	±1:35	±1:39
	Rise 15th	7:20	6:54	6:13	6:25	5:49	5:35	5:48	6:15	6:43	7:12	6:46	7:14
	Set 15th	5:04	5:39	6:09	7:40	8:09	8:30	8:27	7:57	7:10	6:23	4:48	4:40
	Twl	±1:38	±1:34	±1:33	±1:40	±1:53	±2:07	±2:02	±1:52	±1:36	±1:34	±1:37	±1:41
Wilmington *39°44' N* *75°33' W*	Rise 1st	7:23	7:10	6:35	5:46	6:03	5:36	5:38	6:01	6:30	6:59	6:31	7:04
	Set 1st	4:49	5:22	5:54	6:26	7:57	8:24	8:34	8:15	7:34	6:45	5:00	4:38
	Twl	±1:41	±1:37	±1:34	±1:37	±1:48	±2:05	±2:08	±1:54	±1:40	±1:34	±1:35	±1:40
	Rise 15th	7:22	6:55	6:14	6:25	5:48	5:34	5:47	6:14	6:43	7:13	6:47	7:16
	Set 15th	5:02	5:39	6:09	7:41	8:10	8:32	8:29	7:58	7:11	6:23	4:46	4:39
	Twl	±1:40	±1:35	±1:34	±1:42	±1:56	±2:09	±2:02	±1:46	±1:37	±1:35	±1:38	±1:42
FL **Jacksonville** *30°15' N* *81°38' W*	Rise 1st	7:23	7:17	6:53	6:16	6:45	6:25	6:28	6:45	7:03	7:20	6:41	7:05
	Set 1st	5:37	6:03	6:25	6:45	8:04	8:24	8:32	8:20	7:49	7:12	5:39	5:26
	Twl	±1:30	±1:26	±1:24	±1:25	±1:32	±1:39	±1:42	±1:35	±1:28	±1:23	±1:25	±1:29
	Rise 15th	7:24	7:07	6:37	7:00	6:33	6:24	6:35	6:54	7:11	7:29	6:52	7:15
	Set 15th	5:49	6:15	6:35	7:54	8:13	8:30	8:30	8:08	7:32	6:56	5:30	5:28
	Twl	±1:27	±1:25	±1:24	±1:28	±1:36	±1:42	±1:39	±1:31	±1:25	±1:24	±1:27	±1:30
Miami *25°45' N* *80°15' W*	Rise 1st	7:08	7:05	6:44	6:12	6:44	6:29	6:33	6:47	7:01	7:13	6:29	6:50
	Set 1st	5:41	6:05	6:23	6:38	7:52	8:08	8:16	8:07	7:40	7:08	5:39	5:29
	Twl	±1:26	±1:22	±1:19	±1:21	±1:27	±1:34	±1:35	±1:29	±1:23	±1:21	±1:22	±1:25

→ **Sunrises & Sunsets have been adjusted for Daylight-Savings Time**

SunRISE/SET

Sunrises & Sunsets

Florida/Georgia

		JAN	FEB	MAR	APR	MAY	JUN	JUL	AUG	SEP	OCT	NOV	DEC
Miami	Rise 15th	7:09	6:56	6:30	6:58	6:35	6:29	6:39	6:54	7:07	7:20	6:39	7:00
	Set 15th	5:52	6:14	6:30	7:44	7:59	8:14	8:15	7:56	7:25	6:53	5:32	5:32
	Twl	±1:24	±1:22	±1:19	±1:24	±1:30	±1:34	±1:32	±1:26	±1:21	±1:21	±1:24	±1:26
Orlando *28°30' N 81°25' W*	Rise 1st	7:18	7:14	6:51	6:16	6:45	6:28	6:32	6:47	7:04	7:19	6:38	7:01
	Set 1st	5:40	6:05	6:26	6:44	8:01	8:19	8:27	8:16	7:47	7:12	5:41	5:29
	Twl	±1:28	±1:25	±1:22	±1:23	±1:29	±1:37	±1:39	±1:33	±1:25	±1:22	±1:23	±1:27
	Rise 15th	7:19	7:04	6:35	7:00	6:35	6:28	6:38	6:55	7:11	7:26	6:48	7:11
	Set 15th	5:51	6:16	6:34	7:51	8:09	8:25	8:25	8:05	7:31	6:56	5:32	5:31
	Twl	±1:27	±1:23	±1:23	±1:26	±1:34	±1:38	±1:37	±1:29	±1:23	±1:23	±1:26	±1:29
St. Petersburg *27°45' N 82°40' W*	Rise 1st	7:22	7:17	6:55	6:21	6:51	6:35	6:38	6:54	7:09	7:23	6:42	7:04
	Set 1st	5:47	6:11	6:31	6:48	8:05	8:22	8:31	8:20	7:52	7:17	5:47	5:35
	Twl	±1:27	±1:24	±1:16	±1:23	±1:29	±1:36	±1:37	±1:31	±1:24	±1:21	±1:23	±1:27
	Rise 15th	7:23	7:08	6:40	7:06	6:42	6:34	6:45	7:01	7:16	7:31	6:52	7:14
	Set 15th	5:58	6:22	6:39	7:56	8:13	8:28	8:28	8:09	7:35	7:02	5:39	5:38
	Twl	±1:26	±1:22	±1:22	±1:25	±1:32	±1:37	±1:36	±1:28	±1:23	±1:22	±1:25	±1:27
Tallahassee *30°25' N 84°15' W*	Rise 1st	7:34	7:28	7:03	6:26	6:54	6:35	6:38	6:55	7:14	7:30	6:51	7:16
	Set 1st	5:48	6:14	6:36	6:56	8:15	8:34	8:43	8:31	8:00	7:22	5:49	5:36
	Twl	±1:29	±1:25	±1:23	±1:25	±1:32	±1:40	±1:42	±1:35	±1:27	±1:24	±1:26	±1:29
	Rise 15th	7:35	7:17	6:47	7:10	6:43	6:34	6:45	7:04	7:21	7:39	7:03	7:26
	Set 15th	5:59	6:25	6:45	8:05	8:24	8:41	8:41	8:19	7:43	7:06	5:40	5:38
	Twl	±1:28	±1:25	±1:24	±1:28	±1:36	±1:42	±1:39	±1:30	±1:25	±1:24	±1:27	±1:30
GA **Albany** *31°40' N 84°10' W*	Rise 1st	7:37	7:30	7:04	6:25	6:51	6:32	6:35	6:53	7:12	7:30	6:53	7:19
	Set 1st	5:44	6:11	6:35	6:56	8:17	8:37	8:46	8:33	8:01	7:22	5:47	5:33
	Twl	±1:31	±1:27	±1:25	±1:27	±1:34	±1:43	±1:44	±1:36	±1:28	±1:25	±1:27	±1:30
	Rise 15th	7:37	7:19	6:47	7:08	6:40	6:31	6:42	7:02	7:21	7:40	7:05	7:29
	Set 15th	5:56	6:23	6:45	8:06	8:26	8:43	8:43	8:20	7:43	7:05	5:38	5:35
	Twl	±1:29	±1:26	±1:25	±1:29	±1:38	±1:46	±1:41	±1:33	±1:26	±1:25	±1:28	±1:31

→ **Sunrises & Sunsets have been adjusted for Daylight-Savings Time**

SunRISE/SET

Sunrises & Sunsets

Georgia

		JAN	FEB	MAR	APR	MAY	JUN	JUL	AUG	SEP	OCT	NOV	DEC
Atlanta	Rise 1st	7:43	7:34	7:06	6:25	6:49	6:28	6:31	6:49	7:11	7:32	6:57	7:24
33°50' N	Set 1st	5:40	6:09	6:34	6:58	8:21	8:43	8:52	8:38	8:03	7:22	5:45	5:29
84°24' W	Twl	±1:33	±1:28	±1:27	±1:29	±1:37	±1:47	±1:50	±1:41	±1:32	±1:28	±1:29	±1:32
	Rise 15th	7:42	7:22	6:48	7:07	6:37	6:27	6:38	6:59	7:21	7:42	7:10	7:35
	Set 15th	5:52	6:22	6:45	8:09	8:32	8:50	8:49	8:24	7:44	7:04	5:35	5:31
	Twl	±1:32	±1:28	±1:27	±1:32	±1:42	±1:50	±1:46	±1:36	±1:29	±1:27	±1:30	±1:33
Augusta	Rise 1st	7:32	7:24	6:56	6:16	6:40	6:19	6:22	6:40	7:02	7:22	6:47	7:14
33°29' N	Set 1st	5:31	5:59	6:25	6:48	8:11	8:33	8:42	8:28	7:53	7:13	5:36	5:20
81°59' W	Twl	±1:33	±1:29	±1:26	±1:29	±1:37	±1:47	±1:49	±1:40	±1:31	±1:27	±1:28	±1:32
	Rise 15th	7:32	7:12	6:39	6:58	6:28	6:18	6:29	6:50	7:11	7:33	6:59	7:25
	Set 15th	5:43	6:13	6:36	7:59	8:21	8:39	8:39	8:14	7:34	6:54	5:25	5:22
	Twl	±1:32	±1:27	±1:26	±1:31	±1:41	±1:49	±1:45	±1:35	±1:29	±1:28	±1:31	±1:32
Macon	Rise 1st	7:37	7:30	7:03	6:23	6:47	6:27	6:30	6:48	7:09	7:29	6:52	7:19
32°50' N	Set 1st	5:39	6:07	6:32	6:55	8:16	8:38	8:47	8:33	7:59	7:19	5:44	5:28
83°37' W	Twl	±1:32	±1:28	±1:26	±1:28	±1:35	±1:45	±1:47	±1:39	±1:30	±1:27	±1:27	±1:31
	Rise 15th	7:37	7:18	6:45	7:05	6:36	6:26	6:37	6:58	7:18	7:39	7:05	7:30
	Set 15th	5:51	6:20	6:42	8:05	8:27	8:44	8:44	8:20	7:41	7:02	5:33	5:30
	Twl	±1:31	±1:27	±1:26	±1:31	±1:40	±1:47	±1:44	±1:34	±1:27	±1:26	±1:30	±1:32
Savannah	Rise 1st	7:25	7:18	6:52	6:13	6:38	6:19	6:22	6:39	6:59	7:18	6:41	7:07
32°04' N	Set 1st	5:31	5:58	6:22	6:44	8:05	8:26	8:35	8:21	7:49	7:09	5:34	5:20
81°04' W	Twl	±1:31	±1:27	±1:25	±1:27	±1:34	±1:43	±1:45	±1:38	±1:28	±1:26	±1:27	±1:30
	Rise 15th	7:25	7:07	6:35	6:56	6:27	6:18	6:29	6:49	7:08	7:28	6:53	7:17
	Set 15th	5:42	6:11	6:32	7:54	8:15	8:32	8:32	8:08	7:30	6:52	5:24	5:21
	Twl	±1:30	±1:26	±1:26	±1:29	±1:38	±1:45	±1:42	±1:33	±1:27	±1:26	±1:29	±1:32
Waycross	Rise 1st	7:28	7:22	6:57	6:19	6:45	6:26	6:29	6:46	7:06	7:23	6:45	7:10
31°12' N	Set 1st	5:38	6:05	6:28	6:49	8:09	8:29	8:38	8:25	7:53	7:15	5:41	5:27
82°25' W	Twl	±1:31	±1:27	±1:25	±1:26	±1:32	±1:42	±1:44	±1:36	±1:28	±1:24	±1:26	±1:30

→ **Sunrises & Sunsets have been adjusted for Daylight-Savings Time**

SunRISE/SET

Sunrises & Sunsets

Georgia/Hawaii/Idaho

		JAN	FEB	MAR	APR	MAY	JUN	JUL	AUG	SEP	OCT	NOV	DEC
Waycross	Rise 15th	7:29	7:11	6:40	7:02	6:34	6:25	6:36	6:55	7:14	7:32	6:57	7:21
	Set 15th	5:50	6:17	6:38	7:58	8:18	8:35	8:35	8:13	7:36	6:58	5:31	5:29
	Twl	±1:28	±1:26	±1:24	±1:29	±1:38	±1:44	±1:41	±1:32	±1:26	±1:25	±1:28	±1:31
HI **Honolulu** 21°19' N 157°52' W	Rise 1st	7:08	7:09	6:52	6:24	6:00	5:49	5:53	6:05	6:15	6:23	6:35	6:53
	Set 1st	6:01	6:22	6:36	6:46	6:57	7:10	7:18	7:10	6:47	6:19	5:55	5:49
	Twl	±1:23	±1:20	±1:18	±1:18	±1:23	±1:28	±1:29	±1:26	±1:20	±1:17	±1:19	±1:21
	Rise 15th	7:12	7:02	6:40	6:12	5:53	5:49	5:58	6:10	6:19	6:27	6:43	7:01
	Set 15th	6:11	6:30	6:41	6:51	7:03	7:15	7:16	7:01	6:34	6:07	5:50	5:52
	Twl	±1:21	±1:17	±1:18	±1:20	±1:26	±1:30	±1:29	±1:23	±1:19	±1:18	±1:21	±1:23
ID **Boise** 43°43' N 116°09' W	Rise 1st	8:18	8:01	7:21	6:26	6:37	6:06	6:07	6:34	7:09	7:43	7:21	7:59
	Set 1st	5:19	5:56	6:34	7:12	8:47	9:20	9:30	9:07	8:20	7:25	5:35	5:09
	Twl	±1:51	±1:45	±1:42	±1:47	±2:03	±2:27	±2:35	±2:09	±1:49	±1:42	±1:44	±1:50
	Rise 15th	8:15	7:43	6:57	7:02	6:20	6:03	6:17	6:50	7:24	7:59	7:39	8:11
	Set 15th	5:34	6:16	6:51	8:29	9:03	9:28	9:24	8:48	7:55	7:01	5:19	5:09
	Twl	±1:49	±1:42	±1:43	±1:52	±2:14	±2:36	±2:23	±1:58	±1:44	±1:42	±1:47	±1:51
Idaho Falls 43°30' N 112°01' W	Rise 1st	8:01	7:44	7:04	6:09	6:21	5:50	5:51	6:18	6:52	7:26	7:04	7:41
	Set 1st	5:03	5:40	6:17	6:55	8:30	9:02	9:13	8:50	8:03	7:09	5:19	4:53
	Twl	±1:47	±1:42	±1:39	±1:44	±2:00	±2:24	±2:29	±2:08	±1:48	±1:40	±1:42	±1:47
	Rise 15th	7:58	7:26	6:40	6:45	6:03	5:46	6:01	6:33	7:08	7:42	7:22	7:54
	Set 15th	5:18	5:59	6:35	8:12	8:46	9:11	9:07	8:31	7:38	6:45	5:03	4:52
	Twl	±1:46	±1:40	±1:40	±1:49	±2:09	±2:30	±2:20	±1:56	±1:43	±1:40	±1:44	±1:49
Twin Falls 42°30' N 114°30' W	Rise 1st	8:08	7:52	7:13	6:20	6:35	6:03	6:05	6:30	7:03	7:35	7:12	7:48
	Set 1st	5:16	5:52	6:28	7:04	8:38	9:09	9:19	8:58	8:12	7:19	5:31	5:06
	Twl	±1:46	±1:41	±1:38	±1:42	±1:56	±2:18	±2:23	±2:02	±1:46	±1:39	±1:39	±1:45
	Rise 15th	8:05	7:34	6:50	6:57	6:16	6:00	6:14	6:45	7:18	7:51	7:29	8:01
	Set 15th	5:31	6:10	6:45	8:20	8:53	9:17	9:13	8:39	7:47	6:56	5:16	5:06
	Twl	±1:43	±1:39	±1:38	±1:47	±2:06	±2:24	±2:16	±1:54	±1:42	±1:38	±1:42	±1:46

→ **Sunrises & Sunsets have been adjusted for Daylight-Savings Time**

Sunrises & Sunsets

Illinois

		JAN	FEB	MAR	APR	MAY	JUN	JUL	AUG	SEP	OCT	NOV	DEC
IL	Rise 1st	7:18	7:03	6:26	5:34	5:47	5:18	5:19	5:44	6:16	6:47	6:23	6:59
Chicago	Set 1st	4:30	5:06	5:41	6:16	7:49	8:19	8:30	8:09	7:24	6:32	4:45	4:20
41°53' N	Twl	±1:45	±1:40	±1:37	±1:41	±1:54	±2:14	±2:19	±2:00	±1:45	±1:38	±1:39	±1:45
87°40' W	Rise 15th	7:16	6:46	6:03	6:10	5:30	5:15	5:28	5:58	6:31	7:03	6:40	7:11
	Set 15th	4:44	5:23	5:57	7:32	8:04	8:28	8:24	7:51	7:00	6:09	4:30	4:20
	Twl	±1:44	±1:38	±1:38	±1:45	±2:03	±2:21	±2:13	±1:52	±1:40	±1:38	±1:41	±1:45
Danville	Rise 1st	7:13	6:59	6:24	5:34	5:50	5:23	5:25	5:49	6:18	6:47	6:20	6:54
40°10' N	Set 1st	4:36	5:10	5:43	6:15	7:46	8:14	8:24	8:05	7:22	6:33	4:48	4:26
87°40' W	Twl	±1:41	±1:37	±1:34	±1:37	±1:49	±2:06	±2:11	±1:55	±1:42	±1:35	±1:36	±1:40
	Rise 15th	7:11	6:44	6:02	6:12	5:35	5:21	5:34	6:02	6:32	7:01	6:36	7:06
	Set 15th	4:50	5:27	5:58	7:30	8:00	8:22	8:19	7:47	6:59	6:11	4:34	4:26
	Twl	±1:40	±1:35	±1:34	±1:42	±1:57	±2:11	±2:05	±1:49	±1:38	±1:35	±1:39	±1:42
Moline	Rise 1st	7:29	7:14	6:37	5:45	5:59	5:31	5:32	5:57	6:28	6:59	6:34	7:09
41°30' N	Set 1st	4:43	5:18	5:53	6:27	8:00	8:29	8:40	8:19	7:35	6:44	4:57	4:33
90°30' W	Twl	±1:44	±1:39	±1:36	±1:41	±1:53	±2:13	±2:16	±2:00	±1:43	±1:37	±1:39	±1:44
	Rise 15th	7:26	6:57	6:14	6:22	5:43	5:28	5:41	6:11	6:42	7:14	6:51	7:21
	Set 15th	4:57	5:36	6:09	7:42	8:14	8:38	8:34	8:02	7:11	6:21	4:42	4:33
	Twl	±1:42	±1:37	±1:37	±1:46	±2:03	±2:17	±2:10	±1:50	±1:39	±1:37	±1:41	±1:44
Mount Vernon	Rise 1st	7:13	7:01	6:27	5:41	5:59	5:34	5:36	5:58	6:25	6:52	6:22	6:54
	Set 1st	4:46	5:18	5:49	6:19	7:46	8:14	8:24	8:05	7:25	6:38	4:56	4:36
38°19' N	Twl	±1:39	±1:34	±1:32	±1:35	±1:46	±2:00	±2:02	±1:51	±1:38	±1:33	±1:34	±1:38
88°55' W	Rise 15th	7:11	6:46	6:07	6:20	5:44	5:32	5:44	6:10	6:37	7:05	6:36	7:06
	Set 15th	5:00	5:34	6:03	7:32	8:00	8:22	8:19	7:48	7:04	6:18	4:43	4:36
	Twl	±1:36	±1:33	±1:32	±1:39	±1:52	±2:02	±1:58	±1:45	±1:35	±1:33	±1:36	±1:40
Rockford	Rise 1st	7:25	7:10	6:32	5:39	5:51	5:22	5:23	5:48	6:21	6:53	6:29	7:05
42°20' N	Set 1st	4:34	5:10	5:46	6:22	7:55	8:26	8:37	8:16	7:30	6:38	4:50	4:25
89°00' W	Twl	±1:46	±1:41	±1:37	±1:41	±1:56	±2:17	±2:21	±2:02	±1:44	±1:38	±1:40	±1:44

→ **Sunrises & Sunsets have been adjusted for Daylight-Savings Time**

SunRISE/SET

Sunrises & Sunsets

Illinois/Indiana/Iowa

		JAN	FEB	MAR	APR	MAY	JUN	JUL	AUG	SEP	OCT	NOV	DEC
Rockford	Rise 15th	7:23	6:53	6:08	6:15	5:35	5:19	5:33	6:03	6:36	7:09	6:47	7:18
	Set 15th	4:49	5:28	6:02	7:38	8:11	8:34	8:31	7:57	7:06	6:14	4:34	4:24
	Twl	±1:43	±1:39	±1:38	±1:46	±2:04	±2:23	±2:14	±1:53	±1:41	±1:38	±1:42	±1:46
Springfield *39°48' N 89°40' W*	Rise 1st	7:20	7:07	6:32	5:43	5:59	5:33	5:34	5:57	6:27	6:55	6:27	7:01
	Set 1st	4:45	5:18	5:51	6:23	7:53	8:21	8:31	8:12	7:30	6:41	4:57	4:35
	Twl	±1:41	±1:37	±1:34	±1:37	±1:49	±2:05	±2:09	±1:54	±1:41	±1:35	±1:35	±1:40
	Rise 15th	7:18	6:51	6:10	6:21	5:44	5:30	5:43	6:11	6:40	7:09	6:43	7:13
	Set 15th	4:58	5:35	6:06	7:37	8:07	8:29	8:26	7:55	7:07	6:19	4:43	4:35
	Twl	±1:40	±1:35	±1:33	±1:42	±1:56	±2:10	±2:03	±1:47	±1:37	±1:35	±1:38	±1:42
IN **Indianapolis** *39°42' N 86°10' W*	Rise 1st	8:06	7:52	7:18	6:29	5:45	5:19	5:21	5:44	6:13	6:41	7:13	7:47
	Set 1st	5:31	6:05	6:37	7:09	7:39	8:07	8:16	7:58	7:16	6:27	5:43	5:21
	Twl	±1:41	±1:36	±1:33	±1:37	±1:49	±2:04	±2:09	±1:53	±1:40	±1:35	±1:35	±1:40
	Rise 15th	8:04	7:37	6:56	6:07	5:30	5:16	5:29	5:57	6:26	6:55	7:29	7:59
	Set 15th	5:45	6:21	6:52	7:23	7:53	8:14	8:12	7:41	6:53	6:05	5:29	5:21
	Twl	±1:39	±1:35	±1:33	±1:38	±1:55	±2:09	±2:03	±1:41	±1:37	±1:35	±1:38	±1:42
South Bend *41°38' N 86°20' W*	Rise 1st	8:12	7:57	7:20	6:28	5:42	5:13	5:15	5:40	6:11	6:42	7:18	7:53
	Set 1st	5:26	6:01	6:36	7:11	7:44	8:13	8:23	8:03	7:18	6:27	5:40	5:16
	Twl	±1:44	±1:39	±1:36	±1:40	±1:53	±2:14	±2:18	±2:00	±1:45	±1:37	±1:39	±1:44
	Rise 15th	8:10	7:41	6:57	6:05	5:26	5:10	5:24	5:54	6:26	6:58	7:35	8:05
	Set 15th	5:40	6:19	6:52	7:26	7:58	8:21	8:18	7:45	6:54	6:04	5:25	5:16
	Twl	±1:43	±1:37	±1:37	±1:45	±2:03	±2:19	±2:11	±1:51	±1:40	±1:37	±1:41	±1:45
IA **Davenport** *41°30' N 90°40' W*	Rise 1st	7:29	7:14	6:37	5:45	5:59	5:31	5:32	5:57	6:28	6:59	6:34	7:09
	Set 1st	4:43	5:18	5:53	6:27	8:00	8:29	8:40	8:19	7:35	6:44	4:57	4:33
	Twl	±1:45	±1:40	±1:36	±1:41	±1:54	±2:14	±2:18	±2:00	±1:44	±1:38	±1:40	±1:44
	Rise 15th	7:26	6:57	6:14	6:22	5:43	5:28	5:41	6:11	6:42	7:14	6:51	7:21
	Set 15th	4:57	5:36	6:09	7:42	8:14	8:38	8:34	8:02	7:11	6:21	4:42	4:33
	Twl	±1:43	±1:38	±1:38	±1:46	±2:03	±2:19	±2:12	±1:51	±1:40	±1:38	±1:42	±1:45

→ **Sunrises & Sunsets have been adjusted for Daylight-Savings Time**

SunRISE/SET

Sunrises & Sunsets

Iowa/Kansas

		JAN	FEB	MAR	APR	MAY	JUN	JUL	AUG	SEP	OCT	NOV	DEC
Des Moines	Rise 1st	7:41	7:26	6:49	5:58	6:11	5:43	5:44	6:09	6:40	7:11	6:46	7:22
41° 35' N	Set 1st	4:55	5:30	6:05	6:40	8:12	8:42	8:52	8:32	7:48	6:56	5:09	4:45
93° 37' W	Twl	±1:45	±1:40	±1:36	±1:40	±1:54	±2:14	±2:18	±2:00	±1:44	±1:37	±1:39	±1:44
	Rise 15th	7:39	7:10	6:26	6:35	5:55	5:40	5:53	6:23	6:55	7:26	7:03	7:34
	Set 15th	5:09	5:48	6:21	7:55	8:27	8:50	8:47	8:14	7:24	6:33	4:54	4:45
	Twl	±1:43	±1:37	±1:37	±1:45	±2:02	±2:19	±2:11	±1:51	±1:39	±1:38	±1:41	±1:45
Mason City	Rise 1st	7:45	7:28	6:49	5:55	6:06	5:36	5:37	6:03	6:37	7:10	6:48	7:25
43° 09' N	Set 1st	4:48	5:25	6:02	6:39	8:14	8:46	8:56	8:34	7:48	6:54	5:05	4:39
93° 12' W	Twl	±1:47	±1:42	±1:39	±1:43	±1:58	±2:22	±2:27	±2:06	±1:46	±1:40	±1:40	±1:46
	Rise 15th	7:42	7:11	6:25	6:31	5:49	5:32	5:47	6:18	6:52	7:26	7:06	7:38
	Set 15th	5:03	5:44	6:19	7:56	8:30	8:54	8:50	8:16	7:23	6:30	4:49	4:38
	Twl	±1:45	±1:40	±1:40	±1:48	±2:09	±2:29	±2:19	±1:55	±1:42	±1:40	±1:43	±1:48
Sioux City	Rise 1st	7:56	7:40	7:01	6:08	6:21	5:51	5:52	6:18	6:51	7:23	6:59	7:36
42° 32' N	Set 1st	5:03	5:39	6:15	6:52	8:26	8:57	9:07	8:46	8:00	7:07	5:19	4:54
96° 25' W	Twl	±1:46	±1:41	±1:38	±1:41	±1:55	±2:17	±2:23	±2:03	±1:46	±1:39	±1:40	±1:45
	Rise 15th	7:53	7:23	6:38	6:45	6:04	5:48	6:02	6:32	7:05	7:39	7:17	7:48
	Set 15th	5:18	5:58	6:32	8:08	8:41	9:05	9:01	8:27	7:36	6:44	5:03	4:53
	Twl	±1:44	±1:38	±1:39	±1:46	±2:06	±2:24	±2:16	±1:54	±1:41	±1:38	±1:43	±1:46
KS **Kansas City**	Rise 1st	7:38	7:25	6:51	6:03	6:20	5:55	5:57	6:20	6:48	7:15	6:46	7:19
	Set 1st	5:07	5:40	6:12	6:43	8:12	8:39	8:48	8:30	7:49	7:01	5:18	4:57
39° 00' N	Twl	±1:40	±1:36	±1:32	±1:35	±1:46	±2:01	±2:05	±1:52	±1:39	±1:34	±1:34	±1:39
94° 40' W	Rise 15th	7:36	7:10	6:30	6:42	6:06	5:52	6:05	6:32	7:00	7:28	7:02	7:31
	Set 15th	5:21	5:56	6:26	7:56	8:25	8:46	8:44	8:13	7:27	6:40	5:05	4:57
	Twl	±1:37	±1:34	±1:33	±1:40	±1:53	±2:06	±2:00	±1:46	±1:36	±1:34	±1:37	±1:40
Oakley	Rise 1st	8:03	7:50	7:16	6:26	6:45	6:19	6:21	6:44	7:12	7:40	8:11	7:44
39° 08' N	Set 1st	5:32	6:05	6:36	7:07	8:37	9:04	9:13	8:55	8:14	7:26	6:42	6:21
100° 51' W	Twl	±1:40	±1:35	±1:33	±1:36	±1:46	±2:01	±2:05	±1:52	±1:38	±1:34	±1:35	±1:40

➝ **Sunrises & Sunsets have been adjusted for Daylight-Savings Time**

Sunrises & Sunsets

Kansas/Kentucky

		JAN	FEB	MAR	APR	MAY	JUN	JUL	AUG	SEP	OCT	NOV	DEC
Oakley	Rise 15th	8:01	7:35	6:55	7:06	6:30	6:17	6:30	6:57	7:25	7:53	7:27	7:56
	Set 15th	5:45	6:21	6:51	8:21	8:50	9:11	9:09	8:38	7:52	7:04	5:29	5:22
	Twl	±1:38	±1:34	±1:32	±1:39	±1:53	±2:06	±2:00	±1:46	±1:35	±1:34	±1:38	±1:40
Salina	Rise 1st	7:49	7:36	7:02	6:15	6:32	6:07	6:09	6:31	6:59	7:26	6:57	7:30
38°50' N	Set 1st	5:19	5:52	6:23	6:54	8:23	8:50	8:59	8:41	8:00	7:13	5:29	5:09
97°40' W	Twl	±1:40	±1:36	±1:33	±1:36	±1:47	±2:02	±2:06	±1:52	±1:39	±1:34	±1:36	±1:39
	Rise 15th	7:47	7:21	6:41	6:53	6:18	6:04	6:17	6:44	7:12	7:40	7:13	7:41
	Set 15th	5:33	6:08	6:37	8:07	8:36	8:57	8:54	8:24	7:38	6:51	5:16	5:09
	Twl	±1:38	±1:34	±1:33	±1:40	±1:54	±2:06	±2:01	±1:47	±1:36	±1:35	±1:38	±1:41
Wichita	Rise 1st	7:45	7:33	7:01	6:15	6:34	6:09	6:11	6:33	7:00	7:25	6:55	7:26
37°40' N	Set 1st	5:22	5:53	6:23	6:52	8:20	8:45	8:55	8:38	7:58	7:12	5:31	5:11
97°20' W	Twl	±1:39	±1:36	±1:33	±1:36	±1:45	±1:59	±2:02	±1:50	±1:39	±1:34	±1:34	±1:39
	Rise 15th	7:43	7:19	6:40	6:54	6:20	6:07	6:20	6:45	7:11	7:38	7:10	7:37
	Set 15th	5:35	6:09	6:37	8:05	8:32	8:53	8:50	8:22	7:37	6:52	5:18	5:12
	Twl	±1:37	±1:33	±1:32	±1:38	±1:52	±2:02	±1:59	±1:44	±1:35	±1:33	±1:36	±1:40
KY **Bowling Green**	Rise 1st	6:59	6:48	6:16	5:31	5:51	5:28	5:30	5:51	6:17	6:41	6:10	6:40
	Set 1st	4:40	5:11	5:40	6:08	7:35	8:00	8:09	7:52	7:14	6:29	4:48	4:29
	Twl	±1:37	±1:33	±1:30	±1:33	±1:42	±1:55	±1:59	±1:48	±1:36	±1:31	±1:32	±1:37
37°00' N *86°25' W*	Rise 15th	6:58	6:34	5:56	6:11	5:38	5:25	5:38	6:03	6:28	6:54	6:24	6:52
	Set 15th	4:53	5:26	5:53	7:21	7:47	8:07	8:05	7:37	6:53	6:09	4:36	4:30
	Twl	±1:35	±1:31	±1:30	±1:36	±1:48	±2:00	±1:54	±1:41	±1:32	±1:31	±1:34	±1:38
Lexington	Rise 1st	7:54	7:43	7:10	6:23	6:42	6:17	6:19	6:41	7:08	7:34	7:04	7:36
38°06' N	Set 1st	5:29	6:01	6:32	7:01	8:29	8:55	9:05	8:47	8:07	7:21	5:39	5:19
84°30' W	Twl	±1:37	±1:34	±1:32	±1:37	±1:49	±2:06	±2:09	±1:55	±1:40	±1:33	±1:33	±1:36
	Rise 15th	7:53	7:28	6:49	7:02	6:27	6:15	6:27	6:53	7:20	7:47	7:19	7:47
	Set 15th	5:42	6:17	6:45	8:14	8:42	9:03	9:00	8:31	7:46	7:00	5:26	5:19
	Twl	±1:36	±1:32	±1:33	±1:41	±1:56	±2:10	±2:04	±1:48	±1:36	±1:33	±1:35	±1:38

➡ **Sunrises & Sunsets have been adjusted for Daylight-Savings Time**

SunRISE/SET

Sunrises & Sunsets

Kentucky/Louisiana

		JAN	FEB	MAR	APR	MAY	JUN	JUL	AUG	SEP	OCT	NOV	DEC
Louisville	Rise 1st	8:00	7:48	7:15	6:28	6:46	6:21	6:23	6:46	7:13	7:39	7:09	7:41
38°15' N	Set 1st	5:34	6:06	6:36	7:06	8:34	9:01	9:10	8:53	8:13	7:26	5:43	5:23
85°45' W	Twl	±1:39	±1:35	±1:32	±1:35	±1:45	±2:00	±2:03	±1:50	±1:37	±1:33	±1:34	±1:38
	Rise 15th	7:58	7:33	6:54	7:07	6:32	6:19	6:32	6:58	7:25	7:52	7:24	7:53
	Set 15th	5:47	6:22	6:50	8:19	8:47	9:08	9:06	8:36	7:51	7:05	5:31	5:24
	Twl	±1:37	±1:32	±1:32	±1:39	±1:52	±2:03	±1:58	±1:44	±1:35	±1:33	±1:35	±1:39
LA **Alexandria**	Rise 1st	7:09	7:03	6:37	5:59	6:25	6:06	6:09	6:27	6:46	7:04	6:26	6:51
	Set 1st	5:18	5:45	6:08	6:29	7:49	8:10	8:18	8:06	7:34	6:55	5:21	5:07
31°20' N	Twl	±1:31	±1:27	±1:25	±1:26	±1:33	±1:41	±1:44	±1:36	±1:28	±1:25	±1:26	±1:30
92°30' W	Rise 15th	7:09	6:52	6:20	6:42	6:14	6:05	6:16	6:35	6:54	7:13	6:37	7:01
	Set 15th	5:30	5:57	6:18	7:39	7:59	8:16	8:16	7:53	7:16	6:38	5:12	5:09
	Twl	±1:28	±1:26	±1:25	±1:28	±1:38	±1:44	±1:41	±1:32	±1:26	±1:25	±1:28	±1:31
Baton Rouge	Rise 1st	7:01	6:56	6:31	5:54	6:21	6:03	6:06	6:22	6:41	6:58	6:19	6:44
	Set 1st	5:15	5:41	6:03	6:23	7:42	8:02	8:11	7:59	7:27	6:50	5:17	5:03
30°30' N	Twl	±1:30	±1:26	±1:24	±1:25	±1:32	±1:40	±1:42	±1:35	±1:28	±1:23	±1:25	±1:29
91°05' W	Rise 15th	7:02	6:45	6:14	6:37	6:10	6:02	6:12	6:31	6:49	7:07	6:30	6:54
	Set 15th	5:26	5:53	6:13	7:32	7:52	8:08	8:08	7:46	7:10	6:33	5:07	5:05
	Twl	±1:28	±1:24	±1:24	±1:28	±1:36	±1:42	±1:39	±1:32	±1:25	±1:25	±1:28	±1:30
New Orleans	Rise 1st	6:56	6:51	6:26	5:50	6:18	6:00	6:03	6:19	6:37	6:54	6:14	6:38
	Set 1st	5:12	5:38	5:59	6:19	7:38	7:57	8:05	7:54	7:23	6:46	5:13	5:00
30°00' N	Twl	±1:29	±1:25	±1:24	±1:25	±1:31	±1:39	±1:41	±1:34	±1:27	±1:23	±1:25	±1:29
90°05' W	Rise 15th	6:57	6:40	6:10	6:34	6:07	5:59	6:09	6:28	6:45	7:02	6:25	6:48
	Set 15th	5:23	5:49	6:09	7:27	7:47	9:03	8:03	7:41	7:06	6:30	5:04	5:02
	Twl	±1:27	±1:25	±1:23	±1:28	±1:35	±1:42	±1:39	±1:32	±1:25	±1:24	±1:27	±1:30
Port Arthur	Rise 1st	7:12	7:06	6:42	6:05	6:33	6:15	6:18	6:35	6:53	7:09	6:30	6:54
30°00' N	Set 1st	5:27	5:53	6:15	6:35	7:53	8:13	8:21	8:09	7:39	7:02	5:29	5:16
94°00' W	Twl	±1:28	±1:26	±1:24	±1:24	±1:32	±1:39	±1:41	±1:34	±1:27	±1:23	±1:25	±1:29

➜ **Sunrises & Sunsets have been adjusted for Daylight-Savings Time**

SunRISE/SET

Sunrises & Sunsets

Louisiana/Maine

		JAN	FEB	MAR	APR	MAY	JUN	JUL	AUG	SEP	OCT	NOV	DEC
Port Arthur	Rise 15th	7:13	6:56	6:26	6:49	6:23	6:14	6:25	6:43	7:01	7:18	6:41	7:04
	Set 15th	5:39	6:05	6:24	7:43	8:02	8:19	8:19	7:57	7:21	6:45	5:20	5:18
	Twl	±1:27	±1:24	±1:24	±1:28	±1:36	±1:41	±1:39	±1:30	±1:24	±1:24	±1:27	±1:30
Shreveport	Rise 1st	7:17	7:10	6:43	6:04	6:29	6:09	6:12	6:30	6:50	7:09	6:33	6:59
32°30' N	Set 1st	5:21	5:48	6:13	6:35	7:57	8:18	8:27	8:13	7:40	7:00	5:25	5:10
93°50' W	Twl	±1:32	±1:28	±1:26	±1:28	±1:34	±1:44	±1:46	±1:38	±1:29	±1:26	±1:27	±1:31
	Rise 15th	7:17	6:58	6:26	6:46	6:17	6:08	6:19	6:39	6:59	7:19	6:45	7:10
	Set 15th	5:33	6:01	6:23	7:45	8:07	8:24	8:24	8:00	7:22	6:43	5:15	5:11
	Twl	±1:29	±1:27	±1:26	±1:30	±1:39	±1:47	±1:40	±1:34	±1:27	±1:26	±1:29	±1:37
ME **Bangor**	Rise 1st	7:13	6:54	6:13	5:16	5:25	4:52	4:53	5:21	5:57	6:33	6:13	6:53
	Set 1st	4:05	4:44	5:23	6:03	7:40	8:14	8:25	8:01	7:12	6:16	4:24	3:56
44°48' N	Twl	±1:51	±1:46	±1:40	±1:45	±2:02	±2:30	±2:42	±2:15	±1:50	±1:43	±1:44	±1:50
68°42' W	Rise 15th	7:09	6:36	5:47	5:51	5:07	4:48	5:03	5:37	6:14	6:51	6:33	7:06
	Set 15th	4:21	5:04	5:41	7:21	7:57	8:23	8:18	7:41	6:46	5:50	4:07	3:55
	Twl	±1:51	±1:42	±1:40	±1:51	±2:14	±2:41	±2:30	±2:03	±1:45	±1:42	±1:50	±1:55
Calais	Rise 1st	7:08	6:50	6:07	5:10	5:18	4:45	4:46	5:14	5:51	6:28	6:08	6:48
45°11' N	Set 1st	3:58	4:37	5:17	5:57	7:36	8:10	8:20	7:56	7:07	6:10	4:17	3:49
67°20' W	Twl	±1:51	±1:46	±1:42	±1:47	±2:04	±2:36	±2:45	±2:14	±1:52	±1:43	±1:45	±1:50
	Rise 15th	7:05	6:30	5:42	5:44	5:00	4:41	4:56	5:31	6:08	6:45	6:28	7:02
	Set 15th	4:14	4:57	5:36	7:15	7:52	8:19	8:14	7:36	6:40	5:44	4:00	3:46
	Twl	±1:48	±1:43	±1:42	±1:54	±2:18	±2:47	±2:32	±2:02	±1:48	±1:43	±1:48	±1:54
Portland	Rise 1st	7:15	6:58	6:17	5:22	5:33	5:02	5:03	5:30	6:05	6:39	6:17	6:55
43°40' N	Set 1st	4:15	4:52	5:30	6:08	7:44	8:16	8:26	8:04	7:16	6:22	4:32	4:05
70°15' W	Twl	±1:48	±1:43	±1:39	±1:44	±1:59	±2:24	±2:31	±2:07	±1:49	±1:41	±1:42	±1:47
	Rise 15th	7:11	6:40	5:53	5:58	5:16	4:59	5:13	5:46	6:20	6:55	6:35	7:08
	Set 15th	4:30	5:11	5:47	7:25	8:00	8:24	8:20	7:44	6:51	5:57	4:16	4:05
	Twl	±1:46	±1:41	±1:41	±1:49	±2:10	±2:33	±2:21	±1:58	±1:44	±1:41	±1:44	±1:49

➙ **Sunrises & Sunsets have been adjusted for Daylight-Savings Time**

SunRISE/SET

Sunrises & Sunsets

Maine/Maryland/Massachusetts

		JAN	FEB	MAR	APR	MAY	JUN	JUL	AUG	SEP	OCT	NOV	DEC
Presque Isle 46°40' N 68°00' W	Rise 1st	7:17	6:56	6:11	5:11	5:17	4:42	4:42	5:12	5:52	6:30	6:14	6:56
	Set 1st	3:55	4:38	5:18	6:01	7:42	8:18	8:29	8:03	7:11	6:12	4:17	3:46
	Twl	±1:55	±1:46	±1:44	±1:51	±2:10	±2:51	±3:03	±2:22	±1:56	±1:47	±1:47	±1:53
	Rise 15th	7:12	6:36	5:45	5:45	4:58	4:38	4:54	5:30	6:10	6:49	6:34	7:10
	Set 15th	4:11	4:57	5:38	7:20	8:00	8:27	8:22	7:42	6:44	5:45	3:59	3:45
	Twl	±1:53	±1:46	±1:45	±1:58	±2:26	±3:08	±2:45	±2:08	±1:50	±1:46	±1:50	±1:55
MD **Baltimore** 39°18' N 76°37' W	Rise 1st	7:26	7:14	6:39	5:51	6:08	5:42	5:43	6:06	6:35	7:02	6:34	7:07
	Set 1st	4:54	5:27	5:59	6:30	8:00	8:27	8:37	8:19	7:37	6:49	5:05	4:44
	Twl	±1:40	±1:36	±1:33	±1:37	±1:47	±2:03	±2:07	±1:52	±1:39	±1:34	±1:35	±1:39
	Rise 15th	7:25	6:58	6:18	6:30	5:53	5:39	5:52	6:19	6:48	7:16	6:50	7:19
	Set 15th	5:08	5:43	6:13	7:44	8:13	8:35	8:32	8:02	7:15	6:28	4:52	4:44
	Twl	±1:38	±1:35	±1:34	±1:40	±1:55	±2:07	±2:02	±1:46	±1:36	±1:34	±1:38	±1:41
Cumberland 39°40' N 78°43' W	Rise 1st	7:36	7:23	6:48	5:59	6:16	5:49	5:51	6:14	6:43	7:11	6:43	7:16
	Set 1st	5:01	5:35	6:07	6:39	8:09	8:37	8:47	8:28	7:46	6:58	5:13	4:51
	Twl	±1:41	±1:36	±1:34	±1:37	±1:48	±2:04	±2:08	±1:54	±1:41	±1:34	±1:35	±1:40
	Rise 15th	7:34	7:07	6:27	6:38	6:01	5:46	6:00	6:27	6:56	7:25	6:59	7:29
	Set 15th	5:15	5:51	6:22	7:53	8:22	8:44	8:42	8:11	7:24	6:36	4:59	4:52
	Twl	±1:40	±1:35	±1:33	±1:41	±1:56	±2:09	±2:03	±1:46	±1:36	±1:34	±1:39	±1:41
MA **Boston** 42°20' N 71°00' W	Rise 1st	7:14	6:58	6:20	5:27	5:39	5:10	5:11	5:37	6:10	6:41	6:18	6:54
	Set 1st	4:23	4:59	5:34	6:10	7:44	8:15	8:25	8:04	7:18	6:26	4:38	4:13
	Twl	±1:45	±1:40	±1:37	±1:41	±1:55	±2:16	±2:21	±2:02	±1:45	±1:38	±1:40	±1:44
	Rise 15th	7:11	6:41	5:56	6:03	5:23	5:07	5:21	5:52	6:24	6:57	6:35	7:07
	Set 15th	4:37	5:17	5:51	7:26	7:59	8:23	8:19	7:45	6:54	6:02	4:22	4:13
	Twl	±1:43	±1:38	±1:38	±1:46	±2:04	±2:22	±2:14	±1:53	±1:39	±1:38	±1:42	±1:45
New Bedford 41°40' N 70°52' W	Rise 1st	7:11	6:55	6:19	5:26	5:39	5:10	5:13	5:37	6:09	6:41	6:17	6:51
	Set 1st	4:24	4:58	5:34	6:10	7:42	8:11	8:22	8:01	7:16	6:25	4:37	4:14
	Twl	±1:44	±1:40	±1:36	±1:39	±1:53	±2:14	±2:18	±1:59	±1:45	±1:38	±1:40	±1:44

→ **Sunrises & Sunsets have been adjusted for Daylight-Savings Time**

SunRISE/SET

Sunrises & Sunsets

Massachusetts/Michigan

		JAN	FEB	MAR	APR	MAY	JUN	JUL	AUG	SEP	OCT	NOV	DEC
New Bedford	Rise 15th	7:08	6:40	5:56	6:03	5:23	5:07	5:21	5:51	6:24	6:57	6:33	7:04
	Set 15th	4:37	5:17	5:51	7:24	7:56	8:20	8:16	7:43	6:54	6:02	4:22	4:14
	Twl	±1:44	±1:37	±1:37	±1:46	±2:03	±2:18	±2:11	±1:52	±1:38	±1:38	±1:42	±1:45
Springfield	Rise 1st	7:19	7:03	6:26	5:33	5:46	5:17	5:18	5:44	6:16	6:48	6:24	6:59
42°08' N	Set 1st	4:30	5:05	5:41	6:16	7:50	8:20	8:30	8:09	7:24	6:32	4:44	4:20
72°37' W	Twl	±1:45	±1:40	±1:37	±1:41	±1:54	±2:16	±2:21	±2:02	±1:45	±1:38	±1:40	±1:44
	Rise 15th	7:16	6:46	6:02	6:10	5:30	5:14	5:28	5:58	6:31	7:03	6:41	7:12
	Set 15th	4:44	5:23	5:57	7:32	8:05	8:28	8:25	7:51	7:00	6:09	4:29	4:19
	Twl	±1:43	±1:38	±1:38	±1:46	±2:04	±2:22	±2:14	±1:52	±1:41	±1:38	±1:42	±1:46
MI													
Cadillac	Rise 1st	8:17	8:00	7:19	6:23	6:33	6:01	6:02	6:29	7:05	7:40	7:19	7:57
	Set 1st	5:14	5:52	6:30	7:09	8:46	9:19	9:29	9:06	8:18	7:22	5:31	5:04
44°16' N	Twl	±1:49	±1:43	±1:40	±1:45	±2:01	±2:28	±2:36	±2:11	±1:49	±1:42	±1:44	±1:48
85°25' W	Rise 15th	8:14	7:41	6:54	6:58	6:15	5:57	6:12	6:45	7:21	7:57	7:38	8:11
	Set 15th	5:29	6:11	6:48	8:26	9:02	9:27	9:23	8:46	7:52	6:57	5:15	5:03
	Twl	±1:47	±1:41	±1:41	±1:52	±2:13	±2:38	±2:25	±2:00	±1:45	±1:42	±1:45	±1:50
Cheboygan	Rise 1st	8:19	7:59	7:16	6:18	6:26	5:52	5:53	6:22	6:59	7:36	7:18	7:58
45°38' N	Set 1st	5:05	5:45	6:25	7:06	8:45	9:20	9:31	9:06	8:16	7:18	5:25	4:56
84°29' W	Twl	±1:52	±1:46	±1:43	±1:49	±2:07	±2:40	±2:49	±2:15	±1:53	±1:45	±1:46	±1:51
	Rise 15th	8:15	7:40	6:50	6:52	6:07	5:48	6:03	6:38	7:16	7:55	7:38	8:12
	Set 15th	5:21	6:05	6:44	8:25	9:03	9:29	9:24	8:45	7:49	6:52	5:07	4:55
	Twl	±1:49	±1:44	±1:44	±1:54	±2:20	±2:53	±2:36	±2:05	±1:48	±1:44	±1:49	±1:53
Detroit	Rise 1st	8:02	7:46	7:08	6:15	6:27	5:58	5:59	6:25	6:58	7:30	7:06	7:42
42°23' N	Set 1st	5:11	5:47	6:22	6:58	8:32	9:03	9:13	8:52	8:06	7:14	5:25	5:01
83°05' W	Twl	±1:45	±1:40	±1:38	±1:42	±1:56	±2:16	±2:22	±2:02	±1:46	±1:38	±1:41	±1:45
	Rise 15th	7:59	7:29	6:44	6:51	6:11	5:55	6:09	6:40	7:12	7:45	7:23	7:55
	Set 15th	5:25	6:05	6:39	8:14	8:47	9:11	9:07	8:33	7:42	6:50	5:10	5:00
	Twl	±1:43	±1:38	±1:38	±1:47	±2:06	±2:24	±2:15	±1:54	±1:42	±1:39	±1:42	±1:46

→ **Sunrises & Sunsets have been adjusted for Daylight-Savings Time**

Sunrises & Sunsets

Michigan/Minnesota

		JAN	FEB	MAR	APR	MAY	JUN	JUL	AUG	SEP	OCT	NOV	DEC
Lansing 42°47' N 84°40' W	Rise 1st	8:09	7:53	7:14	6:21	6:33	6:03	6:04	6:30	7:03	7:36	7:13	7:50
	Set 1st	5:16	5:52	6:28	7:05	8:39	9:11	9:21	8:59	8:13	7:20	5:31	5:06
	Twl	±1:46	±1:41	±1:38	±1:42	±1:57	±2:19	±2:24	±2:04	±1:46	±1:39	±1:40	±1:45
	Rise 15th	8:06	7:36	6:51	6:57	6:16	6:00	6:14	6:45	7:19	7:52	7:31	8:02
	Set 15th	5:30	6:11	6:45	8:21	8:55	9:19	9:15	8:40	7:48	6:56	5:16	5:05
	Twl	±1:44	±1:38	±1:39	±1:48	±2:07	±2:26	±2:17	±1:56	±1:43	±1:39	±1:42	±1:48
Marquette 46°30' N 87°21' W	Rise 1st	8:32	8:12	7:28	6:29	6:36	6:00	6:02	6:30	7:10	7:48	7:30	8:13
	Set 1st	5:13	5:55	6:36	7:18	8:58	9:35	9:46	9:19	8:28	7:29	5:35	5:04
	Twl	±1:55	±1:47	±1:44	±1:51	±2:11	±2:49	±3:00	±2:17	±1:51	±1:42	±1:45	±1:53
	Rise 15th	8:29	7:52	7:02	7:03	6:17	5:56	6:13	6:49	7:28	8:07	7:52	8:27
	Set 15th	5:29	6:16	6:56	8:37	9:17	9:44	9:39	8:58	8:00	7:03	5:17	5:04
	Twl	±1:53	±1:44	±1:45	±1:58	±2:25	±3:05	±2:40	±2:03	±1:46	±1:42	±1:47	±1:54
Sault Sainte Marie 46°27' N 84°22' W	Rise 1st	8:21	8:01	7:17	6:17	6:23	5:48	5:49	6:19	6:58	7:36	7:19	8:01
	Set 1st	5:01	5:42	6:24	7:07	8:47	9:23	9:34	9:08	8:16	7:17	5:22	4:52
	Twl	±1:55	±1:48	±1:44	±1:50	±2:10	±2:48	±2:59	±2:21	±1:56	±1:47	±1:48	±1:53
	Rise 15th	8:17	7:41	6:50	6:50	6:04	5:44	6:00	6:36	7:16	7:55	7:39	8:15
	Set 15th	5:18	6:03	6:44	8:25	9:05	9:32	9:27	8:47	7:49	6:51	5:04	4:51
	Twl	±1:52	±1:45	±1:45	±1:58	±2:25	±3:04	±2:42	±2:05	±1:48	±1:43	±1:51	±1:55
MN **Duluth** 46°48' N 92°10' W	Rise 1st	7:54	7:33	6:49	5:48	5:54	5:18	5:18	5:49	6:28	7:07	6:51	7:33
	Set 1st	4:31	5:12	5:54	6:38	8:19	8:55	9:06	8:41	7:48	6:49	4:53	4:22
	Twl	±1:55	±1:49	±1:45	±1:51	±2:11	±2:53	±3:07	±2:22	±1:56	±1:47	±1:48	±1:54
	Rise 15th	7:49	7:13	6:22	6:21	5:34	5:14	5:30	6:06	6:46	7:26	7:11	7:47
	Set 15th	4:47	5:33	6:14	7:57	8:37	9:05	8:59	8:19	7:21	6:22	4:35	4:21
	Twl	±1:53	±1:46	±1:46	±1:58	±2:28	±3:11	±2:46	±2:08	±1:50	±1:46	±1:50	±1:55
International Falls 48°36' N 93°25' W	Rise 1st	8:06	7:43	6:55	5:52	5:54	5:16	5:15	5:48	6:31	7:13	7:00	7:45
	Set 1st	4:29	5:12	5:57	6:44	8:28	9:08	9:19	8:51	7:56	6:53	4:54	4:21
	Twl	±2:00	±1:53	±1:49	±1:56	±2:21	±3:29	NONE	±2:35	±2:01	±1:50	±1:51	±1:58

→ **Sunrises & Sunsets have been adjusted for Daylight-Savings Time**

SunRISE/SET

Sunrises & Sunsets

Minnesota/Mississippi

		JAN	FEB	MAR	APR	MAY	JUN	JUL	AUG	SEP	OCT	NOV	DEC
International Falls	Rise 15th	8:01	7:21	6:27	6:23	5:33	5:11	5:27	6:07	6:50	7:34	7:22	7:59
Note: Some Minnesota locations do not experience an end of twilight during the summer	Set 15th	4:46	5:35	6:19	8:05	8:48	9:18	9:11	8:28	7:26	6:25	4:34	4:18
	Twl	±1:57	±1:51	±1:51	±2:05	±2:42	NONE	±3:13	±2:16	±1:55	±1:49	±1:56	±2:01
Minneapolis	Rise 1st	7:52	7:33	6:51	5:54	6:03	5:30	5:31	5:59	6:35	7:11	6:52	7:31
44°58' N 93°20' W	Set 1st	4:43	5:21	6:01	6:41	8:19	8:53	9:04	8:40	7:51	6:54	5:02	4:33
	Twl	±1:50	±1:46	±1:42	±1:47	±2:04	±2:34	±2:42	±2:13	±1:51	±1:43	±1:44	±1:51
	Rise 15th	7:48	7:14	6:26	6:29	5:44	5:26	5:41	6:15	6:52	7:29	7:11	7:45
	Set 15th	4:58	5:41	6:19	7:59	8:36	9:02	8:57	8:20	7:24	6:29	4:45	4:32
	Twl	±1:49	±1:43	±1:43	±1:53	±2:16	±2:44	±2:30	±2:01	±1:46	±1:42	±1:47	±1:51
MS													
Biloxi	Rise 1st	6:52	6:47	6:22	5:45	6:12	5:54	5:57	6:14	6:32	6:49	6:10	6:35
30°24' N 88°53' W	Set 1st	5:06	5:32	5:54	6:14	7:34	7:53	8:02	7:50	7:18	6:41	5:08	4:54
	Twl	±1:30	±1:26	±1:24	±1:25	±1:31	±1:40	±1:42	±1:35	±1:28	±1:23	±1:25	±1:30
	Rise 15th	6:53	6:36	6:06	6:28	6:01	5:53	6:04	6:22	6:40	6:58	6:21	6:45
	Set 15th	5:17	5:44	6:04	7:23	7:43	7:59	7:59	7:37	7:01	6:25	4:59	4:57
	Twl	±1:28	±1:24	±1:24	±1:28	±1:36	±1:42	±1:39	±1:32	±1:26	±1:24	±1:27	±1:30
Jackson	Rise 1st	7:02	6:55	6:28	5:49	6:14	5:55	5:58	6:15	6:36	6:55	6:18	6:44
32°20' N 90°10' W	Set 1st	5:07	5:34	5:58	6:21	7:42	8:03	8:12	7:58	7:25	6:46	5:11	4:55
	Twl	±1:31	±1:28	±1:26	±1:27	±1:34	±1:43	±1:45	±1:38	±1:29	±1:26	±1:26	±1:31
	Rise 15th	7:02	6:43	6:11	6:32	6:03	5:53	6:05	6:25	6:44	7:04	6:30	6:55
	Set 15th	5:18	5:47	6:09	7:30	7:52	8:09	8:09	7:45	7:07	6:28	5:00	4:57
	Twl	±1:30	±1:26	±1:25	±1:30	±1:38	±1:47	±1:43	±1:33	±1:27	±1:26	±1:29	±1:32
Meridian	Rise 1st	6:56	6:49	6:22	5:43	6:08	5:49	5:51	6:09	6:30	6:49	6:12	6:38
32°20' N 88°42' W	Set 1st	5:01	5:28	5:52	6:15	7:36	7:57	8:06	7:52	7:19	6:40	5:05	4:49
	Twl	±1:31	±1:28	±1:26	±1:27	±1:34	±1:43	±1:46	±1:38	±1:29	±1:26	±1:27	±1:31
	Rise 15th	6:56	6:38	6:05	6:26	5:57	5:47	5:59	6:19	6:39	6:58	6:24	6:49
	Set 15th	5:12	5:41	6:03	7:24	7:46	8:03	8:03	7:39	7:01	6:22	4:54	4:51
	Twl	±1:30	±1:26	±1:25	±1:30	±1:38	±1:47	±1:43	±1:34	±1:27	±1:26	±1:29	±1:32

→ **Sunrises & Sunsets have been adjusted for Daylight-Savings Time**

Sunrises & Sunsets

Mississippi/Missouri

		JAN	FEB	MAR	APR	MAY	JUN	JUL	AUG	SEP	OCT	NOV	DEC
Natchez	Rise 1st	7:05	6:59	6:33	5:54	6:21	6:01	6:04	6:22	6:41	6:59	6:22	6:47
31°35' N	Set 1st	5:13	5:40	6:04	6:25	7:46	8:06	8:15	8:02	7:30	6:51	5:17	5:02
91°25' W	Twl	±1:31	±1:27	±1:25	±1:26	±1:32	±1:43	±1:44	±1:36	±1:28	±1:25	±1:26	±1:30
	Rise 15th	7:06	6:47	6:16	6:37	6:09	6:00	6:11	6:31	6:50	7:09	6:34	6:58
	Set 15th	5:25	5:53	6:14	7:34	7:55	8:12	8:12	7:49	7:12	6:34	5:07	5:04
	Twl	±1:29	±1:25	±1:25	±1:29	±1:38	±1:45	±1:41	±1:32	±1:26	±1:25	±1:28	±1:31
Tupelo	Rise 1st	7:01	6:52	6:24	5:42	6:05	5:44	5:46	6:06	6:28	6:49	6:15	6:43
34°15' N	Set 1st	4:56	5:25	5:51	6:16	7:39	8:02	8:11	7:56	7:21	6:39	5:02	4:45
88°42' W	Twl	±1:34	±1:29	±1:27	±1:29	±1:37	±1:48	±1:50	±1:42	±1:32	±1:28	±1:29	±1:33
	Rise 15th	7:01	6:40	6:05	6:24	5:53	5:42	5:54	6:16	6:38	7:00	6:28	6:53
	Set 15th	5:08	5:38	6:03	7:26	7:50	8:08	8:07	7:42	7:02	6:21	4:51	4:47
	Twl	±1:33	±1:29	±1:27	±1:33	±1:42	±1:51	±1:47	±1:36	±1:29	±1:28	±1:31	±1:34
MO **Kansas City**	Rise 1st	7:37	7:25	6:51	6:03	6:20	5:54	5:56	6:19	6:47	7:14	6:46	7:18
	Set 1st	5:07	5:39	6:11	6:42	8:11	8:38	8:48	8:30	7:49	7:01	5:18	4:56
39°03' N	Twl	±1:39	±1:36	±1:33	±1:36	±1:47	±2:02	±2:05	±1:52	±1:38	±1:33	±1:34	±1:39
94°30' W	Rise 15th	7:36	7:10	6:30	6:42	6:06	5:52	6:05	6:32	7:00	7:28	7:01	7:30
	Set 15th	5:20	5:56	6:25	7:56	8:24	8:46	8:43	8:13	7:27	6:40	5:04	4:57
	Twl	±1:38	±1:33	±1:33	±1:39	±1:54	±2:06	±2:00	±1:46	±1:35	±1:33	±1:37	±1:40
St. Joseph	Rise 1st	7:41	7:27	6:53	6:04	6:20	5:53	5:55	6:18	6:47	7:15	6:48	7:21
39°46' N	Set 1st	5:06	5:39	6:11	6:43	8:14	8:41	8:51	8:33	7:51	7:02	5:17	4:55
94°50' W	Twl	±1:40	±1:37	±1:34	±1:37	±1:48	±2:05	±2:09	±1:54	±1:40	±1:34	±1:36	±1:41
	Rise 15th	7:39	7:12	6:31	6:42	6:05	5:51	6:04	6:31	7:00	7:30	7:04	7:33
	Set 15th	5:19	5:56	6:26	7:57	8:27	8:49	8:47	8:16	7:28	6:40	5:04	4:56
	Twl	±1:40	±1:34	±1:34	±1:42	±1:56	±2:09	±2:03	±1:46	±1:37	±1:35	±1:38	±1:42
St. Louis	Rise 1st	7:19	7:07	6:33	5:46	6:04	5:38	5:40	6:02	6:30	6:57	6:28	7:00
38°40' N	Set 1st	4:50	5:23	5:54	6:24	7:53	8:20	8:29	8:11	7:31	6:44	5:01	4:40
90°12' W	Twl	±1:40	±1:35	±1:32	±1:36	±1:46	±2:01	±2:04	±1:51	±1:38	±1:33	±1:34	±1:39

➙ **Sunrises & Sunsets have been adjusted for Daylight-Savings Time**

SunRISE/SET

Sunrises & Sunsets

Missouri/Montana

		JAN	FEB	MAR	APR	MAY	JUN	JUL	AUG	SEP	OCT	NOV	DEC
St. Louis	Rise 15th	7:17	6:52	6:12	6:25	5:49	5:36	5:48	6:15	6:42	7:10	6:43	7:11
	Set 15th	5:04	5:39	6:08	7:38	8:06	8:27	8:25	7:55	7:09	6:23	4:48	4:41
	Twl	±1:40	±1:33	±1:32	±1:39	±1:53	±2:05	±1:59	±1:44	±1:35	±1:33	±1:36	±1:39
Springfield	Rise 1st	7:27	7:16	6:45	5:59	6:19	5:55	5:57	6:18	6:44	7:09	6:38	7:09
37°15' N 93°20' W	Set 1st	5:07	5:38	6:07	6:36	8:03	8:28	8:38	8:21	7:42	6:57	5:16	4:56
	Twl	±1:38	±1:34	±1:31	±1:34	±1:43	±1:57	±1:59	±1:47	±1:37	±1:31	±1:32	±1:37
	Rise 15th	7:26	7:02	6:25	6:39	6:05	5:52	6:05	6:30	6:55	7:21	6:52	7:20
	Set 15th	5:20	5:53	6:21	7:48	8:15	8:35	8:34	8:05	7:21	6:37	5:03	4:57
	Twl	±1:35	±1:32	±1:31	±1:37	±1:50	±2:00	±1:55	±1:42	±1:33	±1:31	±1:34	±1:38
MT **Bonners Ferry**	Rise 1st	8:38	8:15	7:27	6:23	6:25	5:47	5:47	6:20	6:03	7:45	7:32	8:17
48°38' N 116°21' W	Set 1st	5:01	5:44	6:30	7:17	9:01	9:40	9:51	9:23	8:27	7:24	5:25	4:52
Note: Some Montana locations do not experience an end of twilight during the summer	Twl	±1:59	±1:53	±1:49	±1:55	±2:20	±3:31	NONE	±2:35	±2:02	±1:51	±1:52	±1:58
	Rise 15th	8:33	7:53	6:58	6:54	6:04	5:42	5:59	6:39	7:22	8:06	7:54	8:31
	Set 15th	5:18	6:07	6:51	8:37	9:20	9:50	9:43	9:00	7:58	6:56	5:06	4:50
	Twl	±1:56	±1:51	±1:51	±2:05	±2:43	NONE	±3:13	±2:16	±1:55	±1:50	±1:55	±2:01
Bozeman	Rise 1st	8:05	7:45	7:02	6:04	6:11	5:38	5:39	6:08	6:45	7:23	7:04	7:45
45°40' N 111°00' W	Set 1st	4:51	5:31	6:11	6:53	8:31	9:06	9:17	8:52	8:02	7:04	5:10	4:42
	Twl	±1:52	±1:46	±1:43	±1:47	±2:07	±2:40	±2:49	±2:17	±1:52	±1:45	±1:46	±1:51
	Rise 15th	8:01	7:26	6:36	6:38	5:53	5:34	5:49	6:25	7:03	7:41	7:24	7:58
	Set 15th	5:07	5:51	6:30	8:11	8:49	9:15	9:10	8:32	7:35	6:38	4:53	4:41
	Twl	±1:50	±1:44	±1:44	±1:55	±2:21	±2:53	±2:34	±2:04	±1:48	±1:44	±1:49	±1:53
Glendive	Rise 1st	7:45	7:24	6:38	5:37	5:43	5:07	5:07	5:38	6:18	6:58	6:42	7:24
47°07' N 104°40' W	Set 1st	4:20	5:01	5:44	6:28	8:10	8:47	8:58	8:31	7:38	6:38	4:42	4:11
	Twl	±1:56	±1:50	±1:46	±1:52	±2:12	±2:57	±3:13	±2:23	±1:57	±1:48	±1:49	±1:55
	Rise 15th	7:40	7:03	6:11	6:10	5:23	5:02	5:19	5:56	6:36	7:17	7:03	7:38
	Set 15th	4:37	5:23	6:05	7:48	8:28	8:56	8:50	8:09	7:10	6:11	4:24	4:10
	Twl	±1:53	±1:48	±1:46	±1:59	±2:30	±3:19	±2:47	±2:08	±1:49	±1:47	±1:51	±1:57

➥ **Sunrises & Sunsets have been adjusted for Daylight-Savings Time**

SunRISE/SET

Sunrises & Sunsets

Montana/Nebraska

		JAN	FEB	MAR	APR	MAY	JUN	JUL	AUG	SEP	OCT	NOV	DEC
Great Falls	Rise 1st	8:12	7:51	7:05	6:03	6:08	5:32	5:32	6:03	6:44	7:24	7:09	7:52
47°27' N	Set 1st	4:45	5:27	6:10	6:55	8:37	9:14	9:25	8:58	8:05	7:04	5:07	4:36
111°12' W	Twl	±1:56	±1:50	±1:46	±2:54	±2:14	±3:02	±3:21	±2:24	±1:58	±1:49	±1:50	±1:56
	Rise 15th	8:08	7:30	6:37	6:36	5:48	5:27	5:43	6:21	7:02	7:44	7:30	8:06
	Set 15th	5:02	5:49	6:31	8:15	8:55	9:24	9:18	8:36	7:36	6:37	4:49	4:34
	Twl	±1:54	±1:47	±1:48	±2:00	±2:33	±3:28	±2:51	±2:06	±1:51	±1:47	±1:52	±1:58
Helena	Rise 1st	8:13	7:52	7:07	6:07	6:13	5:38	5:38	6:09	6:48	7:27	7:10	7:52
46°40' N	Set 1st	4:51	5:32	6:14	6:57	8:38	9:14	9:25	8:59	8:07	7:07	5:12	4:42
112°00' W	Twl	±1:55	±1:49	±1:45	±1:51	±2:11	±2:51	±3:04	±2:22	±1:56	±1:48	±1:48	±1:53
	Rise 15th	8:08	7:32	6:40	6:40	5:53	5:34	5:50	6:26	7:06	7:46	7:31	8:06
	Set 15th	5:08	5:53	6:34	8:16	8:56	9:24	9:18	8:38	7:39	6:41	4:54	4:41
	Twl	±1:52	±1:46	±1:46	±1:58	±2:27	±3:08	±2:43	±2:08	±1:50	±1:46	±1:51	±1:55
NE **Bassett**	Rise 1st	8:08	7:52	7:13	6:20	6:32	6:03	6:04	6:30	7:03	7:35	7:12	7:49
	Set 1st	5:16	5:52	6:28	7:04	8:38	9:09	9:20	8:58	8:12	7:19	5:31	5:06
42°37' N	Twl	±1:45	±1:40	±1:38	±1:42	±1:56	±2:18	±2:23	±2:04	±1:46	±1:39	±1:40	±1:45
99°30' W	Rise 15th	8:05	7:35	6:50	6:57	6:16	6:00	6:14	6:45	7:18	7:51	7:30	8:01
	Set 15th	5:30	6:10	6:45	8:20	8:54	9:18	9:14	8:39	7:47	6:55	5:15	5:05
	Twl	±1:44	±1:39	±1:38	±1:47	±2:05	±2:25	±2:15	±1:54	±1:43	±1:39	±1:43	±1:47
Grand Island	Rise 1st	7:59	7:44	7:08	6:17	6:32	6:04	6:05	6:30	7:01	7:30	7:05	7:39
40°59' N	Set 1st	5:16	5:51	6:25	6:59	8:31	9:00	9:10	8:50	8:06	7:15	5:29	5:06
98°25' W	Twl	±1:44	±1:38	±1:35	±1:39	±1:51	±2:10	±2:14	±1:58	±1:43	±1:37	±1:39	±1:42
	Rise 15th	7:56	7:28	6:45	6:54	6:16	6:01	6:15	6:44	7:14	7:45	7:21	7:52
	Set 15th	5:31	6:08	6:41	8:14	8:45	9:08	9:04	8:32	7:42	6:53	5:15	5:06
	Twl	±1:41	±1:37	±1:36	±1:43	±2:00	±2:15	±2:08	±1:50	±1:39	±1:36	±1:40	±1:44
Lincoln	Rise 1st	7:51	7:37	7:01	6:10	6:25	5:57	5:59	6:23	6:54	7:24	6:58	7:32
40°50' N	Set 1st	5:10	5:45	6:18	6:52	8:23	8:52	9:02	8:42	7:59	7:09	5:23	5:00
96°42' W	Twl	±1:43	±1:38	±1:35	±1:39	±1:52	±2:10	±2:14	±1:57	±1:42	±1:36	±1:38	±1:41

➜ **Sunrises & Sunsets have been adjusted for Daylight-Savings Time**

SunRISE/SET

Sunrises & Sunsets

Nebraska/Nevada

		JAN	FEB	MAR	APR	MAY	JUN	JUL	AUG	SEP	OCT	NOV	DEC
Lincoln	Rise 15th	7:49	7:21	6:38	6:48	6:09	5:55	6:08	6:37	7:08	7:38	7:14	7:44
	Set 15th	5:24	6:02	6:34	8:07	8:38	9:00	8:57	8:25	7:36	6:46	5:08	5:00
	Twl	±1:41	±1:36	±1:36	±1:43	±1:59	±2:15	±2:07	±1:49	±1:38	±1:37	±1:40	±1:43
Omaha	Rise 1st	7:50	7:35	6:58	6:07	6:21	5:53	5:55	6:19	6:51	7:21	6:56	7:30
41°15' N	Set 1st	5:06	5:41	6:15	6:49	8:21	8:51	9:01	8:41	7:57	7:06	5:19	4:56
96°00' W	Twl	±1:44	±1:38	±1:36	±1:40	±1:52	±2:11	±2:16	±1:58	±1:43	±1:37	±1:39	±1:43
	Rise 15th	7:47	7:19	6:36	6:44	6:05	5:50	6:04	6:33	7:05	7:36	7:12	7:43
	Set 15th	5:20	5:58	6:31	8:04	8:36	8:59	8:55	8:23	7:33	6:43	5:05	4:56
	Twl	±1:42	±1:37	±1:37	±1:44	±2:01	±2:17	±2:10	±1:51	±1:39	±1:37	±1:40	±1:44
Scottsbluff	Rise 1st	7:22	7:07	6:29	5:37	5:50	5:21	5:23	5:48	6:20	6:51	6:27	7:03
41°55' N	Set 1st	4:34	5:10	5:45	6:20	7:53	8:23	8:33	8:12	7:28	6:36	4:48	4:24
103°35' W	Twl	±1:45	±1:39	±1:36	±1:41	±1:54	±2:15	±2:20	±2:01	±1:45	±1:38	±1:40	±1:44
	Rise 15th	7:20	6:50	6:06	6:14	5:34	5:18	5:32	6:03	6:35	7:07	6:44	7:15
	Set 15th	4:49	5:28	6:01	7:36	8:08	8:31	8:28	7:54	7:04	6:13	4:33	4:24
	Twl	±1:42	±1:37	±1:38	±1:45	±2:04	±2:20	±2:12	±1:53	±1:40	±1:37	±1:42	±1:45
NV **Ely**	Rise 1st	6:59	6:46	6:12	5:24	5:41	5:15	5:17	5:40	6:08	6:36	6:07	6:40
	Set 1st	4:28	5:01	5:32	6:03	7:33	8:00	8:09	7:51	7:10	6:22	4:38	4:17
39°10' N	Twl	±1:40	±1:35	±1:33	±1:36	±1:47	±2:03	±2:07	±1:53	±1:39	±1:34	±1:35	±1:39
114°50' W	Rise 15th	6:57	6:31	5:50	6:02	5:26	5:13	5:26	5:53	6:21	6:49	6:23	6:52
	Set 15th	4:41	5:17	5:47	7:17	7:46	8:07	8:05	7:34	6:47	6:00	4:25	4:18
	Twl	±1:38	±1:34	±1:32	±1:40	±1:54	±2:08	±2:00	±1:46	±1:37	±1:34	±1:38	±1:40
Las Vegas	Rise 1st	6:52	6:41	6:11	5:27	5:48	5:25	5:27	5:48	6:12	6:36	6:04	6:33
36°10' N	Set 1st	4:37	5:08	5:36	6:03	7:28	7:53	8:02	7:46	7:08	6:24	4:44	4:26
115°05' W	Twl	±1:35	±1:30	±1:29	±1:31	±1:40	±1:52	±1:55	±1:44	±1:34	±1:30	±1:31	±1:35
	Rise 15th	6:51	6:28	5:51	6:07	5:34	5:23	5:35	5:59	6:23	6:48	6:18	6:45
	Set 15th	4:50	5:22	5:48	7:15	7:40	8:00	7:58	7:31	6:48	6:04	4:31	4:27
	Twl	±1:34	±1:30	±1:29	±1:35	±1:46	±1:56	±1:51	±1:40	±1:31	±1:30	±1:34	±1:37

→ **Sunrises & Sunsets have been adjusted for Daylight-Savings Time**

Sunrises & Sunsets

Nevada/New Hampshire/New Jersey

		JAN	FEB	MAR	APR	MAY	JUN	JUL	AUG	SEP	OCT	NOV	DEC
Reno 39°30' N 119°50' W	Rise 1st	7:20	7:07	6:32	5:43	6:00	5:34	5:36	5:59	6:28	6:56	6:28	7:01
	Set 1st	4:47	5:20	5:52	6:24	7:53	8:21	8:30	8:12	7:30	6:41	4:58	4:36
	Twl	±1:40	±1:36	±1:33	±1:36	±1:48	±2:04	±2:08	±1:53	±1:39	±1:35	±1:35	±1:40
	Rise 15th	7:18	6:51	6:10	6:22	5:45	5:32	5:45	6:12	6:41	7:10	6:44	7:13
	Set 15th	5:00	5:36	6:07	7:37	8:07	8:28	8:26	7:55	7:07	6:20	4:44	4:37
	Twl	±1:40	±1:35	±1:33	±1:41	±1:55	±2:09	±2:02	±1:46	±1:37	±1:34	±1:38	±1:41
Winnemucca 41°00' N 117°45' W	Rise 1st	7:16	7:01	6:25	5:34	5:49	5:21	5:23	5:47	6:18	6:48	6:22	6:57
	Set 1st	4:34	5:08	5:42	6:16	7:48	8:17	8:27	8:07	7:23	6:33	4:47	4:23
	Twl	±1:43	±1:39	±1:36	±1:40	±1:51	±2:11	±2:15	±1:58	±1:43	±1:36	±1:38	±1:42
	Rise 15th	7:14	6:45	6:02	6:12	5:33	5:18	5:32	6:01	6:32	7:03	6:39	7:09
	Set 15th	4:48	5:26	5:58	7:31	8:02	8:25	8:22	7:49	7:00	6:10	4:32	4:24
	Twl	±1:41	±1:36	±1:36	±1:43	±2:01	±2:16	±2:08	±1:51	±1:38	±1:37	±1:40	±1:43
NH **Berlin** 44°29' N 71°10' W	Rise 1st	7:20	7:03	6:22	5:26	5:36	5:04	5:05	5:32	6:08	6:42	6:21	7:00
	Set 1st	4:17	4:55	5:33	6:12	7:48	8:21	8:32	8:09	7:21	6:26	4:35	4:07
	Twl	±1:49	±1:43	±1:40	±1:46	±2:03	±2:31	±2:38	±2:12	±1:50	±1:41	±1:43	±1:49
	Rise 15th	7:17	6:44	5:57	6:01	5:18	4:59	5:15	5:48	6:24	6:59	6:40	7:13
	Set 15th	4:32	5:14	5:51	7:29	8:06	8:30	8:26	7:50	6:55	6:01	4:18	4:07
	Twl	±1:47	±1:41	±1:42	±1:52	±2:13	±2:40	±2:27	±2:00	±1:45	±1:41	±1:45	±1:49
Manchester 42°58' N 71°29' W	Rise 1st	7:17	7:01	6:22	5:28	5:40	5:10	5:11	5:37	6:10	6:43	6:21	6:58
	Set 1st	4:22	4:59	5:35	6:12	7:47	8:18	8:29	8:06	7:20	6:27	4:38	4:12
	Twl	±1:47	±1:41	±1:39	±1:43	±1:57	±2:21	±2:26	±2:05	±1:47	±1:40	±1:41	±1:46
	Rise 15th	7:14	6:43	5:58	6:04	5:23	5:06	5:21	5:52	6:26	7:00	6:38	7:10
	Set 15th	4:37	5:18	5:53	7:29	8:02	8:27	8:23	7:48	6:56	6:03	4:22	4:12
	Twl	±1:45	±1:39	±1:39	±1:48	±2:08	±2:27	±2:17	±1:56	±1:42	±1:40	±1:44	±1:48
NJ **Altantic City** 39°25' N 74°25' W	Rise 1st	7:18	7:05	6:31	5:42	5:59	5:33	5:34	5:57	6:26	6:54	6:26	6:59
	Set 1st	4:45	5:18	5:50	6:22	7:51	8:19	8:29	8:10	7:29	6:40	4:56	4:35
	Twl	±1:40	±1:36	±1:33	±1:36	±1:48	±2:03	±2:07	±1:53	±1:39	±1:34	±1:36	±1:39

➡ **Sunrises & Sunsets have been adjusted for Daylight-Savings Time**

SunRISE/SET

Sunrises & Sunsets

New Jersey/New Mexico

		JAN	FEB	MAR	APR	MAY	JUN	JUL	AUG	SEP	OCT	NOV	DEC
Atlantic City	Rise 15th	7:16	6:50	6:09	6:21	5:44	5:30	5:43	6:10	6:39	7:07	6:41	7:11
	Set 15th	4:58	5:34	6:05	7:36	8:05	8:26	8:24	7:53	7:06	6:19	4:43	4:35
	Twl	±1:40	±1:35	±1:33	±1:40	±1:55	±2:08	±2:02	±1:46	±1:36	±1:34	±1:38	±1:42
NM													
Albuquerque	Rise 1st	7:15	7:06	6:37	5:54	6:16	5:54	5:57	6:16	6:40	7:02	6:28	6:57
	Set 1st	5:06	5:36	6:03	6:29	7:53	8:16	8:25	8:10	7:34	6:51	5:13	4:55
35°05' N	Twl	±1:35	±1:30	±1:28	±1:30	±1:39	±1:50	±1:53	±1:43	±1:33	±1:29	±1:30	±1:34
106°47' W	Rise 15th	7:15	6:53	6:18	6:35	6:03	5:52	6:04	6:27	6:50	7:13	6:42	7:08
	Set 15th	5:19	5:50	6:15	7:40	8:04	8:23	8:22	7:56	7:14	6:32	5:01	4:57
	Twl	±1:33	±1:29	±1:28	±1:33	±1:44	±1:53	±1:49	±1:37	±1:30	±1:29	±1:32	±1:34
Clovis	Rise 1st	6:59	6:50	6:22	5:40	6:03	5:42	5:44	6:03	6:26	6:47	6:13	6:41
34°20' N	Set 1st	4:54	5:23	5:49	6:14	7:37	8:00	8:09	7:54	7:19	6:37	4:59	4:43
103°10' W	Twl	±1:33	±1:29	±1:27	±1:29	±1:38	±1:48	±1:51	±1:41	±1:32	±1:28	±1:29	±1:32
	Rise 15th	6:59	6:38	6:03	6:22	5:51	5:40	5:52	6:14	6:36	6:58	6:26	6:52
	Set 15th	5:06	5:36	6:00	7:24	7:48	8:06	8:05	7:40	6:59	6:18	4:48	4:44
	Twl	±1:32	±1:29	±1:28	±1:33	±1:42	±1:51	±1:47	±1:37	±1:30	±1:28	±1:31	±1:34
Farmington	Rise 1st	7:27	7:16	6:45	6:00	6:20	5:56	5:59	6:20	6:45	7:09	6:38	7:08
36°45' N	Set 1st	5:09	5:39	6:08	6:36	8:02	8:27	8:37	8:20	7:42	6:57	5:17	4:58
108°28' W	Twl	±1:37	±1:34	±1:30	±1:32	±1:43	±1:56	±1:57	±1:47	±1:35	±1:31	±1:32	±1:36
	Rise 15th	7:26	7:02	6:25	6:40	6:06	5:54	6:07	6:31	6:56	7:21	6:52	7:19
	Set 15th	5:21	5:54	6:21	7:48	8:14	8:34	8:33	8:05	7:21	6:37	5:05	4:59
	Twl	±1:36	±1:31	±1:30	±1:37	±1:49	±1:59	±1:53	±1:41	±1:32	±1:31	±1:33	±1:37
Las Cruces	Rise 1st	7:09	7:01	6:35	5:56	6:21	6:01	6:04	6:22	6:42	7:01	6:24	6:51
32°18' N	Set 1st	5:13	5:41	6:05	6:27	7:48	8:09	8:18	8:05	7:32	6:52	5:17	5:02
106°50' W	Twl	±1:32	±1:27	±1:26	±1:28	±1:35	±1:44	±1:46	±1:38	±1:29	±1:26	±1:27	±1:31
	Rise 15th	7:09	6:50	6:18	6:38	6:09	6:00	6:11	6:31	6:51	7:11	6:37	7:01
	Set 15th	5:25	5:53	6:15	7:37	7:58	8:16	8:15	7:52	7:13	6:35	5:07	5:04
	Twl	±1:30	±1:27	±1:26	±1:30	±1:39	±1:46	±1:43	±1:33	±1:28	±1:26	±1:29	±1:32

→ **Sunrises & Sunsets have been adjusted for Daylight-Savings Time**

SunRISE/SET

Sunrises & Sunsets

New Mexico/New York

		JAN	FEB	MAR	APR	MAY	JUN	JUL	AUG	SEP	OCT	NOV	DEC
Roswell	Rise 1st	7:02	6:54	6:27	5:46	6:10	5:49	5:52	6:11	6:32	6:52	6:17	6:44
33°26' N	Set 1st	5:02	5:30	5:55	6:19	7:41	8:03	8:12	7:58	7:24	6:43	5:06	4:50
104°32' W	Twl	±1:32	±1:28	±1:27	±1:28	±1:37	±1:47	±1:48	±1:40	±1:30	±1:27	±1:28	±1:32
	Rise 15th	7:02	6:42	6:09	6:28	5:58	5:48	5:59	6:21	6:42	7:03	6:30	6:55
	Set 15th	5:13	5:43	6:06	7:29	7:51	8:09	8:09	7:44	7:05	6:25	4:56	4:52
	Twl	±1:32	±1:27	±1:27	±1:32	±1:41	±1:49	±1:45	±1:35	±1:28	±1:27	±1:30	±1:33
Albany	Rise 1st	7:25	7:09	6:31	5:37	5:50	5:20	5:21	5:47	6:20	6:52	6:29	7:06
	Set 1st	4:33	5:09	5:45	6:21	7:55	8:26	8:37	6:15	7:29	6:36	4:48	4:23
42°35' N	Twl	±1:45	±1:40	±1:38	±1:42	±1:56	±2:18	±2:23	±2:04	±1:46	±1:39	±1:41	±1:45
73°47' W	Rise 15th	7:22	6:52	6:07	6:14	5:33	5:17	5:31	6:02	6:35	7:08	6:47	7:18
	Set 15th	4:47	5:27	6:02	7:37	8:11	8:35	8:31	7:56	7:05	6:13	4:33	4:23
	Twl	±1:44	±1:39	±1:38	±1:47	±2:05	±2:25	±2:15	±1:55	±1:42	±1:39	±1:42	±1:46
Buffalo	Rise 1st	7:46	7:30	6:51	5:58	6:10	5:39	5:40	6:06	6:40	7:12	6:50	7:26
42°55' N	Set 1st	4:52	5:28	6:05	6:42	8:16	8:47	8:58	8:36	7:50	6:57	5:08	4:42
78°50' W	Twl	±1:46	±1:41	±1:38	±1:42	±1:57	±2:21	±2:26	±2:04	±1:46	±1:39	±1:41	±1:46
	Rise 15th	7:44	7:13	6:28	6:34	5:52	5:36	5:50	6:21	6:55	7:29	7:07	7:39
	Set 15th	5:06	5:47	6:22	7:58	8:32	8:56	8:52	8:18	7:25	6:33	4:52	4:42
	Twl	±1:45	±1:39	±1:39	±1:48	±2:07	±2:27	±2:17	±1:55	±1:43	±1:39	±1:43	±1:47
New York City	Rise 1st	7:20	7:06	6:30	5:39	5:54	5:27	5:28	5:53	6:23	6:53	6:27	7:01
40°45' N	Set 1st	4:39	5:14	5:47	6:21	7:52	8:21	8:31	8:11	7:28	6:38	4:52	4:29
74°00' W	Twl	±1:43	±1:38	±1:35	±1:39	±1:51	±2:09	±2:14	±1:57	±1:42	±1:36	±1:38	±1:42
	Rise 15th	7:18	6:50	6:08	6:17	5:39	5:24	5:38	6:06	6:37	7:07	6:43	7:13
	Set 15th	4:53	5:31	6:03	7:36	8:07	8:29	8:26	7:54	7:05	6:16	4:38	4:29
	Twl	±1:41	±1:36	±1:35	±1:43	±1:59	±2:14	±2:07	±1:49	±1:38	±1:36	±1:40	±1:44
Rochester	Rise 1st	7:43	7:26	6:47	5:52	6:04	5:34	5:35	6:01	6:35	7:08	6:46	7:23
43°10' N	Set 1st	4:46	5:23	6:00	6:37	8:12	8:44	8:54	8:32	7:45	6:52	5:02	4:37
77°40' W	Twl	±1:47	±1:42	±1:38	±1:43	±1:58	±2:22	±2:27	±2:06	±1:47	±1:40	±1:42	±1:46

NY

→ **Sunrises & Sunsets have been adjusted for Daylight-Savings Time**

313

Sunrises & Sunsets

New York/North Carolina

		JAN	FEB	MAR	APR	MAY	JUN	JUL	AUG	SEP	OCT	NOV	DEC
Rochester	Rise 15th	7:40	7:08	6:23	6:28	5:47	5:30	5:45	6:16	6:50	7:25	7:04	7:36
	Set 15th	5:01	5:42	6:17	7:54	8:28	8:52	8:48	8:13	7:20	6:28	4:47	4:36
	Twl	±1:45	±1:39	±1:40	±1:48	±2:08	±2:29	±2:19	±1:56	±1:43	±1:40	±1:43	±1:48
Syracuse	Rise 1st	7:36	7:20	6:41	5:47	5:58	5:28	5:29	5:55	6:29	7:02	6:40	7:17
43° 04' N	Set 1st	4:41	5:17	5:54	6:31	8:06	8:38	8:48	8:26	7:39	6:46	4:57	4:31
76° 11' W	Twl	±1:46	±1:42	±1:38	±1:43	±1:57	±2:20	±2:27	±2:05	±1:47	±1:40	±1:41	±1:46
	Rise 15th	7:33	7:02	6:17	6:23	5:41	5:25	5:39	6:11	6:44	7:18	6:58	7:29
	Set 15th	4:56	5:36	6:11	7:48	8:22	8:46	8:42	8:07	7:15	6:22	4:41	4:31
	Twl	±1:44	±1:39	±1:40	±1:48	±2:07	±2:28	±2:18	±1:56	±1:42	±1:40	±1:43	±1:47
Watertown	Rise 1st	7:39	7:21	6:41	5:45	5:55	5:24	5:25	5:52	6:27	7:02	6:40	7:19
43° 58' N	Set 1st	4:37	5:14	5:52	6:31	8:07	8:40	8:50	8:27	7:39	6:44	4:54	4:27
75° 57' W	Twl	±1:49	±1:43	±1:40	±1:45	±2:01	±2:27	±2:34	±2:09	±1:50	±1:42	±1:43	±1:48
	Rise 15th	7:35	7:03	6:16	6:20	5:38	5:20	5:35	6:08	6:43	7:19	6:59	7:32
	Set 15th	4:52	5:34	6:10	7:48	8:23	8:48	8:44	8:08	7:14	6:20	4:38	4:27
	Twl	±1:47	±1:40	±1:41	±1:51	±2:12	±2:36	±2:24	±1:58	±1:44	±1:41	±1:44	±1:49
NC **Asheville**	Rise 1st	7:40	7:30	7:00	6:16	6:38	6:15	6:18	6:38	7:02	7:25	6:52	7:21
	Set 1st	5:28	5:58	6:25	6:52	8:17	8:41	8:50	8:34	7:57	7:14	5:35	5:17
35° 39' N	Twl	±1:36	±1:31	±1:29	±1:32	±1:41	±1:51	±1:54	±1:45	±1:33	±1:29	±1:30	±1:34
82° 30' W	Rise 15th	7:39	7:17	6:41	6:57	6:25	6:14	6:26	6:49	7:13	7:37	7:06	7:32
	Set 15th	5:40	6:12	6:38	8:03	8:28	8:47	8:46	8:19	7:37	6:54	5:23	5:18
	Twl	±1:34	±1:30	±1:28	±1:35	±1:46	±1:55	±1:50	±1:38	±1:31	±1:29	±1:33	±1:36
Charlotte	Rise 1st	7:32	7:22	6:53	6:10	6:32	6:10	6:12	6:32	6:55	7:18	6:44	7:13
35° 16' N	Set 1st	5:22	5:51	6:19	6:45	8:09	8:32	8:42	8:27	7:50	7:07	5:29	5:11
80° 46' W	Twl	±1:34	±1:31	±1:28	±1:30	±1:39	±1:51	±1:53	±1:42	±1:33	±1:29	±1:29	±1:34
	Rise 15th	7:31	7:10	6:34	6:51	6:19	6:08	6:20	6:43	7:06	7:29	6:58	7:24
	Set 15th	5:34	6:05	6:31	7:56	8:20	8:39	8:38	8:12	7:30	6:48	5:17	5:12
	Twl	±1:34	±1:30	±1:28	±1:33	±1:45	±1:54	±1:50	±1:38	±1:30	±1:29	±1:32	±1:36

➝ **Sunrises & Sunsets have been adjusted for Daylight-Savings Time**

SunRISE/SET

Sunrises & Sunsets

North Carolina/North Dakota

		JAN	FEB	MAR	APR	MAY	JUN	JUL	AUG	SEP	OCT	NOV	DEC
Kitty Hawk	Rise 1st	7:14	7:04	6:33	5:49	6:10	5:47	5:50	6:10	6:35	6:58	6:26	6:55
36°04' N	Set 1st	5:00	5:30	5:58	6:25	7:50	8:14	8:24	8:08	7:30	6:46	5:07	4:49
75°42' W	Twl	±1:35	±1:31	±1:29	±1:31	±1:40	±1:53	±1:55	±1:45	±1:35	±1:31	±1:31	±1:34
	Rise 15th	7:13	6:50	6:14	6:30	5:57	5:45	5:58	6:21	6:45	7:10	6:40	7:06
	Set 15th	5:12	5:44	6:10	7:37	8:02	8:21	8:20	7:53	7:10	6:27	4:55	4:50
	Twl	±1:34	±1:30	±1:30	±1:35	±1:46	±1:57	±1:52	±1:40	±1:31	±1:30	±1:33	±1:36
Raleigh	Rise 1st	7:25	7:15	6:44	6:01	6:22	6:00	6:02	6:22	6:47	7:10	6:37	7:06
35°47' N	Set 1st	5:12	5:42	6:10	6:37	8:02	8:25	8:35	8:19	7:42	6:58	5:19	5:01
78°39' W	Twl	±1:35	±1:32	±1:29	±1:30	±1:39	±1:52	±1:54	±1:45	±1:34	±1:30	±1:31	±1:34
	Rise 15th	7:24	7:01	6:25	6:42	6:09	5:58	6:10	6:33	6:57	7:21	6:51	7:17
	Set 15th	5:25	5:57	6:22	7:48	8:13	8:32	8:31	8:04	7:22	6:39	5:07	5:02
	Twl	±1:33	±1:29	±1:29	±1:35	±1:46	±1:56	±1:50	±1:39	±1:31	±1:30	±1:33	±1:37
Wilmington	Rise 1st	7:18	7:09	6:40	5:59	6:22	6:01	6:03	6:23	6:45	7:06	6:32	7:00
34°14' N	Set 1st	5:13	5:42	6:08	6:33	7:56	8:18	8:27	8:13	7:37	6:56	5:18	5:02
77°54' W	Twl	±1:33	±1:29	±1:27	±1:29	±1:37	±1:49	±1:51	±1:41	±1:33	±1:28	±1:30	±1:33
	Rise 15th	7:17	6:56	6:22	6:40	6:10	5:59	6:11	6:33	6:55	7:17	6:45	7:10
	Set 15th	5:25	5:56	6:20	7:43	8:07	8:25	8:24	7:59	7:18	6:38	5:08	5:03
	Twl	±1:32	±1:28	±1:27	±1:33	±1:42	±1:51	±1:47	±1:36	±1:29	±1:27	±1:30	±1:34
Winston-Salem	Rise 1st	7:32	7:22	6:51	6:07	6:28	6:05	6:08	6:28	6:53	7:16	6:44	7:14
	Set 1st	5:18	5:48	6:16	6:43	8:09	8:33	8:42	8:26	7:49	7:04	5:25	5:07
36°07' N	Twl	±1:35	±1:31	±1:29	±1:31	±1:40	±1:53	±1:56	±1:45	±1:34	±1:31	±1:31	±1:34
80°15' W	Rise 15th	7:31	7:08	6:32	6:48	6:15	6:03	6:16	6:39	7:04	7:28	6:58	7:25
	Set 15th	5:30	6:02	6:29	7:55	8:20	8:40	8:38	8:11	7:28	6:45	5:13	5:08
	Twl	±1:34	±1:31	±1:29	±1:35	±1:47	±1:56	±1:52	±1:40	±1:31	±1:30	±1:33	±1:36
ND **Bismarck**	Rise 1st	8:28	8:07	7:22	6:22	6:28	5:53	5:53	6:23	7:03	7:42	7:26	8:08
	Set 1st	5:06	5:47	6:29	7:13	8:53	9:30	9:41	9:15	8:22	7:23	5:27	4:57
46°49' N	Twl	±1:55	±1:49	±1:45	±1:51	±2:12	±2:53	±3:07	±2:23	±1:57	±1:47	±1:48	±1:53
100°49' W													

➡ **Sunrises & Sunsets have been adjusted for Daylight-Savings Time**

Sunrises & Sunsets

North Dakota/Ohio

		JAN	FEB	MAR	APR	MAY	JUN	JUL	AUG	SEP	OCT	NOV	DEC
Bismarck	Rise 15th	8:24	7:47	6:56	6:55	6:08	5:48	6:04	6:41	7:21	8:01	7:46	8:22
	Set 15th	5:22	6:08	6:49	8:32	9:12	9:39	9:33	8:53	7:55	6:56	5:09	4:55
	Twl	±1:53	±1:46	±1:46	±1:59	±2:28	±3:12	±2:47	±2:09	±1:50	±1:46	±1:51	±1:56
Grand Forks 48°00' N 97°03' W	Rise 1st	8:18	7:55	7:09	6:06	6:09	5:32	5:32	6:04	6:46	7:27	7:13	7:57
	Set 1st	4:46	5:28	6:13	6:58	8:41	9:20	9:31	9:03	8:09	7:07	5:09	4:37
	Twl	±1:58	±1:52	±1:47	±1:55	±2:18	±3:12	±3:44	±2:31	±2:00	±1:50	±1:51	±1:57
Note: Some North Dakota locations do not experience an end of twilight during the summer	Rise 15th	8:13	7:34	6:41	6:38	5:49	5:27	5:44	6:23	7:05	7:48	7:35	8:11
	Set 15th	5:02	5:51	6:34	8:19	9:01	9:30	9:23	8:41	7:40	6:39	4:50	4:35
	Twl	±1:56	±1:49	±1:49	±2:02	±2:36	NONE	±3:02	±2:14	±1:54	±1:49	±1:54	±1:59
Williston 48°10' N 103°35' W	Rise 1st	7:45	7:22	6:35	5:32	5:35	4:58	4:58	5:30	6:12	6:54	6:40	7:24
	Set 1st	4:12	4:54	5:39	6:25	8:08	8:47	8:58	8:30	7:35	6:33	4:35	4:03
	Twl	±1:58	±1:52	±1:47	±1:54	±2:19	±3:15	±3:55	±2:32	±2:01	±1:50	±1:51	±1:57
Note: Some North Dakota locations do not experience an end of twilight during the summer	Rise 15th	7:40	7:01	6:07	6:04	5:15	4:53	5:10	5:49	6:32	7:14	7:02	7:38
	Set 15th	4:29	5:17	6:00	7:45	8:27	8:57	8:50	8:08	7:06	6:05	4:16	4:01
	Twl	±1:55	±1:49	±1:50	±2:03	±2:39	NONE	±3:04	±2:14	±1:55	±1:49	±1:54	±1:59
OH **Akron** 41°07' N 81°31' W	Rise 1st	7:51	7:37	7:00	6:09	6:24	5:56	5:57	6:22	6:53	7:23	6:57	7:32
	Set 1st	5:08	5:43	6:17	6:51	8:23	8:52	9:02	8:42	7:59	7:08	5:22	4:58
	Twl	±1:44	±1:39	±1:36	±1:40	±1:52	±2:11	±2:16	±1:59	±1:42	±1:37	±1:38	±1:43
	Rise 15th	7:49	7:20	6:38	6:47	6:08	5:53	6:07	6:36	7:07	7:38	7:14	7:44
	Set 15th	5:23	6:01	6:33	8:06	8:38	9:00	8:57	8:25	7:35	6:45	5:07	4:58
	Twl	±1:41	±1:36	±1:36	±1:44	±2:00	±2:16	±2:08	±1:50	±1:39	±1:37	±1:40	±1:44
Cincinnati 39°10' N 84°26' W	Rise 1st	7:57	7:44	7:10	6:22	6:39	6:13	6:15	6:38	7:06	7:34	7:06	7:38
	Set 1st	5:26	5:59	6:30	7:02	8:31	8:58	9:08	8:49	8:08	7:20	5:37	5:15
	Twl	±1:40	±1:36	±1:33	±1:36	±1:47	±2:03	±2:06	±1:53	±1:39	±1:34	±1:35	±1:40
	Rise 15th	7:56	7:29	6:49	7:01	6:24	6:11	6:24	6:51	7:19	7:48	7:21	7:50
	Set 15th	5:39	6:15	6:45	8:15	8:44	9:06	9:03	8:33	7:46	6:59	5:23	5:16
	Twl	±1:38	±1:34	±1:33	±1:40	±1:54	±2:07	±2:02	±1:46	±1:36	±1:34	±1:38	±1:40

→ **Sunrises & Sunsets have been adjusted for Daylight-Savings Time**

SunRISE/SET

Sunrises & Sunsets
Ohio/Oklahoma

		JAN	FEB	MAR	APR	MAY	JUN	JUL	AUG	SEP	OCT	NOV	DEC
Columbus	Rise 1st	7:54	7:40	7:05	6:16	6:32	6:05	6:07	6:31	7:00	7:28	7:01	7:35
39°57' N	Set 1st	5:18	5:52	6:24	6:57	8:27	8:55	9:05	8:46	8:03	7:14	5:30	5:08
83°01' W	Twl	±1:41	±1:36	±1:34	±1:36	±1:49	±2:06	±2:09	±1:54	±1:41	±1:35	±1:36	±1:40
	Rise 15th	7:52	7:25	6:43	6:54	6:17	6:03	6:16	6:44	7:13	7:43	7:17	7:47
	Set 15th	5:32	6:08	6:39	8:11	8:41	9:03	9:00	8:28	7:41	6:52	5:16	5:08
	Twl	±1:40	±1:35	±1:34	±1:42	±1:57	±2:10	±2:03	±1:48	±1:37	±1:35	±1:39	±1:42
Toledo	Rise 1st	8:01	7:46	7:09	6:17	6:31	6:02	6:04	6:29	7:00	7:31	7:06	7:42
41°37' N	Set 1st	5:15	5:50	6:25	7:00	8:32	9:02	9:12	8:52	8:07	7:16	5:29	5:05
83°33' W	Twl	±1:44	±1:39	±1:36	±1:40	±1:54	±2:14	±2:18	±2:00	±1:45	±1:37	±1:39	±1:44
	Rise 15th	7:59	7:29	6:46	6:54	6:15	5:59	6:13	6:43	7:15	7:46	7:23	7:54
	Set 15th	5:29	6:08	6:41	8:15	8:47	9:10	9:07	8:34	7:43	6:53	5:14	5:05
	Twl	±1:42	±1:37	±1:37	±1:45	±2:02	±2:19	±2:11	±1:51	±1:40	±1:37	±1:41	±1:44
OK **Blackwell**	Rise 1st	7:43	7:32	7:00	6:15	6:35	6:11	6:14	6:35	7:00	7:25	6:54	7:24
	Set 1st	5:24	5:55	6:24	6:52	8:18	8:43	8:53	8:36	7:58	7:12	5:32	5:13
36°55' N	Twl	±1:37	±1:33	±1:30	±1:32	±1:43	±1:56	±1:57	±1:47	±1:36	±1:32	±1:32	±1:37
97°20' W	Rise 15th	7:41	7:18	6:40	6:55	6:21	6:09	6:22	6:46	7:12	7:37	7:08	7:35
	Set 15th	5:37	6:10	6:37	8:04	8:30	8:50	8:48	8:21	7:37	6:53	5:20	5:14
	Twl	±1:35	±1:31	±1:30	±1:36	±1:49	±1:59	±1:54	±1:41	±1:32	±1:31	±1:34	±1:37
Oklahoma City	Rise 1st	7:39	7:29	7:00	6:16	6:38	6:16	6:19	6:39	7:02	7:25	6:52	7:21
	Set 1st	5:29	5:58	6:26	6:52	8:16	8:40	8:49	8:33	7:57	7:14	5:35	5:17
35°25' N	Twl	±1:34	±1:31	±1:28	±1:30	±1:40	±1:51	±1:54	±1:44	±1:33	±1:29	±1:30	±1:34
97°30' W	Rise 15th	7:39	7:16	6:41	6:57	6:25	6:14	6:26	6:49	7:13	7:36	7:06	7:32
	Set 15th	5:41	6:12	6:38	8:03	8:28	8:47	8:45	8:19	7:37	6:55	5:24	5:19
	Twl	±1:33	±1:30	±1:28	±1:34	±1:44	±1:54	±1:50	±1:38	±1:30	±1:29	±1:32	±1:36
Tulsa	Rise 1st	7:35	7:25	6:54	6:10	6:31	6:08	6:10	6:31	6:56	7:19	6:47	7:17
36°10' N	Set 1st	5:21	5:51	6:19	6:46	8:12	8:36	8:45	8:29	7:52	7:07	5:28	5:09
96°00' W	Twl	±1:35	±1:32	±1:29	±1:31	±1:40	±1:52	±1:56	±1:45	±1:34	±1:31	±1:31	±1:35

➙ **Sunrises & Sunsets have been adjusted for Daylight-Savings Time**

SunRISE/SET

Sunrises & Sunsets

Oklahoma/Oregon

		JAN	FEB	MAR	APR	MAY	JUN	JUL	AUG	SEP	OCT	NOV	DEC
Tulsa	Rise 15th	7:34	7:11	6:35	6:51	6:18	6:06	6:18	6:42	7:07	7:31	7:01	7:28
	Set 15th	5:33	6:05	6:32	7:58	8:23	8:43	8:41	8:14	7:31	6:48	5:16	5:11
	Twl	±1:34	±1:31	±1:29	±1:35	±1:47	±1:57	±1:52	±1:40	±1:31	±1:30	±1:33	±1:36
OR **Burns** *43°40' N* *119°04' W*	Rise 1st	7:30	7:13	6:32	5:38	5:48	5:17	5:19	5:46	6:20	6:54	6:32	7:10
	Set 1st	4:30	5:08	5:45	6:23	7:59	8:31	8:42	8:19	7:31	6:37	4:47	4:21
	Twl	±1:49	±1:42	±1:40	±1:45	±1:59	±2:25	±2:31	±2:07	±1:49	±1:41	±1:42	±1:47
	Rise 15th	7:27	6:55	6:08	6:13	5:31	5:14	5:29	6:01	6:36	7:11	6:51	7:23
	Set 15th	4:45	5:27	6:03	7:40	8:15	8:40	8:35	8:00	7:06	6:13	4:31	4:20
	Twl	±1:47	±1:40	±1:40	±1:49	±2:10	±2:32	±2:22	±1:57	±1:44	±1:40	±1:44	±1:49
Medford *42°20' N* *122°52' W*	Rise 1st	7:41	7:25	6:46	5:54	6:06	5:37	5:39	6:04	6:37	7:09	6:45	7:21
	Set 1st	4:50	5:26	6:02	6:38	8:11	8:42	8:52	8:31	7:45	6:53	5:05	4:40
	Twl	±1:45	±1:40	±1:37	±1:41	±1:56	±2:16	±2:22	±2:02	±1:46	±1:38	±1:40	±1:45
	Rise 15th	7:38	7:08	6:23	6:30	5:50	5:34	5:48	6:19	6:52	7:25	7:03	7:34
	Set 15th	5:05	5:44	6:18	7:53	8:26	8:50	8:46	8:12	7:21	6:29	4:49	4:40
	Twl	±1:43	±1:38	±1:39	±1:47	±2:06	±2:24	±2:14	±1:54	±1:41	±1:39	±1:43	±1:45
Ontario *44°01' N* *117°01' W*	Rise 1st	7:23	7:05	6:25	5:29	5:39	5:08	5:09	5:36	6:12	6:46	6:25	7:03
	Set 1st	4:21	4:59	5:37	6:15	7:52	8:24	8:35	8:12	7:24	6:29	4:38	4:11
	Twl	±1:49	±1:43	±1:40	±1:45	±2:01	±2:27	±2:33	±2:09	±1:49	±1:41	±1:43	±1:48
	Rise 15th	7:20	6:47	6:00	6:04	5:22	5:04	5:19	5:52	6:27	7:03	6:43	7:16
	Set 15th	4:36	5:18	5:55	7:32	8:08	8:33	8:28	7:52	6:58	6:04	4:22	4:11
	Twl	±1:47	±1:41	±1:40	±1:51	±2:12	±2:35	±2:24	±1:58	±1:44	±1:41	±1:45	±1:49
Portland *45°35' N* *122°40' W*	Rise 1st	7:51	7:32	6:49	5:51	5:58	5:25	5:26	5:55	6:32	7:09	6:51	7:31
	Set 1st	4:38	5:18	5:58	6:39	8:18	8:52	9:03	8:38	7:48	6:51	4:57	4:29
	Twl	±1:52	±1:46	±1:42	±1:48	±2:07	±2:40	±2:49	±2:16	±1:53	±1:44	±1:46	±1:51
	Rise 15th	7:47	7:12	6:23	6:25	5:40	5:21	5:37	6:12	6:49	7:27	7:10	7:44
	Set 15th	4:54	5:38	6:17	7:57	8:35	9:01	8:56	8:18	7:21	6:25	4:40	4:28
	Twl	±1:49	±1:44	±1:44	±1:55	±2:20	±2:52	±2:35	±2:04	±1:48	±1:44	±1:49	±1:53

➡ **Sunrises & Sunsets have been adjusted for Daylight-Savings Time**

SunRISE/SET

Sunrises & Sunsets

Pennsylvania

		JAN	FEB	MAR	APR	MAY	JUN	JUL	AUG	SEP	OCT	NOV	DEC
PA **Erie** *42°10' N* *80°07' W*	Rise 1st	7:49	7:34	6:56	6:03	6:16	5:47	5:48	6:14	6:46	7:18	6:54	7:30
	Set 1st	4:59	5:35	6:11	6:46	8:20	8:50	9:00	8:39	7:54	7:02	5:14	4:49
	Twl	±1:46	±1:40	±1:37	±1:41	±1:55	±2:16	±2:21	±2:02	±1:45	±1:38	±1:40	±1:45
	Rise 15th	7:46	7:17	6:32	6:40	5:59	5:44	5:58	6:28	7:01	7:33	7:11	7:42
	Set 15th	5:14	5:53	6:27	8:02	8:35	8:58	8:55	8:21	7:30	6:39	4:59	4:49
	Twl	±1:43	±1:38	±1:38	±1:46	±2:04	±2:23	±2:14	±1:53	±1:41	±1:38	±1:42	±1:46
Harrisburg *40°18' N* *76°52' W*	Rise 1st	7:30	7:16	6:41	5:51	6:07	5:40	5:42	6:06	6:35	7:04	6:37	7:11
	Set 1st	4:53	5:27	5:59	6:32	8:03	8:31	8:41	8:21	7:39	6:50	5:05	4:42
	Twl	±1:41	±1:36	±1:35	±1:37	±1:49	±2:07	±2:11	±1:57	±1:42	±1:35	±1:36	±1:41
	Rise 15th	7:28	7:00	6:19	6:29	5:52	5:37	5:51	6:19	6:48	7:18	6:53	7:23
	Set 15th	5:07	5:43	6:15	7:46	8:17	8:39	8:36	8:04	7:16	6:28	4:51	4:43
	Twl	±1:39	±1:35	±1:35	±1:43	±1:57	±2:12	±2:05	±1:49	±1:38	±1:35	±1:39	±1:42
Philadelphia *40°00' N* *75°10' W*	Rise 1st	7:22	7:09	6:34	5:44	6:01	5:34	5:36	5:59	6:28	6:57	6:30	7:03
	Set 1st	4:46	5:20	5:53	6:25	7:55	8:23	8:33	8:14	7:32	6:43	4:58	4:36
	Twl	±1:41	±1:37	±1:34	±1:37	±1:49	±2:07	±2:10	±1:55	±1:41	±1:35	±1:36	±1:41
	Rise 15th	7:21	6:53	6:12	6:23	5:45	5:31	5:45	6:12	6:42	7:11	6:46	7:15
	Set 15th	5:00	5:37	6:08	7:39	8:09	8:31	8:28	7:57	7:09	6:21	4:44	4:36
	Twl	±1:40	±1:35	±1:34	±1:42	±1:57	±2:11	±2:04	±1:48	±1:37	±1:35	±1:39	±1:43
Pittsburgh *40°25' N* *79°55' W*	Rise 1st	7:43	7:29	6:54	6:04	6:19	5:52	5:54	6:17	6:47	7:17	6:50	7:24
	Set 1st	5:04	5:39	6:12	6:45	8:16	8:44	8:54	8:35	7:52	7:02	5:17	4:54
	Twl	±1:42	±1:37	±1:34	±1:37	±1:49	±2:08	±2:12	±1:56	±1:41	±1:35	±1:36	±1:41
	Rise 15th	7:41	7:13	6:31	6:41	6:04	5:49	6:03	6:31	7:01	7:31	7:06	7:36
	Set 15th	5:18	5:56	6:27	7:59	8:30	8:52	8:49	8:17	7:29	6:40	5:03	4:54
	Twl	±1:40	±1:35	±1:34	±1:42	±1:58	±2:13	±2:06	±1:49	±1:37	±1:35	±1:39	±1:43
Scranton *41°22' N* *75°41' W*	Rise 1st	7:29	7:14	6:37	5:46	6:00	5:32	5:33	5:58	6:29	7:00	6:34	7:09
	Set 1st	4:44	5:19	5:54	6:28	8:00	8:30	8:40	8:20	7:35	6:44	4:58	4:34
	Twl	±1:44	±1:39	±1:35	±1:40	±1:53	±2:12	±2:16	±1:59	±1:44	±1:38	±1:39	±1:44

→ **Sunrises & Sunsets have been adjusted for Daylight-Savings Time**

SunRISE/SET

319

Sunrises & Sunsets

Pennsylvania/Rhode Island/South Carolina

		JAN	FEB	MAR	APR	MAY	JUN	JUL	AUG	SEP	OCT	NOV	DEC
Scranton	Rise 15th	7:26	6:58	6:14	6:23	5:44	5:29	5:42	6:12	6:43	7:15	6:51	7:22
	Set 15th	4:58	5:37	6:10	7:43	8:15	8:38	8:35	8:02	7:12	6:22	4:43	4:34
	Twl	±1:42	±1:37	±1:36	±1:45	±2:01	±2:17	±2:09	±1:51	±1:39	±1:37	±1:41	±1:44
RI **Providence** 41°50' N 71°28' W	Rise 1st	7:14	6:58	6:21	5:29	5:42	5:13	5:15	5:40	6:12	6:43	6:18	6:54
	Set 1st	4:26	5:01	5:36	6:12	7:44	8:15	8:25	8:04	7:19	6:27	4:40	4:16
	Twl	±1:45	±1:40	±1:37	±1:40	±1:54	±2:13	±2:19	±2:01	±1:45	±1:38	±1:40	±1:44
	Rise 15th	7:11	6:41	5:58	6:06	5:26	5:10	5:24	5:54	6:26	6:58	6:36	7:06
	Set 15th	4:40	5:19	5:53	7:27	7:59	8:23	8:19	7:46	6:55	6:04	4:25	4:16
	Twl	±1:43	±1:38	±1:37	±1:45	±2:03	±2:20	±2:13	±1:53	±1:40	±1:38	±1:42	±1:45
SC **Charleston** 32°47' N 79°56' W	Rise 1st	7:22	7:15	6:48	6:08	6:33	6:13	6:15	6:33	6:54	7:14	6:37	7:04
	Set 1st	5:25	5:52	6:17	6:40	8:01	8:23	8:32	8:18	7:45	7:05	5:29	5:13
	Twl	±1:32	±1:28	±1:26	±1:28	±1:36	±1:45	±1:47	±1:39	±1:29	±1:26	±1:27	±1:32
	Rise 15th	7:22	7:03	6:30	6:50	6:21	6:11	6:22	6:43	7:03	7:24	6:50	7:15
	Set 15th	5:36	6:05	6:28	7:50	8:12	8:29	8:29	8:05	7:26	6:47	5:19	5:15
	Twl	±1:31	±1:27	±1:26	±1:30	±1:40	±1:47	±1:44	±1:34	±1:28	±1:26	±1:29	±1:32
Columbia 34°00' N 81°00' W	Rise 1st	7:30	7:21	6:53	6:12	6:35	6:14	6:16	6:35	6:58	7:18	6:43	7:11
	Set 1st	5:26	5:55	6:20	6:45	8:08	8:30	8:39	8:25	7:50	7:08	5:31	5:15
	Twl	±1:33	±1:29	±1:28	±1:29	±1:37	±1:47	±1:50	±1:40	±1:32	±1:28	±1:29	±1:32
	Rise 15th	7:29	7:09	6:35	6:53	6:23	6:12	6:24	6:45	7:07	7:29	6:56	7:22
	Set 15th	5:38	6:08	6:32	7:55	8:18	8:37	8:36	8:11	7:31	6:50	5:21	5:16
	Twl	±1:32	±1:28	±1:27	±1:33	±1:43	±1:50	±1:46	±1:36	±1:28	±1:28	±1:30	±1:34
Myrtle Beach 33°43' N 78°50' W	Rise 1st	7:20	7:12	6:44	6:03	6:27	6:06	6:08	6:27	6:49	7:10	6:34	7:02
	Set 1st	5:18	5:46	6:12	6:36	7:59	8:21	8:30	8:16	7:41	7:00	5:23	5:07
	Twl	±1:33	±1:29	±1:27	±1:29	±1:37	±1:47	±1:49	±1:40	±1:30	±1:27	±1:28	±1:32
	Rise 15th	7:20	7:00	6:26	6:45	6:15	6:04	6:16	6:37	6:59	7:20	6:47	7:13
	Set 15th	5:30	6:00	6:23	7:46	8:09	8:27	8:27	8:02	7:22	6:42	5:12	5:08
	Twl	±1:32	±1:28	±1:27	±1:32	±1:42	±1:49	±1:46	±1:35	±1:28	±1:27	±1:31	±1:33

→ **Sunrises & Sunsets have been adjusted for Daylight-Savings Time**

SunRISE/SET

Sunrises & Sunsets

South Dakota

		JAN	FEB	MAR	APR	MAY	JUN	JUL	AUG	SEP	OCT	NOV	DEC
SD **Aberdeen** 45°30' N 98°30' W	Rise 1st	8:14	7:55	7:12	6:14	6:22	5:49	5:49	6:18	6:56	7:32	7:14	7:54
	Set 1st	5:02	5:41	6:21	7:02	8:41	9:16	9:26	9:02	8:11	7:14	5:21	4:52
	Twl	±1:51	±1:46	±1:43	±1:49	±2:05	±2:38	±2:48	±2:15	±1:53	±1:45	±1:46	±1:51
	Rise 15th	8:10	7:36	6:46	6:48	6:03	5:45	6:00	6:35	7:13	7:51	7:33	8:07
	Set 15th	5:17	6:01	6:40	8:21	8:58	9:25	9:20	8:41	7:45	6:48	5:04	4:51
	Twl	±1:50	±1:44	±1:44	±1:54	±2:20	±2:50	±2:34	±2:04	±1:48	±1:44	±1:48	±1:53
Mitchell 43°40' N 98°00' W	Rise 1st	8:06	7:48	7:08	6:13	6:24	5:53	5:54	6:21	6:56	7:30	7:08	7:46
	Set 1st	5:06	5:43	6:21	6:59	8:35	9:07	9:17	8:55	8:07	7:13	5:23	4:56
	Twl	±1:49	±1:43	±1:39	±1:44	±1:59	±2:24	±2:31	±2:07	±1:49	±1:40	±1:42	±1:47
	Rise 15th	8:02	7:30	6:44	6:49	6:07	5:50	6:04	6:37	7:12	7:46	7:26	7:59
	Set 15th	5:21	6:03	6:39	8:16	8:51	9:15	9:11	8:35	7:42	6:48	5:07	4:56
	Twl	±1:46	±1:40	±1:40	±1:49	±2:10	±2:33	±2:21	±1:58	±1:44	±1:41	±1:44	±1:49
Pierre 44°23' N 100°20' W	Rise 1st	8:17	7:59	7:18	6:22	6:32	6:00	6:01	6:29	7:04	7:39	7:19	7:57
	Set 1st	5:13	5:51	6:30	7:09	8:46	9:19	9:29	9:06	8:17	7:22	5:31	5:03
	Twl	±1:50	±1:43	±1:40	±1:45	±2:01	±2:30	±2:38	±2:11	±1:50	±1:42	±1:43	±1:50
	Rise 15th	8:14	7:41	6:53	6:57	6:14	5:57	6:11	6:45	7:21	7:57	7:37	8:10
	Set 15th	5:28	6:11	6:48	8:26	9:02	9:27	9:23	8:46	7:52	6:57	5:14	5:03
	Twl	±1:48	±1:41	±1:41	±1:52	±2:14	±2:39	±2:26	±2:00	±1:45	±1:42	±1:46	±1:50
Rapid City 44°00' N 103°00' W	Rise 1st	7:27	7:09	6:28	5:33	5:43	5:12	5:13	5:40	6:15	6:50	6:28	7:07
	Set 1st	4:25	5:02	5:40	6:19	7:55	8:28	8:38	8:15	7:27	6:32	4:42	4:15
	Twl	±1:49	±1:43	±1:40	±1:45	±2:01	±2:27	±2:34	±2:09	±1:50	±1:42	±1:43	±1:48
	Rise 15th	7:23	6:51	6:04	6:08	5:25	5:08	5:23	5:56	6:31	7:07	6:47	7:20
	Set 15th	4:40	5:22	5:58	7:36	8:11	8:36	8:32	7:56	7:02	6:08	4:26	4:14
	Twl	±1:47	±1:41	±1:41	±1:51	±2:13	±2:36	±2:24	±1:58	±1:44	±1:41	±1:45	±1:50
Sioux Falls 43°35' N 96°40' W	Rise 1st	8:00	7:43	7:03	6:08	6:19	5:48	5:49	6:16	6:50	7:24	7:02	7:40
	Set 1st	5:01	5:38	6:15	6:53	8:29	9:01	9:11	8:49	8:01	7:07	5:17	4:51
	Twl	±1:48	±1:42	±1:40	±1:45	±1:59	±2:25	±2:31	±2:08	±1:49	±1:41	±1:43	±1:47

→ **Sunrises & Sunsets have been adjusted for Daylight-Savings Time**

Sunrises & Sunsets

South Dakota/Tennessee

		JAN	FEB	MAR	APR	MAY	JUN	JUL	AUG	SEP	OCT	NOV	DEC
Sioux Falls	Rise 15th	7:57	7:25	6:38	6:43	6:01	5:44	5:59	6:31	7:06	7:41	7:21	7:53
	Set 15th	5:16	5:57	6:33	8:10	8:45	9:09	9:05	8:30	7:36	6:43	5:01	4:50
	Twl	±1:46	±1:40	±1:40	±1:49	±2:10	±2:32	±2:22	±1:57	±1:44	±1:41	±1:45	±1:49
TN	Rise 1st	7:49	7:40	7:11	6:28	6:50	6:28	6:31	6:50	7:14	7:36	7:02	7:31
Chattanooga	Set 1st	5:40	6:10	6:37	7:02	8:27	8:50	8:59	8:44	8:08	7:25	5:47	5:29
35°02' N	Twl	±1:35	±1:30	±1:28	±1:31	±1:39	±1:50	±1:53	±1:43	±1:33	±1:29	±1:30	±1:34
85°17' W	Rise 15th	7:49	7:27	6:52	7:09	6:38	6:27	6:38	7:01	7:24	7:47	7:16	7:42
	Set 15th	5:53	6:24	6:49	8:14	8:38	8:57	8:56	8:29	7:48	7:06	5:36	5:31
	Twl	±1:33	±1:29	±1:28	±1:33	±1:44	±1:53	±1:48	±1:38	±1:30	±1:29	±1:31	±1:34
Knoxville	Rise 1st	7:46	7:36	7:06	6:22	6:43	6:21	6:23	6:43	7:08	7:31	6:58	7:28
35°58' N	Set 1st	5:33	6:03	6:31	6:58	8:23	8:47	8:56	8:41	8:04	7:20	5:40	5:22
83°57' W	Twl	±1:35	±1:31	±1:29	±1:31	±1:40	±1:52	±1:55	±1:44	±1:33	±1:29	±1:31	±1:34
	Rise 15th	7:46	7:23	6:47	7:03	6:30	6:19	6:31	6:54	7:18	7:42	7:12	7:39
	Set 15th	5:45	6:17	6:43	8:09	8:35	8:54	8:53	8:26	7:43	7:00	5:28	5:23
	Twl	±1:34	±1:30	±1:30	±1:36	±1:46	±1:55	±1:49	±1:40	±1:31	±1:30	±1:33	±1:36
Memphis	Rise 1st	7:08	6:59	6:30	5:47	6:09	5:47	5:49	6:09	6:33	6:55	6:21	6:50
35°07' N	Set 1st	4:59	5:29	5:56	6:21	7:46	8:09	8:18	8:03	7:27	6:44	5:06	4:48
90°00' W	Twl	±1:34	±1:30	±1:28	±1:31	±1:39	±1:50	±1:53	±1:43	±1:33	±1:29	±1:29	±1:34
	Rise 15th	7:08	6:46	6:11	6:28	5:56	5:45	5:57	6:20	6:43	7:06	6:35	7:01
	Set 15th	5:11	5:43	6:08	7:33	7:57	8:16	8:15	7:49	7:07	6:25	4:54	4:49
	Twl	±1:34	±1:29	±1:28	±1:33	±1:44	±1:53	±1:49	±1:38	±1:30	±1:29	±1:32	±1:35
Nashville	Rise 1st	6:58	6:48	6:18	5:33	5:54	5:31	5:33	5:54	6:19	6:42	6:10	6:40
36°12' N	Set 1st	4:43	5:14	5:42	6:09	7:35	7:59	8:08	7:52	7:15	6:31	4:51	4:33
86°46' W	Twl	±1:36	±1:31	±1:29	±1:32	±1:40	±1:54	±1:56	±1:45	±1:34	±1:30	±1:31	±1:35
	Rise 15th	6:58	6:35	5:58	6:14	5:41	5:29	5:41	6:05	6:29	6:54	6:24	6:51
	Set 15th	4:56	5:28	5:54	7:21	7:46	8:06	8:04	7:37	6:55	6:11	4:39	4:34
	Twl	±1:34	±1:31	±1:30	±1:35	±1:47	±1:57	±1:52	±1:40	±1:31	±1:30	±1:33	±1:36

➙ **Sunrises & Sunsets have been adjusted for Daylight-Savings Time**

SunRISE/SET

Sunrises & Sunsets

Texas

		JAN	FEB	MAR	APR	MAY	JUN	JUL	AUG	SEP	OCT	NOV	DEC
TX **Corpus Christi** 27°50' N 97°28' W	Rise 1st	7:21	7:17	6:54	6:20	6:50	6:34	6:37	6:53	7:09	7:23	6:41	7:04
	Set 1st	5:46	6:11	6:30	6:48	8:04	8:22	8:30	8:19	7:51	7:16	5:46	5:34
	Twl	±1:27	±1:23	±1:22	±1:23	±1:29	±1:36	±1:38	±1:32	±1:24	±1:21	±1:23	±1:27
	Rise 15th	7:22	7:07	6:40	7:05	6:41	6:33	6:44	7:00	7:15	7:30	6:51	7:13
	Set 15th	5:57	6:21	6:39	7:55	8:12	8:27	8:28	8:08	7:35	7:01	5:38	5:37
	Twl	±1:26	±1:23	±1:21	±1:25	±1:32	±1:38	±1:35	±1:28	±1:22	±1:22	±1:25	±1:27
Dallas 32°50' N 96°50' W	Rise 1st	7:30	7:22	6:55	6:15	6:40	6:20	6:23	6:41	7:02	7:21	6:45	7:12
	Set 1st	5:32	6:00	6:24	6:47	8:09	8:30	8:39	8:26	7:52	7:12	5:36	5:21
	Twl	±1:32	±1:28	±1:27	±1:29	±1:35	±1:46	±1:47	±1:38	±1:30	±1:27	±1:28	±1:31
	Rise 15th	7:30	7:10	6:38	6:58	6:28	6:19	6:30	6:51	7:11	7:31	6:57	7:22
	Set 15th	5:44	6:13	6:35	7:57	8:19	8:37	8:36	8:12	7:33	6:54	5:26	5:23
	Twl	±1:31	±1:27	±1:26	±1:32	±1:41	±1:47	±1:45	±1:35	±1:28	±1:27	±1:29	±1:32
El Paso 31°50' N 106°30' W	Rise 1st	7:06	6:59	6:33	5:55	6:20	6:01	6:04	6:22	6:41	7:00	6:22	6:48
	Set 1st	5:13	5:40	6:04	6:26	7:46	8:07	8:16	8:03	7:30	6:51	5:16	5:02
	Twl	±1:31	±1:27	±1:25	±1:27	±1:34	±1:43	±1:45	±1:37	±1:29	±1:25	±1:27	±1:30
	Rise 15th	7:07	6:48	6:16	6:37	6:09	6:00	6:11	6:31	6:50	7:09	6:34	6:59
	Set 15th	5:25	5:53	6:14	7:35	7:56	8:13	8:13	7:50	7:12	6:34	5:07	5:04
	Twl	±1:29	±1:26	±1:25	±1:29	±1:38	±1:45	±1:42	±1:32	±1:27	±1:25	±1:28	±1:31
Houston 29°50' N 95°20' W	Rise 1st	7:17	7:11	6:47	6:11	6:39	6:21	6:24	6:41	6:58	7:15	6:35	6:59
	Set 1st	5:33	5:59	6:21	6:40	7:58	8:17	8:26	8:14	7:44	7:07	5:35	5:21
	Twl	±1:29	±1:25	±1:23	±1:24	±1:32	±1:40	±1:41	±1:34	±1:27	±1:23	±1:24	±1:29
	Rise 15th	7:18	7:01	6:31	6:55	6:28	6:20	6:31	6:49	7:06	7:23	6:46	7:09
	Set 15th	5:44	6:10	6:30	7:48	8:07	8:24	8:24	8:02	7:27	6:51	5:26	5:24
	Twl	±1:28	±1:24	±1:23	±1:28	±1:36	±1:41	±1:38	±1:30	±1:25	±1:24	±1:26	±1:29
Lubbock 33°40' N 101°53' W	Rise 1st	7:52	7:44	7:16	6:35	6:59	6:38	6:41	7:00	7:21	7:42	7:07	7:34
	Set 1st	5:50	6:19	6:44	7:08	8:31	8:53	9:02	8:48	8:13	7:32	5:55	5:39
	Twl	±1:33	±1:29	±1:27	±1:29	±1:37	±1:47	±1:49	±1:40	±1:31	±1:27	±1:29	±1:32

➡ **Sunrises & Sunsets have been adjusted for Daylight-Savings Time**

SunRISE/SET

Sunrises & Sunsets

Texas/Utah

		JAN	FEB	MAR	APR	MAY	JUN	JUL	AUG	SEP	OCT	NOV	DEC
Lubbock	Rise 15th	7:52	7:32	6:58	7:17	6:47	6:37	6:48	7:10	7:31	7:52	7:19	7:45
	Set 15th	6:02	6:32	6:55	8:19	8:41	8:59	8:59	8:34	7:54	7:13	5:45	5:41
	Twl	±1:32	±1:28	±1:27	±1:31	±1:42	±1:49	±1:45	±1:35	±1:29	±1:28	±1:30	±1:33
San Angelo *31°30' N* *100°30' W*	Rise 1st	7:41	7:35	7:09	6:31	6:57	6:38	6:41	6:58	7:18	7:36	6:58	7:24
	Set 1st	5:50	6:17	6:40	7:01	8:22	8:42	8:51	8:38	8:06	7:27	5:53	5:39
	Twl	±1:31	±1:27	±1:25	±1:26	±1:33	±1:43	±1:43	±1:36	±1:28	±1:25	±1:26	±1:30
	Rise 15th	7:42	7:24	6:52	7:14	6:46	6:37	6:48	7:07	7:26	7:45	7:10	7:34
	Set 15th	6:01	6:29	6:50	8:11	8:31	8:48	8:48	8:25	7:48	7:10	5:43	5:41
	Twl	±1:29	±1:26	±1:25	±1:29	±1:38	±1:45	±1:41	±1:33	±1:26	±1:25	±1:28	±1:31
San Antonio *29°30' N* *98°30' W*	Rise 1st	7:29	7:24	7:00	6:24	6:52	6:35	6:38	6:54	7:11	7:27	6:47	7:11
	Set 1st	5:47	6:12	6:34	6:53	8:11	8:29	8:38	8:26	7:56	7:20	5:48	5:35
	Twl	±1:28	±1:25	±1:23	±1:24	±1:30	±1:40	±1:40	±1:34	±1:26	±1:22	±1:24	±1:28
	Rise 15th	7:30	7:13	6:44	7:08	6:42	6:34	6:44	7:02	7:19	7:36	6:58	7:21
	Set 15th	5:58	6:23	6:42	8:01	8:19	8:35	8:36	8:15	7:39	7:04	5:39	5:37
	Twl	±1:27	±1:24	±1:24	±1:27	±1:35	±1:41	±1:37	±1:29	±1:24	±1:23	±1:26	±1:30
UT **Cedar City** *37°41' N* *113°03' W*	Rise 1st	7:48	7:36	7:03	6:17	6:36	6:12	6:14	6:36	7:02	7:28	6:58	7:29
	Set 1st	5:25	5:56	6:26	6:55	8:23	8:48	8:58	8:40	8:01	7:15	5:34	5:14
	Twl	±1:38	±1:34	±1:31	±1:34	±1:44	±1:58	±2:00	±1:48	±1:37	±1:32	±1:32	±1:37
	Rise 15th	7:46	7:22	6:43	6:57	6:22	6:10	6:23	6:48	7:14	7:41	7:13	7:40
	Set 15th	5:38	6:12	6:40	8:08	8:35	8:56	8:53	8:25	7:40	6:55	5:21	5:15
	Twl	±1:36	±1:32	±1:31	±1:37	±1:50	±2:04	±1:57	±1:43	±1:34	±1:32	±1:35	±1:38
Richfield *38°50' N* *112°00' W*	Rise 1st	7:47	7:34	7:00	6:12	6:30	6:05	6:07	6:29	6:57	7:24	6:55	7:28
	Set 1st	5:17	5:50	6:21	6:52	8:21	8:47	8:57	8:39	7:58	7:10	5:27	5:07
	Twl	±1:40	±1:35	±1:32	±1:35	±1:46	±2:00	±2:05	±1:51	±1:39	±1:34	±1:35	±1:39
	Rise 15th	7:45	7:19	6:39	6:51	6:15	6:02	6:15	6:42	7:10	7:38	7:11	7:39
	Set 15th	5:31	6:06	6:35	8:05	8:34	8:55	8:52	8:22	7:36	6:49	5:14	5:07
	Twl	±1:36	±1:33	±1:33	±1:40	±1:53	±2:06	±2:01	±1:46	±1:36	±1:34	±1:36	±1:40

➧ **Sunrises & Sunsets have been adjusted for Daylight-Savings Time**

Sunrises & Sunsets

Utah/Vermont/Virginia

		JAN	FEB	MAR	APR	MAY	JUN	JUL	AUG	SEP	OCT	NOV	DEC
Salt Lake City	Rise 1st	7:52	7:37	7:01	6:11	6:26	5:59	6:00	6:24	6:55	7:24	6:58	7:33
	Set 1st	5:11	5:46	6:19	6:53	8:24	8:53	9:03	8:43	8:00	7:09	5:24	5:01
40° 45' N *111° 58' W*	Twl	±1:43	±1:38	±1:35	±1:39	±1:51	±2:09	±2:14	±1:57	±1:42	±1:37	±1:38	±1:42
	Rise 15th	7:50	7:21	6:39	6:49	6:10	5:56	6:09	6:38	7:08	7:39	7:15	7:45
	Set 15th	5:25	6:03	6:35	8:07	8:36	9:01	8:58	8:25	7:36	6:47	5:09	5:01
	Twl	±1:41	±1:36	±1:36	±1:44	±2:02	±2:14	±2:07	±1:50	±1:39	±1:36	±1:41	±1:44
VT **Barre**	Rise 1st	7:26	7:08	6:27	5:31	5:41	5:09	5:10	5:38	6:13	6:48	6:27	7:06
	Set 1st	4:22	5:00	5:38	6:17	7:54	8:27	8:37	8:14	7:26	6:31	4:40	4:12
44° 15' N *72° 30' W*	Twl	±1:49	±1:43	±1:41	±1:46	±2:01	±2:28	±2:36	±2:11	±1:50	±1:41	±1:43	±1:48
	Rise 15th	7:22	6:49	6:02	6:06	5:23	5:06	5:20	5:53	6:29	7:05	6:46	7:19
	Set 15th	4:37	5:19	5:56	7:35	8:10	8:36	8:31	7:55	7:00	6:06	4:23	4:12
	Twl	±1:47	±1:42	±1:42	±1:51	±2:14	±2:37	±2:25	±1:59	±1:45	±1:41	±1:45	±1:49
Burlington	Rise 1st	7:29	7:11	6:30	5:34	5:43	5:11	5:12	5:40	6:18	6:51	6:30	7:09
44° 27' N *73° 14' W*	Set 1st	4:24	5:02	5:41	6:20	7:57	8:31	8:41	8:18	7:29	6:33	4:42	4:15
	Twl	±1:50	±1:44	±1:41	±1:46	±2:02	±2:29	±2:37	±2:11	±1:50	±1:43	±1:44	±1:49
	Rise 15th	7:26	6:53	6:05	6:09	5:25	5:08	5:22	5:56	6:32	7:08	6:49	7:22
	Set 15th	4:39	5:22	5:59	7:38	8:14	8:39	8:35	7:58	7:03	6:08	4:25	4:14
	Twl	±1:48	±1:42	±1:42	±1:51	±2:13	±2:39	±2:26	±2:00	±1:45	±1:43	±1:46	±1:50
VA **Norfolk**	Rise 1st	7:18	7:07	6:36	5:51	6:11	5:48	5:50	6:11	6:36	7:00	6:29	6:59
	Set 1st	5:00	5:31	6:00	6:27	7:54	8:18	8:28	8:11	7:33	6:48	5:08	4:49
36° 40' N *76° 15' W*	Twl	±1:37	±1:33	±1:29	±1:32	±1:41	±1:54	±1:57	±1:47	±1:35	±1:31	±1:32	±1:37
	Rise 15th	7:17	6:53	6:16	6:31	5:58	5:46	5:58	6:22	6:47	7:13	6:43	7:10
	Set 15th	5:13	5:46	6:13	7:40	8:06	8:25	8:24	7:56	7:12	6:28	4:56	4:50
	Twl	±1:35	±1:31	±1:29	±1:35	±1:47	±1:58	±1:53	±1:41	±1:32	±1:31	±1:34	±1:38
Richmond	Rise 1st	7:25	7:13	6:41	5:55	6:14	5:50	5:52	6:14	6:40	7:05	6:35	7:06
37° 33' N *77° 27' W*	Set 1st	5:03	5:34	6:04	6:33	8:00	8:26	8:35	8:18	7:39	6:53	5:11	4:52
	Twl	±1:37	±1:34	±1:31	±1:34	±1:43	±1:57	±2:00	±1:49	±1:37	±1:32	±1:33	±1:37

➥ **Sunrises & Sunsets have been adjusted for Daylight-Savings Time**

Sunrises & Sunsets

Virginia/Washington

		JAN	FEB	MAR	APR	MAY	JUN	JUL	AUG	SEP	OCT	NOV	DEC
Richmond	Rise 15th	7:23	6:59	6:21	6:35	6:00	5:48	6:01	6:26	6:52	7:18	6:50	7:17
	Set 15th	5:16	5:49	6:17	7:45	8:12	8:33	8:31	8:02	7:17	6:32	4:59	4:53
	Twl	±1:35	±1:32	±1:31	±1:37	±1:50	±2:01	±1:55	±1:43	±1:35	±1:32	±1:35	±1:38
Roanoke	Rise 1st	7:34	7:23	6:51	6:05	6:25	6:01	6:03	6:24	6:50	7:15	6:44	7:15
37° 19' N	Set 1st	5:13	5:44	6:14	6:42	8:09	8:35	8:44	8:27	7:48	7:03	5:22	5:02
79° 55' W	Twl	±1:38	±1:34	±1:30	±1:34	±1:43	±1:56	±1:59	±1:48	±1:37	±1:31	±1:32	±1:37
	Rise 15th	7:33	7:09	6:31	6:45	6:11	5:59	6:11	6:36	7:02	7:28	6:59	7:27
	Set 15th	5:26	6:00	6:27	7:55	8:22	8:42	8:40	8:12	7:27	6:43	5:09	5:03
	Twl	±1:36	±1:31	±1:31	±1:37	±1:49	±2:00	±1:55	±1:41	±1:34	±1:31	±1:35	±1:38
WA **Bellingham**	Rise 1st	8:03	7:39	6:51	5:47	5:49	5:11	5:11	5:44	6:27	7:10	6:57	7:42
48° 45' N	Set 1st	4:25	5:08	5:54	6:41	8:25	9:05	9:16	8:48	7:51	6:48	4:49	4:16
122° 27' W	Twl	±2:00	±1:53	±1:50	±1:56	±2:21	±3:35	NONE	±2:36	±2:03	±1:52	±1:52	±2:00
Note: Some Washington locations do not experience an end of twilight during the summer	Rise 15th	7:57	7:17	6:23	6:19	5:28	5:06	5:23	6:03	6:47	7:30	7:19	7:56
	Set 15th	4:42	5:31	6:16	8:02	8:45	9:15	9:08	8:24	7:22	6:20	4:30	4:14
	Twl	±1:58	±1:51	±1:50	±2:05	±2:44	NONE	±3:15	±2:18	±1:56	±1:50	±1:55	±2:01
Seattle	Rise 1st	7:58	7:36	6:49	5:48	5:52	5:16	5:16	5:47	6:28	7:08	6:53	7:37
47° 41' N	Set 1st	4:29	5:11	5:55	6:40	8:22	8:59	9:10	8:43	7:49	6:48	4:51	4:19
122° 15' W	Twl	±1:57	±1:50	±1:46	±1:53	±2:15	±3:07	±3:29	±2:28	±1:59	±1:49	±1:50	±1:57
	Rise 15th	7:53	7:15	6:22	6:20	5:32	5:11	5:27	6:05	6:47	7:29	7:15	7:51
	Set 15th	4:46	5:33	6:15	7:59	8:40	9:09	9:03	8:21	7:21	6:21	4:33	4:18
	Twl	±1:54	±1:47	±1:48	±2:02	±2:35	±3:40	±2:56	±2:12	±1:53	±1:48	±1:52	±1:58
Spokane	Rise 1st	7:38	7:16	6:30	5:28	5:32	4:55	4:56	5:27	6:08	6:49	6:34	7:17
47° 45' N	Set 1st	4:09	4:51	5:35	6:20	8:02	8:40	8:51	8:24	7:30	6:28	4:32	4:00
117° 25' W	Twl	±1:57	±1:50	±1:46	±1:54	±2:16	±3:08	±3:31	±2:29	±1:59	±1:50	±1:50	±1:56
	Rise 15th	7:33	6:55	6:02	6:00	5:12	4:51	5:07	5:45	6:27	7:09	6:55	7:32
	Set 15th	4:26	5:13	5:55	7:40	8:21	8:49	8:43	8:02	7:01	6:01	4:13	3:58
	Twl	±1:54	±1:48	±1:49	±2:02	±2:35	±3:46	±2:58	±2:12	±1:53	±1:48	±1:52	±1:58

➙ **Sunrises & Sunsets have been adjusted for Daylight-Savings Time**

SunRISE/SET

Sunrises & Sunsets

Washington/West Virginia/Wisconsin

		JAN	FEB	MAR	APR	MAY	JUN	JUL	AUG	SEP	OCT	NOV	DEC
Yakima 46°42' N 120°30' W	Rise 1st	7:47	7:26	6:41	5:41	5:47	5:12	5:12	5:43	6:22	7:01	6:44	7:26
	Set 1st	4:25	5:06	5:48	6:31	8:12	8:48	8:59	8:33	7:41	6:41	4:46	4:16
	Twl	±1:55	±1:49	±1:45	±1:51	±2:11	±2:52	±3:05	±2:22	±1:56	±1:48	±1:48	±1:53
	Rise 15th	7:42	7:06	6:14	6:14	5:27	5:08	5:24	6:00	6:40	7:20	7:05	7:40
	Set 15th	4:41	5:27	6:08	7:51	8:30	8:58	8:52	8:12	7:13	6:15	4:28	4:15
	Twl	±1:53	±1:46	±1:46	±1:57	±2:27	±3:09	±2:45	±2:08	±1:50	±1:46	±1:51	±1:55
WV **Charleston** 38°24' N 81°36' W	Rise 1st	7:44	7:32	6:58	6:11	6:29	6:04	6:06	6:28	6:56	7:22	6:53	7:25
	Set 1st	5:16	5:49	6:20	6:50	8:18	8:45	8:55	8:37	7:56	7:09	5:26	5:06
	Twl	±1:40	±1:35	±1:32	±1:35	±1:45	±2:00	±2:03	±1:50	±1:38	±1:33	±1:34	±1:39
	Rise 15th	7:43	7:17	6:38	6:50	6:15	6:02	6:14	6:41	7:08	7:36	7:08	7:37
	Set 15th	5:30	6:05	6:34	8:03	8:31	8:52	8:50	8:20	7:34	6:48	5:13	5:07
	Twl	±1:37	±1:33	±1:32	±1:39	±1:52	±2:04	±1:58	±1:40	±1:35	±1:33	±1:36	±1:39
Wheeling 40°02' N 80°41' W	Rise 1st	7:45	7:31	6:56	6:07	6:23	5:56	5:58	6:21	6:51	7:19	6:52	7:26
	Set 1st	5:08	5:42	6:15	6:47	8:18	8:46	8:56	8:36	7:54	7:05	5:20	4:58
	Twl	±1:41	±1:37	±1:34	±1:37	±1:49	±2:06	±2:09	±1:55	±1:41	±1:35	±1:36	±1:41
	Rise 15th	7:43	7:16	6:34	6:45	6:07	5:53	6:06	6:34	7:04	7:33	7:08	7:38
	Set 15th	5:22	5:59	6:30	8:01	8:31	8:53	8:51	8:19	7:31	6:43	5:06	4:58
	Twl	±1:40	±1:35	±1:34	±1:42	±1:57	±2:11	±2:04	±1:48	±1:38	±1:35	±1:39	±1:43
WI **Eau Claire** 44°46' N 91°30' W	Rise 1st	7:44	7:25	6:44	5:47	5:56	5:23	5:24	5:52	6:28	7:04	6:44	7:23
	Set 1st	4:36	5:14	5:54	6:34	8:11	8:45	8:56	8:32	7:43	6:47	4:55	4:27
	Twl	±1:51	±1:46	±1:41	±1:46	±2:03	±2:32	±2:39	±2:12	±1:50	±1:42	±1:44	±1:50
	Rise 15th	7:40	7:07	6:19	6:22	5:38	5:20	5:34	6:08	6:45	7:21	7:03	7:37
	Set 15th	4:51	5:34	6:12	7:51	8:28	8:54	8:49	8:12	7:17	6:22	4:38	4:26
	Twl	±1:49	±1:43	±1:42	±1:53	±2:15	±2:42	±2:29	±2:01	±1:45	±1:42	±1:47	±1:51
Green Bay 44°30' N 88°00' W	Rise 1st	7:29	7:11	6:30	5:33	5:43	5:10	5:11	5:39	6:15	6:50	6:29	7:08
	Set 1st	4:23	5:01	5:40	6:19	7:56	8:30	8:41	8:17	7:29	6:33	4:41	4:14
	Twl	±1:50	±1:44	±1:41	±1:46	±2:02	±2:31	±2:37	±2:11	±1:49	±1:42	±1:44	±1:49

➙ **Sunrises & Sunsets have been adjusted for Daylight-Savings Time**

Sunrises & Sunsets

Wisconsin

		JAN	FEB	MAR	APR	MAY	JUN	JUL	AUG	SEP	OCT	NOV	DEC
Green Bay	Rise 15th	7:25	6:52	6:05	6:08	5:25	5:07	5:21	5:55	6:31	7:07	6:48	7:22
	Set 15th	4:38	5:21	5:58	7:37	8:13	8:39	8:34	7:57	7:03	6:08	4:25	4:13
	Twl	±1:48	±1:42	±1:42	±1:52	±2:14	±2:40	±2:27	±2:00	±1:45	±1:42	±1:45	±1:50
Ironwood	Rise 1st	7:45	7:24	6:40	5:40	5:47	5:12	5:12	5:41	6:21	6:59	6:42	7:24
46°30' N	Set 1st	4:24	5:05	5:47	6:30	8:10	8:46	8:57	8:32	7:40	6:41	4:46	4:15
90°10' W	Twl	±1:55	±1:48	±1:44	±1:50	±2:10	±2:50	±3:01	±2:21	±1:55	±1:46	±1:47	±1:53
	Rise 15th	7:40	7:04	6:14	6:14	5:27	5:07	5:23	5:59	6:38	7:18	7:02	7:38
	Set 15th	4:40	5:26	6:06	7:48	8:28	8:55	8:50	8:11	7:12	6:14	4:28	4:14
	Twl	±1:53	±1:45	±1:46	±1:58	±2:25	±3:06	±2:43	±2:07	±1:50	±1:45	±1:50	±1:55
Madison	Rise 1st	7:29	7:13	6:34	5:40	5:51	5:21	5:22	5:48	6:22	6:55	6:32	7:09
43°05' N	Set 1st	4:33	5:10	5:47	6:24	7:59	8:30	8:41	8:19	7:33	6:39	4:50	4:24
89°25' W	Twl	±1:47	±1:42	±1:38	±1:43	±1:57	±2:21	±2:27	±2:05	±1:46	±1:39	±1:41	±1:46
	Rise 15th	7:26	6:55	6:10	6:16	5:34	5:18	5:32	6:03	6:37	7:11	6:50	7:22
	Set 15th	4:48	5:29	6:04	7:40	8:15	8:39	8:35	8:00	7:08	6:15	4:34	4:23
	Twl	±1:45	±1:39	±1:40	±1:49	±2:07	±2:28	±2:18	±1:56	±1:42	±1:39	±1:43	±1:48
Milwaukee	Rise 1st	7:24	7:07	6:28	5:34	5:46	5:15	5:16	5:42	6:16	6:49	6:27	7:04
43°09' N	Set 1st	4:27	5:04	5:41	6:18	7:53	8:25	8:35	8:14	7:27	6:33	4:44	4:18
87°58' W	Twl	±1:47	±1:42	±1:39	±1:43	±1:58	±2:22	±2:27	±2:05	±1:46	±1:40	±1:41	±1:46
	Rise 15th	7:21	6:50	6:04	6:10	5:28	5:12	5:26	5:57	6:31	7:05	6:45	7:17
	Set 15th	4:42	5:23	5:58	7:35	8:09	8:33	8:30	7:55	7:02	6:09	4:28	4:17
	Twl	±1:45	±1:40	±1:40	±1:48	±2:09	±2:29	±2:18	±1:55	±1:43	±1:40	±1:43	±1:48
Wausau	Rise 1st	7:37	7:18	6:37	5:40	5:48	5:15	5:16	5:44	6:21	6:57	6:37	7:16
44°57' N	Set 1st	4:28	5:07	5:46	6:26	8:04	8:38	8:49	8:25	7:36	6:39	4:47	4:19
89°40' W	Twl	±1:51	±1:45	±1:42	±1:47	±2:04	±2:34	±2:42	±2:13	±1:51	±1:43	±1:44	±1:50
	Rise 15th	7:33	7:00	6:11	6:14	5:30	5:11	5:26	6:00	6:37	7:14	6:56	7:30
	Set 15th	4:43	5:27	6:05	7:44	8:21	8:47	8:42	8:05	7:10	6:14	4:30	4:18
	Twl	±1:49	±1:42	±1:42	±1:53	±2:17	±2:44	±2:31	±2:02	±1:45	±1:42	±1:47	±1:51

→ **Sunrises & Sunsets have been adjusted for Daylight-Savings Time**

SunRISE/SET

Sunrises & Sunsets

Wyoming/Puerto Rico/Canada

		JAN	FEB	MAR	APR	MAY	JUN	JUL	AUG	SEP	OCT	NOV	DEC
WY **Buffalo** 44°25' N 106°50' W	Rise 1st	7:44	7:26	6:44	5:48	5:58	5:26	5:27	5:55	6:30	7:05	6:45	7:24
	Set 1st	4:39	5:17	5:56	6:35	8:12	8:45	8:55	8:32	7:43	6:48	4:56	4:29
	Twl	±1:50	±1:44	±1:40	±1:46	±2:01	±2:30	±2:38	±2:11	±1:50	±1:42	±1:44	±1:49
	Rise 15th	7:40	7:07	6:19	6:23	5:40	5:22	5:37	6:11	6:47	7:23	7:04	7:37
	Set 15th	4:54	5:37	6:14	7:52	8:28	8:54	8:49	8:12	7:18	6:23	4:40	4:28
	Twl	±1:48	±1:41	±1:41	±1:52	±2:14	±2:39	±2:27	±2:00	±1:45	±1:42	±1:45	±1:51
Casper 42°52' N 106°20' W	Rise 1st	7:36	7:20	6:41	5:47	5:59	5:29	5:31	5:57	6:30	7:03	6:40	7:17
	Set 1st	4:42	5:19	5:55	6:32	8:06	8:38	8:48	8:26	7:40	6:46	4:57	4:32
	Twl	±1:50	±1:43	±1:38	±1:42	±1:57	±2:19	±2:25	±2:04	±1:46	±1:40	±1:42	±1:46
	Rise 15th	7:33	7:02	6:17	6:23	5:42	5:26	5:40	6:12	6:45	7:19	6:58	7:29
	Set 15th	4:57	5:37	6:12	7:48	8:22	8:46	8:42	8:07	7:15	6:23	4:42	4:32
	Twl	±1:44	±1:39	±1:39	±1:48	±2:07	±2:26	±2:17	±1:55	±1:42	±1:39	±1:43	±1:47
Rock Springs 41°40' N 109°10' W	Rise 1st	7:44	7:29	6:51	5:59	6:13	5:45	5:46	6:11	6:43	7:14	6:49	7:24
	Set 1st	4:57	5:33	6:07	6:42	8:15	8:45	8:55	8:34	7:50	6:58	5:11	4:47
	Twl	±1:45	±1:39	±1:37	±1:41	±1:53	±2:13	±2:19	±2:01	±1:44	±1:38	±1:39	±1:44
	Rise 15th	7:41	7:12	6:28	6:36	5:57	5:42	5:56	6:25	6:57	7:29	7:06	7:37
	Set 15th	5:12	5:50	6:24	7:58	8:30	8:53	8:49	8:16	7:26	6:35	4:56	4:47
	Twl	±1:42	±1:38	±1:37	±1:45	±2:02	±2:19	±2:11	±1:52	±1:39	±1:38	±1:41	±1:45
Puerto Rico **San Juan** 18°28' N 66°08' W	Rise 1st	6:57	6:58	6:44	6:19	5:57	5:47	5:52	6:02	6:10	6:15	6:24	6:40
	Set 1st	6:00	6:19	6:30	6:38	6:46	6:57	7:05	6:59	6:39	6:13	5:52	5:47
	Twl	±1:21	±1:18	±1:17	±1:17	±1:21	±1:26	±1:27	±1:23	±1:18	±1:16	±1:18	±1:20
	Rise 15th	7:00	6:52	6:33	6:08	5:51	5:48	5:56	6:06	6:12	6:18	6:31	6:49
	Set 15th	6:08	6:25	6:34	6:42	6:51	7:02	7:04	6:52	6:27	6:02	5:47	5:51
	Twl	±1:21	±1:17	±1:16	±1:18	±1:24	±1:27	±1:26	±1:19	±1:17	±1:17	±1:20	±1:21
Canada **Calgary** 51°0' N 114°10' W	Rise 1st	8:40	8:13	7:21	6:12	6:10	5:28	5:27	6:02	6:50	7:37	7:29	8:18
	Set 1st	4:41	5:28	6:18	7:10	8:59	9:42	9:54	9:23	8:22	7:15	5:11	4:33
	Twl	±2:07	±1:59	±1:55	±2:03	±2:36	NONE	NONE	±2:58	±2:10	±1:56	±1:58	±2:06

→ **Sunrises & Sunsets have been adjusted for Daylight-Savings Time**

Sunrises & Sunsets

Canada

		JAN	FEB	MAR	APR	MAY	JUN	JUL	AUG	SEP	OCT	NOV	DEC
Calgary	Rise 15th	8:33	7:49	6:51	6:42	5:47	5:22	5:40	6:24	7:12	8:00	7:53	8:33
	Set 15th	4:59	5:53	6:42	8:33	9:20	9:53	9:45	8:58	7:51	6:44	4:49	4:30
	Twl	±2:05	±1:56	±1:56	±2:14	±3:15	NONE	NONE	±2:29	±2:01	±1:56	±2:01	±2:08
Chicoutimi *48°28' N 71°05' W*	Rise 1st	7:36	7:14	6:26	5:23	5:25	4:47	4:47	5:19	6:01	6:44	6:30	7:15
	Set 1st	4:00	4:43	5:28	6:15	7:59	8:38	8:50	8:22	7:26	6:24	4:25	3:52
	Twl	±1:59	±1:52	±1:50	±1:55	±2:19	NONE	NONE	±2:34	±2:02	±1:50	±1:51	±1:59
Note: Some locations in Canada do not experience an end of twilight during the summer	Rise 15th	7:31	6:52	5:58	5:54	5:04	4:42	4:58	5:38	6:21	7:04	6:52	7:29
	Set 15th	4:17	5:06	5:50	7:35	8:18	8:48	8:42	7:59	6:57	5:55	4:05	3:50
	Twl	±1:56	±1:50	±1:50	±2:05	±2:42	NONE	±3:09	±2:15	±1:55	±1:50	±1:54	±1:59
Edmonton *53°30' N 113°30' W*	Rise 1st	8:50	8:19	7:22	6:07	5:59	5:12	5:09	5:50	6:43	7:36	7:33	8:27
	Set 1st	4:25	5:17	6:12	7:10	9:04	9:53	10:06	9:30	8:24	7:11	5:01	4:19
	Twl	±2:16	±2:06	±2:01	±2:12	±3:02	NONE	NONE	NONE	±2:21	±2:03	±2:05	±2:14
	Rise 15th	8:42	7:53	6:49	6:34	5:33	5:04	5:24	6:13	7:08	8:01	8:00	8:44
	Set 15th	4:45	5:45	6:38	8:36	9:28	10:05	9:55	9:02	7:50	6:38	4:37	4:14
	Twl	±2:13	±2:03	±2:04	±2:26	NONE	NONE	NONE	±2:49	±2:09	±2:02	±2:09	±2:17
Halifax *44°38' N 63°35' W*	Rise 1st	7:51	7:33	6:52	5:56	6:05	5:32	5:33	6:01	6:37	7:12	6:52	7:31
	Set 1st	4:45	5:23	6:02	6:42	8:19	8:52	9:03	8:40	7:51	6:55	5:03	4:36
	Twl	±1:50	±1:44	±1:41	±1:46	±2:03	±2:32	±2:39	±2:12	±1:50	±1:42	±1:44	±1:49
Note: Some locations in Canada do not experience an end of twilight during the summer	Rise 15th	7:48	7:15	6:27	6:31	5:47	5:28	5:43	6:17	6:53	7:29	7:11	7:44
	Set 15th	5:00	5:43	6:20	7:59	8:35	9:01	8:57	8:20	7:25	6:30	4:47	4:35
	Twl	±1:48	±1:42	±1:42	±1:52	±2:16	±2:42	±2:28	±2:00	±1:45	±1:42	±1:45	±1:50
Kamloops *50°40' N 120°20' W*	Rise 1st	8:03	7:37	6:45	5:37	5:36	4:54	4:54	5:28	6:15	7:02	6:53	7:41
	Set 1st	4:07	4:54	5:43	6:34	8:22	9:05	9:17	8:46	7:46	6:39	4:36	4:00
	Twl	±2:07	±1:58	±1:54	±2:02	±2:34	NONE	NONE	±2:54	±2:09	±1:56	±1:58	±2:04
	Rise 15th	7:57	7:13	6:15	6:07	5:13	4:48	5:07	5:51	6:38	7:26	7:17	7:56
	Set 15th	4:25	5:18	6:06	7:57	8:44	9:16	9:07	8:19	7:15	6:09	4:15	3:57
	Twl	±2:04	±1:56	±1:56	±2:12	±3:08	NONE	NONE	±2:30	±2:00	±1:54	±2:00	±2:06

→ **Sunrises & Sunsets have been adjusted for Daylight-Savings Time**

SunRISE/SET

Sunrises & Sunsets

Canada

		JAN	FEB	MAR	APR	MAY	JUN	JUL	AUG	SEP	OCT	NOV	DEC
Montreal	Rise 1st	7:35	7:16	6:33	5:35	5:43	5:09	5:09	5:38	6:15	6:52	6:34	7:14
45°31' N	Set 1st	4:21	5:01	5:41	6:22	8:01	8:36	8:47	8:23	7:32	6:35	4:42	4:13
73°34' W	Twl	±1:52	±1:47	±1:43	±1:48	±2:06	±2:39	±2:48	±2:15	±1:53	±1:44	±1:45	±1:51
	Rise 15th	7:31	6:56	6:07	6:09	5:24	5:05	5:20	5:55	6:33	7:10	6:53	7:28
	Set 15th	4:37	5:21	6:00	7:40	8:18	8:45	8:40	8:02	7:06	6:09	4:24	4:11
	Twl	±1:50	±1:44	±1:44	±1:55	±2:20	±2:51	±2:34	±2:03	±1:47	±1:44	±1:48	±1:53
Prince George	Rise 1st	8:30	7:58	7:00	5:44	5:35	4:47	4:44	5:25	6:20	7:13	7:12	8:07
53°55' N	Set 1st	4:01	4:53	5:49	6:47	8:43	9:33	9:46	9:09	8:02	6:48	4:37	3:54
122°50' W	Twl	±2:17	±2:08	±2:02	±2:14	±3:08	NONE	NONE	NONE	±2:23	±2:04	±2:06	±2:15
	Rise 15th	8:21	7:31	6:26	6:11	5:09	4:39	4:59	5:50	6:45	7:39	7:39	8:24
Note: Some locations in Canada do not experience an end of twilight during the summer	Set 15th	4:21	5:21	6:16	8:13	9:08	9:45	9:35	8:41	7:27	6:14	4:12	3:49
	Twl	±2:14	±2:04	±2:04	±2:30	NONE	NONE	NONE	±2:53	±2:12	±2:04	±2:11	±2:19
Quebec	Rise 1st	7:30	7:10	6:25	5:24	5:30	4:54	4:54	5:24	6:04	6:43	6:27	7:09
46°52' N	Set 1st	4:07	4:48	5:30	6:14	7:55	8:32	8:43	8:17	7:25	6:25	4:29	3:58
71°13' W	Twl	±1:55	±1:49	±1:46	±1:51	±2:12	±2:53	±3:08	±2:23	±1:56	±1:47	±1:48	±1:55
	Rise 15th	7:26	6:49	5:58	5:58	5:10	4:50	5:05	5:42	6:22	7:03	6:48	7:23
	Set 15th	4:23	5:09	5:50	7:33	8:13	8:41	8:36	7:56	6:57	5:58	4:11	3:57
	Twl	±1:53	±1:47	±1:47	±1:58	±2:28	NONE	±2:47	±2:08	±1:50	±1:46	±1:51	±1:55
Regina	Rise 1st	8:59	8:33	7:42	6:35	6:33	5:52	5:51	6:26	7:13	7:59	7:49	8:37
50°27' N	Set 1st	5:05	5:51	6:40	7:31	9:18	10:01	10:13	9:42	8:43	7:37	5:34	4:58
104°35' W	Twl	±2:05	±1:58	±1:54	±2:02	±2:32	NONE	NONE	±2:52	±2:08	±1:54	±1:57	±2:04
	Rise 15th	8:53	8:10	7:12	7:05	6:11	5:46	6:04	6:47	7:34	8:21	8:13	8:52
Note: Some locations in Canada do not experience an end of twilight during the summer	Set 15th	5:23	6:16	7:03	8:53	9:40	10:12	10:04	9:18	8:12	7:07	5:13	4:55
	Twl	±2:03	±1:55	±1:55	±2:12	±3:04	NONE	NONE	±2:26	±2:00	±1:53	±1:59	±2:06
Rouyn-Noranda	Rise 1st	8:07	7:44	6:57	5:54	5:57	5:19	5:19	5:51	6:34	7:15	7:02	7:46
48°20' N	Set 1st	4:32	5:16	6:00	6:47	8:30	9:09	9:20	8:53	7:57	6:55	4:57	4:24
79°00' W	Twl	±1:59	±1:51	±1:49	±1:55	±2:19	±3:20	NONE	±2:33	±2:02	±1:50	±1:51	±1:58

→ **Sunrises & Sunsets have been adjusted for Daylight-Savings Time**

Sunrises & Sunsets

Canada

		JAN	FEB	MAR	APR	MAY	JUN	JUL	AUG	SEP	OCT	NOV	DEC
Rouyn-Noranda	Rise 15th	8:02	7:23	6:29	6:26	5:36	5:14	5:31	6:10	6:53	7:36	7:24	8:01
	Set 15th	4:49	5:38	6:22	8:07	8:50	9:19	9:12	8:30	7:28	6:27	4:37	4:22
	Twl	±1:56	±1:50	±1:49	±2:04	±2:38	NONE	±3:07	±2:15	±1:55	±1:49	±1:54	±1:59
St. John's *47°35' N 52°40' W*	Rise 1st	7:49	7:27	6:42	5:40	5:44	5:07	5:07	5:38	6:19	6:59	6:44	7:28
	Set 1st	4:20	5:02	5:45	6:30	8:13	8:50	9:02	8:35	7:41	6:40	4:44	4:11
	Twl	±1:58	±1:50	±1:47	±1:54	±2:15	±3:05	NONE	±2:28	±1:59	±1:49	±1:49	±1:57
	Rise 15th	7:44	7:07	6:14	6:12	5:24	5:02	5:18	5:56	6:38	7:19	7:06	7:42
	Set 15th	4:36	5:24	6:06	7:50	8:31	9:00	8:54	8:13	7:13	6:13	4:25	4:10
	Twl	±1:55	±1:47	±1:49	±2:01	±2:34	NONE	±2:56	±2:12	±1:52	±1:47	±1:52	±1:58
Saskatoon *52°10' N 106°38' W*	Rise 1st	9:16	8:47	7:53	6:41	5:36	4:52	4:50	5:28	6:18	7:08	8:02	8:53
	Set 1st	5:05	5:54	6:46	7:41	8:32	9:18	9:31	8:57	7:54	6:44	5:38	4:58
	Twl	±2:12	±2:02	±1:58	±2:07	±2:46	NONE	NONE	±3:18	±2:15	±2:00	±2:01	±2:10
	Rise 15th	9:08	8:22	7:21	6:10	5:12	4:45	5:04	5:50	6:41	7:32	8:27	9:09
	Set 15th	5:24	6:20	7:11	8:05	8:55	9:29	9:21	8:31	7:20	6:12	5:15	4:54
	Twl	±2:08	±1:59	±2:00	±2:20	±4:11	NONE	NONE	±2:38	±2:06	±1:59	±2:04	±2:12
Sudbury *46°30' N 81°00' W*	Rise 1st	8:08	7:48	7:04	6:04	6:10	5:35	5:35	6:05	6:44	7:22	7:06	7:47
	Set 1st	4:48	5:28	6:10	6:53	8:33	9:09	9:21	8:55	8:03	7:04	5:09	4:39
	Twl	±1:54	±1:49	±1:44	±1:50	±2:11	±2:50	±3:00	±2:21	±1:55	±1:46	±1:47	±1:53
	Rise 15th	8:04	7:28	6:37	6:37	5:50	5:30	5:46	6:22	7:02	7:41	7:26	8:01
	Set 15th	5:04	5:49	6:30	8:12	8:51	9:19	9:13	8:34	7:36	6:38	4:51	4:37
	Twl	±1:52	±1:46	±1:45	±1:57	±2:26	±3:05	±2:44	±2:07	±1:49	±1:45	±1:50	±1:55
Thunder Bay *48°20' N 89°15' W*	Rise 1st	8:48	8:26	7:39	6:35	6:38	6:00	6:00	6:32	7:14	7:56	7:43	8:27
	Set 1st	5:13	5:56	6:41	7:27	9:11	9:50	10:02	9:34	8:39	7:36	5:38	5:05
	Twl	±1:59	±1:52	±1:49	±1:56	±2:19	±3:20	NONE	±2:33	±2:01	±1:50	±1:51	±1:58
	Rise 15th	8:43	8:04	7:10	7:07	6:17	5:55	6:12	6:51	7:34	8:17	8:05	8:42
	Set 15th	5:30	6:19	7:02	8:48	9:30	10:00	9:54	9:11	8:10	7:08	5:18	5:03
	Twl	±1:56	±1:50	±1:50	±2:03	±2:41	NONE	±3:06	±2:15	±1:54	±1:49	±1:54	±1:59

Note: Some locations in Canada do not experience an end of twilight during the summer

➙ **Sunrises & Sunsets have been adjusted for Daylight-Savings Time**

SunRISE/SET

		JAN	FEB	MAR	APR	MAY	JUN	JUL	AUG	SEP	OCT	NOV	DEC
Toronto *43°39' N 79°20' W*	Rise 1st	7:51	7:34	6:54	5:59	6:10	5:39	5:40	6:06	6:41	7:15	6:53	7:31
	Set 1st	4:51	5:28	6:06	6:44	8:20	8:52	9:03	8:40	7:53	6:59	5:08	4:42
	Twl	±1:49	±1:43	±1:39	±1:45	±1:59	±2:25	±2:31	±2:08	±1:48	±1:40	±1:43	±1:47
	Rise 15th	7:48	7:16	6:30	6:35	5:52	5:35	5:50	6:22	6:57	7:31	7:11	7:44
	Set 15th	5:06	5:47	6:24	8:01	8:36	9:01	8:57	8:21	7:28	6:34	4:52	4:41
	Twl	±1:47	±1:41	±1:40	±1:49	±2:10	±2:32	±2:21	±1:57	±1:43	±1:40	±1:44	±1:49
Winnipeg *49°54' N 97°09' W*	Rise 1st	8:27	8:02	7:12	6:06	6:05	5:25	5:24	5:58	6:44	7:29	7:18	8:05
	Set 1st	4:38	5:23	6:11	7:00	8:47	9:29	9:41	9:11	8:12	7:07	5:06	4:30
	Twl	±2:04	±1:57	±1:52	±2:00	±2:29	NONE	NONE	±2:46	±2:07	±1:54	±1:55	±2:02
Note: Some locations in Canada do not experience an end of twilight during the summer	Rise 15th	8:21	7:39	6:42	6:36	5:43	5:19	5:37	6:18	7:04	7:50	7:41	8:20
	Set 15th	4:56	5:47	6:34	8:22	9:08	9:39	9:32	8:47	7:42	6:38	4:45	4:27
	Twl	±2:00	±1:54	±1:53	±2:10	±2:57	NONE	NONE	±2:22	±1:59	±1:52	±1:58	±2:04

Mexico

		JAN	FEB	MAR	APR	MAY	JUN	JUL	AUG	SEP	OCT	NOV	DEC
Chihuahua *28°40' N 106°03' W*	Rise 1st	7:57	7:52	7:29	6:54	7:23	7:07	7:10	7:26	7:42	7:57	7:16	7:40
	Set 1st	6:19	6:44	7:04	7:22	8:40	8:58	9:06	8:55	8:26	7:50	6:19	6:07
	Twl	±1:27	±1:24	±1:23	±1:24	±1:29	±1:37	±1:39	±1:33	±1:25	±1:22	±1:24	±1:28
	Rise 15th	7:58	7:43	7:14	7:39	7:13	7:06	7:16	7:33	7:49	8:05	7:27	7:49
	Set 15th	6:29	6:54	7:13	8:30	8:48	9:04	9:04	8:44	8:09	7:34	6:10	6:09
	Twl	±1:27	±1:23	±1:22	±1:26	±1:34	±1:39	±1:37	±1:28	±1:23	±1:23	±1:26	±1:29
Hermosillo *29°10' N 111°00' W*	Rise 1st	7:18	7:13	6:49	6:14	6:42	6:25	6:28	6:45	7:02	7:17	6:37	7:01
	Set 1st	5:37	6:03	6:24	6:42	8:00	8:19	8:27	8:16	7:46	7:10	5:38	5:26
	Twl	±1:28	±1:25	±1:23	±1:24	±1:30	±1:38	±1:40	±1:33	±1:25	±1:22	±1:24	±1:28
	Rise 15th	7:19	7:03	6:34	6:58	6:32	6:24	6:35	6:53	7:09	7:25	6:48	7:10
	Set 15th	5:48	6:14	6:32	7:50	8:09	8:25	8:25	8:04	7:29	6:54	5:29	5:28
	Twl	±1:27	±1:24	±1:23	±1:27	±1:34	±1:40	±1:37	±1:29	±1:24	±1:23	±1:27	±1:29
Monterrey *25°40' N 100°30' W*	Rise 1st	7:29	7:26	7:05	6:33	7:05	6:51	6:54	7:09	7:22	7:34	6:50	7:11
	Set 1st	6:03	6:26	6:44	6:59	8:13	8:29	8:37	8:28	8:01	7:29	6:01	5:51
	Twl	±1:25	±1:22	±1:20	±1:21	±1:27	±1:34	±1:34	±1:29	±1:23	±1:20	±1:21	±1:25

➙ **Sunrises & Sunsets have been adjusted for Daylight-Savings Time**

SunRISE/SET

Sunrises & Sunsets

Mexico

		JAN	FEB	MAR	APR	MAY	JUN	JUL	AUG	SEP	OCT	NOV	DEC
Monterrey	Rise 15th	7:30	7:17	6:51	7:19	6:57	6:51	7:00	7:15	7:28	7:41	7:00	7:21
	Set 15th	6:13	6:36	6:51	8:05	8:20	8:35	8:36	8:17	7:46	7:15	5:53	5:54
	Twl	±1:24	±1:20	±1:19	±1:24	±1:30	±1:34	±1:31	±1:26	±1:21	±1:20	±1:24	±1:25
Tamaulipas	Rise 1st	7:15	7:14	6:55	6:26	7:00	6:47	6:50	7:03	7:15	7:25	6:39	6:58
23°30' N	Set 1st	5:59	6:20	6:36	6:49	8:01	8:16	8:24	8:16	7:51	7:21	5:55	5:46
98°20' W	Twl	±1:24	±1:21	±1:19	±1:20	±1:25	±1:30	±1:31	±1:26	±1:21	±1:18	±1:20	±1:23
	Rise 15th	7:17	7:06	6:42	7:13	6:52	6:47	6:56	7:09	7:20	7:30	6:48	7:08
	Set 15th	6:08	6:29	6:43	7:55	8:08	8:21	8:23	8:06	7:37	7:07	5:48	5:50
	Twl	±1:23	±1:19	±1:19	±1:21	±1:27	±1:32	±1:30	±1:24	±1:19	±1:20	±1:22	±1:24

→ **Sunrises & Sunsets have been adjusted for Daylight-Savings Time**

Facing page. Mercury seen through the branches of a desert ocotillo plant just before the rising of the Sun.

Astronomical Glossary

Absolute Magnitude. The magnitude of a star if it were placed at a distance of 10 parsecs from Earth. The Sun's absolute magnitude is +4.8, and most stars range from −5 to +15. Absolute magnitude is used for comparing the actual brightness of stars.

Absolute Zero. The coldest possible temperature, at which all molecular motion stops. Absolute zero is 0K, −273° C or −459° F.

Albedo. The amount of sunlight reflected from a Planet, moon or asteroid. Albedo is normally expressed as a decimal between 0 and 1 (or the equivalent percentage). A mirror would have an albedo of 1 (reflects 100% of sunlight); Venus has a high albedo of 0.65 (65%); the Earth, 0.37 (37%) and the Moon, 0.11 (11%).

Altazimuth Telescope Mount. A mount that moves in altitude and azimuth, allowing a telescope to move "up" and "down" vertically (altitude) and rotate horizontally to any compass point (azimuth). Everyone is familiar with this mount because it is the type used with binoculars at tourist attractions. This mount has become increasing popular because of its simplicity and low cost. Most professional telescopes today use computer controlled altazimuth mounts.

Altitude. For an altazimuth telescope mount, altitude refers to the movement of the telescope "up" and "down" vertically from the horizon to directly overhead. Altitude also refers to a measurement system, where the height of an object above the horizon is expressed in arc degrees. This measurement system ranges from 0° at the horizon to 90° at the zenith (of the observer).

Angstrom (Å). A unit of measurement that once was widely used to express the wavelength of light. The angstrom is being replaced by the nanometer (abbreviated nm). An angstrom is 10^{-10} meters; a nanometer is 10^{-9} meters, so 10 Å = 1 nm.

Annular Eclipse. An eclipse of the Sun by the Moon in which the whole Moon moves in front of the Sun but does not completely cover the Sun. Because the Moon's orbit is an ellipse, its distance to the Earth varies. Annular eclipses occur when the Moon is a little farther away than normal, making its arc diameter a little smaller than the Sun's. During a total eclipse of the Sun, the Moon's arc diameter is slightly larger than the Sun's.

Aphelion. The point in a Planet's, asteroid's or comet's orbit where it is farthest from the Sun. Since all celestial objects have elliptical orbits, they have a closest and farthest point from the object they orbit.

Facing page. Liftoff of the Voyager 2 space probe atop a Titan/Centaur rocket on August 20, 1977. Voyager 2 encountered all the outer planets except Pluto. The future of astronomy lies with exploratory spacecraft like this and other instrumentation that can be placed above Earth's atmosphere.

Astronomical Glossary

Apochromatic. Optical term that refers to the highest quality telescope optics which are free of spherical, chromatic and other optical aberrations. The term is usually associated with refractor telescopes.

Apogee. The point in the orbit of the Moon or an artificial satellite where it is farthest from the Earth. Since all celestial objects have elliptical orbits, they have a closest and farthest point from the object they orbit.

Arc Degree (°). Unit of angular measurement used in astronomy. One arc degree is the same as one compass point degree. There are 360 arc degrees in a circle; each arc degree is divided into 60 arc minutes; and each arc minute is divided into 60 arc seconds. Arc seconds are further divided into tenths. The word "arc" is usually omitted when using this measurement system, but this omission can cause confusion when minutes (time) are used in the same dialog with arc minutes. The Sun and Moon are both about 1/2 of an arc degree (30 arc minutes) in angular diameter. Notation example: 6° 26' 3.2"

Arc Minute ('). 1/60 of an arc degree. The Moon is about 30 arc minutes in diameter.

Arc Second ("). 1/3600 of an arc degree or 1/60 of an arc minute.

Ascending Node. The point at which the orbit of a Solar System member, like one of the Planets, crosses the celestial equator or ecliptic from south to north (in declination). See also Descending Node.

Asterism. A recognizable or distinguished group of stars. Often a subgroup of a constellation. The Big Dipper is an asterism of the constellation Ursa Major.

Asteroid. A large, irregularly shaped "rock" that circles the Sun. Most asteroids orbit in a belt between Mars and Jupiter. The largest asteroid, Ceres, is 568 miles (914 km) in diameter and takes approximately 4.6 years to circle the Sun. Asteroids are also referred to as minor planets.

Asteroid Belt. Most asteroids orbit the Sun in a belt between Mars and Jupiter. These asteroids represent remnants left over from the formation of the Solar System.

Astrology. Astrology is not astronomy! Astronomy is a science; astrology is not. Astrology is a system of predictions based on Planetary and lunar positions. Although astronomy and astrology share some terminology and concepts, astrology's foundation is not based on the scientific gathering and analysis of information; hence it is an arbitrary system. Until modern times, astronomy and astrology were linked together. In the early 1600s, Johannes Kepler, who discovered the laws that govern the orbits of the Planets, used astrology to help earn a living. Kings, queens and nobles hired astrologers to predict their futures (obviously, making positive or favorable predictions helped an astrologer

Astronomical Glossary

to stay in business). Astrological predictions offer a feeling of control and power in a chaotic world.

Astronomical Unit (AU). Unit of distance in astronomy. One astronomical unit is 92,955,800 miles (1.48 billion km), the average distance from the Earth to the Sun.

Aurora (plural: Aurorae). A beautiful display of illumination in the night sky caused by charged particles from the Sun spilling into the atmosphere. These displays are concentrated around the polar regions of the Earth. In the northern hemisphere, the aurorae are called Aurora Borealis (Northern Lights) and in the southern hemisphere, Aurora Australis. Their red and green colors can shimmer, move and pulsate in large diffuse patches, ribbons or folded curtains. Their shape and intensity can change in minutes.

Autumnal Equinox. Occurs on or near September 23. At this time, the Sun is crossing the celestial equator from north to south. This occasion is one of two during the year (the other is at the vernal equinox) when day and night are equal in length.

Averted Vision. An observing technique which helps one see faint objects. Instead of looking directly at a faint object, you look slightly away from it, using peripheral vision for viewing. In the dark, our peripheral vision is more sensitive to faint light than direct vision.

Azimuth. For an altazimuth telescope mount, azimuth refers to the rotation of the telescope in a circle, around the horizon to any compass point. Azimuth is also part of a measurement system. Azimuth starts with 0° at true North and arcs eastwardly, through 360° of the compass.

Barlow Lens. A barlow lens increases the magnification of eyepieces, usually by a preset factor of 2 or 3. Barlows are popular because one barlow effectively doubles the range of magnification possible from a set of eyepieces. Barlow lenses fit into a telescope's eyepiece holder. Eyepieces are then inserted into the barrel of the barlow.

Barred Spiral Galaxy. Similar to a spiral galaxy except that the center bulge has a straight arm, or "bar" passing through it. The curved arms then radiate off the ends of the bar. Our Milky Way galaxy is a moderately barred spiral galaxy.

Bayer Letters. The formal name of the lowercase Greek letters assigned to the brightest stars in each of the constellations.

Big Bang. The predominant theory detailing the creation of the Universe. This theory states that all the matter in the Universe was once compressed together and then rapidly expanded or exploded to form the galaxies that exist today.

Binary Star. A pair of stars where one revolves around the other

Astronomical Glossary

(actually, each star revolves around a mutual center of gravity). Binary stars have revolutions that can last just days or thousands of years.

Black Hole. An astronomical body with a density so great that the resulting gravity will not even let light escape from its surface. Black holes cannot be directly observed, but there are telltale signs that indicate their presence. A black hole can be created from a star with as little as three times the mass of our Sun. As massive stars age and burn out, their remaining matter collapses upon themselves, creating black holes, the densest objects in the Universe. Some galaxies have giant black holes at their centers. A rudimentary idea of a black hole was formed in the late 1700s.

Brown Dwarf. A "star" that never ignited because it did not have sufficient mass to produce nuclear fusion. It is essentially a ball of hydrogen gas. Brown dwarfs are difficult to locate because they do not give off visible light.

Catadioptric Telescope. Any telescope that uses a combination of lenses and mirrors to focus light.

CCD (Charged-Coupled Device). A term often used for the digital imaging technology used in astronomy. This is the same technology as digital cameras.

Celestial Equator. A great circle that is the projection of the Earth's equator onto the sky. The celestial equator has declination 0° (corresponding to a latitude of 0°).

Celestial Horizon. The meeting of the sky and the horizon. At sea, the celestial horizon is unobstructed and perfectly round.

Celestial Meridian. A celestial meridian is a great circle that divides the sky into eastern and western halves. This circle passes through the observer's zenith and the North and South Celestial Poles. On Earth, a meridian is a longitude line.

Celestial Sphere. At one time, it was thought the Sun, Moon, Planets, comets and stars resided on the inside of a giant sphere called the Celestial Sphere. Today, it is a convenient term to indicate the visible Universe.

Chromatic Aberration. Optical term referring to the inability of a refracting lens to focus all colors of light at the same point. This aberration is particularly noticeable in lower-quality binoculars/refractor telescopes and eyepieces as orange and blue halos around viewed objects.

Coma (Comet). The large, cloudy veil that forms around the nucleus of a comet when it gets close to the Sun. The coma is the brightest part of a comet.

Astronomical Glossary

Coma (Telescope). An optical aberration that occurs in short focal length reflectors, causing stars toward the edge of an eyepiece's field of view to appear elongated instead of as points of light.

Comet. Sometimes referred to as "dirty snowballs," because they are composed mostly of dust and ices. As comets approach the Sun, the ices vaporize, creating the bright, reflective, gaseous coma and tail. Most comets have highly elliptical orbits and take hundreds to thousands of years to revolve around the Sun.

Conjunction. The alignment of two or more Solar System members as viewed from Earth. Conjunction usually applies to the Sun, Moon and Planets.

When two or more Planets, the Moon and a Planet (or Planets) or the Sun and a Planet (or Planets) appear very close to one another in the sky, they are said to be in conjunction.

The inferior Planets, Mercury and Venus, are at Inferior Conjunction when they are directly between the Earth and the Sun. They are at Superior Conjunction when they are on the opposite side of the Sun from the Earth. In both cases, these Planets will rise and set with the Sun.

A superior Planet, Mars through Pluto, is in conjunction when it is on the opposite side of the Sun from the Earth (Sun and Planet rise and set at the same time).

Constellation. A group of visible stars that has been assigned a name. The stars in a constellation usually form a pattern that aides in their recognition. The visible stars were first categorized into constellations thousands of years ago and are associated with lore. Today the constellations are not just named groups of stars, but also include the area of sky around the stars. Each constellation has a boundary just like each state in the United States. Probably the most easily recognizable constellation is Orion because of its bright stars and striking pattern. There are a total of 88 constellations. They are listed on pages 33–37.

Corona. The "atmosphere" of the Sun above the photosphere (visible surface). It extends outward from the Sun for several million miles and is visible during a total solar eclipse as the irregular white halo surrounding the Moon.

Cosmology. The study of the Universe as a whole, on its grand scale.

Cosmogony. The study of the origin and evolution of the Universe.

Crater. A concave depression on a planet, moon or asteroid created from the impact of a comet, asteroid or meteoroid.

Crater Rays. Bright streaks that radiate from some craters on the Moon. They are the result of the ejection of reflective material from craters during their formation (from cometary or meteoroid impacts).

Astronomical Glossary

Crescent. A phase of the Moon between New Moon and either First or Last Quarter.

Dawn. The time in the morning around sunrise.

Daylight-Savings Time. The advancing of clocks from Standard Time by one hour. Most of the world changes to Daylight-Savings Time. In the US, the clocks are advanced from the first Sunday in April through the last Saturday in October. The practice of advancing the clocks occurs for social, rather than scientific reasons.

Declination (also Dec or δ). Latitude-type coordinate used to indicate the position of an object in the sky. Declination is equivalent to and is expressed in the same manner as latitude. 0° declination is at the celestial equator (0° latitude is at the equator). The north celestial pole has declination +90°, the south celestial pole, −90°. Declination is used in conjunction with Right Ascension to determine coordinates of celestial objects.

Deep Sky Objects. Refers to galaxies, nebulae, globular clusters and open clusters. Although the term connotes objects that are distant and faint, some deep sky objects are bright and span a large area of the sky. The Andromeda galaxy, for example, spans more than six Moon diameters and can be seen with the naked eye. The stars, Planets and other members of our Solar System are not considered deep sky objects.

Descending Node. The point at which the orbit of a Solar System member, like one of the Planets or a comet, crosses the celestial equator or ecliptic from north to south (in declination). See also Ascending Node.

Dobsonian Telescope. Named after John Dobson, who in the 1970s popularized astronomy through larger, simpler and cheaper Newtonian telescopes. The key to this concept was the use of simple but effective altazimuth mounts.

Double Star. Double stars can be optical or binary. Optical doubles are two stars that appear visually very close to each other because they just happen to be in the same line of sight. On the other hand, binary doubles, also called binary stars, are a pair of stars that revolve around each other.

Dusk. The time around sunset.

Dwarf Star. Our Sun is a typical dwarf star. The term "dwarf" refers to luminosity rather than to size. More than 90% of stars are classified as "dwarfs," but they represent the average stars.

Earthshine. Sunlight reflected off the Earth which slightly illuminates the dark side of the Moon facing Earth (that is, the side that is not being directly lit by sunlight). Earthshine is especially noticeable when the Moon is a crescent. During this time, the highlands and maria can be glimpsed on the dark side through a telescope.

Astronomical Glossary

Eccentricity. A number between 0 and 1 used to indicate the elongation of an ellipse. An eccentricity of 0 indicates a circle; and ellipses with eccentricities close to 1 would look similar in shape to a submarine.

Ecliptic. The apparent path that the Sun describes in the sky over the course of a year. The ecliptic is a great circle (cuts the sky into two halves) and crosses 12 constellations — the constellations of the zodiac. The Sun appears to revolve around the Earth once a day, but this movement does not "create" the ecliptic. The ecliptic is described from the Earth revolving around the Sun. Since the background stars remain stationary, it appears from the Earth as if the Sun slowly moves in a circle against the background stars over the course of a year.

Ellipse. An oval or elongated circle. All celestial orbits (of planets, moons, comets, binary stars) are ellipses and not circles. An elliptical orbit may be very close to a circle, as is the case of Venus' orbit, or highly elongated as with comets.

Elongation. The arc angle distance between the Sun and a Solar System member (Planet, Moon, comet or asteroid) as viewed from Earth.

Emission Nebula. A nebula that produces its own light from the stimulation of its gas by ultraviolet radiation from a nearby star or stars.

Equatorial Mount. A type of mount that facilitates observing and photographing celestial objects because an observer has to make only one movement to keep an object centered in the eyepiece. Equatorial mounts have two perpendicular axes. The polar axis points to the north celestial pole; the other axis is positioned 90° to the polar axis. Until the mid-1970s, the majority of telescopes at professional observatories were equatorial mounts. Today, most professional telescopes have computer-controlled altazimuth mounts because they cost less than equatorial mounts. Equatorial mounts are also called German equatorial mounts because the idea originated in Germany.

Equinox. See Vernal Equinox or Autumnal Equinox.

f/number. See Focal Ratio.

Field of View. The expanse of sky that can be seen through binoculars or a telescope. Expressed in degrees (arc degrees), field of view can be true or apparent. True field of view is the actual amount of sky that can be seen through a telescope or binoculars. For example, if you look through a telescope and you see the whole Full Moon, nothing more and nothing less, then the true field of view for that eyepiece is 1/2° or 30 arc minutes (30'). Apparent field of view is a design attribute of an eyepiece. The greater an eyepiece's apparent field of view (usually ranges from 50° to 83°), the larger is the true field of view. A difference

Astronomical Glossary

in apparent field of view is like the difference between looking out a large and small window.

First Quarter. Phase of the Moon, halfway between New and Full, when the Moon is "half" lighted on the right or eastern side.

Fission. The splitting apart of atoms which was the process employed in early nuclear weapons. This is not the mechanism that fuels stars.

Flamsteed Numbers. Numbers assigned to the stars, by constellation, to aid in identification. Flamsteed numbers are an expansion of the system that identifies the brightest stars with Greek letters.

Focal Length. The distance from the primary mirror or objective lens to the point where light comes to a focus. Usually expressed in millimeters.

Focal Ratio (f/ratio). The ratio of the focal length of a telescope to the diameter of the primary mirror or objective lens. A focal ratio is calculated by dividing the diameter of the primary or objective into the focal length of the telescope (the units of measurement must be the same for the focal length and primary/objective diameter).

Full Moon. Phase of the Moon when the lighted side presents a full, circular disk in the sky. The Full Moon rises as the Sun sets.

Fusion. The process that fuels the stars and our Sun. Fusion occurs when four hydrogen atoms fuse to form one helium atom. The resulting helium atom is 1% less in mass than the four hydrogen atoms. The energy from the Sun comes from this 1% difference in mass. Fusion is triggered by the tremendous pressure from the sheer mass of stars.

Galactic Cluster. Relatively young open clusters found in the spiral arms of our galaxy. The spiral arms have the highest concentrations of hydrogen gas, where stars are born.

Galaxy. A basic grouping in the Universe. Galaxies represent a collection of billions to hundreds of billions of stars that are gravitationally bound. They are generally circular, like a disk or spherical in shape. All galaxies are outside of our Milky Way galaxy.

Giant Star. This term refers more to a star's relative luminosity than its actual size. A giant star is in a later stage in the evolution of average dwarf stars, like the Sun, where the star is brighter than normal.

Gibbous. The phase of the Moon between First and Last Quarter, (through Full Moon). During this time, the Moon is considered to be respectively a waxing and waning gibbous Moon.

Globular Cluster. This deep sky object is a tight group of up to a million stars resembling a ball (like a cotton ball). Globular clusters are not galaxies, but are parts of galaxies. The globular cluster M13 in Hercules is just visible to the naked eye at a dark location.

GMT. See Universal Time.

Astronomical Glossary

Great Circle. Any circle in the sky that divides the sky in half (creating two equal hemispheres). Examples are the celestial equator and the ecliptic.

Green Flash. A flash of green light that sometimes appears at the moment the Sun dips below the horizon. Green flashes are more often seen at sea.

Greenwich Mean Time. See Universal Time.

Harvest Moon. The Full Moon closest to the autumnal equinox, around September 23.

Hertzsprung-Russell Diagram. A famous diagram in astronomy that shows the relationship between the luminosity and surface temperature of stars.

Hubble Space Telescope (HST). Launched into orbit 375 miles (600 km) above Earth in 1990, this 94-inch (2.4 meters) diameter telescope has revolutionized astronomy by providing the most detailed images of the Universe.

Huygens Eyepiece. The first true eyepiece, invented by Christian Huygens in the 1700s, uses two lens elements.

IC (Index Catalogue of Nebulae and Star Clusters). A listing of more than 5,000 deep sky objects compiled by J. L. E. Dreyer in 1908 and still in use. The majority of IC objects are faint galaxies. Also see NGC.

Inferior Conjunction. See Conjunction.

Inferior Planets. Mercury and Venus — the two Planets that orbit closer to the Sun than Earth.

Inner Planets. The four Planets — Mercury, Venus, Earth and Mars — that orbit inside the asteroid belt.

Ion. An atom or molecule that has gained a positive or negative charge by acquiring or losing outer electrons.

Jupiter. The 5th Planet from the Sun. Jupiter is famous for its Great Red Spot, cloud bands and four bright moons. Comet Shoemaker-Levy 9 collided with Jupiter in July 1994. Astronomers believe that Jupiter may act like a gravitational magnet and has probably incurred the largest proportion of comet and meteoroid impacts in our Solar System, thus giving Earth a chance to harbor life.

Kellner Eyepiece. A "medium line" eyepiece with three or more lens elements. Kellner eyepieces are superior to Ramsden eyepieces but do not perform as well as Orthoscopic or Plössl eyepieces.

Kelvin (K). A temperature system based on absolute zero (the lowest temperature possible) and the Celsius scale. 0K is absolute zero; 273K is 0° C and 373K is 100° C. Note that the little circle used to denote degrees is not used with the K.

Astronomical Glossary

Last Quarter. Phase of the Moon, between Full and New, when the Moon is half lighted on the left or western side. Also referred to as Third Quarter.

Libration. A slight up-and-down and side-to-side movement of the Moon that enables observers on Earth to see more than just half of its surface — in fact, close to 59%. The Moon's elliptical orbit combined with its small axial tilt allow for glimpses around its edges.

Light-Year (l.y.). Unit of distance in astronomy. One light year is the distance light travels in one year. Since light travels at the rate of 186,282 miles per second, it will travel 5,880,000,000,000 miles (almost 6 trillion miles) in one year. It takes light 1.3 seconds to travel the distance from the Earth to the Moon and 8.3 minutes to travel from the Sun to the Earth. Our Solar System is about 11 light hours in diameter and our galaxy is about 100,000 light years in diameter.

Local Group. A group of about 30 galaxies that includes our galaxy and the Andromeda galaxy. Galaxies are clumped together in groups throughout the Universe.

Lunar Eclipse. The blockage of the sunlight illuminating the Moon by Earth's shadow. Lunar eclipses can occur only at Full Moon and do not occur every month because the Moon's orbit is inclined to Earth's orbit. This usually places the Moon above or below Earth's shadow.

Maksutov Reflector. A catadioptric telescope that has a deeply concave front correcting lens. Maksutov reflectors can provide better image quality over a larger field of view than Newtonian and Schmidt-Cassegrain reflectors.

Mare (plural: Maria). Original name given by Galileo to the smooth, dark plains on the Moon because they resemble bodies of water. Mare is the Latin word for sea. The maria were created by lava flow.

Mars. The 4th Planet from the Sun. Mars appears reddish but is actually pale brown. Mars became well known for its "canals," the result of erroneous observations made in the early 1900s. The canals do not exist. Mars is the most hospitable Planet in our Solar System (after Earth) and its north polar cap contains huge amounts of frozen water. Mars may have harbored primitive life in the past, and will hopefully be visited by humans before 2050.

Mercury. The closest Planet to the Sun. Mercury resembles the Moon because it is pitted with craters and has no atmosphere.

Meridian. See Celestial Meridian.

Messier Objects. A collection of 110 deep sky objects recorded and described around 1750 by Charles Messier of France. These objects include the brightest galaxies, nebulae, globular clusters and open clusters. Messier was a comet hunter, and cataloged these objects so other comet hunters would not mistake them for comets. Astronomers and scientists of the 1700s did not know what galaxies and nebulae were, but they knew these blurry objects did not move around the sky as did comets.

Meteor. The light trail in the sky created when a meteoroid enters Earth's atmosphere. Often called a shooting star.

Meteorite. A rock from space that has fallen to the ground.

Meteoroid. The term used to describe a space rock before it enters the Earth's atmosphere and becomes a white streak known as a meteor. Most meteoroids are about the size of a grain of sand and burn up completely in the Earth's atmosphere.

Meteor Shower. Meteors that appear to originate from a particular spot in the sky. Twelve major meteor showers occur every year. These showers are the result of the Earth passing through semi-permanent swarms of cometary debris that orbit the Sun.

Micrometeorite. A meteoroid as small as or smaller than a grain of sand.

Milky Way. A hazy, cloudy (milky) band that circles the night sky. This band is a permanent part of the sky and has an average width of five arc degrees (10 Moon diameters). The Milky Way is impossible to see in larger cities because of light and air pollution; however, it is very prominent in country skies. It appears milky because it is composed of countless stars — the bulk of the stars in our galaxy. With a telescope or binoculars, one can see that there are many more stars in the region of the Milky Way than in other areas of the sky. The Milky Way is also the name of our galaxy.

Minor Planet. The preferred term for an asteroid by astronomers.

Multiple Star. Three or more stars that are gravitationally bound and revolve around one another.

Nadir. The point directly below an observer. We each have our own nadir.

Nebula (plural: Nebulae). Gaseous cloud, comprised mostly of hydrogen, that resides in galaxies. Most nebulae are irregular in shape; however, some are spherical shells of hydrogen left by the collapse of a giant star. In spiral galaxies, the highest concentration of hydrogen gas is in the arms, where most new stars are born.

Neptune. The 8th Planet is a gas giant and was discovered in 1871. It is slightly smaller than Uranus and has a very faint ring system.

Neutron Star. An extremely dense star created from the supernova explosion of a massive star. The compression from the explosion merges electrons and protons into neutrons. The mass of a neutron star

Astronomical Glossary

ranges from 1.4 to 3 times that of our Sun, but it only has a diameter of about 12 miles (19 km). Since neutron stars give off very little light, they are often studied as pulsars with radio telescopes. Pulsar is a descriptive term for a neutron star that is highly magnetized and spins rapidly, anywhere from 4 to 200 times a second.

NGC (New General Catalogue of Nebulae and Star Clusters). A listing of nearly 8,000 deep sky objects compiled by J. L. E. Dreyer in 1888 and still used today. The majority of NGC objects are galaxies and open clusters. Overall, they are not as faint as Dreyer's list of 5,000 IC objects (Index Catalogue of Nebulae and Star Clusters). See IC.

New Moon. The Moon is considered New when it is between the Earth and Sun. It cannot be seen at this time because it is near the Sun.

Newtonian Telescope. The simplest and most widely used reflector telescope. First built by Isaac Newton in 1668, this telescope uses a parabolic mirror to focus light.

Northern Lights. See Aurora.

Nova. A nova explosion is cyclical, caused by the repeated infusion of hydrogen gas from a giant star to a white dwarf (binary pair).

Occultation. The eclipsing of one celestial body by another. The Moon frequently occults stars and the Planets. Less frequent are occulations of a star by the Planets or an asteroid.

Open Cluster. A group of up to several thousands stars that were born together and reside in close proximity to one another. Several open clusters are visible to the naked eye. The Pleiades in Taurus is the best known; however, most open clusters can be seen only with binoculars or a telescope.

Opposition. The alignment of one or more superior Planets (Mars through Pluto) with the Earth and Sun. These Planets are in opposition when they are directly "behind" the Earth, away from the Sun. The superior Planets are closest to the Earth at opposition and they rise in the east as the Sun is setting in the west.

Orthoscopic Eyepiece. A four-element lens eyepiece that was very popular during the 60s and 70s. The Plössl lens design has superseded the orthoscopic eyepiece in popularity because it has a wider field of view.

Outer Planets. Jupiter, Saturn, Uranus, Neptune and Pluto: the Planets that orbit outside the asteroid belt.

Parabolic. The adjective of the noun parabola, which is a mathematical shape that describes a curve found frequently in nature. This shape has the unique property of allowing incoming light to focus at the same point — something that a simple circle shape cannot do. The primary mirrors of Newtonian reflectors are parabolic.

Astronomical Glossary

Parsec. Unit of distance in astronomy. One parsec is about 3.2 light years. The parsec is derived by using the astronomical unit and trigonometry. It is the distance that one astronomical unit would have to be from the Earth in order for it to appear 1 arc second in length (1/3600 of 1 compass degree). The Moon is about 1,800 arc seconds.

Penumbra (Eclipse). The shadow adjacent to the dark umbra shadow. If you are in the penumbra shadow during a solar eclipse, you will see the Sun partially blocked by the Moon.

Penumbra (Sunspot). The lighter part of a sunspot that immediately surrounds the dark inner umbra.

Perigee. The closest point that the Moon or an artificial satellite comes to the Earth. Since all orbiting bodies have elliptical orbits, they have a closest and farthest point from the object they orbit.

Perihelion. The point in a Planet's, asteroid's or comet's orbit where it is closest to the Sun. Since all Solar System members have elliptical orbits, they have a closest and farthest point from the Sun.

*David H. Levy's Guide to the Stars **planisphere** is one of the best available. It was written for beginners in mind and has loads of information on the back. It consists of two pieces of plastic, riveted together, that are rotated for the observing time and date (hours and dates are along the circumference). Available in two sizes, an easy-to-read 16-inch diameter and smaller 11-inch diameter.*

Photosphere. The visible surface of the Sun. The photosphere is 125 miles deep (200 km), reaches a temperature of 10,000° F (5,500° C) and is comprised of granules, or cells, about 650 miles (1,050 km) in diameter. Sunspots are on the photosphere.

Planetary Nebula. A huge spherical shell, a ring or opposed lobes of hydrogen gas left by the collapse of a red giant or supergiant star. The gas is stimulated to emit its own light by ultraviolet radiation from the collapsed star. Planetary nebulae can measure a light year or more in diameter (or greatest length) and can be seen with small telescopes.

Planisphere. A circular star chart that is used to find the constellations. The word planisphere refers to a sphere of stars plotted on a flat plane. Planispheres are handy charts for beginners and amateurs because unlike star charts in books, they can be adjusted to show the stars visible for a specific hour and day of the year.

Astronomical Glossary

Plössl Eyepiece. The most popular optical design for eyepieces. It utilizes four lens elements and provides a large apparent field of view (50° or greater).

Pluto. The 9th Planet in our Solar System. Discovered in 1930 by Clyde Tombaugh in Flagstaff, Arizona, after an extensive photographic search of the sky. Pluto's orbit is greatly inclined compared to the other Planets. Its moon, Charon, is more than half Pluto's diameter.

Population I and II Stars. Population I stars, which include our Sun, are relatively young stars and contain a higher abundance of metals than the older Population II stars. Population I stars are often found in the arms of spiral galaxies. Globular clusters are composed mainly of the older Population II stars.

Precession. The Earth spins on its axis like a top. At the same time, the Earth's axis is slowly wobbling around a "giant" circle, similar to a top wobbling as it slows down. This wobble is known as precession and is caused by the gravitational pull from the Moon and Sun. The precession wobble describes a 47° arc diameter circle in the sky and it takes approximately 25,800 years for the Earth's axis to move and complete this circle. Today, the Earth's axis points toward Polaris, the North Star. In about 12,000 years, the axis will be pointing to the star Vega, in the constellation Lyra. Some ancient civilizations, including the Egyptians, knew about precession.

Prominence. Protrusion of ionized gas from the surface of the Sun. Large prominences can easily extend 10 to 30 Earth diameters from the photosphere and can loop back to the surface, creating beautiful arches.

Proper Motion. The apparent motion of the stars in the sky in relationship to the Sun. This motion is not the daily motion of the stars around the Earth, but represents the movement of stars with respect to one another. Generally, the stars that are closest to our Sun have the largest proper motions. Proper motion is measured in thousands of years.

Pulsar. See Neutron Star.

Pyrex. Annealed pyrex is the preferred glass for reflector telescope mirrors. Pyrex is significantly more stable with temperature variations than plate glass.

Quadrature. A separation in the sky of 90° between Solar System members. A superior Planet (Mars through Pluto) would be at quadrature with the Sun if the Planet were at the zenith as the Sun was rising or setting.

Quasar. Extremely bright galaxy that outputs enormous amounts of energy over the entire electromagnetic spectrum. Quasars are the farthest and among the oldest objects in the Universe. The energy from quasar galaxies is produced from the interaction of enoromous amounts of matter being pulled into giant black holes at the galaxies' centers.

Radio Telescope. An instrument used to study celestial objects by mapping their radio waves instead of light rays. Radio astronomy uses very large dish antennae.

Ramsden Eyepiece. An inexpensive eyepiece that uses two lens elements. Ramsden eyepieces often are included with inexpensive telescopes. They are not generally used today.

Redshift. A lengthening or stretching of the wavelength of light in the spectrum of a celestial body that is moving away from Earth. The redshift can be used to determine the speed of receding objects.

Reflecting Telescope. Any telescope that uses a concave mirror as the primary means for focusing light.

Refractor Telescope. Any telescope that uses a glass objective lens as the primary means for focusing light. Camera lenses and Galileo's telescope are refracting instruments. Refracting telescopes are more expensive per aperture inch than other telescopes. For the price of a quality 4-inch refractor, you could purchase a 16 to 18-inch Dobsonian reflector.

Retrograde. An apparent backward movement in the sky (as viewed from Earth) of the superior Planets (Mars through Pluto). As the superior Planets move in their orbits around the Sun, they appear to move slowly eastward against the background of stars. However, for several months each year, these Planets reverse their course and move westward, then resume their eastward course. This apparent backward/westward movement is called retrograde motion. This effect is created by a faster orbiting Earth "passing" the slower orbiting superior Planets.

Richest-Field Telescope (RFT). A telescope with a low focal ratio, generally ranging from f/4 to f/6. You can see more sky in the eyepiece of a RFT than with higher focal ratio telescopes.

Right Ascension (also RA or α). West-to-east coordinate used in conjunction with Declination to determine the position of an object in the sky. Right Ascension is equivalent to longitude but is expressed differently. It is derived by dividing the celestial sphere into 24 hours. Each hour is further divided into 60 minutes and each minute into 60 seconds. Zero hours (0h) starts at the vernal equinox. Examples of R.A. are 12h 23.7m and 1h 14m 23s.

Rille. Fairly straight, long "lines" on the Moon's maria produced from faults on these plains.

Saturn. The 6th Planet is magnificent in the sky with its beautiful ring system. Until the 1980s, it was thought these rings were unique to

Astronomical Glossary

Saturn. The other gas giants (Jupiter, Uranus and Neptune) also have ring systems, but none are as spectacular as Saturn's.

Schmidt-Cassegrain Telescope (SCT). This catadioptric telescope has two mirrors and a front correcting lens. Its folded optical path makes it one of the most compact telescopes. The 8-inch SCT is a very popular amateur telescope.

Seeing. An observing term indicating the atmospheric viewing condition of the night sky. Good, fair, poor, transparent and turbulent are adjectives often used with seeing.

Setting Circles. Circular, graduated scales sometimes attached to the right ascension and declination axes of equatorial mounts that aid in locating celestial objects by using their RA and Dec coordinates.

Sidereal. The true orbital or rotational period of a Planet, moon, asteroid or comet. This is the time it takes to complete one revolution or rotation. Earth's sidereal rotational period (23 hours, 56 minutes, 4 seconds) is obtained by measuring successive passages of a star in a fixed telescope. This is not used for clock time because if it were, in six month's time, noon would occur at midnight (4 minutes x 180 days = 12 hour change).

Solar Eclipse. Occurs when the Moon moves in front of the Sun, which can happen only at New Moon. There are three types of solar eclipses: total, partial and annular. A total eclipse occurs when the Sun is completely blocked by the Moon. An annular eclipse occurs when the Moon passes completely in front of the Sun, but does not totally cover the Sun. Partial eclipses occur when the Moon covers only a portion of the Sun.

Solar Flare. A spontaneous eruption on the surface of the Sun that releases enormous amounts of energy and energetic particles into the Solar System. These eruptions cause the aurorae as well as radio and communication disruptions.

Solar System. A system composed of a star and revolving planets, asteroids and comets. We normally use the term to refer to our Solar System; however, astronomers have found numerous nearby stars with their own orbiting planets.

Solar Wind. A wind in the Solar System caused by the release of charged photons and electrons from the Sun. The solar wind is partially responsible for pushing a comet's tail away from the Sun.

Solstice. The time of year when the Sun is at its highest or lowest point in the sky. Also see Summer Solstice and Winter Solstice.

Spectrum. The light from the Sun, Planets, stars, nebulae and galaxies can be directed through a prism (or diffraction grating) to obtain a spectrogram (photographic or digital image of a spectrum). Spectrograms look like long, horizontal bands marked with numerous dark parallel lines.

Astronomical Glossary

The arrangement of these lines is used to identify the chemical makeup as well as the velocity of celestial objects.

Spherical Aberration. The inability of an optical system to focus all light rays at the same point. For example, the light rays from the outer edge of an objective mirror or lens may focus short or long compared to the light rays that pass near the center of the objective.

Sporadic Meteor. A meteor not associated with a shower. Between three and seven sporadic meteors can be observed every hour.

Standard Time. Local time, the time on our clocks. The continental United States has four standard time zones.

Star Cluster. An open cluster, galactic cluster or a globular cluster.

Sublimate. To change directly from a solid to a gas or from a gas to a solid without becoming liquid. The volatiles in a comet sublimate to create the coma and tail.

Summer Solstice. The day on which the Sun reaches its highest point in the sky (at noon), approximately June 21. The day with the most amount of sunlight (in the northern hemisphere).

Sunspots. Dark spots on the surface of the Sun. Sunspots rotate with the Sun. They continuously form, grow, decrease in size, and dissolve away. Often larger than the Earth, sunspots are cooler than the surrounding brighter photosphere (about 6,300° F or 3,500° C compared to 10,000° F or 5,500° C) and have intense magnetic fields.

Supergiant Star. A star with a diameter of around a 1,000 times that of our Sun. Because of their size, supergiants are very luminous; but they have low densities. Betelgeuse in Orion is a supergiant star.

Superior Conjunction. See Conjunction.

Superior Planets. The Planets that orbit beyond Earth — Mars, Jupiter, Saturn, Neptune, Uranus and Pluto.

Supernova (plural: Supernovae). An explosion of a massive star, at the end of its life, of such intensity that the light emitted can outshine the star's galaxy. A supernova is about 1,000 times brighter than a nova, and can remain brilliant for several weeks. Supernovae occur infrequently and are observed more often in galaxies other than our own. Supernovae have absolute magnitudes around −19.

Synodic Period. A relative period of revolution as viewed from Earth. For example, the time a superior Planet takes to go from one opposition to the next, the time from one inferior conjunction with Venus to the next, or the time from one Full Moon to the next Full Moon. All of these examples represent revolution periods that are not a complete revolution around the Sun or Earth, but appear to be a complete revolution as viewed from Earth.

Astronomical Glossary

Syzergy. The alignment of three or more Solar System members. New Moon and Full Moon are examples of three bodies lining up — the Sun, Earth and Moon.

Terminator. The "border" on the Moon between the lighted side and the dark side. The terminator is visible to observers on Earth when the Moon is in a phase other than Full or New. Craters near the terminator appear sharp and contrasty because of their shadows.

Terrestrial Planets. Mercury, Venus, Earth and Mars. These four Planets share many characteristics.

Third Quarter. See Last Quarter.

Twilight. The transition time between day and night either before sunrise or after sunset. There are three officially defined twilights — civil, nautical and astronomical. Each is based on the Sun's arc angle distance below the horizon.

Umbra (Eclipse). An observer must be inside the Moon's umbra shadow to witness a total solar eclipse. The Moon must pass into Earth's umbra shadow for a total lunar eclipse to occur. The penumbra shadow immediately surrounds the umbra shadow.

Umbra (Sunspot). The inner and darkest part of a sunspot. The umbra is surrounded by the lighter penumbra.

Universal Time (UT). The occurrence of astronomical events is expressed in Universal Time in order to avoid confusion with time zones and Daylight-Savings Time. Universal Time was adopted by an international conference in 1884 and is the local time at the Old Royal Observatory in Greenwich, near London, England. Expressed using the 24-hour clock, Universal Time must be converted to Local Standard Time to adjust for time zone differences. The WWV radio station in Fort Collins, Colorado, as well as CHU in Ottawa, Ontario, Canada broadcast Universal Time 24 hours a day. These radio signal broadcasts are known as Coordinated Universal Time (UTC). Universal Time is sometimes referred to as Greenwich Mean Time (GMT).

Uranus. The 7th Planet from the Sun was discovered by William Herschel in 1781. This gas giant is the third largest Planet in our Solar System and has a faint ring system.

Variable Star. A star whose brightness changes over a period of time. Stars change in brightness for various reasons. Some stars, like Algol in Perseus, change in brightness because they are eclipsed by dimmer companion stars. Other stars called Cepheid variables vary in brightness because they periodically expand and contact up to 30% in size.

Venus. The 2nd Planet from the Sun is the brightest Planet in the sky, reaching magnitude −4.6. Venus once was referred to as Earth's sister

Astronomical Glossary

Planet because its diameter is about the same as Earth's. However, this connotation is not used anymore because Venus' environment is totally hostile to life. Completely covered with clouds of sulfuric acid, Venus has an atmospheric pressure 90 times greater than Earth's and a surface temperatures reaching 900° F (480° C).

Vernal Equinox. One of two points in the sky where the ecliptic (the apparent path of the Sun over the course of a year) crosses the celestial equator. The other is the autumnal equinox. The vernal equinox is located in the constellation Pisces and represents the beginning of spring, when the Sun crosses the celestial equator from south to north. The vernal equinox is also the starting point for all celestial coordinates (R.A. 0h, Declination 0°). The Sun is at the vernal equinox on approximately March 21. Day and night are equal in length on this day.

Vulcan. A nonexistent planet that some thought might orbit between the Sun and Mercury.

Waning. Shrinking, decreasing. The Moon wanes as it decreases in size from Full to New. Opposite of waxing.

Waxing. Increasing, growing. The Moon is waxing as it increases in size from a Crescent to Full. Opposite of waning.

White Dwarf. The final stage in the life of some lower mass stars before they becomes cold, dark objects. White dwarfs have high densities; they are about the size of the Earth with the mass of our Sun. Sirius, the brightest star in the sky, has a white dwarf binary companion.

Winter Solstice. The day on which the Sun reaches its lowest point in the sky (at noon), which occurs approximately December 22. For the northern hemisphere, this is the day with the least amount of sunlight.

Zenith. The highest point in the sky, directly overhead. Everyone has his or her own zenith (unless you are carrying someone on your shoulders, then you share a zenith).

Zodiac. Twelve constellations make up the zodiac. These constellations lie along a great circle in the sky called the ecliptic, the apparent path the Sun travels in the sky over the course of a year. The ecliptic is created from the Earth's yearly revolution around the Sun.

Historical Timeline

4240 BC   The Egyptians institute the first 365-day calendar. It includes twelve 30-day months and five festival days.

3000 BC   The Babylonians predict eclipses.

2296 BC   Chinese observers make the first known record of a comet sighting.

763 BC   Babylonians make the earliest known record of a solar eclipse.

500 BC   The Pythagoreans teach that Earth is a sphere and not a disk.

380 BC   Democritus, a Greek philosopher, recognizes that the Milky Way consists of numerous stars, that the Moon is similar to Earth, and that matter is composed of atoms.

352 BC   Chinese observers report a supernova, the earliest such record.

270 BC   Aristarchus of Samos (Greek island near Turkey) challenges Aristotle's teachings by asserting that the Sun is the center of the Solar System and that the Planets revolve around the Sun.

240 BC   Chinese astronomers make the first known record of a visit from Halley's Comet.

170 BC   The Greek Seleucus is the last known astronomer to champion the heliocentric theory of the Solar System until Copernicus.

165 BC   Chinese astronomers record sunspots.

140 AD   Ptolemy of Egypt (Claudius Ptolemaeus, 100–175 AD) writes *Megale Syntaxis tes Astronomias* (Great Astronomical Composition), which becomes the most important astronomy text of the Middle Ages. It so impresses the Arabs that they call it *Almagest* (The Greatest). The work describes a model of Planetary motion in which the Earth is the center of the Universe, and the Sun and Moon orbit in perfect circles.

635   The Chinese record that a comet's tail always points away from the Sun.

1054   The Chinese, Japanese and Arabs observe the supernova that forms the Crab nebula in the constellation Taurus, on July 4. It is visible for 22 months.

1250   Alfonso X of Castile (Spain) orders the compilation of tables, which become known as the *Alfonsine Tables,* listing the positions and movement of the Planets. Fifty astronomers work on this project.

Historical Timeline

1300   Eyeglasses become common.

1504   Christopher Columbus of Spain uses Regiomontanus' *Ephemerides Astronomicae* to predict a total lunar eclipse and frighten a group of Native Americans.

1543   Nicolas Copernicus (1473–1543) of Poland publishes *De Revolutionibus Orbium Coelestium* (On the Revolutions of Celestial Bodies). It offers a heliocentric model. Copernicus delays publishing the work almost until his death for fear of reprisals from the church.

1572   Tycho Brahe (1546–1601) of Denmark observes a supernova in the constellation Cassiopeia in 1572 and publishes *De Nova Stella* (On the New Star), giving an exact description of his observation. Tycho was a consummate observer who recorded the positions of the Planets and stars which Kepler later used to formulate the fundamental laws of orbits.

1599   Tycho Brahe moves to the court of Holy Roman Emperor Rudolph II in Prague.

1600   Johannes Kepler (1571–1630) of Germany begins assisting Tycho Brahe at his Prague observatory.

1604   Johannes Kepler observes a supernova in the constellation Ophiuchus — the last supernova observed in our galaxy.

1609   Galileo Galilei (1564–1642) of Italy builds one of the earliest refractor telescopes and observes four of Jupiter's moons, Saturn's rings, individual stars of the Milky Way and the phases of Venus. Kepler's book, *Astronomia Nova* (New Astronomy) contains his views that the Planets revolve around the Sun in elliptical orbits and that these orbits sweep out equal areas in equal time intervals.

1656   Christian Huygens (1629–1695), a Dutch scientist, discovers that Saturn's odd "handles" are actually rings. He also discovers Saturn's largest satellite, Titan, and observes dark patches in the Orion Nebula as well as surface features on Mars.

1668   Isaac Newton (1643–1727) of England makes the first reflecting telescope.

1675   Greenwich Observatory is founded by King Charles II of England. He appoints John Flamsteed (1646–1719) as the first Astronomer Royal.

1682   Edmond Halley of England observes "The Great Comet." He predicts in 1705 that it will return in 1758, and it is then named after him.

Historical Timeline

1781 Charles Messier (1730–1817) of France catalogs more than a hundred star clusters and nebulae that might be mistaken for comets. William Herschel (1738–1822) of England discovers Uranus on March 13, although he first believes it to be a comet.

1794 Ernst Chladni, a German-born Hungarian, shows that meteors are extraterrestrial.

1798 Pierre Simon de Laplace of France predicts the existence of black holes.

1801 Giuseppe Piazzi of Italy discovers the first asteroid, Ceres.

1821 The Catholic church lifts its ban on teaching the Copernican system.

1822 The Catholic church removes Galileo's *Dialogue Concerning the Two Chief World Systems* from the *Index of Prohibited Books* 190 years after its publication.

1839 The Harvard College Observatory is founded, the first official observatory in the United States. A 15-inch (38 cm) refractor is installed in 1847. It is one of the two largest in the world at the time.

1846 Johann Galle of Germany discovers Neptune using the predictions of its position by Urbain Le Verrier of France and John Couch Adams of England.

1851 Baron von Humboldt's *Kosmos* gives currency to Heinrich Samuel Schwabe's 1843 discovery of the 11-year sunspot cycle.

1863 William Huggins of England uses the spectra of stars to show that the same elements that exist in stars also exist on Earth.

1864 John Herschel, son of William Herschel, publishes a catalog of nebulae and star clusters that contains more than 5,000 entries.

1868 Pietro Secchi of Italy completes the first spectroscopic survey of the stars, cataloging the spectrograms of about 4,000 stars.

1873 Richard Proctor suggests that the craters on the Moon were formed by the impacts of meteorites instead of by volcanoes as was previously assumed.

1877 Giovanni Schiaparelli of Italy thinks he discovers canals or channels on Mars. This observation is considered a possibility for years, but eventually fails to be confirmed.

Historical Timeline

1882   David Gill photographs Halley's comet and notices the multitude of stars surrounding the comet — the idea of stellar cataloging by photography is born.

1884   An international meeting in Washington, DC, sets the Prime Meridian through Greenwich, England.

1887   The Lick 36-inch (91 cm) refracting telescope is completed on Mount Hamilton near San Francisco, California.

1888   Johan L. E. Dreyer (1852–1926), a Danish astronomer working in Ireland, publishes *A New General Catalogue of Nebulae and Clusters of Stars* containing 7,840 nebulae and star clusters.

1891   Maximilian Wolf makes the first discovery of an asteroid (Brucia) from photographs.

1894   Percival Lowell (1855–1916) founds his observatory at Flagstaff, Arizona, and starts searching for a hypothetical ninth Planet. He also maps what he believes to be canals on Mars.

1897   George Hale (1868–1938) sets up the Yerkes Observatory in Williams Bay, Wisconsin. The Yerkes telescope at 40 inches (1 meter) is still the largest refracting telescope ever built.

1900   James Keeler photographs a large number of nebulae and discovers that some have a spiral structure (The nebulae with spiral structure are galaxies).

1908   Hale installs a 60-inch (1.5 meters) reflecting telescope at Mount Wilson Observatory, near Pasedena, California.

1912   Studies of short-period variable stars in the Small Magellanic Cloud by Henrietta Leavitt lead to the period-luminosity law of Cepheid variables — a key that is used to unlock the distances to the stars.

1913   Henry Russel announces his theory of stellar evolution which was independently theorized by Hertzsprung in 1905. This concept becomes the famous Hertzsprung-Russell diagram depicting the relationship and evolution of stars.

1914   Arthur Eddington suggests in *Stellar Movements and the Structure of the Universe* that spiral nebulae are galaxies.

1917   George Hale installs a 100-inch (2.5 meter) reflecting telescope at Mount Wilson Observatory in California. It will be the world's largest telescope until 1948. Karl Schwarzschild develops the equations that predict the

Historical Timeline

existence of black holes from Einstein's General Theory of Relativity.

1924   Edwin Hubble (1889–1953) demonstrates that galaxies are true independent systems rather than parts of our Milky Way system.

1927   Georges Lemaître, a Belgian priest and astrophysicist, proposes the first version of the Big Bang theory, that the Universe was created by the explosion of a concentration of matter and energy which he called the "cosmic egg" or "primeval atom."

1929   Edwin Hubble establishes that the more distant a galaxy is, the faster it is receding from Earth (Hubble's law), confirming that the Universe is expanding.

1930   Clyde Tombaugh discovers Pluto from Flagstaff, Arizona.

1931   Experiments by Karl Jansky with an improvised aerial lead to the founding of radio astronomy.

1938   German physicists Hans Bethe and Carl von Weizsäcker independently propose that the cause of the energy produced by stars is the nuclear fusion of hydrogen into helium. J. Robert Oppenheimer and George Volkoff predict the existence of rapidly rotating neutron stars which are discovered in 1967 by Jocelyn Bell and become known as pulsars.

1939   J. Robert Oppenheimer calculates that if the mass of a star is more than 3.2 times the mass of the Sun, a collapse of the star would create what would come to be known as a black hole.

1942   Grote Reber makes the first radio maps of the Universe, and locates individual radio sources.

1946   A V-2 rocket carries a spectrograph to record a spectrogram of the Sun to a height of 34 miles (55 km).

1947   Lyman Spitzer, Jr., speculates that astronomers might put telescopes of various kinds in orbit around Earth on artificial satellites.

1948   The 200-inch (5 meter) Hale reflecting telescope at Palomar, California is completed.

1949   Fred Whipple suggests that comets are "dirty snowballs" consisting of ice or ammonia ice and rock dust. A rocket testing ground is established at Cape Canaveral, Florida.

1955   The US Vanguard project for launching artificial satellites is announced.

Historical Timeline

1957 — The first artificial satellite, *Sputnik I*, is launched by the Soviet Union on October 4.

1958 — American physicist Eugene Parker demonstrates that there is a "solar wind" of particles thrown out by the Sun. Wernher von Braun's team launches the first American satellite to reach a successful orbit around Earth.

1960 — Allan Sandage discovers a starlike object of 16th magnitude that emits radio waves. This object is later identified as a quasar.

1961 — Soviet cosmonaut Yuri Gagarin becomes the first human being to orbit Earth during his 1.8-hour mission in *Vostok I*. Alan Shepard, Jr., becomes the first US astronaut in space as his *Mercury 3* capsule *Freedom 7* completes a 15-minute suborbital flight on May 5.

1962 — The US space probe *Mariner 2* becomes the first object made by humans to voyage to another Planet when it reaches the vicinity of Venus. John Glenn, Jr., is the first American to orbit Earth in his *Mercury 6* space capsule *Friendship 7* on February 20.

1963 — Valentina Tereshkova-Nikolayeva of the Soviet Union becomes the first woman in space, making 48 orbits in 78 hours on June 16.

1965 — *Mariner IV* reaches the vicinity of Mars on July 15, passing within 7,500 miles (12,000 km) of the Planet.

1966 — *Luna 9* (Soviet Union) becomes the first spacecraft to soft land on the Moon.

1968 — Astronomers find a pulsar with a period of 0.033 seconds in the center of the Crab nebula in Taurus, the site of the 1054 supernova.

1969 — American astronaut Neil Armstrong becomes the first human to stand on the Moon on July 20.

1970 — *Venera 7* (Soviet Union) becomes the first spacecraft to soft land on a Planet, Venus.

1972 — The first Earth-resources satellite, *Landsat I*, is launched.

1973 — The first *Skylab* is launched on May 25 by a Saturn rocket. A 3-man crew conducts medical and other experiments for 28 days.

1975 — The first pictures from the surface of Venus are received from the Russian probes *Venera 9* and *Venera 10*.

Historical Timeline

1976   US space probes *Viking 1* and *2* land on Mars and begin sending back direct pictures and other information from the surface of the Planet. Space probes *Voyager 1* and *2* are launched on a journey to Jupiter and the outer Planets.

1978   James Christy and Robert Harrington discover Charon, Pluto's moon.

1981   The first Space Shuttle, *Columbia,* is launched on April 12 with John Young and Robert Crippen as crew.

1983   The *Challenger* space shuttle flight launched on June 18 carries the first 5-person crew and the first American woman in space, Sally Ride. The remote manipulator structure is used to deploy and retrieve a satellite.

1986   The space shuttle *Challenger* explodes 73 seconds after launch on January 28, killing six astronauts and teacher S. Christa McAuliffe.

1987   Bruce Campbell, Gordon Walker and Stephenson Yang announce the discovery of planet-size bodies orbiting Gamma Cephei and Epsilon Eridani.

1989   The space probe *Galileo* is launched toward Jupiter and enters orbit in 1995.

1990   *Hubble Space Telescope* (HST) is launched into orbit around Earth.

1994   Comet Shoemaker-Levy 9, discovered by Gene and Carolyn Shoemaker along with David Levy in March of 1993, slams into Jupiter.

1995   Comet Hale-Bopp is discovered by Dr. Thomas Bopp and Alan Hale.

1997   *Pathfinder* becomes the first roving vehicle on another Planet, Mars. The space probe *Cassini* is launched to Saturn and is due to enter orbit around the ringed Planet in 2004.

1998   The *Lunar Prospector* orbits the Moon and detects a signature that indicates frozen water may exist at both poles.

1998/99   Construction on the *International Space Station* begins.

Online Support

Online support for this book is at:

www.whatsouttonight.com

Visit for
Recap of Sky for the Current Month
& More

Recommended Reading & Resources

PLANISPHERES (Beginning Star Charts)
David H. Levy's Guide to the Stars
By David Levy & Ken Graun
Ken Press

STAR ATLAS
Sky Atlas 2000.0
By Wil Tirion
Sky Publishing Corporation

PLANETARY INFORMATION
The New Solar System, 4th Edition
Edited by J. Kelly Beatty et al.
Sky Publishing Corporation

MESSIER OBJECTS
Deep-Sky Companions: The Messier Objects
By Stephen James O'Meara
Sky Publishing Corporation

POPULAR MONTHLY ASTRONOMY MAGAZINES
Astronomy   (800) 533-6644   www.astronomy.com
Sky & Telescope   (800) 253-0245   www.skypub.com

References

Abell, George O. *Exploration of the Universe.* 3rd Ed. New York: Holt, Rinehart and Winston, 1964.

Bauval, Robert, and Adrian Gilbert. *The Orion Mystery: Unlocking the Secrets of the Pyramids.* New York: Crown Publishers, Inc., 1994.

Beatty, J. Kelly, and Andrew Chaikin, eds. *The New Solar System.* 3rd. Ed. Cambridge: Sky Publishing Corp., 1990.

Becvár, Antonín. *Atlas of the Heavens.* Cambridge: Sky Publishing Corp., 1962.

Beyer, William H., and Samuel M. Selby, eds. *Standard Mathematical Tables.* 24th ed. Cleveland: CRC Press, 1974.

Bishop, Roy, ed. *Observer's Handbook 1998.* Toronto: The Royal Astronomical Society of Canada, 1997.

Brown, Sam. *All About Telescopes.* Barrington: Edmund Scientific Co., 1967.

Cambridge Astronomy Dictionary. Cambridge: Cambridge UP, 1995

Du Pont Reagents. *A Condensed Laboratory Handbook.* Wilmington: E. I. du Pont de Nemours & Co., 1971.

Halliday, David, and Robert Resnick. *Fundamentals of Physics.* New York: John Wiley & Sons, Inc., 1970.

Harrington, Philip S. *Eclipse! The What, Where, When, Why & How Guide to Watching Solar & Lunar Eclipses.* New York: John Wiley & Sons, Inc., 1997.

Hellemans, Alexander, and Bryan Bunch. *The Timetables of Science: A Chronology of the Most Important People and Events in the History of Science.* New York: Simon & Schuster, 1988.

Levy, David H. *Comets: Creators and Destroyers.* New York: Simon & Schuster, 1998.

Lovi, George, and Graham Blow. *Monthly Star Charts: 24 All-Sky Charts for Star Watchers Worldwide.* Cambridge: Sky Publishing Corp., 1995.

Mallas, John H., and Evered Kreimer. *The Messier Album.* Cambridge: Sky Publishing Corp., 1978.

New World Atlas. Englewood Cliffs: Prentice-Hall, 1984.

North, Gerald. *Astronomy Explained.* London: Springer, 1997

Norton, Arthur P. *Norton's Star Atlas and Reference Handbook.* 17th ed. Cambridge: Sky Publishing Corp., 1973.

National Maritime Museum. *The Old Royal Observatory Greenwich: Guide to the Collections.* London: Merrell Holberton, 1998.

References

O'Meara, Stehen J. *The Messier Objects.* Cambridge: Sky Publishing Corp., 1998.

Ottewell, Guy. *Astronomical Calendar 1999.* Greenville: Author, 1997.

Percy, John R., ed. *The Observer's Handbook 1971.* Toronto: The Royal Astronomical Society of Canada, 1971.

Scagell, Robin, Ed. *City Astronomy. Sky & Telescope* Observer's Guides. Cambridge: Sky Publishing Corp., 1994.

Sinnot, Roger W., ed. *NGC 2000.0.* Cambridge: Sky Publishing Corp., 1988.

– *Millennium Star Atlas: an All-Sky Atlas Comprising One Million Stars to Visual Magnitude Eleven from the Hipparcos and Tycho Catalogues and Ten Thousand Nonstellar Objects. vols. I to III.* Cambridge: Sky Publishing Corp., 1997.

Trinklein, Frederick E., and Charles M. Huffer. *Modern Space Science.* New York: Holt, Rinehart and Winston, Inc., 1961.

United States Naval Observatory. *The Astronomical Almanac.* Washington: GPO, 1997.

Voyager II. Vers. 2.0. Computer software. Carina Software, 1988. Mac OS 6.0.7 or higher 6MB, CD-ROM.

Watters, Thomas R. *Planets.* Smithsonian Guides Series. New York: Simon & Schuster, 1995.

Notes

Photo Credits

Photos without credits are by the author. Page numbers are bolded.

Cover: Anglo-Australian Observatory/Royal Observatory Edinburgh.
4: AURA/NASA/ESA. **7:** Jeff Hester and Paul Scowen (Arizona State University) and NASA. **8:** AURA/NOAO/NSF. **14:** AURA/STScI/NASA.
15: NASA/ARC. **16:** NASA/ESA. **18:** NASA. **20:** JPL. **21:** NASA.
22: JPL. **26:** JPL. **29:** JPL. **30:** JPL. **80:** NASA. **82:** NASA. **83:** UCO/Lick Observatory. **86:** UCO/Lick Observatory. **87:** NASA. **88:** NASA. **89, 90, 91, 93–97:** UCO/Lick Observatory. **104:** NASA. **112:** JPL. **120:** NASA.
121: NASA/ARC. **122:** AURA/NASA/ESA. **125:** JPL. **126:** JPL. **129:** JPL.
132: JPL. **133 & 134:** A. Stern (SwRI), M. Buie (Lowell Obs.), NASA/ESA. **144:** AURA/NASA/ESA. **145:** JPL. **156:** JPL. **157:** JPL.
166: JPL. **170:** NASA. **178:** NASA/ARC. **180:** NASA. **182:** JPL.
188: AURA/NOAO/NSF. **187:** NASA/JPL. **188:** From the collections of Don Yeomans. **190:** J. C. Casado. **196:** AURA/NOAO/NSF.
201: T. Rimmele, M. Hanna/AURA/NOAO/NSF. **216:** Celestron International. **219:** Celestron International. **222:** Celestron International.
230: Bill Schoening/AURA/NOAO/NSF. **231:** AURA/NOAO/NSF.
232 clockwise: Bill Schoening, Vanessa Harvey/REU Program/AURA/NOAO/NSF; N. A. Sharp/AURA/NOAO/NSF; N. A. Sharp/AURA/NOAO/NSF. **233:** Bill Schoening/AURA/NOAO/NSF. **240:** AURA/NOAO/NSF. **242:** Scott Tucker. **246:** AURA/NOAO/NSF. **250:** Anglo-Australian Observatory/Royal Observatory Edinburgh. **252:** Bill Schoening/AURA/NOAO/NSF. **256:** Bill Schoening, Vanessa Harvey/REU Program/AURA/NOAO/NSF. **260:** AURA/NOAO/NSF. **262:** AURA/NOAO/NSF.
266: Philip Farnam. **270:** Scott Tucker. **272:** Background, David Talent/AURA/NOAO/NSF; top two circles, AURA/NOAO/NSF; bottom circle, Scott Tucker. **336:** JPL.

Index